Clouds above the Hill

Clouds above the Hill, a longtime best-selling novel in Japan, is now translated into English for the first time. An epic portrait of Japan in crisis, it combines graphic military history and highly readable fiction to depict an aspiring nation modernizing at breakneck speed. Acclaimed author Shiba Ryōtarō devoted an entire decade of his life to this extraordinary blockbuster, which features Japan's emergence onto the world stage by the early years of the twentieth century.

In Volume II, Meiji Japan is on a collision course with Russia, as Russian troops stationed in Manchuria ignore repeated calls to withdraw. Admiral Tōgō leads a blockade and subsequent skirmish at the strategically vital and heavily fortified Port Arthur, while Yoshifuru's cavalry in Manchuria maneuvers for position as it approaches the Russian Army lines. The two armies clash at the battle of Liaoyang, where Japan seals a victory that shocks the world.

Anyone curious as to how the "tiny, rising nation of Japan" was able to fight so fiercely for its survival should look no further. *Clouds above the Hill* is an exciting, human portrait of a modernizing nation that goes to war and thereby stakes its very existence on a desperate bid for glory in East Asia.

Shiba Ryōtarō (1923–1996) is one of Japan's best-known writers, acclaimed for his direct tone and insightful portrayals of historic personalities and events. He was drafted into the Japanese Army, served in the Second World War, and subsequently worked for the newspaper *Sankei Shimbun*. He is most famous for his numerous works of historical fiction.

Translated by Juliet Winters Carpenter, Andrew Cobbing, and Paul McCarthy
Edited by Phyllis Birnbaum

Shiba Ryōtarō is Japan's best-loved author, and *Clouds above the Hill* is his most popular and influential work. In it he celebrates the transformative spirit of Meiji Japan and examines Japan's unexpected victory in the Russo-Japanese War, providing a thoughtful and thought-provoking perspective on those dramatic times and the people at their center. This distinguished translation of a modern classic is a landmark event.

Donald Keene, University Professor Emeritus,
Columbia University, USA

Shiba Ryōtarō wrote that from the Meiji Restoration of 1868 through the Russo-Japanese War of 1904–1905, Japan transformed its premodern "brown sugar" society into a modern "white sugar" one, eagerly scooping up crystals of the new substance in the drive to create society anew. During the Pacific War, by contrast, the nation's leaders merely went through empty motions, and Japan collapsed. This book looks back on that earlier era through the lens of the later tragedy, depicting the struggles and growth to maturity of Japan's young men.

Tanaka Naoki, President of the Center for International
Public Policy Studies, Japan

When the siege of Port Arthur was over and Japan had won, the commanding generals from both sides came together face to face at Shuishiying. They paid honor to each other's bravery and expressed mutual condolences, and before parting they shook hands. I have visited that very place, which seems to me less the site of a Japanese victory than a monument to the souls of fallen soldiers on both sides. I have no doubt that *Clouds above the Hill* was also written to honor those souls.

Anno Mitsumasa, author and illustrator of
children's books in Japan

Clouds above the Hill

A historical novel of the Russo-Japanese War, Volume II

Shiba Ryōtarō

Translated by Juliet Winters Carpenter
and Paul McCarthy

Edited by Phyllis Birnbaum

First published in hardback 2013
First published in paperback 2015
by Routledge
2 Park Square, Milton Park, Abingdon, Oxon OX14 4RN

Simultaneously published in the USA and Canada
by Routledge
711 Third Avenue, New York, NY 10017

Routledge is an imprint of the Taylor & Francis Group, an informa business

© 1979 The original work in the Japanese language, Shiba Ryōtarō
© 2013 The translation of the work in the English language, Japan Documents

The right of Shiba Ryōtarō to be identified as author of this work has been asserted by him in accordance with sections 77 and 78 of the Copyright, Designs and Patents Act 1988.

All rights reserved. No part of this book may be reprinted or reproduced or utilised in any form or by any electronic, mechanical, or other means, now known or hereafter invented, including photocopying and recording, or in any information storage or retrieval system, without permission in writing from the publishers.

Trademark notice: Product or corporate names may be trademarks or registered trademarks, and are used only for identification and explanation without intent to infringe.

British Library Cataloguing in Publication Data
A catalogue record for this book is available from the British Library

Library of Congress Cataloging in Publication Data
Shiba, Ryotaro, 1923–1996.
  [Saka no ue no kumo. English]
  Clouds above the hill: a historical novel of the Russo-Japanese War/
  Shiba Ryotaro; translated by Paul McCarthy, Andrew Cobbing and
  Juliet Winters Carpenter ; edited by Phyllis Birnbaum.
  p. cm.
  "The original work in the Japanese language, Shiba Ryotaro."
  1. Shiba, Ryotaro, 1923–1996.—Translations into English. 2. Japan—Politics and government—1868–1912. I. McCarthy, Paul, 1944– II. Cobbing, Andrew. III. Carpenter, Juliet Winters. IV. Birnbaum, Phyllis. V. Title.
  PL861.H68S2513 2012
  895.6'35—dc23
  2012033404

ISBN: 978-0-415-50884-1 (hbk)
ISBN: 978-1-138-85890-9 (pbk)
ISBN: 978-0-203-06872-4 (ebk)

Typeset in Scala Sans and Times New Roman
by Florence Production Ltd, Stoodleigh, Devon

Contents

PRINCIPAL CHARACTERS — vii
CHRONOLOGY OF MAJOR EVENTS — xi
JAPANESE AND RUSSIAN FLEETS IN 1904 — xiii
A NOTE FROM THE EDITOR — xv
MAPS — xviii

Part 3, translated by Paul McCarthy — 1

1 Bright moonlit night — 3
2 "Gombei" — 19
3 Diplomacy — 34
4 Winds and clouds — 58
5 Toward war — 85
6 Shellfire — 101
7 Port Arthur — 122
8 The army — 150
9 Makarov — 177

Part 4, translated by Juliet Winters Carpenter — 195

1 Yellow dust — 197
2 Liaoyang — 245

	3	Port Arthur	284
	4	Shaho	309
	5	The storming of Port Arthur	348
		GLOSSARY	397

Principal Characters—Volumes I and II

Akiyama Hisakata (Yasoku) (1822–1890): father of Yoshifuru and Saneyuki.
Akiyama Saneyuki (1868–1918): Yoshifuru's younger brother; staff officer of the Japanese Combined Fleet at the time of the Russo-Japanese War.
Akiyama Yoshifuru (1859–1930): Saneyuki's older brother; father of the modern Japanese cavalry; defeated Russian Cossacks in the Russo-Japanese War.
Alexeyev, Yevgeny Ivanovich (1843–1918): Russian tsar's viceroy in the Far East.
Arima Ryōkitsu (1861–1944): vice chief of staff of the Japanese Combined Fleet in the Russo-Japanese War.
Cervera y Topete, Pascual (1839–1909): commander of the Spanish fleet in the Spanish–American War.
Ding Ruchang (1836–1895): admiral in the Chinese Navy at the end of the Qing dynasty.
Fujii Shigeta (1858–1945): chief of staff of General Kuroki's First Army.
Grippenberg, Oskar-Ferdinand Kazimirovich (1838–1916): commander of the Russian Second Army in Manchuria.
Hayashi Tadasu (1850–1912): Japan's ambassador to Britain at the time of the Russo-Japanese War.
Hekigotō (see Kawahigashi Hekigotō).
Hirose Takeo (1868–1904): naval officer; close friend of Saneyuki; killed during the second blocking operation at Port Arthur; remembered as a war hero, he was revered as a "war god" until Japan's defeat in the Second World War in 1945.

Hisamatsu family: former lords of the Matsuyama domain in Iyo province.
Iguchi Shōgo (1855–1925): staff officer of Japan's Manchurian Army during the Russo-Japanese War.
Ijichi Kōsuke (1854–1917): chief of staff of General Nogi's Third Army.
Itō Hirobumi (1841–1909): head of the Privy Council; prime minister at the time of the First Sino-Japanese War.
Itō Sukeyuki (1843–1914): fleet commander during the First Sino-Japanese War.
Kamimura Hikonojō (1849–1916): commander in chief of the Second Squadron of the Japanese Combined Fleet during the Russo-Japanese War.
Kataoka Shichirō (1854–1920): commander of the Third Squadron of the Japanese fleet.
Katō Tomosaburō (1861–1923): chief of staff of Admiral Kamimura's Second Squadron.
Katō Tsunetada (1859–1923): diplomat and Shiki's uncle.
Katsura Tarō (1847–1913): prime minister at the time of the Russo-Japanese War.
Kawahigashi Hekigotō (1873–1937): haiku poet.
Kawakami Sōroku (1848–1899): vice chief of the Army General Staff during the First Sino-Japanese War; known for his genius in military tactics.
Kodama Gentarō (1852–1906): chief of staff at General Headquarters of Japan's Manchurian Army during the Russo-Japanese War.
Komura Jutarō (1855–1911): foreign minister at the time of the Russo-Japanese War.
Kovalevskaya, Ariadna Vladimirovna: beautiful young Russian noblewoman who fell in love with Japanese naval officer Hirose Takeo.
Kuga Katsunan (1857–1907): journalist and head of the newspaper *Nippon*; Shiki's lifelong friend and protector.
Kuroki Tamemoto (1844–1923): commander of the Japanese First Army in the Russo-Japanese War.
Kuropatkin, Alexei Nikolayevich (1848–1925): Russian war minister and the commander in chief of the Russian Manchurian Army during the Russo-Japanese War.
Kyoshi (see Takahama Kyoshi).
Lansdowne, Lord Henry Charles Keith Petty-Fitzmaurice (1845–1927): British foreign secretary.
Li Hongzhang (1823–1901): China's best-known statesman and diplomat in the latter part of the nineteenth century.
Linevich, Nikolai Petrovich (1838–1908): commander in chief of the Russian Manchurian Army in the early phase of the Russo-Japanese War.

Makarov, Stepan Osipovich (1848–1904): commander in chief of the Russian fleet at Port Arthur and author.
Masaoka Shiki (1867–1902): poet and critic credited with modernizing Japan's two traditional short poetic forms, haiku and tanka.
Matsukawa Toshitane (1860–1928): staff officer of Japan's Manchuria Army.
Meckel, Klemens Wilhelm Jacob (1842–1906): German military officer and advisor to the Japanese Army.
Mishchenko, Pavel Ivanovich (1853–1918): commander of the Cossack cavalry brigade involved in many battles of the Russo-Japanese War.
Nagaoka Gaishi (1858–1933): vice chief of the Army General Staff during the Russo-Japanese War; proud of his mustache, which was said to be the world's second longest.
Natsume Sōseki (1867–1916): Shiki's friend; became a great Japanese novelist.
Nicholas II (1868–1918): Russian tsar at the time of the Russo-Japanese War.
Nogi Maresuke (1849–1912): commander of the Japanese Third Army during the Russo-Japanese War.
Nozu Michitsura (1841–1908): commander of the Japanese Fourth Army during the Russo-Japanese War.
Ochiai Toyosaburō (1861–1934): chief of staff of General Nozu's Fourth Army.
Oku Yasukata (1846–1930): commander of the Japanese Second Army during the Russo-Japanese War.
Ōyama Iwao (1842–1916): army minister at the time of the Russo-Japanese War.
Rozhestvensky, Zinovy Petrovich (1848–1909): favorite of Tsar Nicholas II and commander of the Russian Baltic Fleet, which traveled via the Cape of Good Hope all the way to the Sea of Japan.
Ritsu (1870–1941): Shiki's sister.
Sada (1827–1905): mother of Yoshifuru and Saneyuki.
Saigō Tsugumichi (1843–1902): navy minister at the time of the First Sino-Japanese War; younger brother of Satsuma hero Saigō Takamori.
Saneyuki (see Akiyama Saneyuki).
Schiff, Jacob (1847–1920): Jewish financier who contributed to Japan's war effort.
Shiki (see Masaoka Shiki).
Shimamura Hayao (1858–1923): chief of staff of the Japanese Combined Fleet at the time of the Russo-Japanese War.

Stakelberg, Georgi Karlovich (1851–1913): commander of the First Siberian Army Corps.

Stark, Oskar Viktorovich (1846–1928): commander of the Pacific Fleet at the start of the Russo-Japanese War.

Stoessel, Anatoly Mikhailovich (1848–1915): commander of the Russian forces at Port Arthur.

Takahama Kyoshi (1874–1959): haiku poet and editor of the journal *Hototogisu*.

Takahashi Korekiyo (1854–1936): vice governor of the Bank of Japan at the time of the Russo-Japanese War; later prime minister and finance minister.

Tamura Iyozō (1854–1903): vice chief of the Army General Staff from 1902; died of overwork just before the outbreak of war with Russia.

Terauchi Masatake (1852–1919): army minister at the time of the Russo-Japanese War.

Tōgō Heihachirō (1847–1934): commander in chief of the Japanese Combined Fleet in the Russo-Japanese War.

Uehara Yūsaku (1856–1933): chief of staff of General Nozu's Fourth Army.

Uryū Sotokichi (1857–1937): commander of the Fourth Division of the Japanese Combined Fleet in the Russo-Japanese War.

Vitgeft, Vilgelm Karlovich (1847–1904): acted as commander in chief of the Russian fleet at Port Arthur after Makarov's death.

Wilhelm II (1859–1941): German kaiser.

Witte, Sergei Yulyevich (1849–1915): Russian finance minister 1892–1903; strong opponent of the Russo-Japanese War.

Yae: Shiki's mother.

Yamagata Aritomo (1838–1922): architect of the modern Japanese Army and chief of the Army General Staff during the Russo-Japanese War.

Yamamoto Gombei (1852–1933): Satsuma-born officer responsible for modernization of the Japanese Navy; navy minister at the time of the Russo-Japanese War.

Yoshifuru (see Akiyama Yoshifuru).

Yuan Shikai (1859–1916): Chinese army leader; first president of the Republic of China.

Chronology of Major Events

1603	Establishment of the Tokugawa shogunate
1825	Shogunate issues order to repel foreign ships
1853	U.S. Commodore Perry's warships appear in Edo Bay (now Tokyo Bay)
1854	Perry reopens Japan to the Western world, ending the period of national seclusion that began in 1639 and lasted more than two hundred years
1868	Collapse of the Tokugawa shogunate Meiji Restoration
1868–1869	Boshin War
1877	Satsuma Rebellion
1889	Promulgation of the Meiji Constitution
1894	Outbreak of the First Sino-Japanese War (August) Yalu River naval battle (September)
1895	Destruction of the Chinese fleet at Weihaiwei (February) Peace treaty signed at Shimonoseki (April) Triple Intervention (April–May)—Japan forced by Russia, France, and Germany to relinquish the Liaodong Peninsula
1898	Spanish–American War
1900	Boxer Rebellion in China
1902	Anglo-Japanese Alliance signed in London (January)
1904	Outbreak of the Russo-Japanese War (February) Battle over the crossing of the Yalu (April) Siege of Port Arthur (August–January 1905) Battle of the Yellow Sea (August) Battle of Ulsan (August)

Battle of Liaoyang (August–September)
Battle of Shaho (October)
Russian Baltic Fleet departs the Baltic Sea (October)

1905 Battle of Heigoutai (January)
Battle of Mukden (March)
Tōgō's Combined Fleet defeats the Baltic Fleet at Tsushima off the coast of Kyushu (May)
Peace treaty signed in Portsmouth (September)

JAPANESE AND RUSSIAN FLEETS IN 1904

At the beginning of the Russo-Japanese War in February 1904, the Japanese fleet was organized into three squadrons.

The First Squadron was under the direct command of Admiral Tōgō Heihachirō, who was also overall commander of the entire Combined Fleet. The First Squadron included Japan's six new battleships: *Mikasa*, *Asahi*, *Fuji*, *Shikishima*, *Hatsuse*, and *Yashima*.

The Second Squadron, under Admiral Kamimura Hikonojō, included Japan's six new armored cruisers: *Izumo*, *Azuma*, *Tokiwa*, *Iwate*, *Asama*, and *Yakumo*.

While both squadrons contained numerous supporting warships—large and small "protected cruisers," dispatch vessels, gunboats, and large numbers of destroyers and torpedo boats—the battleships and armored cruisers are the ships that count. Battleships are the biggest, strongest, and most heavily armed and armored, usually carrying a main armament of four 12-inch and numerous smaller guns. Armored cruisers are often just as big, but faster and more lightly armed, typically with four 8-inch guns. They carry an armor "belt" along their sides, like those of the battleships, only not as thick.

In contrast, "protected cruisers" are smaller, with no vertical armor belt but only a horizontal armor "protective deck" covering their vitals at waterline level. Gunboats and dispatch vessels are smaller than cruisers; the latter (like Tōgō's *Tatsuta*) are fast and act as scouts or to carry messages. Destroyers and torpedo boats are light, small, and very fast vessels whose main armament is the torpedo.

The Japanese also formed a Third Squadron—a reserve or supporting force, consisting of obsolete and second-line warships commanded by Kataoka Shichirō. Thus, it contained the ships that played dominant roles in the First Sino-Japanese War of 1894–1895, including the captured Chinese battleship *Zhenyuan*, called *Chin'en* in Japanese.

The Russian Pacific Fleet was basically divided between its two bases. At Port Arthur were seven new battleships, under a succession of commanders (Oskar Stark, Stepan Makarov, Yevgeny Alexeyev, Vilgelm Vitgeft, and Robert Viren). The battleships were: *Tsesarevich*, *Retvizan*, *Pobeda*, *Poltava*, *Peresvet*, *Petropavlosk*, and *Sevastopol*. This force had numerous supporting ships including one armored cruiser, the *Bayan*.

At Vladivostok, the Russians had three powerful armored cruisers under Georgi Stakelberg and Nikolai von Essen as part of the Vladivostok Squadron: *Rurik*, *Rossiya*, and *Gromoboy*.

During the early months of the Russo-Japanese War, the Japanese First and Second squadrons sometimes operated as separate forces. Tōgō's battleships watched, threatened, and harassed the Russian battle fleet at Port Arthur. Meanwhile, Kamimura's armored cruisers sought to intercept von Essen's daring raids out of Vladivostok into Japanese and Korean waters.

When the Russian battle fleet finally came out, seeking to escape to Vladivostok on August 10, 1904, during the battle of the Yellow Sea, it was beaten by Tōgō's force and permanently bottled up in Port Arthur.

By the time of the August 10 battle, the Japanese had lost the two battleships *Hatsuse* and *Yashima* to mines, dangerously altering the balance of strength, and the Russians had lost the *Petropavlosk* to the same cause. However, by August 10, the two Japanese battleships had been replaced in Tōgō's First Squadron by the armored cruisers *Nisshin* and *Kasuga*, newly purchased from Italy. And, on August 14, Kamimura finally caught and crippled von Essen's Vladivostok armored cruiser force. This ended naval action in the East for the rest of 1904, leaving the Japanese a vital breathing space to prepare for the arrival of Russian reinforcements from Europe, namely, the Baltic Fleet.

Robert Patrick Largess

A Note from the Editor

This translation project has benefited from the expertise and assistance of a number of people, most importantly, Takechi Manabu, of the Center for Intercultural Communication, who has checked the translations, researched background information, and created most of the introductory materials. He is a devoted fan of *Clouds above the Hill*; Shiba Ryōtarō and our project are fortunate indeed to have his invaluable help. Noda Makito checked the translations in Volume IV.

Lynne Riggs, also of the Center for Intercultural Communication, has been our indefatigable behind-the-scenes adviser and liaison with various business concerns. Assisted by Imoto Chikako, she obtained appropriate images for the covers and the required permissions. Anne Bergasse and Kiwaki Tetsuji of Abinitio Design are the cover designers.

We are grateful for the cooperation of the Shiba Ryōtarō Memorial Foundation, with special thanks to Uemura Motoko, who helped answer our various questions.

Tamara Agvanian has toiled as our official Russian expert, going to great lengths to track down the English equivalents for the Russian names and terms in our text; Miguel Romá joined the search for other non-Japanese names. Komiyama Emiko of Komiyama Printing Company created the map graphics. HyunSook Yun was a great help with Korean names and terms. Bruce Carpenter looked up Chinese sources, interpreted Chinese poems, and provided vital advice.

Robert Patrick Largess was our military consultant, finding the appropriate English for the many guns, ships, and other military terms in the text; he compiled our explanatory "Japanese and Russian Fleets in 1904" and "Japanese and Russian Fleets at Tsushima." In addition, his vast knowledge in other fields has served to improve these translations in many ways.

xvi A NOTE FROM THE EDITOR

My personal thanks to Teruko Craig and Stuart Kiang for their helpful, speedy advice.

Above all, everyone who has contributed to this translation of *Clouds above the Hill* thanks Saitō Sumio of Japan Documents, whose enthusiasm and determination have brought this project to fruition. He did not only decide to have this immense novel translated and succeed in organizing a translation team, but he has also been a tremendously loyal supporter of our efforts. His patience, generosity, and most importantly, his calm in the face of assorted difficulties have made this work a great pleasure for all.

* * *

Clouds above the Hill was originally published as a serial in the newspaper *Sankei Shimbun* from April 22, 1968 to August 4, 1972. Traces of the serialization remained when the entire novel was published in book form; those traces can be seen in this translation as well. The section breaks are often indications of the end of a day's installment, although there are times when we've merged sections or moved the breaks around. At the start of a new section, Shiba frequently summarized what had gone on just before to help readers who had missed the previous installment. We've tried to eliminate some of these repetitions, but they are too numerous to eliminate entirely.

In the main, we have used pinyin to transcribe Chinese place and personal names; exceptions are well-known places and names like Port Arthur, Mukden, and Genghis Khan. Some of the famous sites around Port Arthur are in English.

Shiba alternates between the metric and imperial systems in his measurements, but we've made certain measures consistent: we've used the imperial system for naval guns; metric for land guns.

Japanese names are in Japanese order, the family name followed by the given name. Ages are cited in the traditional Japanese method of calculating ages—a child is one on the date of birth and two the following New Year's Day.

We have not corrected any errors Shiba may have made regarding historical fact or translations from other languages. "General Staff" refers to the Army General Staff unless otherwise noted.

Phyllis Birnbaum

First Sino-Japanese War

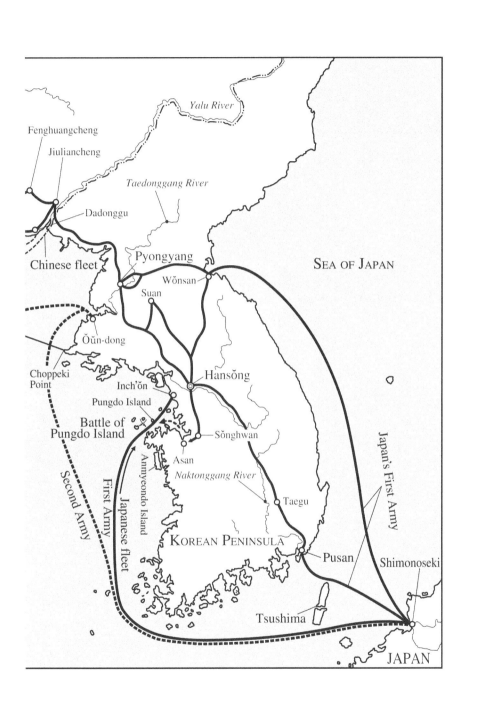

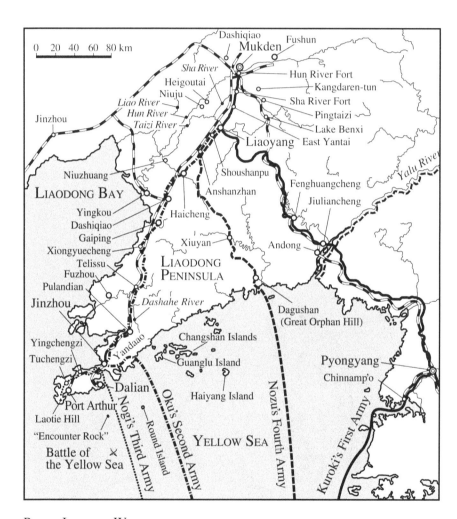

Russo-Japanese War

Part 3

Translated by Paul McCarthy

1

BRIGHT MOONLIT NIGHT

Saneyuki returned from his duties abroad in the summer of 1900. He was then assigned to the permanent fleet as a staff officer and promoted to lieutenant commander in the next year, 1901.

"I'm amazed the navy puts up with our Jun, with all his little ways." This is what his mother Sada often murmured around this time as she looked at the photos he frequently sent her from Yokosuka. Saneyuki never adopted a proper pose, and, in some, he was seated with one arm hanging over the back of his chair. In others, while properly dressed in a uniform displaying his service ribbons, he did not stand but sat cross-legged on the grass, gazing blankly at the ground.

He was then beginning to immerse himself ever more deeply in the study of naval strategy. His enthusiasm knew no bounds. Perhaps out of embarrassment, he claimed that strategy was "the greatest pleasure in my life." Since military men were in fact bureaucrats, there was no need for him to work so hard. He could just have performed his daily duties in the navy and thus received regular promotions. His strategic studies were a thing apart from his daily work—hence perhaps, in that sense, his "greatest pleasure."

We should remember that there were amazingly few men in the Japanese Navy of the time who were seen, either by themselves or others, as strategists. Only two men, both with more seniority than Saneyuki, were acknowledged as such: Shimamura Hayao and Yamaya Tanin. And, of course, there were no works on naval strategy by Japanese apart from a simple one written by Yamaya Tanin.

Thus, Saneyuki felt he had to research naval strategy by himself (though no one ordered him to do so). It would all have to be developed painstakingly by him alone. He tried to read every military classic, no matter where it came from. Most of these works dealt with land armies, but he felt there was no difference between strategy on land and sea. He had been clear about this from the time of his studies in the United States. He read the Chinese military classics *The Art of War* and the *Wuzi* over and over, and he read all the major Western works as well, including those on military history and strategy. He recommended to others as well such works as Wilhelm von Blume's *Strategy: A Study* and Stepan Makarov's *Discussion of Questions in Naval Tactics*. Later, he would fight and always win out over Vice Admiral Makarov, the author of the book he had read so devotedly; while perhaps mere coincidence, this had an air of destiny about it too.

He also read Japanese traditional works on warfare and always cited those by the Yamaga school as the most excellent. And he read with great care the accounts of the struggles between Uesugi Kenshin and Takeda Shingen, skilled military leaders who crossed swords on occasion during the sixteenth century. Not only that, but he also avidly read works dealing with martial arts like horsemanship and archery.

"Horsemanship and archery are martial arts for the individual," he always said, "but if you take the trouble to extract their basic principles, they can be applied to military theory as well."

"Akiyama's genius lies in the power of induction from specific facts," his colleagues in the navy said. And truly his special gift was the ability to classify miscellaneous pieces of information and then derive one or two pure principles from them. This special gift of his would one day intersect with Japan's destiny, and Saneyuki, supremely confident man that he was, had a premonition of this early on.

* * *

The above gives an indication of what "Akiyama's military science" actually was.

There is a story about the time Saneyuki developed stomach and intestinal problems shortly after returning to Japan, and was admitted to the Nagayo Hospital. When Lieutenant Commander Ogasawara Naganari came to visit him, Saneyuki asked, "Don't you have any books on pirates' tactics in your home?" Ogasawara Naganari was the head of the Ogasawara family, who had been the daimyo of Karatsu in Kyushu under the old regime. Saneyuki was sure they must have many old books around the house.

"I'll have a look," promised Ogasawara, who, after returning home and asking several old retainers, discovered a quite rare volume. It was a manuscript in five or six fascicles entitled *Old Piratical Tactics of the Nojima School*.

Now the Inland Sea had been a nest of pirates, who had flourished during the Gempei War in the late twelfth century. During that time, they were first allied with the Heike but later joined the Genji, annihilating the Heike fleet at the battle of Dannoura under the direction of the Genji general Minamoto no Yoshitsune. After the peace of the Kamakura period came the disorder of the Northern and Southern Courts period, and with it even more power to the pirates. The various pirate groups of the Inland Sea were united by Murakami Yoshihiro of Iyo. A skilled tactician, he gave rise to the Murakami school of tactics. The Murakami clan eventually divided into three branches, from Innoshima, Kurushima, and Nojima.

Nojima was an appendage of the considerably larger island of Oshima in Iyo. The whole of Nojima was fortified and became the stronghold of the Murakami clan's Nojima branch. Here was born the Nojima school of tactics.

In the hospital, Saneyuki became so immersed in reading this work that he seemed about to drown in it. When Ogasawara Naganari came to visit him again, Saneyuki repeatedly told him, "My eyes have been opened!" Ogasawara later said to others that Japan's naval strategy had been created while Akiyama was convalescing.

The pirates' strategies and tactics were fascinating. What particularly impressed Saneyuki was the adage "Use all of our power against one part of the enemy's." This was the pirates' fundamental strategy. According to the old text, the best boat formation for this was the "long snake," which was equivalent to the column formation in modern naval terminology. You stretch your ships out in a long vertical line as you move toward the enemy. This formation makes shifting easier and is convenient for encircling given portions of the enemy's force, which was what most impressed Saneyuki. It became the root of Akiyama's naval strategy, and the tactical formation most used in the battle of Tsushima.

Afterward, Ogasawara was appointed a member of the committee charged with compiling a history of this naval battle. He conferred with Saneyuki as to the maps to be included in detailed descriptions of the various encounters with the enemy. "These tactics smell of piracy!" Ogasawara laughingly remarked at one point.

"White sugar is made from brown sugar," Saneyuki brusquely responded.

And this was how Saneyuki created his "Akiyama-style military techniques."

* * *

There is another anecdote about how Saneyuki made use of pirate tactics in the strategies he devised. Premodern pirates distinguished between the "tiger formation" and the "leopard formation" in devising their tactics. They apparently believed that leopards were the female mates of male tigers, so that the distinction really was between "husband formation" and "wife formation." The "tiger" was the main formation, which would stay hidden behind an island, for example. The weaker "leopard" formation would sail around the area where the enemy fleet was expected. When the enemy in fact appeared, the "leopard" would pretend to flee, all the while drawing the enemy closer to the "tiger." Watching for its chance, the "tiger" would suddenly appear, attack, and tear the enemy to pieces.

This was the same tactic used when Russia's Baltic Fleet appeared in the seas off Japan. The Third, Fourth, Fifth and Sixth squadrons were sent out as "leopards" to engage the enemy fleet and draw it toward the "tigers" of the First and Second squadrons, ready and waiting to the north of Okinoshima. The plan worked splendidly.

Many other elements in Saneyuki's strategies were derived from traditional ways of waging war. The pirates believed in "attacking not the ship but the minds of the sailors." This greatly impressed Saneyuki, who felt it accorded with *The Art of War*'s view that defeating the enemy without actually fighting was the best strategy of all. He made it one of the fundamentals of his own military strategy. A great deal of energy was required to concentrate on sinking enemy ships and killing soldiers and sailors. The pirates' strategy was to "deprive the enemy of the will to fight and so win the battle." Saneyuki felt this indeed was the key to victory.

He also learned a lot from the Kōshū-style tactics of Takeda Shingen. He didn't rely on his own solitary study for this but found a teacher who could explain the details to him, namely, Utsunomiya Saburō. Utsunomiya had been a samurai attached to the Owari domain, born into a family versed in the Kōshū-style school of tactics. Later, he switched to the study of Western tactics, serving the shogunate in its last days. He played a major role in the military reforms enacted in the Kishū domain and was a truly versatile person. Since he had studied chemistry as well, he made a career as a chemist after the Restoration, becoming a professor at the School of Engineering, the predecessor of the Faculty of Engineering at the University of Tokyo. By the time Saneyuki studied under him, however, Utsunomiya was already an old man and had retired from all public positions.

Kōshū-style tactics included the use of "the wheel," when one's own group sent fresh forces out one after the other, in the manner of a wheel turning, to confront the enemy's front line. Saneyuki adopted this tactic as well and put it to good use in the battle of Tsushima.

Another Kōshū-style tactic was to use a clearly superior force to prevent the enemy from taking control of a given area—a tactic derived from the shōgi, with its distinction between "gold" and "silver" pieces, the former one rank higher than the latter. During the naval battle of Inch'ŏn right after the beginning of the Russo-Japanese War, Saneyuki used his "gold" against the enemy's "silver."

* * *

Incredibly, it was not until July 1902 that the Naval Staff College introduced a course in strategy. This marked the beginning of strategic studies in the Japanese Navy, and Saneyuki was chosen as the first lecturer in this field. Everyone in the navy believed that Akiyama was by far the most appropriate person for the appointment.

The head of the Naval Staff College was Sakamoto Toshiatsu, who had visited America on his way to a study tour of Europe and met Saneyuki when he was a naval lieutenant in Washington. "Would you consider entering the Naval Staff College?" he asked Saneyuki.

The best students to enter the Naval Staff College were chosen from among lieutenant commanders and lieutenants, so this was not a strange request in any way. But Saneyuki looked steadily at this senior officer's face as he said, with a slightly strange look on his own, "Do you think I'll learn anything there?"

Sakamoto thought for a moment, before concluding, "Actually, he's probably right!" He had had many chances to hear what Saneyuki had to say in the embassy parlor during his stay in Washington and was impressed each time.

"He's more suited to be a lecturer than a student," he thought and without delay decided to appoint Lieutenant Commander Akiyama Saneyuki as lecturer in strategic studies at the school. Thus, Saneyuki was freed from service in the fleet, returned to Tokyo, and began to teach at the Naval Staff College. His residence was the house in Takanawa Kuruma-chō in Shiba that he had previously rented.

His mother Sada looked forward to living with Saneyuki, her youngest and favorite son, so the move to Tokyo was an important event to her. "So, Jun, does it mean that you won't be, you know, on board ship for a while, then?" she pressed.

"That's right, I won't be. But when I do go to sea again, it may be for a war." Russia's high-pressure diplomatic dealings with Japan already smelled of gunpowder.

Meanwhile, his older brother Yoshifuru was in Tianjin.

"What if there's a war . . . ?" murmured Sada. If both her older and younger sons had to leave home and go to war, it would be terrible, she added.

Saneyuki commuted from the house in Takanawa to the Naval Staff College, and, as soon as he entered the school gates, he felt the urge to urinate. There was a cherry tree at the entrance to the school, and Saneyuki would urinate at that spot almost every day. The school janitor didn't like it, but he couldn't really say anything. There was someone else from Matsuyama at the school, and he explained to the other students, "His father always did that, too!"

The late Yasoku had continued to urinate in the road even though the police at the time were becoming strict and would demand a fine on the spot if they discovered such a thing. One day, Yasoku was caught in the act and, embarrassed, paid the patrolman the fine but then added some extra coins with the words, "Let me do just this much more," and continued to urinate until he was done. This became a well-known story in Matsuyama, and that Matsuyama student had heard all about it.

* * *

The lectures in strategy that Saneyuki gave at the Naval Staff College were so superb that they seemed outstanding forever after. He used no texts. Not only was he teaching naval strategic studies that he himself had systematized, but he also repeatedly told the students the secret of how he was able to systematize them.

"If you read a variety of strategic texts and a great number of military histories, the basic principles will become clear to you. Each of you should devise your own strategies. If it's not your own, a strategy won't be of much use in time of real need."

He tested them and didn't necessarily give them bad marks even if their answers were different from his own ideas. Even those with more seniority in the navy than Saneyuki came to audit his lectures.

Yashiro Rokurō had been Saneyuki's instructor at the Naval Academy, but he became an auditor and eagerly listened to Saneyuki's lectures. Yashiro was known as a stouthearted, heroic figure who vigorously questioned anything he had doubts about. Saneyuki would answer, and if Yashiro was unsatisfied he would stand up again and take on Saneyuki directly; so an argument would be carried on between the lectern and the floor.

There were times when neither side would give in, and Saneyuki would declare to this former mentor of his from Naval Academy days, "How extraordinarily stupid! I thought better of you. I'm amazed that you don't understand something as simple as this!" Yashiro was a captain, while Saneyuki was only a lieutenant commander.

Yashiro fell silent. He was the sort of person who might have resorted to a physical fight, but instead he stood silent, lost in thought, and then went home without a word.

The next day, his eyes red and bleary, he came to apologize. "Akiyama, you were right!" he said in a loud voice there in the middle of the classroom. He had spent the whole night thinking the matter through, and that was his conclusion.

"Yes," said Saneyuki brusquely. Usually, if one's superior has admitted defeat and been embarrassed like this, the man of lower rank will say something to cover for his superior. But Saneyuki's attitude was cold, totally without human warmth, as if he were hitting a nail home with a hammer.

"He is a genius, to be sure," some decided when they saw Saneyuki's response to Yashiro, "but there's something wrong with his character."

Saneyuki would have shot back, "What need is there for human warmth in matters of strategy?"

Saneyuki's lectures on strategy were backed up with watertight theory, and his seminars, using charts and military simulations, were graphic and concrete. There was always a hypothetical enemy: the Russian fleet.

Using the knowledge he had gained during his travels in Russia regarding the capacity of their warships, the characteristic movements of their fleet, and their ways of conceiving a battle plan, as well as the various documentary materials about Russia that the Japanese Navy had managed to acquire, Saneyuki "reproduced" the Russian fleet within his classroom. He studied along with his students how best to fight this enemy in the hope of discovering specific ways to achieve its annihilation.

During the Russo-Japanese War, these students were appointed as staff officers of the various squadrons and carried out "Akiyama-style strategy" under Saneyuki's direction. They were thus able to ensure that the entire navy would move in concert on the battlefield.

* * *

After moving to Tokyo, Saneyuki paid a visit to Shiki's house in Negishi. Seeing Shiki on his sickbed, Saneyuki was thunderstruck at how much he had weakened physically since they had last met. Shiki kept his eyes closed. When he opened them, he became feverish and dizzy—that was how severe his symptoms were.

And then there was the pain. According to Shiki's sister Ritsu, the pain was intense, as if holes were being drilled into the sick man's spine and pelvis. By then, no trace of girlishness remained in Ritsu. She was tired out from her care of her brother, and so her skin had become jaundiced and her facial expressions as slow and stilted as some middle-aged woman's.

"So, how are things going?" asked Shiki, eyes still closed. "Been doing anything interesting?"

"Oh, the same old things," Saneyuki answered. There seemed no point in telling Shiki about Saneyuki's becoming a lieutenant commander and leaving shipboard duties to become a lecturer in strategy at the Naval Staff College. To an invalid, such worldly concerns would seem dazzling and incomprehensible. "Dazzling" here has the sense of "vulgar and worldly," which Saneyuki, who envied the life of a Buddhist priest in his later years, understood from long before.

"Is there going to be a war with Russia?"

"If there is, ten percent of Japanese may die in it."

"As many as that?" Shiki at last opened his eyes.

* * *

That day's visit turned out to be the last meeting between Saneyuki and Shiki, though Shiki survived for about one more month. He knew he was dying. When intense pain assaulted him, he would cry out, but he never showed sorrow over his impending death. For about a year, he had been suffering, but when we look at the letters and notes he wrote when not in pain, we find expressions of his views about life and death.

The following is from a letter to a haiku poet named Ishii Rogetsu of Akita Prefecture. Rogetsu had reproached Shiki for shouting out that he wanted to die when the pain was too great, and this is how Shiki replied:

"Though others insist they do not want me to die"—the point of Rogetsu's reproaches—"how can the loss of my life mean so little to me myself? If I say that I no longer want this precious, precious life, that I want to die as quickly as possible, don't you realize it's because of this unbearable pain?"

Around this same time, Nakae Chōmin, an advocate of freedom and popular rights, came down with cancer and was told by his doctor that he had about a year and a half to live. From his bed, he wrote and published thoughts on life and death under the title *One Year and a Half*. It was well received, and Shiki asked a friend to go and buy a copy for him, which he then read.

"He's nothing much, compared to me," he said, with a smile that took those around him by surprise. He dropped the book by his pillow. "Chōmin's a mediocre, frivolous man."

Most people thought that Chōmin was splendidly fulfilling his vocation as a writer by continuing to write even though he had received a death sentence.

"Why make so much of him?" Shiki asked. "If he writes during his illness, it's just to make himself feel a little better." This was the frank opinion of someone who was also facing a mortal illness.

Chōmin suffered from cancer of the throat.

"Master Chōmin has one hole in his throat. Now me, I've got so many holes in my belly and my back and my buttocks that I'm like a beehive. The one and a half years part is probably the same for both of us. But Master Chōmin doesn't know beans about beauty yet."

Shiki was saying that he possessed a certain beauty in himself. And, in fact, even lying in his sickbed, he probably outdid any healthy man in his continuing quest for beauty. He would gaze at the grass in the garden and the birdcage by the window; he would compose haiku and express his thoughts about the beauties of nature; taking morphine to ease his pain, he would take up his sketchbook and draw the little bit of nature he could see from his pillow.

"If you understand beauty, you will know true pleasure," he wrote. Chōmin, he claimed, knew nothing of this.

In *One Year and a Half*, Chōmin described how he ate apricots with his wife. Shiki, comparing this with his own state of mind, commented, "That is certainly pleasure of one sort, but it conceals a kind of moral-ethical principle." Chōmin was resigned to reality and placed himself within the spiritual empty space that resulted from perfect resignation. But Shiki's pleasure was greater in that he could draw and compose poetry within that same space. "Since my pleasure is greater, I'm greater" was his boast. What an innocent he already had become!

In November of the previous year, Shiki had sent Natsume Sōseki in London the following letter: "I'm sure I'll never be able to meet you again. And, if by some chance we can meet, I doubt I'd be able to speak with you then. To tell the truth, living has become painful for me."

"Painful" refers to the intense pain of Shiki's illness. From the beginning of the year, when the pain came, Shiki cried out in tears without caring what others might think.

"I hear they still torture people in Korea and China," he told Kyoshi. "Well, I experience that every day, every hour."

This young disciple, whom Shiki called "Kiyoshi," tended to Shiki virtually full time during the poet's last year.

"I don't know why, but I've loved the natural world ever since I was a child, Kiyoshi." Shiki would tell him about his views regarding the appreciation of nature as fully as his energy level would permit on any given day, but his talk would always be retrospective. "But why do I love the beauties of nature so much—why, Kiyoshi? I have been in love with beauty since I was a child, but the house was totally without charm, and the furnishings had nothing beautiful about them. Well, there were the hanafuda, of course. I was envious of other families and asked myself why I had to be born into so poor a household. Was that why I gave up on manmade beauty and set my heart on flowers and clouds—the beauties of nature?"

These were the sorts of topics Shiki talked about.

In early September, he became weaker and weaker. Even so, he kept on writing short entries in his journal, entitled "A 6-foot Sickbed." Or rather, he kept dictating them. Disciples like Kyoshi and Hekigotō, who took turns staying with him, wrote them out.

On the night of September 13, it was Kyoshi's turn. He was sleeping in the guestroom next to Shiki's sickroom. As the shoji screen grew light with the dawn, Shiki woke up. The call of a seller of fermented *nattō* beans floated past. Even such a small event made Shiki glad, and he wanted to have some part in it. His part was that of buyer.

"Buy some nattō from him, won't you?"

Yae rose and went out.

Kyoshi came in with paper and a writing brush to take dictation. After the dictation, Shiki spoke nostalgically with Kyoshi about the morning scenes he had observed when he was in the hospital in Suma. As they spoke, a single leaf of the luffa vine in the garden trembled a bit. Shiki immediately noticed.

"The dew must have fallen from it." That's why the leaf moved. This was the only kind of change in Shiki's universe now. Autumn was already coming.

Every day, several disciples came to pay their respects. One of them would stay the night, but, after the incident of the luffa leaf, Shiki hardly spoke at all.

* * *

Shiki died at one in the morning on September 19, 1902. The doctor and various visitors had come throughout the previous day, and Shiki, who lay in his sickroom seemingly asleep, nonetheless seemed to be aware of their voices.

"Who's here now?" he would ask his sister Ritsu.

"Kiyoshi, and Hei, and . . . " she would answer, giving each one's name, and Shiki would nod his head, his face now entirely without expression.

When night came, everyone went home except Kyoshi, whose turn it was to spend the night there. Shiki lay inside a mosquito net. Perhaps he was sleeping, since he was so quiet. Around midnight, Kyoshi spread the futon in the next room but couldn't get to sleep. He went out into the garden. It was already past midnight.

Dew seemed to be falling on the trellis of the luffa in the garden, and two or three leaves had a special sheen. This was due to the near-full moon of the seventeenth night, which was rising brightly in the sky. It was the seventeenth night by the old, lunar calendar.

When Kyoshi returned to the parlor that served as sickroom, he found the small dark figure of Shiki's mother Yae sitting there. She had slept for two or three hours in her own room some time before and got up to relieve Kyoshi of his bedside vigil.

"Get some rest now, Kiyoshi, since we'll have to ask you to sit up with him again later."

Kyoshi looked through the mosquito net. Shiki seemed to be fast asleep.

"You, too, Ritsu . . . " Yae urged her daughter to go to bed as well.

Kyoshi went into the next room and lay down. The sky of the seventeenth night, which he had just been looking at, still vividly occupied his thoughts. It had been fearfully bright, with the large moon floating up. Kyoshi may have slept just a bit. When he was between sleeping and waking, a panic-stricken voice called his name from the other room. It was Yae. Kyoshi leaped from the futon.

It turned out that Ritsu had not yet gone to bed and had been talking quietly with her mother, fanning herself against the heat. Suddenly she had felt an urge to look through the mosquito net, and, when she did so, she found that Shiki was no longer breathing.

She called out to him, weeping, trying to bring him back, but Shiki did not respond.

"Ritsu, call the doctor!" Yae's voice was strong but steady as she gave the order. Yet, when she called out to Kyoshi just afterward, it was in a very agitated voice.

Ritsu ran barefoot to a neighbor's house to use the telephone.

Kyoshi was a man whose face expressed little emotion. He gazed steadily at Shiki's face, then finally stood up. He had to go summon Hekigotō and Samukawa Sokotsu, who were staying nearby.

When he stepped outside, he saw that the moon of the seventeenth night was shining brightly, after Shiki's death, as before it.

* * *

Beneath that bright moon, Kyoshi hurried off, his geta clattering on the pavement. Having let Hekigotō and Sokotsu know of Shiki's death, he returned to the house.

His footsteps were heavy. "I don't want to go back there," he thought. Shiki was already a corpse, and for Kyoshi it seemed somehow too cruel to even be there in the midst of Yae's and Ritsu's cries of grief. And yet he had to go back. There were just the two women now in the Masaoka household, and the funeral and other practical details would all have to be dealt with by Kyoshi and his friends.

To his right as he walked was a bamboo fence, while to his left there was the long black wooden wall of the former Kaga domain's residence. The moonlight fell full upon that wooden wall, and, if you looked at it alone, the wall was so bright that night seemed hardly there. Within the brightness of that wall, Kyoshi sensed for an instant something moving and slipping away.

"The soul of Master Shiki!" thought Kyoshi. The soul must now be rising up, up through the air.

> Shiki's gone!
> under the bright moon
> of the seventeenth night

Kyoshi murmured this haiku to himself as he walked. It was an extempore poem with no trace of sham. Kyoshi was exemplifying the "sketching from real life" that Shiki had insisted upon throughout his own literary life. When he got back to the Masaoka house, Kyoshi found both Yae and Ritsu sitting next to Shiki's body with blank looks on their faces.

Yae had not shed one tear earlier, but when she saw Kyoshi coming into the parlor after having stepped out of his geta in the entranceway, it seemed as if a spiritual support that had been sustaining her up to then suddenly collapsed.

"Kiyoshi!" she called yet couldn't look at him. She averted her face to stare at the dark wall beside her.

Kyoshi seated himself nearby. In the silence, Yae lowered her head. She seemed to be trying not to cry, and the effort made her thin shoulders shake.

"Noboru loved you most. And you were always so good to him."

Yae seemed to be speaking for Shiki himself. When she said this, her shoulders began to shake more violently, but she did not cry out.

Kyoshi remained silent. There was nothing else he could do, he felt, until the others came. Only, from time to time, he would look at Shiki's body.

"I saw you going up into the sky just now, you know." He spoke silently to Shiki, as if a secret had passed between them. Then he remembered one of Shiki's poems:

> People laugh and call me "monkey from Shikoku"
> a baby, the child of a monkey from Shikoku—
> that's me!

Shiki had secretly deprecated himself for being a provincial, but there is a pride in this poem that virtually shouts, "This country bumpkin has changed the whole world of haiku and waka in Japan!" Shiki didn't leave a death poem, but Kyoshi felt that this one verse summed up his life of thirty-five years.

Shiki had loved to give direction to others in everything, and he had left written instructions as to how his funeral was to be conducted. "Public announcements of the funeral are unnecessary." This was because both his house and the neighborhood were small. If a lot of people saw an announcement and came to the funeral, it would be hard to move the casket. Shiki had been the sort who did everything by rough estimates, and he had thought that twenty or thirty people should be the limit at his own funeral. Shiki had no religion. He had learned a little about Zen, but the idea that he should be able to deal with his own problems without help from religion came completely naturally to him.

Just because he believed in doing things naturally, however, he did not object to having a Buddhist priest come and recite sutras at this funeral. A priest of any sect would do. But as for having elegies read before his coffin, or his life history rehearsed, that too was "unnecessary."

A Buddhist posthumous name was also "unnecessary"—not in order to stress at all costs Shiki's lack of religious faith, but, typical of Shiki, for practical reasons. When Shiki had been researching Japanese poets of the past in order to make a chronology, he found that the posthumous names could not be fitted into the space he'd allotted for them since they tended to be quite long. This had caused him problems, and he did not want one of his own.

With regard to the gravestone, he was aware that many men of culture made a point of using natural stones rather than the standard tablets fashioned by human hands, but he thought that in bad taste. A very ordinary stone was best. He had always tried to find beauty in the ordinary, completely unaffected world of common sense. As to the wake, "Keeping vigil all night before the coffin is unnecessary" was what he first wrote, but then, perhaps thinking he was being too strict, he added, "If an all-night vigil must be kept, let it be done by turns, not by everyone at once." And, thinking it showy for people to be seen crying in front of the coffin during the vigil, he urged, "People should talk and laugh normally throughout." Everyone knew these things, and Kyoshi and his other old friends intended to do their best to have the deceased's wishes respected.

Kyoshi continued to sit there in silence. After about twenty minutes, Kuga Katsunan came from next door, and Hekigotō and Sokotsu also arrived from nearby. Each of them had been caring for Shiki in his last year, and all they needed to do was silently bow to Yae and then sit quietly at the bedside.

After a time, Katsunan asked the younger men what arrangements they would make for the funeral.

"We're young and ignorant about these things," said Hekigotō, meaning they needed direction from Katsunan who, then in his forties, answered, "Maybe so. Getting older entails knowing about funerals."

Shiki had benefited from Katsunan's kindness ever since coming to Tokyo for the entrance exams at the Preparatory School. And, at the very end too, he would once again depend on Katsunan.

* * *

The Akiyamas were immediately informed of Shiki's death, but, as luck would have it, Saneyuki was away in Yokosuka and didn't receive the sad news directly. Two men, probably teachers from their appearance, happened to be sitting next to him on the Yokosuka line train while discussing Shiki's death.

A stunned Saneyuki asked, "Excuse me, but is the Shiki you are speaking of Masaoka Shiki, by any chance?"

"Yes. Shiki has passed away." The teachers were extremely polite in their reply. "We've just begun studying haiku, actually."

"When was it?"

"When did we begin studying haiku, you mean?"

"No, when did Shiki die?"

"Here . . . " One of the men showed Saneyuki a newspaper, the September 20 issue of *Nippon*. Saneyuki glanced at it and saw the headline, "Masaoka Shiki Dies," with a black line printed alongside. It was a long article of about eighty lines praising Shiki's accomplishments in life.

"So he's dead . . . " Saneyuki sat there vacantly, quite unlike himself. Then he remembered to return the newspaper with thanks. The day of the funeral was not given in the article.

He went back to Takanawa, where his mother Sada took one look at his face and immediately told him the details of the funeral—it would be at nine o'clock in the morning of the next day, the twenty-first, at the Masaoka home in Negishi.

"I see," said Saneyuki with an angry look and went to his room.

"What'll happen to Noboru's family, I wonder," Sada said as she followed him, cleaning off some dust that had collected at the threshold.

"It'll be hard for them" was Saneyuki's immediate thought. Still, Shiki's maternal relatives, the Ōharas, were among the most wealthy and secure of the former Matsuyama retainers, so they might look after the mother and younger sister now that Shiki was gone.

"I'll bet he didn't save a penny himself," Saneyuki reflected.

But Sada was talking of something other than finances, it seemed. She was afraid that the Masaoka family would die out. Shiki had been single and without children.

"And you need to think about the same thing, Jun." She was talking about marriage.

"Mother, it's not fitting to move so quickly from talk of a funeral to talk of a wedding, you know."

"Oh, but it is! Weddings and funerals are just two sides of one and the same coin."

"What strange reasoning!" he said to himself. But if you thought about it, they might both be aspects of one and the same thing. Sada had been urging Saneyuki to marry for some time. She could not free herself from the old ways of thinking of samurai families. For her, producing children to carry on the line was the best offering one could make to one's ancestors.

Shiki's house in Kami-Negishi was deep inside a warren of back lanes, and the house itself was small. Shiki had regarded twenty to thirty people as the upper limit of mourners it could accommodate, but as many as one hundred fifty people came, having seen the death notice in the newspapers.

"It was a pipe dream," whispered Hekigotō to Kyoshi. The two of them had discussed keeping the funeral as simple as possible, in accordance with Shiki's will. That seemed doubtful now. "A pipe dream" was an expression in vogue among students of that day.

Shiki had felt himself to be "a student" all his life, while Kyoshi and Hekigotō really were authentic students. It was their intention, as students, to give the "student" Shiki a fitting funeral. Yet over one hundred mourners came, the same as at any ordinary funeral.

The ceremony itself, however, was simple. At a little past nine in the morning, when the customary sutra recitation was finished, the casket left the house.

"Oh, don't forget—we need to let Natsume Sōseki in London know," Kyoshi whispered to Hekigotō.

"And what about Akiyama Jun? He's not here."

"He's on board ship somewhere, isn't he?"

"No," replied Hekigotō, who made it his business to keep up-to-date on the doings of his friends from Matsuyama, "he's at the Naval Staff College."

"Oh yes, Master Shiki said something about that."

Just then, a small man with a swaggering walk appeared from beyond the funeral procession. His hair was cropped short, and he was dressed like a student, with no haori coat and his hakama pulled up toward his shins. In one hand, he carried a walking stick as thick as a log and came toward them with a long, easy stride.

"Isn't that Jun over there?" These words had hardly been uttered when the man came close enough for them to tell that it was indeed Saneyuki.

He had come a bit late. Coming closer, he looked at Kyoshi and the others, then averted his gaze, and immediately approached the coffin. He seemed almost to glare at it for a moment, then bobbed his head.

He continued to stand there. The funeral procession went on, but he didn't try to join it. After the procession had passed by, Saneyuki stood alone, making no move to follow. With the procession gone, Saneyuki stood alone in the empty lane.

"Everybody dies, Noboru. I'm going to die, too," he murmured. This was Saneyuki's prayer for the repose of his friend's soul.

Then he went on to the Masaoka house. Yae, Ritsu, and Mrs. Kuga were sitting with blank looks on their faces in the room where the coffin had been. Saneyuki silently entered and knelt, placing his hands on the floor to make a formal bow, and tried to offer his condolences. Somehow, though, the words would not come, so he fell silent again and edged forward to the incense burner, where he took a pinch of incense to offer to Shiki's spirit.

Then he left.

He didn't go to the temple where Shiki was to be interred—the Dairyūji in Tabata, an area then known as the village of Takinogawa.

2

"GOMBEI"

I'm still troubled about just how to write this novel.

Shiki has died.

Yoshifuru and Saneyuki will in time take part in the Russo-Japanese War.

If possible, I'd like to go on to describe the war itself, while keeping those two always at the center. But my subject would then be too large and unfocused, and a novel is not a very convenient means of adequately handling such a subject.

So we will have to distance ourselves from our protagonists from time to time. That was why, in a previous volume, we spent almost too many pages on Russia and Russian matters, and on Tsar Nicholas II. The energy that gave rise to the Russo-Japanese War may well have sprung from history itself, but one of the forces behind that phase of history was Nicholas II.

It is hardly possible to make an objective judgment about which side started the war. Nevertheless, if one wants to roughly assign the blame for it, the answer must be that Russia bore eighty percent and Japan twenty percent of the blame, and Nicholas II must bear the responsibility for almost all of that Russian eighty percent. The tsar's character and judgment must take the blame for inviting this great calamity. That is why I devoted so many pages to him.

Now let us look at the Japanese side.

Most of the politicians on the Japanese side never dreamed that Japan could go to war with Russia and win. Itō Hirobumi, an outstanding statesman of his day, was nicknamed "The Russophobe."

Itō must have really been afraid of Russia. As one of the disciples of Yoshida Shōin from Chōshū, he had been an advocate of the exhortation "Revere the Emperor, Expel the Barbarians" in the final days of the shogunate. He was a low-ranking activist but had ample experience of all of Chōshū's troubles at the time.

When, in 1863, under the rubric of "Expel the Barbarians," Chōshū shelled a foreign ship passing through the Shimonoseki Straits, Itō was in London. After reading about the incident in the *Times*, he returned home immediately only to see the latest battles in Chōshū's lost war against the foreigners, who had retaliated. Chōshū had turned against the shogunate early on and was pressed to the very brink of extinction as a domain in the shogunate's first anti-Chōshū campaign. But once Chōshū had the good fortune to link itself with Satsuma, which was also pro-imperial and anti-shogunate, it managed a miraculous rebirth.

Having drunk to the full this bitter cup, Itō added to his great natural gifts a superb sense of how to deal with foreign affairs. He saw how Chōshū had, near the end of the shogunate, escaped the jaws of death, come back to life, and been able to stand with the victors in the national struggle because of its ties with Satsuma. As one of the leaders of the new Japan, Itō saw that there was a need for another ally who could do for the nation what Satsuma had done for Chōshū. Other leaders were looking to Britain, but Itō stressed the need for Russia. Russia had invaded the Far East and was exerting great pressure there. By allying itself with this oppressor in the Far East, Japan itself could escape invasion and oppression—this was Itō's idea. But it was not adopted by those in power at the time, and Japan allied itself with Britain.

And what about the military?

* * *

We will touch on the army's preparations for war with Russia later. The real issue was the navy. Japan is surrounded by seas and oceans, its most significant geographical characteristic. An enemy's naval forces can attack at will from Japan's seacoasts and even penetrate deep into Tokyo Bay, as was the case when Perry's ships threatened the city of Edo.

"If we were to put pressure on Japan . . . " These words, heard within the Russian Navy around this time, meant that if the Japanese Navy vanished, the Russians could surround the archipelago with some twenty warships, thus rendering Japan helpless and giving Russia the opportunity to dictate the terms for capitulation.

Japan needed to strengthen its navy. The planner and promoter of this effort was one and the same man—Yamamoto Gombei. Before talking about him, however, I need to present some amazing material to the reader.

We're speaking of the national budget of Japan, which represented a sort of financial madness. The First Sino-Japanese War ended in 1895, and the total annual spending for that wartime year was over ninety-one million six hundred thousand yen. The next year, 1896, Japan was at peace. Naturally, one would have wanted to give the people some relief, yet the annual budget was over two hundred million yen, more than twice the previous wartime year. The percentage of the total budget devoted to the military, which had previously been thirty-two percent, had jumped to forty-eight percent.

Herein lies the tragedy of the Meiji period.

When we look back on the world of Meiji, we see a kind of fatal darkness there. These financial problems caused the poverty of the people, their amazingly low income levels. In order for a non-industrial nation like Japan to draw up such a burdensome budget, the people's livelihood had to suffer. This huge budget to prepare for war (and it continued right up to the Russo-Japanese War) represented a kind of miracle, but the greater miracle was the Japanese people's ability to endure these hardships. This was possible because the Japanese had grown accustomed to poverty. At the time, children, except those who lived in some urban areas, did not customarily wear shoes. They wore handmade straw sandals or went barefoot. In the "snow country," with its cold winters, they wore straw shoes, also handmade. And in the countryside, not only were children so primitively shod, but most adults also went about in the same manner.

Food was mostly rice, barley, and two types of millet. The supplementary dishes were incredibly poor. Moreover, feudal ideas of loyalty still held, and refraining as much as possible from stressing one's own personal desires was deemed a virtue. Only in certain Tokyo salons did the concept of respect for the individual come up for serious discussion.

Other factors contributed to this state of affairs as well, but we must conclude that few historical periods offered such perfect conditions for converting the entire nation into a war machine.

* * *

The passing of a certain historical age means the disappearance of the various conditions that created that age. When these have disappeared, then understanding the age that has passed becomes, for people of a later age, still more challenging than comprehending contemporary foreign lands.

For example, Japan had to return the Liaodong Peninsula, gained as a result of victory in the war against Qing China, due to the Triple Intervention by Western powers. After that, the phrase "sleeping on firewood and eating bears' gall bladders" came into vogue. In the Spring and Autumn period in ancient China, Fucha of Wu attacked King Goujian of Yue to take revenge on behalf of his father. In order not to forget his need for revenge, King Fucha always slept on a bed of firewood, thus inflicting pain on himself. When he succeeded in revenging himself fully, King Goujian of Yue sought to focus his sense of shame by always eating the gall bladder of bears so that their bitter taste would help maintain his thirst for revenge against King Fucha.

To understand how much the Japanese of Meiji hated the Russian Empire, one would need to go back to that time and live through what the Japanese experienced. The phrase "sleeping on firewood and eating bears' gall bladders" was not only in vogue—it provided the energy of the age.

That energy welled up from among the people. Those in the government had to try to control the fierce pressure from below. Itō Hirobumi, for one, said, "There's no point paying attention to all sorts of brilliant ideas and theories that are being bandied about. I now must deal with cannons and warships." Confronting a major power whose military force was incomparably greater than Japan's, the government could not be too much swayed by the pressure from below exerted by Japanese public opinion.

The ambitious plans to build warships for the Japanese Navy were created and put into practice at a time when this sort of national mood prevailed in the country. A ten-year plan for warship construction was launched in 1896. The total amount of the annual national budget increased year by year. Fifty-five percent of total expenditures for 1897 went for military spending; in 1899, military spending rose to three times 1895 levels. In terms of the nation's standard of living, this might have been termed a "starvation budget." Yet, strange to say, it engendered almost no opposition in any form at the time.

"Inconceivable!" was the comment in French Navy circles just after the Triple Intervention, with regard to Japan's enthusiasm for constructing warships. "It's impossible for a country as weak as Japan to have a fleet that could compare with the Great Powers' navies, nor would Japan attempt to build one."

That was the view.

In point of fact, Japan's navy at the time of the First Sino-Japanese War was extremely weak and inferior. The term "first-class battleship" in general refers to a ship of over 10,000 tons. Japan didn't have any, whereas Russia had ten. Second-class battleships are over 7,000 tons. Japan had zero, Russia, eight. Third-class battleships are under 7,000 tons. Japan had zero, Russia, ten. Armored cruisers are over 6,000 tons. Japan had zero, Russia, ten. All Japan had was protected cruisers and below. And, with this as a basis, it intended to create a great navy within ten years.

* * *

Occasionally in world history, a people achieves miraculous feats that are unimaginable to later generations. The miracle achieved by Japan in the ten years from the First Sino-Japanese War to the Russo-Japanese War has probably never been equaled by any other nation. Although the Japanese Navy at the time of the First Sino-Japanese War was one in name only, just before the outbreak of the Russo-Japanese War ten years later, Japan had succeeded in building a navy large enough for the nation to rank fifth among the five great naval powers of the world.

"It is almost unbelievable what the Japanese have done," observed the British naval expert Archibald S. Hurd. By the outbreak of the Russo-Japanese War, Japan had six first-class battleships and six armored cruisers, all first-time additions to the fleet. A new navy had been created, with a six-six system, that is, six battleships and six cruisers. This in itself was amazing, but, in addition, these warships were all products of the most up-to-date planning and design. Thus, hardly any unarmored protected cruisers, considered old-fashioned by then, had been built, even though the British Navy was still building ships of this sort for itself. We could almost say that the Japanese built their navy at the sacrifice of food and drink.

The planner of this new Japanese Navy was Yamamoto Gombei, who, at the time of these ambitious shipbuilding plans, had only just become a rear admiral. The people themselves must get credit for providing the energy behind this project, but the planning and promotion of the new Japanese Navy fell to this one man, a native of Satsuma.

At the time of the Boshin War, Yamamoto Gombei served as an infantryman in the Satsuma forces, fighting in both the Echigo and the northeastern regions. After the war ended, he went to Tokyo. Finding nothing else to do, he decided to become a sumo wrestler and asked to become the student of the champion wrestler Jimmaku Kyūgorō, but he was turned down. He had been good at sumo wrestling ever since his boyhood in the castle town of Kagoshima and had even received a sumo name, "Flower Cart."

After that, influenced by Saigō Takamori, the great commander of Satsuma men, he went to see Katsu Kaishū, with an introduction from Saigō, and learned about the navy from him. He entered the Naval School that had just been founded in Tsukiji, though he seems not to have cared much for the navy at that time.

Like a typical Satsuma youth of the time, he was always fighting with other students while at the school. He was good at mathematics, among his academic subjects, and good at climbing masts, among his practical ones. After becoming a probationary sublieutenant, he was sent to the German warship *Vineta* and then to the *Leipzig*; he received his commission while part of the *Leipzig*'s crew. He was a survivor of the Boshin campaigns and therefore a bit older than most other commissioned officers. He was commissioned in 1877, when he was already twenty-six.

* * *

At the time that Yamamoto Gombei was undergoing naval training on board the German warship *Leipzig*, which is to say around 1877, the German Navy itself was not up to much. "The handling of the ships was superb," Gombei later commented, "but the Germans were far behind when it came to strategy, troop disposition, and the like."

Lectures on strategy were given on board, but the content was poor. They were mere imitations of army strategy, a kind of direct translation into naval terms. Even when they were explaining actions peculiar to the navy, they used examples from the army. Germany was an army-centered nation, and not until the turn of the century did they set out to build a great navy.

Gombei liked to ask direct, challenging questions, and he would push particular points so stubbornly that he often found himself debating the instructor. The instructor in strategy was not in the least put out by this, however, and seemed rather in awe of Gombei's brainpower. The other officers too showed him great respect; having participated in the Boshin War as a very young soldier and successfully dodged bullets there, he could talk about problems on the battlefield with real authority.

"Gombei is a brave warrior," all the Germans agreed.

While Gombei was a member of the crew, the *Leipzig* was rushed to Nicaragua to support a struggle that Germany had launched against that Central American country. This turned into a real war, but a land war. An infantry detachment and two large pieces of artillery were transported from the warship so they could take part, and the captain of the *Leipzig* expressed the hope that Gombei would participate in the land campaign. He was to direct the use of the artillery. But permission from the Japanese government was required, and Japan opposed allowing one of its overseas naval students to take part in another country's war, a war unconnected to Japan's own interests. Gombei was therefore refused permission to participate. As a result, he had to leave the *Leipzig* and return to Japan.

"The German Navy did not offer adequate training to forces engaged in a land war," Gombei later said. "That's why they wanted to make use of me, with my actual experience of war."

For the next ten years, Gombei's career was no different from any other naval officer's. He became divisional officer on a warship, then executive officer; he served on the committee charged with sailing foreign-made warships to Japan and was commissioned as captain of a ship. What changed his destiny, and that of the Japanese Navy, was his appointment as adjutant to the navy minister in 1887, at the age of thirty-six. He was then a lieutenant commander.

From then on, he was in charge of military administration. Even during this period, though, he went to sea as captain of the *Takao* and the *Takachiho*. He was finally removed from seagoing duties in 1891 at the age of forty, when, as a naval captain, he became director of the navy minister's secretariat. He was generally referred to as "director of the navy." From this time forward, he showed his astuteness in accomplishing the great work of building the Japanese Navy.

* * *

Yamamoto Gombei's ability to effect a great reform of the navy while still a mere captain or rear admiral is a most interesting feature of the Meiji period navy. Beginning shore duty at the Naval Ministry, he first served under Navy Minister Saigō Tsugumichi. Later as well, this Tsugumichi became Gombei's direct superior. The two of them formed a fine combination.

Tsugumichi was the younger brother of Saigō Takamori. As the shogunate was drawing to a close, he was known as Saigō Shingo and engaged in anti-shogunate activities alongside Takamori. He didn't stand out much, except as a young man who was quite attentive to details. He showed his real abilities after the Restoration. The Meiji journalist Ikebe Sanzan counted him as one of the three great political figures of the age. Partly because Tsugumichi was too big a man for his time, and partly because there was something of the Daoist about him—playing the fool and hiding his own accomplishments—he was never given his full due either in his own lifetime or since.

"Too big a man" is a very Asian way of describing someone, but at some point after the Meiji period, the topic of great men of Meiji was raised at a private dinner given by the foreign minister of the time.

"If we're talking about a man's professional stature, then Ōyama Iwao must be at the top," someone said.

"No," countered someone else. "Saigō Tsugumichi, another Satsuma man, was five times greater than Ōyama!" And no one present contradicted him.

But a man who had known Saigō Takamori said, "By comparison with his older brother Takamori, even Tsugumichi was like a single star in the night sky next to the moon."

Everyone present felt quite dizzy imagining the extraordinary greatness of the man Saigō Takamori, it is said. Takamori and Tsugumichi were siblings, while Ōyama was their cousin. Their bloodlines seemed to share some curious power. All three of them were typical Satsuma men, natural leaders.

And, if they shared the same leadership qualities, the three of them also used the same methods. First, they would look for a man of great ability in practical matters, to whom they could safely leave such concerns. That person would be chosen without much regard for their own personal feelings or private advantage. Next, they would create a broad space so this practical man of affairs could handle things as he thought best and would leave everything to him. They themselves would be in charge only of the policy that created such a space. In the event of the man of affairs making a mess of things, they took it for granted that they should kill themselves to take responsibility. Admiral Tōgō Heihachirō was from Kajiyachō in Kagoshima, as were these three other men, and he adopted the same policy, so typical of Satsuma men.

In Saigō Tsugumichi, this tendency was even stronger. He served as navy minister three times between 1885 and 1898, though he knew nothing about the navy. He was at first a lieutenant general in the army, and he became navy minister with that rank and status.

Relations between Japan and Qing China were growing more difficult, however, and Japan had to strengthen its navy. At that point, Tsugumichi called on Yamamoto Gombei. "Do everything as you think best. If you have some problems that are hard for you to handle, call on me, and I'll clean them up for you." When Gombei's reforms seemed too radical, and there were complaints from all sides, Tsugumichi appropriately dealt with the politics of those matters in his own characteristic way.

*　*　*

Gombei's biggest task before the First Sino-Japanese War was the mass firing of superannuated, incompetent officials in the Naval Ministry. "There's no way to win a war without a massive cleanup in the ministry," he told Tsugumichi, "and the appointment of really able people to the various top posts."

In the navy of that time, there was a large number of worthless high- and medium-grade officers. People referred to the Japanese Navy of the time as the "Satsuma navy," and many men had received high or medium rank in the navy simply because they were from Satsuma, due to the services the Satsuma domain had rendered to the imperial cause before the Restoration. They didn't understand the structure of a warship, much less how to run one properly, yet they received high salaries and held important posts.

Among the superannuated were also men who had been associated with the former shogunate navy. Right after the Restoration, they were very highly regarded since so few people in the new government had any mastery of naval skills, but, at the same time, they couldn't keep up with the ongoing progress of the world's navies. There were high-ranking officers who knew only how to sail old Dutch-style wind-driven ships, and middle-ranking ones who had zero knowledge of attack weapons like torpedoes and the boats that carried them.

All of them were Gombei's seniors and superiors. He made a list of such men with as many as ninety-six high- and medium-ranking officers on it. When he showed his list to Saigō Tsugumichi as the minister in charge, even this broad-minded man hesitated. "Well now, Mr. Yamamoto . . ." True, this bunch might not know anything about modern naval science, but they had certainly made their contributions in the founding days of the Restoration.

"The government should decorate them for their contributions then. But giving them real work and responsibilities leads to a mass of problems," Gombei insisted. He planned to fill the vacancies left by these people's departure with young officers who had received a standard education in military science.

"They'll really resent you for this, you know."

"Of course they'll be resentful. But if the nation is ruined, that'll be the end of everything."

After Tsugumichi agreed to the proposal, Gombei didn't leave the firings to Tsugumichi but handled them on his own. He summoned the people concerned to his office at the Naval Ministry and told them himself. He was only a captain at the time.

His seniors from Satsuma were particularly difficult, some of them pounding the table and shouting things like, "Why, you . . . This is an outrageous usurpation of authority! How can you, a mere captain, presume to fire vice admirals and rear admirals? This goes against national order!"

Gombei would not give in. He had a dagger concealed on his person, and just glared at them with the fierce eyes of a panther, implacably repeating his declaration. The "Satsuma navy" was, in fact, killed and buried at the hands of Yamamoto Gombei, a native of Satsuma.

It is said that later, when the Russian Baltic Fleet sailed to the Far East, there were many superannuated officers on the Russian side who didn't know how to handle anything more modern than a sailing ship. In Japan, such persons had all been swept from office in 1893, just before the First Sino-Japanese War.

* * *

At the time of this great shake-up in 1893, the name "Captain Tōgō Heihachirō" appeared on the list of those who were to be removed from command. Tōgō had graduated from a British merchant marine college and was reputed to be very knowledgeable about international law. But perhaps because he was by nature so taciturn, he had no reputation, either positive or negative, in regard to his strategic abilities. Moreover, he suffered from many illnesses and had been absent from his duties a fair amount for medical treatment.

"What about this man?" asked Navy Minister Saigō Tsugumichi.

Like Tsugumichi and Tōgō, Gombei was also from Kajiyachō in Kagoshima, and so had had rather a lot of contact with Tōgō. From early on, Gombei had gained some sense of Tōgō's likely talents as a leader. "Let's observe him a bit."

"Observe him?"

"Why not put him on board the *Naniwa*? It's now docked at Yokosuka."

And so Tōgō was again made captain of the *Naniwa* and remained in that position throughout the First Sino-Japanese War. We've discussed how, early in the war, Tōgō attacked and sank a British steamship called the *Kowshing* that was filled with Qing soldiers, thereby creating an international incident. Various newspapers in Britain criticized this "outrage," and the Earl of Kimberley, the foreign secretary, pursued the issue of the Japanese government's responsibility in the matter with Ambassador Aoki Shūzō. Eventually, as more came to be known about the incident, it became clear that the *Naniwa*'s actions were in keeping with international law, and the British calmed down.

Nonetheless, Yamamoto Gombei, as "director" of the navy, did not let the matter rest. He had the *Naniwa* return from the war zone and summoned Tōgō to the Naval Ministry. "It is true that your handling of the matter was not wrong under international law, but it hardly seems a decision arrived at after prudent consideration."

Tōgō was not only from the same town as Gombei but was also a captain with roughly the same amount of experience, so he did not hold back in his response. "My handling of the matter was correct." From his point of view, there was no room for such criticisms since he had decided to sink the ship after considering all the relevant international laws.

"As you say, your actions were correct under international law," said Gombei, nodding. "And bolstering your view, public opinion in Britain, which was so outraged at first, has gradually come around to seeing the rightness of what you did. But, remember, the captain of a warship represents the nation as he carries out his duties."

Gombei went on to explain to Tōgō that a warship or a fleet should always act with due consideration of international repercussions. "Had you demanded that the *Kowshing* take down the British flag before you sank it, your actions would not have angered British public opinion as much as they did. And, in any event, I would have taken different measures—not sinking the ship but seizing it. What about that? Then there would have been no diplomatic problems whatsoever."

Tōgō remained silent but smiled slightly, indicating in this way that he yielded to Gombei's argument. And Gombei seems to have been highly impressed with the meticulousness, the decisiveness, and, above all, the obedience that Tōgō had shown.

* * *

When Yamamoto Gombei was young, he was wild, unyielding, and somewhat out of control. Most of his classmates at the Naval School found themselves challenged to fight and got punched around a good deal by Gombei. Partly, this was the "Satsuma style." At primary and middle schools in Satsuma, the fights would begin at the start of a new school year when the composition of a class changed. Many fights would break out each day, and these would continue until the students' relative strengths were determined, and the very strongest one clearly emerged. Only then would peace prevail in the class. This was true not only in the days of the shogunate but right up to the end of the Pacific War.

Both Gombei and Tōgō Heihachirō were former Satsuma soldiers who had participated in the Boshin War, but Tōgō was five years older. When he returned to Japan after graduating from the British merchant marine college, Tōgō served for a time on the same warship as Gombei, who had already graduated from the Naval School, though then his rank in the navy was lower than Tōgō's.

Gombei was indignant about this. "It's absurd! Do they actually think Tōgō's naval knowledge and skills are better than mine?"

One day, they got into an argument on the deck. "That's ridiculous!" Gombei tried to use his logical skills, not an easy task for a Japanese, to overcome Tōgō, his superior. Tōgō too would not give in, and no conclusion was reached.

All that was left was to fight it out—which would have been fine in Satsuma, but, since both of them were naval officers, they couldn't act like tough adolescents.

"Okay—let's see who's better at climbing the mast!" shouted Gombei.

Tōgō agreed.

Gombei was panther-like in both appearance and temperament, and, when it came to climbing a mast, he was truly unbeatable, just like that fierce cat. He quickly climbed up to the masthead.

Tōgō, however, had not climbed even halfway up. He was awkward and unskillful to a degree surprising in someone who had trained in Britain, with its superb navy. Also, one leg of his trousers was torn right to the cuff—as if he had caught it on something as he climbed. The contest was over, and he might well have come down from his spot halfway up, but he continued to climb, faltering all the way. Only when he had reached the masthead did he declare, "I lose!" and start down again. Gombei, for his part, smoothly descended the mast, easily beating Tōgō at that as well.

When it was all over, Gombei praised Tōgō to those present in the officers' cabin, quite as if *he* were the man higher in rank. "Tōgō shows real promise." Gombei offered these words of praise because "He doesn't give up till the very end. The enemy had already made it to the masthead, but, who knows, I might have had an attack of appendicitis and fallen straight to the deck. I'm sure he wasn't hoping that would happen, but a commander of a fighting force needs just that sort of tenacity."

* * *

Yamamoto Gombei was unquestionably one of the greatest men in the history of the world's navies. He planned and built the new navy virtually from nothing, and, as the "owner" of the Japanese Navy, he planned the "sea war" aspect of the First Sino-Japanese War.

The Qing navy possessed some extraordinarily large warships like the *Dingyuan* and the *Zhenyuan*, but the bulk of its fleet was a mix of light and heavy ships. Their ships' speed was generally slow, and the degree of slowness varied greatly from ship to ship. All this, Gombei noticed.

Given the need to assemble a unified Japanese fleet that could win against the Qing, Gombei first of all placed orders abroad for ships that were as fast as possible. Since he had a low budget, the ships were all to be one size smaller than their Qing counterparts. They were swift, though, and the Japanese fleet was on average faster than the Qing fleet. There had been a great improvement in the Japanese fleet's maneuverability. To put it in stark terms, the idea was to attack a herd of rhinos with a pack of agile wolves. That was how the Japanese fleet was designed. The same was true of their armament. The enemy had huge, heavy-caliber guns, but the Japanese side could equip its ships with many smaller, quick-firing guns that might not deal a death blow to the enemy, but could, by lobbing a huge number of small-caliber shells at an enemy ship in a short time, knock down its superstructure, prevent crew activity on deck, start fires on board, and thus render the enemy ship incapable of battle. This was Gombei's concept, which succeeded very well.

He also proved himself very adept at personnel matters. Itō Sukeyuki, commander of the Combined Fleet during the First Sino-Japanese War, was a cautious man, at times more cautious than he needed to be, and this caused problems. For this reason, Gombei dispatched Chief of the Navy General

Staff Kabayama Sukenori, who was in charge of naval operations, and put him on board the steamship *Saikyō Maru*, which accompanied the fleet. Kabayama was an aggressive, even fierce leader, and Gombei judged that putting the two of them together would keep Itō from exercising excessive caution. But, to ensure that two chains of command did not develop, he left the control of on-the-spot operations at sea in Itō's hands alone and made Kabayama simply on-site inspector.

During this period, Gombei was using as he saw fit various officers who had far greater seniority in the navy than he had. From first to last, Saigō Tsugumichi left everything to Gombei.

"If he hadn't had Saigō Tsugumichi as his protector, a difficult, eccentric man like Gombei would probably have ended his career with the rank of captain of a protected cruiser. On the other hand, there's no telling what the outcomes of the Sino-Japanese and Russo-Japanese Wars might have been." This was the general view that came to prevail in the navy.

In terms of the history of the Meiji period and the development of the Japanese Navy, the contribution of this one man, Yamamoto Gombei, cannot be evaluated too highly.

* * *

Gombei planned and designed the Japanese Navy twice, in preparation for the First Sino-Japanese War and then the Russo-Japanese War. Each feat took ten years to accomplish. Earlier, we referred to Gombei as the "owner" of the navy, but if we were to use a metaphor from professional baseball, he might be called the "manager." In that case, the "owner" would be Saigō Tsugumichi.

Shortly after Saigō left the army to become navy minister, Gombei thought to himself, "It's a pain, but I'll have to train him again to be minister." So he wrote a massive report about the current management of naval affairs and the prospects for the future, and presented that as a "textbook for the minister."

Sometime later, he asked Saigō, "Sir, have you read the document I submitted the other day?"

With his usual little smile playing about his lips, Saigō answered, "No," and crinkled his eyes pleasantly.

Another few days passed. Gombei asked the same question. But no, Saigō had not read it. This made Gombei angry. When he was angry, it showed clearly in his eyes.

Saigō gazed at Gombei with interest, then leaned across the table between them and said in a low voice, "Mr. Yamamoto, if I became really knowledgeable about naval matters, it would cause problems for everyone, don't you agree? I don't know anything about the navy, but the rest of you do. Whatever you decide is best, I will push through the cabinet meetings. Won't that do?"

This was during the third Itō Hirobumi cabinet. At a cabinet meeting, the Naval Ministry presented a huge budget request called the "Naval Expansion Plan." It amounted to two hundred million yen, a preposterous sum.

Prime Minister Itō looked displeased, and Finance Minister Inoue Kaoru scowled, declaring, "We need you to be serious about this matter, Mr. Saigō!"

When Saigō asked him what he meant by that, Inoue raised his voice to object to such an outlandish budget request. "How dare you ask for two hundred million yen?"

Saigō, not to be outdone, raised *his* voice. "Mr. Inoue, neither you nor Mr. Itō knows anything about naval matters. There's no point discussing them with people like you!"

Itō and Inoue were both greatly offended, and replied that since they didn't understand such matters, it was up to Saigō, as navy minister, to offer a reasonable explanation.

Saigō then laughed out loud and said, "In fact, I don't understand the matter myself!" Everyone was stunned by this admission, but Saigō went on. "There's a rear admiral in the navy by the name of Yamamoto Gombei. I'll have him present himself later to explain things." It was then that the cabinet first became aware of Gombei's existence.

* * *

Saigō Tsugumichi, the creator of the navy, was that kind of man. He may have seemed, at first glance, something of a fool about the details of administrative methodology, but Itō Hirobumi knew better than anyone that, though Saigō might not seem clever, he was a very wise man.

When Itō came upon some interesting views on world politics, for example, he felt like discussing them with Saigō before anyone else. Saigō was a good listener; he recognized Itō's great ability from early on and showed him sincere respect, though both men belonged to the same generation. When Itō found himself in political difficulties, Saigō was often able to save him by relying on his own unconventional and quick-witted nature.

If we are to describe the relationship between them in terms "who owed whom," we must say that Saigō was never in Itō's debt his entire life, but Itō was often indebted to Saigō. For this reason, Itō, who always called everyone by the informal title *kun*, used the more formal and polite *san* for Saigō alone. Itō always treated Saigō like an older brother.

Saigō was good at seeing through to the essence of a problem. He would grasp the essential point and, for the rest, relax like a man enjoying a spring breeze in the countryside. In later years, Saigō said of Itō, "He was a very knowledgeable and distinguished person. But in an emergency, he tended to go a little crazy." This was an insightful evaluation of Itō.

Strangely, Saigō Tsugumichi, who knew nothing about naval affairs, first became navy minister in the Itō cabinet in 1885, took office again in 1893, and then served as navy minister in three successive cabinets—those of Matsukata Masayoshi, Itō Hirobumi, and Ōkuma Shigenobu. There were no statesmen in the navy who could maintain the necessary balance in relation to the army, and we can say for certain that things went well for the navy precisely because Saigō took charge.

The battleship *Mikasa* was ordered from the British shipbuilder Vickers in 1898, but the naval budget had already been used up by then, and it was impossible to raise the necessary advance payment—a source of great anxiety to Gombei. He was forty-seven at the time and serving as navy minister. Saigō was then the home minister. (Saigō, in fact, served as minister for education, for the army, for agricultural and commercial affairs, for the navy, for home affairs—in short, in virtually every post except those of finance minister and prime minister.)

Gombei had tried everything and finally asked Saigō if he didn't have some wise counsel to give.

"You must purchase that ship, Mr. Yamamoto!" Saigō answered. "We'll divert part of the budget for that purpose. It's unconstitutional, of course. But if the Diet should refuse to allow it, you and I will go to the Double Bridge in front of the Imperial Palace and perform seppuku there together. If by our deaths we can secure this capital ship, that will be fine!"

This decision by Saigō made the building of the *Mikasa* possible. And this was the kind of relationship that existed between the two men, Saigō and Gombei, in the great work of building the Japanese Navy.

3

DIPLOMACY

Russia, having settled itself in Manchuria, was extending its reach to the northern part of Korea. Naturally, that conflicted with Japan's national interests. "National interests"—no term has been so much used in the international arena from the early nineteenth to the early twentieth centuries as this one. For these one hundred years, diplomacy, conspiracies, and wars were carried on among the nations in its name. This period was the most brilliant time in world history for diplomats and military men.

The Industrial Revolution began in Great Britain in the eighteenth century and, of course, from the nineteenth century on, it changed the very nature of European culture, producing a kind of "Warring States" period centering on the industrialized nations of Europe. If they did not gain colonies and markets in the undeveloped world, these nations would go into a decline. This was the type of "physiology" the European nations had developed. In a word, "imperialism."

Russia's southward expansion was a geopolitical instinct on its part but also the result of the type of stimuli we are now talking about. The Russian Empire at this juncture, however, had not yet developed its industries to the point where it needed to find an external outlet for any surplus products. Nonetheless, history provided a great stimulus. We can say that the reception of this historical stimulus, added to a natural instinct to move southward, caused Russia to embark on its highly adventurous territorial expansion, which Witte rightly called an act of madness. When a nation once begins to move in this direction, the self-control needed to know when to stop is greatly weakened.

Korea was the place where Japan's national interests were at stake. We must here take a few lines to explain: Korea was not Japan's colonial territory. Militarily, though, it was a safety cushion against pressures on the Japanese archipelago from the continent. To be viewed in this way could not have been acceptable to the Korean people resident on the peninsula. A nation, however, is fundamentally limited by its geography. Geographical limitations form a fundamental portion of a nation's character as well as a fundamental portion of its posture in regard to foreign nations. And, most unfortunately, countries give priority to such geopolitical considerations rather than to any good intentions they may have.

Japan not only regarded the Korean Peninsula as a defensive cushion but also wanted to make Yi dynasty Korea a market for its products. What the other powers had tried to do to China, Japan tried to do to Korea. Absurdly, even though it was some thirty years after the Restoration, Japan's industrial capacity remained very immature with almost no products worth selling. Japan's modus operandi was an imitation of the European powers'—it was "practicing" imperialism on Korea. Japan believed that it would in time transform itself into a powerful country by long and astute imitation of Europe. Naturally, then, in the civilization of the late nineteenth and early twentieth centuries, Korea became a country of vital importance to Japan.

* * *

Thus, the root causes of the Russo-Japanese War lay in Manchuria and Korea. Having taken Manchuria, Russia would move next against Korea. This is as clear as day. Had Japan lost the Russo-Japanese War, Korea would undoubtedly have become a Russian possession.

Can we then say that, had Japan lost, it would itself have been occupied by Russia? Entertaining various hypotheses regarding an epoch that is already past seems meaningless, but, looking back, it seems unlikely that Russia would have gone so far as to occupy Japan since there was a sea barrier in between. Perhaps only the British, as another island nation, would have understood the inner workings of this matter. There are indications that the British Foreign Office's view at the outbreak of the war was that Russia probably would not take over Japan even if Japan lost. The reason was geographic: Japan was an island country and thus troublesome to take over without a land connection. On the other hand, Japan would surely have had to pay a huge indemnity to Russia that would have rendered its industrial economy stagnant until the 1950s or 1960s. In addition, Russia would have taken Hokkaido and the port of Tsuruga on the Sea of Japan. Tsushima Island near Korea would have been leased to Russia.

Through diplomacy, Itō Hirobumi tried to find a way to ease the intense pressure caused by Russia's southward expansion, and came to the conclusion that an offensive and defensive alliance with imperial Russia would be best. This was unquestionably a leap in logic, akin to your being confronted with an armed gang of robbers who had pushed their way into the neighboring village and then your going with head bowed to negotiate with them, in the hope that perhaps they might leave just your village and the neighboring village alone. The robbers would think that you had some nerve to try such a thing, while the villagers would regard you as gutless.

Nonetheless, Itō felt there was no other course open to Japan. Itō was a supreme realist, so, in a situation like this, his fear remained simply fear. This was his weakness, and this was why he was labeled "The Russophobe," which did not bother him one bit. "Russia will surely attack," he said. "For a country like Japan, whose power and military resources don't amount to even one of Russia's little fingers, acting all high and mighty makes no sense."

But Japanese have a fondness for outward display, one of the ways in which they resemble the French. Even though this may just be a kind of diplomacy for show, the Japanese have been fond of performing great feats and striking grand poses vis-à-vis much stronger foreign powers. At times, they have resorted to military means to challenge enemies whom they could hardly expect to win out against and thus sought to promote Japan's status. And, in every period, those in opposition or out of power at the time have preferred those methods, while those in power have tried to suppress them. Thus, with regard to foreign relations, the more cautious policies of the authorities and the radical views of the opposition have been clearly opposed to one another.

Itō, in fact, had never been so badly thought of as during this period.

* * *

Naturally, the world of European diplomacy was shocked by the abnormal situation that existed at that time—the Far East fast becoming a Russian playground and all its resources Russia's belongings. Yet Japan's government seemed unaware of this fact. They believed that no other country would help Japan in the face of the Russian advance. The Japanese themselves regarded the Far East as a backward, provincial part of the world and thought that the European powers would not lift a finger to help even if the Russians ran wild in such a place.

In fact, Britain's interest in the situation in the Far East was quietly on the rise. Gathering the world's wealth, Britain had become the most highly developed industrial nation, and that had changed its ways of thinking.

When Europe had been laid waste by the Napoleonic Wars, a flood of products flowed from Britain, "the world's factory," to continental Europe. This vastly increased Britain's wealth, strengthened its productive capabilities, and caused the demand for its ever-increasing stream of products to grow, as India and China became available markets for them.

Russia, however, was moving southward, not only in the Far East but in the direction of India as well. If something was not done to stop this, Britain would lose a major market, and its goods would pile up, unsold, in its warehouses. Britain's basic attitude in its foreign policy was to nip in the bud each and every such threat to its interests.

In doing so, Britain employed shrewdness above all, avoiding as far as possible direct means like warfare, and, when war was unavoidable, using skillful diplomacy to have other countries do the actual fighting. And, if finally forced to commit its own troops, Britain made overtures to other countries with common interests and formed alliances with them, rather than fighting alone.

Observing Russia's outrageous acts in the Far East, Britain wanted to nip this movement in the bud while not going to war with Russia. It tried to deal with the matter by diplomatic means so as to ensure "the balance of power in the Far East," to use a favorite platitude of British diplomacy. Britain first thought of Germany, which, since robbing China of Jiaozhou Bay and building a military base in Qingdao, had acquired interests in the Far East. Why not an Anglo-German alliance against Russia as the hypothetical enemy? It was the German chargé d'affaires in Britain Hermann von Eckardstein who first suggested, "Even better would be an Anglo-German–Japanese alliance." Britain did not have a high opinion of Japan's power as a nation, but if the Germans were willing to join in, nothing could be better.

Britain was, at the time, being kept busy with the Boer War in South Africa, with little time or energy to deal with the Far East. If Germany, newly flourishing and with enhanced military power, would act to stabilize the Far East, Britain would be delighted.

* * *

This was an age of brilliant diplomats, but there were sometimes phony ones as well, and Chargé d'Affaires Eckardstein had something of the latter type about him. He had not received the standard training for a diplomat but had become one out of an amateur's interest. Because he was trusted by the kaiser, who held immense, dictatorial power, Eckardstein was able to do this, even in highly bureaucratic Germany. He used his personal funds to entertain in the London diplomatic world and was rich enough to carry it off.

Eckardstein confided his idea about an alliance to Joseph Chamberlain, the British colonial minister. At first, he spoke only of an Anglo-German alliance, without mentioning Japan. "That is the only way to maintain the balance of power in Asia," he argued, pointing out the need to check Russia. Hearing this, Chamberlain was clearly interested.

At the same time, however, Eckardstein was visiting Japan's ambassador to Britain, Hayashi Tadasu, and suggesting something similar, only this time it was for a triple alliance of Britain, Germany, and Japan. "Through such an alliance, Japan would be guaranteed a free hand in Korea—because, in the event of war by one member of the alliance against a fourth country, the other two members of the alliance would agree to maintain neutrality." Eckardstein clearly regarded war between Japan and Russia—Eckardstein's "fourth country"—as inevitable.

To an isolated nation like Japan, no idea could have been more welcome. Hayashi immediately sought directives from his government.

The Japanese Foreign Ministry proceeded to discuss the matter with the German representative Georg von Wedel, just to be on the safe side. Wedel knew nothing about it and, amazed, asked Berlin for confirmation. The German Foreign Ministry knew nothing of the plan either. In short, Eckardstein had been putting on a one-man show.

Yet, even though this had been a deceptive drama staged by the overhasty Eckardstein, one could say that the Anglo-Japanese Alliance itself ultimately emerged as a result of this deception. Chamberlain took Eckardstein's words seriously and cabled Kaiser Wilhelm II, thus opening direct negotiations via cable between the two powers.

The kaiser's response was unexpected. "That would be counter to Germany's interests. Russia is allied with France, and, if we make Russia our enemy, Germany would be caught between two hostile powers. In case of war, would Britain come to our aid? Your navy might be able to attempt some action in the Baltic Sea, but you would hardly be able to enter the Black Sea. Thus, Germany would be isolated, without military assistance from you. Even with Russia alone as our enemy, Germany's position would be perilous. If we were then attacked by the French Army from the rear, our situation would be hopeless. For the security of the German Empire, I wish to remain friends with Russia." This was the substance of the kaiser's response.

* * *

So Germany's negative attitude toward an anti-Russian alliance had become clear. Of course, the Japanese Foreign Ministry knew nothing about this exchange between Britain and Germany. To Japan, however, Germany seemed very close and reliable when it came to academic and strategic studies but distant when it came to foreign policy. Germany did not seem capable of assuming a major role under present conditions in the Far East, and Japan never had great hopes that it would do so in any case.

The question was Britain's role. The Foreign Ministry wanted an alliance with Britain. But would that country with its preeminent national power and level of civilization agree to ally itself on an equal level with a country located in a Far Eastern backwater, a country just beginning to develop some industrial potential, a country whose foreign minister himself had characterized it as only "half civilized"?

The foreign minister in question was Aoki Shūzō. He was a native of the Chōshū domain and the son of the domain's official physician. One of the first to study Western medicine, he served as a doctor in the Chōshū army during the shogunate's second campaign against that rebellious domain. After the Restoration, he entered the Foreign Ministry and later became an ambassador. As such, he acquired more experience than anyone else in the ministry. He served as ambassador to Germany, Britain, Austria, Holland, and Denmark, and, during the three decades beginning in 1870, he worked hard to revise the unequal treaties, which had been the greatest task for the Japanese government since the beginning of the Meiji period.

Aoki served as foreign minister in 1889 and 1898. But, given Aoki's impressive diplomatic career, his actual accomplishments as foreign minister were fewer than might have been expected. He remains something of a mystery. Aoki was an energetic reader. He himself said that his reading "ranged over the whole world," going far beyond the limits of his specialties in politics and diplomacy to include even natural science. In terms of richness of knowledge of the world, he was far and away the best among the statesmen and military men hailing from the former Chōshū domain.

He did not, however, have much tolerance for other people. An extraordinarily arrogant man, he regarded Itō Hirobumi and Yamagata Aritomo as hopeless fools, though they were *genrō*—distinguished elder statesman—and also natives of Chōshū. And all the more so, then, did he disparage his colleagues and subordinates at the Foreign Ministry. In fact, the Japanese themselves seemed to him a barbarous people. Since these attitudes were mixed with a kind of troubled patriotism, quite naturally his words and actions tended toward hysteria.

When he was foreign minister in 1900, he addressed an unprecedented memorial to the emperor himself, without even consulting Prime Minister Yamagata. "Now, as Russia threatens Japan," Aoki wrote,

> what is the actual state of our nation? Though we won the war against the Qing and managed to become one of the powers, in reality we are only half civilized. Your subject's residence and the Imperial Palace are only a short distance apart, but when I look from my carriage, I find that eighty to ninety percent of the Japanese who walk the streets are still clothed in barbarous

traditional dress. In this semi-civilized state, we will certainly not be able to overthrow the oppression of the mighty Russian Empire. If we are to save the nation, a great reconstruction is needed. Petty diplomatic maneuvers will do nothing to resolve the critical state of Japan's fortunes.

This was the essence of Aoki's memorial. Though it may represent the kind of hysteria directed inward at one's own country that is often found among diplomats, it does express an aspect of the actual state of Japan at the time.

* * *

In the midst of this secret but feverish hope for an alliance with Britain that prevailed among the leaders of the Japanese government at the time, Ambassador Hayashi Tadasu was doing his best in London. Hayashi Tadasu was a former vassal of the shogunate and thus quite unlike Aoki Shūzō, who was from the pro-imperial Chōshū domain. Hayashi was the adopted son of the vassal Hayashi Dōkai, and in his youth, toward the end of the shogunate, he had studied English in Yokohama. No doubt due to these early studies, he later acquired the reputation of being the best English speaker in the Foreign Ministry and the most skillful writer of English as well. When in 1866 the shogunate decided to send several young men to study in Britain, he was one of those chosen to go. He was only seventeen.

When the shogunate collapsed, Hayashi was ordered home. Arriving in Yokohama, he saw that Enomoto Takeaki, an admiral in the former shogunate's navy, was at the head of a fleet anchored off Shinagawa. Hayashi seized the opportunity to join these shogunate-loyalist insurgents and went to Hakodate in Hokkaido, holing up in the Goryōkaku Fort. Judging from this, he must have been (to use a term popular in those days) "a man of passionate temperament."

Enomoto, seeking international understanding, wrote a defense of his actions and had Hayashi translate it into English. This was then sent to Sir Harry Parkes, the British minister plenipotentiary to Japan. We may say that this marked the very start of Hayashi Tadasu's diplomatic endeavors. He was just nineteen at the time, but Parkes, reading the English text, was so surprised at its quality that he concluded, "There must be an Englishman in among the insurgent forces of the former shogunate!"

In the end, the attempt at resistance was a failure, and Hayashi surrendered along with Enomoto and his men. He and some five hundred others were taken into the custody of the Tsugaru domain and confined in a temple in Aomori. But Kuroda Kiyotaka from Satsuma, who was a staff officer of the victorious imperial forces, learned that among the rebels held in confinement was a man named Hayashi who could speak and write English like an

Englishman. Kuroda quietly summoned Hayashi and offered to send him alone for service under the new regime in Tokyo.

"If the others can be released along with me," Hayashi said in refusal, "that'll be fine, but if I'm the only one, I must decline."

Once this encounter became well known, it created a very positive image of Hayashi Tadasu among important men from Satsuma and throughout his life led to his being regarded as a man one could trust. After becoming a diplomat, he greatly benefited from the patronage and protection of the Satsuma clique in the government, which made his work easier.

In 1891, Hayashi became vice foreign minister, in 1897, ambassador to Russia, and, in 1900, ambassador to Great Britain. As is clear from his career record, he was one of the most active men in the field of diplomacy prior to both the First Sino-Japanese and the Russo-Japanese Wars.

When Akiyama Saneyuki was sent to Britain by the navy, Hayashi was stationed in London as ambassador. In the United States, Saneyuki had had contact with Hoshi Tōru but was little influenced by him. By contrast, when he later came in contact with Komura Jutarō and then, in Britain, with Hayashi Tadasu, he was very much influenced by both men's views of the modern nation-state. He was filled with admiration for Hayashi's ability to judge a situation accurately and respond to it appropriately. "If you went into the military," he told Hayashi, "you might well become the greatest of generals or admirals of the fleet."

* * *

"Britain seems interested in an alliance," Hayashi informed the Foreign Ministry. When he had been posted to Great Britain, Hayashi suspected that this issue would come up, and so he had gone to Itō Hirobumi before his departure and took care to sound him out on it. Since Itō was an advocate of a Russo-Japanese alliance, Hayashi was afraid that any efforts he made in London for an Anglo-Japanese alliance might be rendered pointless.

Unexpectedly, Itō's response was "I don't mind if you do that."

Itō probably felt that the idea of negotiating for an equal alliance between Japan and a nation like Great Britain was too dazzling. It was the stuff of dreams, not of politics.

Mutsu Munemitsu, who had directed Japan's foreign relations since the First Sino-Japanese War, had died of tuberculosis in August 1897, but, when the subject of an alliance between Britain and Japan came up, even he had always said, "The idea has a beautiful ring to it. But I wonder if it is really possible." His conclusion was that it was not.

"Try thinking about this from Britain's point of view," he would suggest. Britain was no Don Quixote willing to sacrifice itself to save the foreign land of Japan from its troubles. Japan was looking to have its security guaranteed. Well then, Britain too would demand some guarantee of its own security. Was Japan powerful enough to provide that? Britain would, naturally, want Japan to defend Britain's interests in Asia. But Britain's interests in Asia extended from the Chinese mainland to Singapore and on to India, so Japan would need to have the power to dispatch its army and naval forces over that immensely wide area. Only when Japan had such power should an alliance with Britain be talked about. Seeking such an alliance at present would make Japan an international laughingstock. Such was Mutsu's opinion.

Itō felt the same way, which was why he hoped for a Russo-Japanese alliance. If, however, Hayashi wanted to pursue the matter of an alliance with Britain, Itō would not object. If by any chance Hayashi's attempt succeeded, that would be Japan's great good fortune, so Itō did nothing to oppose Hayashi's plans.

Hayashi was posted to London. Soon after his arrival, there were some faint hopeful signs—even if this was the doing of the overhasty German diplomat. Hayashi handled the matter adroitly and, having received permission from his government, immediately paid a visit to Lord Lansdowne, the foreign secretary. Lansdowne was a thin man with small eyes—he looked a bit like Japan's own Komura Jutarō, in fact. He was not a political showman but, rather, of a scholarly bent.

Britain's attitude seemed, to Japan, nearly miraculous. During Hayashi's visit, Lord Lansdowne stated, "Britain too acknowledges the need for an alliance, as you have suggested." At that time, Britain had no alliances with any European powers. Both Britain itself and other powers acknowledged its position of "honorable isolation." If Britain was willing to change its foreign policy and make an alliance with Japan, it must have had real fears about Russia's unlimited aggression in the Far East.

That was Hayashi Tadasu's view. He thought that Britain might be more willing to go along with Japan's proposals than could normally have been expected.

"However," continued Lansdowne, "what about including Germany?"

This "what about?" was not a mere request for Hayashi's opinion but rather clearly seemed to be an insistence that Germany be involved. The implication was that only if Germany's army and navy participated would Asia be secure vis-à-vis Russia. Japan alone would be of little help.

Hayashi was careful not to enter into too deep a discussion of Germany's participation, however, and merely showed mild interest, nodding and remarking, "I see." If Britain could bring Germany along and form a tripartite alliance, this would be the best outcome for Japan as well.

At any rate, the fundamental issue was settled. There was no need to speak at greater length at this point. Lansdowne ended by saying, "After Japan presents a concrete plan regarding the nature of the alliance, our side will give it the most serious consideration," and the two men parted.

On his way home, Hayashi had a thought: "So, in the event of war between Japan and Russia, even if we don't actually win, we won't suffer a crushing defeat."

When, later, Hayashi tried to broach the issue, Britain was no longer interested in discussing an invitation to Germany to join the alliance. The matter seemed to have been totally forgotten. Hayashi did not know, of course, about the exchange of telegrams between Colonial Secretary Chamberlain and the German kaiser. Britain's offer had been refused by Germany. This involved a loss of face, and Britain kept it secret for a long time.

At any rate, Britain was willing to form an alliance even with Japan alone. Hayashi had sent a long telegram to Japan when the Anglo-German–Japanese alliance was under discussion, and at this point he sent a still more detailed telegram to his government.

Around this time, there was a change of cabinets in Japan. When the discussion of a possible tripartite alliance took place, the cabinet was under the direction of Itō Hirobumi, but it dissolved after six and a half months, to be replaced by the Katsura Tarō cabinet. Japan had been pushed to the brink of bankruptcy by its exorbitant military budget, and this was the underlying cause of the dissolution of the Itō cabinet. It was Hayashi's great good luck that Prime Minister Katsura, an advocate of an Anglo-Japanese alliance, was the recipient of his telegram suggesting just that.

* * *

Katsura Tarō first became prime minister on June 2, 1901, after Itō Hirobumi dissolved his cabinet. Katsura was from Chōshū and had participated in the Boshin War, though only as an ordinary, anonymous young officer. Later, he entered the national army and was gradually promoted. During this period, he worked to make the Japanese Army model itself on the German one. He was more suited to military administration than to action on the field and would have been more suited to a political than a military career.

People later harshly criticized Katsura as being like "a professional jester with a saber at his waist," and it is true that he was always ready to show a smiling face in order to bring others around. That plus his habit of slapping people on the back to show his amiability earned him the nickname "Smile and Slap." He was a master "fixer."

Katsura was not one of the eminent genrō of the Meiji period. The forming of cabinets was almost always left to the genrō, and from their perspective, as well as that of the wider society, allowing such a young, inexperienced man to become prime minister was dangerous.

Someone complained about this to Saigō Tsugumichi, who was a kind of semi-genrō at the time, suggesting that Katsura didn't have the weight to be prime minister.

"As for 'weight,'" replied Saigō with a laugh, "if you dress him in a formal tailcoat and put him in a carriage drawn by the requisite number of horses, the weight will come of itself. That's all that's required, I believe!"

Katsura, at any rate, became prime minister against the background of this sort of general unease, and this feeling only increased after he formed his cabinet. Being so young himself, he was unable to persuade major figures to join his cabinet—the members were all minor ones. "Young and ardent" would be a positive way of describing them.

Katsura chose his foreign minister from the ranks of ambassadors, naming Komura Jutarō to this position. (Finance Minister Sone Arasuke shared this responsibility for a time.) The home minister was Utsumi Tadakatsu, the communications minister, Yoshikawa Akimasa, the agriculture minister, Hirata Tōsuke, the justice minister, Kiyoura Keigo, the education minister, Kikuchi Dairoku. These were all relative unknowns, and hence the Katsura cabinet was termed "second rate" and "a junior cabinet." Yet this youthful cabinet carried out the successful war against Russia.

Katsura had four troublesome "mothers-in-law": the distinguished genrō Yamagata Aritomo, Itō Hirobumi, Matsukata Masayoshi, and Inoue Kaoru. Each of them regarded himself as a protector of the new prime minister, but they all had different personalities and political views, and Katsura, as the "new bride," must have found it hard to faithfully serve them all. Nonetheless, he managed to win them over with great skill.

At just this time, a telegram came from Ambassador Hayashi Tadasu in London asking if he should proceed with arrangements for an alliance with Britain. Now, truly, Katsura had to win the genrō over. Particularly difficult would be the task of persuading Itō Hirobumi away from his advocacy of a Russo-Japanese alliance.

"The hardest part of foreign relations," Komura Jutarō said in describing this period, "is the domestic rather than the foreign part." How true that was!

* * *

Katsura Tarō, employing his considerable skills in conciliation, was quite circumspect in gaining control of Itō Hirobumi. As soon as the telegram came from Hayashi Tadasu in London, he rushed to Ōiso to show it to Itō right away. (Itō was living in the Sōrōkaku villa in Ōiso at the time.)

Having read the telegram, Itō said, with a look of surprise, "When I was in office, this same man Hayashi sent a telegram proposing an Anglo-German–Japanese alliance. Now, not long after, he is talking about an Anglo-Japanese alliance, without Germany. Something must have happened in the meantime."

Katsura nodded vigorously. The realities of European politics were always hard for Japan to grasp, however, and Katsura was unable to give a proper response to Itō's doubts. Itō, for his part, understood the situation and did not demand a response from the newly appointed prime minister. He had been, in effect, talking to himself when he made that last remark.

"I wonder if we should take the contents of this telegram seriously?"

"Since Hayashi himself is handling it, I think there can be no mistake about it."

"But what does Britain really intend?" This was the point in doubt. "Mr. Katsura, they are, you know, Anglo-Saxons, an extremely proud race. Will they really abandon their famed policy of 'honorable isolation' and form an alliance with another country? An equal alliance? And with members of the 'yellow race,' to boot? It would be an unprecedented step in the history of British diplomacy."

It seemed incredible to Itō, realist that he was, that Britain would make such a historic leap.

"But Britain seems to have burned its fingers quite a bit over the Boer War in South Africa. I daresay this proposal is a side effect of that," suggested Katsura. "These are facts. So Britain finds itself too occupied elsewhere to spend much energy on the Far East, and most likely wants Japan to fill that void and stop Russia's unlimited advance southward there. The British believe they can use Japan for their benefit. Why should Japan not similarly use Britain?"

"If all this is true," commented Itō.

"Yes—assuming this is Britain's true intention. How do you feel about it, Excellency? Can you give your support to the plan?"

"Of course. I advocated a Russo-Japanese alliance because I believed it was the more likely to be realized. But, if Britain is serious about an alliance, that would of course be even better."

This was all Katsura needed to hear. If Itō chose to hinder the plan, then, no matter how well negotiations were going in London, it would all come to naught in Japan.

Katsura returned to Tokyo. There would be a meeting of the genrō the next day at Katsura's villa in Hayama. It was August 4, at the very height of the summer heat. Just as the dew was vanishing in the strong rays of the morning sun, those elder statesmen arrived.

Katsura's villa was newly built, and the trees in the groves around the pond were not yet very attractive. Yamagata Aritomo had come from his summer retreat in Ōiso. Waka and designing traditional gardens were his hobbies, and as soon as he arrived, he toured the garden, giving his opinion of its various features. Katsura, as owner of the villa, trailed along after him, nodding gratefully at each comment.

Itō Hirobumi came from his villa in Kanazawa near Yokohama; Inoue Kaoru, from Okitsu. These three genrō were all from Chōshū, while Matsukata Masayoshi was from Satsuma. He had come from his summer retreat in Kamakura.

Before the group had seated themselves to begin discussion, Katsura, wishing to ingratiate himself with Itō, asked, "Excellency, could I ask you to give a name to this humble villa of mine?" Since Itō did not seem at all averse to the idea, Katsura brought out a brush, inkstone set, and a piece of silk for him to write on. Itō was quite proud of his calligraphy. He thought for a while about an appropriate name and then, taking up the brush, wrote in large characters "Chōunkaku"—the Pavilion of Eternal Clouds.

This put Itō into a good mood, and, when Katsura exclaimed his praise for the name, Itō was even more pleased and wrote an extempore Chinese poem for Prime Minster Katsura Tarō, the owner of this newly constructed villa, dashing it off on a piece of ordinary writing paper that was at hand.

> What will be, will be—public opinion is like tangled threads.
> When you have seen the great ocean, this disturbance seems like one in a small pond.
> Why should the prime minister not have days and months of leisure?
> Let us leave off talk of military things and discuss only poetry!

"Well done indeed!" said Yamagata, who was skilled in waka since he was a descendant of a family specializing in the Japanese classics. But he had recently been devoting himself to the study of classical Chinese poetry, later going on to become a regular contributor to the Chinese poetry journal the *Balustrade of a Hundred Flowers*.

At last, the meeting began. Itō started out rather aggressively. Though he had said just the previous day that he had no objection to an alliance with Britain, he began to voice views that seemed hostile to the idea, much to Katsura's surprise.

"An Anglo-Japanese alliance is all very well, but won't it seem as if we are viewing Russia as the hypothetical enemy?" He was worried about injuring the feelings of Russia more than was absolutely necessary. That's how afraid of Russia Itō was.

But this was an odd argument to make. Making an offensive and defensive alliance with Britain would naturally offend Russia. That should have been understood all along. Besides, Russia would keep on advancing even if there were no alliance between Japan and Britain. Since Japan would have to fight Russia at some point, by itself if need be, it would only be to Japan's benefit if Britain would agree to an alliance. Katsura explained all this in a roundabout way so as not to injure Itō's pride.

In the end, Itō agreed. The other three elder statesmen had been advocates of the alliance with Britain from the very beginning, so of course there were no objections. The meeting ended with the decision to move toward such an alliance.

* * *

As one of the genrō, Itō Hirobumi had formally agreed to the negotiations with Britain. But this great realist could not rid himself of the feeling, "Is an alliance with Britain actually possible?" He quietly decided that he himself should carry on personal negotiations with the Russians, leaving the Japanese government out of it for the time being. Here we see one of Itō's most intriguing characteristics.

A complete realist in politics can never be anything more than a second-rate politician—indeed, we should perhaps call him not a politician but a businessman. The quality of the man is determined by what kind of ideals he holds, but, since politics cannot be separated from realities, a man who gives too much weight to ideals tends to end as a mere wishful thinker, or a poet, or a hysterical zealot who denies the realities of the situation.

Itō was a realist, but as evidence that he was not one to carry on the business of politics only through realism, we have only to look at his earlier actions. When, near the end of the shogunate, xenophobic ideas were the "reality" of the radical faction in his native Chōshū, Itō boldly explained world realities to his countrymen and made them enter into negotiations with the combined fleet of the four foreign nations, which they had earlier attacked and which had devastatingly bombarded them in return.

Then, in the late 1870s and 1880s, surrounded by leading figures who detested the idea of popular rights, he was the coolest and strongest advocate of constitutionalism, and after the establishment of the Meiji Constitution, he became the founder of one of the political parties that Yamagata Aritomo, for example, so much disliked. Thus, ideals and realities were always kept in harmony in Itō's case.

With regard to the great diplomatic issue then confronting Japan, Itō agreed that an alliance with Britain would be the best option for Japan, but he regarded this as no more than an unrealistic hope. Why would Great

Britain enter into an offensive and defensive alliance, accepting as an equal a provincial Asian country like Japan?

Itō thought that an alliance with Russia was more feasible. Though it possessed the largest army in the world, Russia was still culturally underdeveloped, at least from a Western European point of view. In that respect, Russia's situation was not so very different from Japan's, and so Japan should find Russia more approachable. In addition, Russia, the direct offender in its continued oppression of Asia, would be more quickly and easily persuaded to moderate its criminal conduct through direct negotiation. This was what Itō believed.

"Fortunately, I am no longer Japan's prime minister." He was free to act. Moreover, "Itō Hirobumi of Japan" was well known in international political circles, and other countries would not treat Itō's initiatives cavalierly even though they were undertaken "by a private individual."

Itō decided he would go to Russia. But he told only Prime Minister Katsura Tarō about his secret plan, not saying a word about it to the Foreign Ministry. Katsura, however, was not happy about this sign of Itō's tendency to decide things entirely on his own.

Luckily for Itō, he already had plans for a trip abroad. Yale University in the United States, as part of its one-hundredth-year celebrations, had chosen to award honorary doctorates to distinguished people from various countries, and Itō was one of those selected. Itō used the award as an excuse to go first to the United States and then planned to visit Russia on his way home.

* * *

Itō Hirobumi left for the United States on September 18, 1901. At the end of October, he attended the awards ceremony for the honorary degree at Yale and then boarded a steamship in New York for the passage to Europe. Since negotiations for an alliance between Britain and Japan were then going on in London, it would have been natural for him to go to Britain, but instead he made directly for France.

After taking lodgings in Paris, he sent a cable to Ambassador Hayashi Tadasu in London, ordering him to come at once to Paris to let Itō know how the negotiations with Britain were going. Hayashi came, and Itō learned from him how things stood. Negotiations with Great Britain were going so smoothly that Itō was stunned. Learning that the details of which country would do what in terms of the alliance were already being discussed, Itō made a face and said, "Hayashi, you're getting us in ridiculously deep, you know."

"What do you mean, Excellency?"

"Never mind about that—the point is, I'm on my way to the Russian capital to see if negotiations with the Russians are possible or not."

Hayashi was so surprised he almost leaped from his seat. He was carrying on the negotiations in London in accordance with the wishes of his government, and the negotiations had been almost entirely successful. So what could be the meaning of Japan's most powerful statesman (even given that Itō was no longer prime minister) criticizing what Hayashi had done and declaring that he himself was on his way to Russia?

"But, Excellency," began Hayashi, proceeding to explain again that the Anglo-Japanese Alliance was on the point of becoming a fact. And, if Great Britain learned that Japan was also negotiating with Russia, Britain's great enemy in the area of Asian diplomacy, Britain's attitude would immediately change for the worse, and Japan would lose face and the trust of the European nations.

"All right, then," said Itō with a slight smile. "I'll give up my plans to negotiate with Russia." Skill in shifting his position in accordance with the actual situation was one of Itō's salient political characteristics. He went on to say that he would not even go to St. Petersburg.

Hayashi thought, however, that that would not do. Having once informed the Russian government that he would be coming, for Itō now to cancel his visit without good reason would be impolite by international standards. So Hayashi advised Itō to go as planned.

"Why not just exchange courtesies with the Russians as a private individual? It might actually be . . . " Hayashi went on to say that Itō might actually aid in the ongoing Anglo-Japanese negotiations, because the British were proving to be quite stubborn regarding the details of who would be responsible for what. Hayashi was doing his best, but the negotiations had come to a standstill on these fine points. He told Itō that if "Prince Itō of Japan" were seen to go to Russia, Great Britain might hurry a bit to find a compromise solution.

So that was what Itō intended to do. After spending a few days in Paris, he set off for St. Petersburg.

* * *

Itō Hirobumi's ultimate goal was to avoid a Russo-Japanese war, thus saving Japan from destruction, but conditions in Russia at the time were such that Russia was not at all likely to accede to Itō's wishes. First of all, the court and the military were quite carried away by "Invade the Far East" fever. At court, Bezobrazov, labeled a "wicked minister" by Witte, had worked his way into the confidence of the tsar and, under cover of imperial authority, had begun treating the other ministers like his messenger boys.

This soldier turned adventurer thought of the empire as a large-scale business venture (as so many military men are prone to do), and imperialism was to him the sole product of this venture. He had formerly been the manager of the Yalu River Lumber Company, with the backing of the local army. At the same time, he was a dreamer who proposed the most splendid of grand plans to the tsar.

"Britain's present prosperity is due to its absorption of India. Imperial Russia's control of the globe will be possible only if Manchuria, the Primorsky Region, and Korea can become our India!"

Before speaking to the tsar, Bezobrazov had contacted all the members of the imperial family with influence at court, as well as their wives, and spread the news of this "patriotic enterprise." Moreover, he made these imperial relatives advisors to, or stockholders in, his own business on the Yalu. In short, he made sure that their support for his "patriotic enterprise" would also result in a flow of wealth into the imperial family's coffers. The tsar not only approved Bezobrazov's plans regarding expansion, but he also became one of the most eager fans of this great Russian patriot. And so the future course of the Russian Empire was decided.

The military too followed along the same course. When, in its naïve way of thinking, the military of any country or any age becomes enthusiastic about some invasion, it tends to treat politicians or ordinary citizens who are opposed to that invasion as if they were unpatriotic. During this period, even War Minister Kuropatkin, whose political posture was relatively moderate, took that view.

All the Russian military, of course, realized that a war with Japan was bound to occur if these plans were carried out. It went without saying that the Russians would smash Japan militarily. The military would be responsible for this defeat of Japan, yet, strangely, not a single Russian military expert made an accurate judgment of Japan's military power. No one had even bothered to make an objective analysis of the situation.

When a nation's military is mad for an invasion, it may neglect to undertake a military analysis of the enemy country, though precisely that should be its special concern. Even an attempt at such an analysis may come to seem like foolishness in the eyes of those in the grip of political fervor. The Russian military's evaluation of the strength of Japan's army and navy, as a result of its observation and analysis, was as given below.

The military attachés at the various embassies were of course responsible for on-the-spot observation and analysis of the other nation's military strength. Army Colonel Vannovsky was the military attaché at the Russian embassy in Tokyo from 1900 until the start of the war. He reported to the Russian War Ministry that "The Japanese Army is in its infancy . . . It will take a hundred years for the Japanese Army to build the moral foundation that would allow it to reach the level of even the weakest army in Europe." Vannovsky is talking not about the Japanese Army's equipment or battle readiness but about the military morale that is behind all of that.

"Morale" here means the officers' and men's spirit of loyalty to their country and the ethics of command within the military—for example, the willingness to obey one's superiors and the organization as a whole. Vannovsky claimed that, in respect to these vital matters, Japan not only ranked below the weakest of European nations but would require one hundred years to catch up!

In fact, the spirit of loyalty and obedience was almost excessive in the Japanese military of the day, yet Vannovsky lacked the ability to observe even this most evident of facts, and his report became the basis of the Russian military's view of Japan from then on.

In 1903, an influential observer came from Russia to assess Japan's navy. In April, a grand naval review was held in Kobe, and the cruiser *Askold* was sent from Russia to observe it. Captain K. A. Grammatchikov was in charge of the cruiser, and, after observing the naval review, he told the Russian ambassador Roman Rozen, "To be sure, the Japanese Navy has purchased warships from abroad and is thus materially well equipped. But their spirit as naval military men is by no means equal to ours. And their operational and transport skills are infantile."

Observations by British naval officers around the same time, however, were quite the opposite, stating that Japanese operational and transport skills were at so high a level that only the British Navy itself could compare with them on a world level. And the truth of the British evaluation was proved by the destruction of the Russian Baltic Fleet by Japan shortly thereafter.

Again, in June 1903, Kuropatkin, regarded as the best general in the Russian Army, arrived in Japan and observed the Japanese Army in the most detailed way, and judged Japan to have one of the weakest militaries in the world. "One Russian soldier will serve to deal with three Japanese. Our army could assemble four hundred thousand men in Manchuria within thirteen days, and we are prepared to do so. This is three times larger than the number necessary to defeat the Japanese Army. The war that is likely to come will be not so much a real war as a military pleasure stroll!"

One wonders what part of their brains these Russian military men were using when they made these observations and judgments. Military men of whatever nation tend to be captive to fixed ideas, and the Russians certainly were no exception to this rule.

* * *

It was in this atmosphere, or under such historical conditions, that Itō Hirobumi went to St. Petersburg, with only faint hopes of success. He had virtually staked his life on avoiding war between Russia and Japan.

The Russian side, however, showed an unexpected attitude toward him: they warmly welcomed him. The day Itō arrived at his St. Petersburg hotel Witte paid him a visit. It would have been customary for the foreign visitor to inquire about a convenient day and time, and then pay the Russian minister a visit. But Witte ignored all that and went to see Itō on his own.

Witte was the only member of the Russian government who was eager to avoid war with Japan, and he knew, of course, that Itō held the same view. He must have wanted to make sure that Itō had the right ideas in his mind when he met the other major Russian policymakers starting the following day.

"I am very happy that Your Excellency has come here," Witte began when he met Itō in a private room at the hotel. "I'd like us to speak with complete frankness about the problems in the Far East."

Good-natured Itō, disarmed by Witte's attitude, gave his views on how peace could be preserved in the Far East and criticized Russia's aggressive policies.

"I completely agree," Witte answered calmly, much to Itō's surprise. "But you know, Excellency, that in Russia, as in every country, there are conservative and more radical groups struggling for political power." By "radical," Witte meant the opportunistic imperialists who had gained favor with the tsar. They were led by Vyacheslav Plehve and Aleksandr Bezobrazov. "With their radical ideas, they are trying to lay their hands on Korea, but even *they* are not contemplating an invasion of Japan."

That might be so, thought Itō, but if such radical ideas took hold, an invasion of Japan itself could well follow.

"They have gained favor with the tsar, but the most honorable of the ministers are wary of them. We might call them 'the men of good sense.' These include, for example, the newly appointed foreign minister Vladimir Lamsdorf and the war minister Alexei Kuropatkin. They are eager to continue good relations with Japan."

"Ah, I see ... " thought Itō. Knowing full well that the essence of diplomacy lay in letting the other party know clearly one's own intentions, feelings, and interests, Itō said, "But talk of good relations between Russia and Japan is too abstract to be helpful. Such abstractions won't solve the present crisis in Korea." Itō went on to say that the only real solution would be for Russia to withdraw from Korea.

* * *

The next day, Itō met Foreign Minister Lamsdorf. His predecessor Count Muravyov had, under pressure from the military, been responsible for adoption of the drastic policy of seizing Port Arthur and Dalian from China. He was, however, an easygoing man, like many Russians, and a heavy drinker. One evening, drinking champagne at someone's home, he drank so much that he burst a blood vessel and died on the spot.

Lamsdorf succeeded him. In Witte's opinion, he was a businesslike man with none of the frivolity of his predecessor. Witte did not think he would go along with the military's more radical plans, but Itō's impression upon meeting him was quite different. Lamsdorf seemed to have been influenced by the aggressive tendencies that prevailed at the time and showed no signs of the conciliatory attitude that Witte had spoken of the previous day.

"Prince Itō," Lamsdorf said, "your views on Korean security and independence suggest to me that Japan plans to take over Korea completely and leave Russia with nothing. That would make an agreement between our two countries next to impossible." Lamsdorf seemed to be suggesting that, fundamentally, Russia wanted to take over approximately half of the Korean Peninsula.

Still, Lamsdorf spoke throughout of his desire for Russia and Japan to settle the Korean crisis through diplomacy rather than military action, and sought to make that clear to Itō, who was very pleased to hear this. But we must note here that Lamsdorf's words on this occasion were nothing more than a diplomatic gambit.

Behind Lamsdorf stood the Russian military, whose commander in chief, War Minister Kuropatkin, was not the advocate of peace between Russia and Japan that Witte made him out to be, a fact made clear in Witte's own memoirs. Actually, Kuropatkin had suggested that Lamsdorf "offer Itō 'the bread of peace.'" For, if war broke out, a vast number of troops would have to be sent to the presumed battlefields in Manchuria via the Trans-Siberian Railway, and its construction would not be completed within the year. War must be avoided at all costs until the completion of the railroad. Peace between Russia and Japan would be a strategic necessity until then.

Itō, it goes without saying, knew nothing of all this. He left Russia full of confidence that a crisis between Japan and Russia over Korea could be avoided through peaceful diplomatic means. He went to Germany and sent a cable to Prime Minister Katsura from Berlin, advising, "Postpone signing the Anglo-Japanese treaty. An agreement with Russia seems possible."

Both Prime Minister Katsura Tarō and Foreign Minister Komura Jutarō were dumbfounded at this private diplomacy of Itō's.

* * *

Itō waited at his Berlin hotel. During his visit to Russia, the Russians had promised that they would respond in writing to Itō's diplomatic feelers. Experienced diplomat though he was, Itō waited hopefully. "It will certainly be good news . . . " He was as naïvely hopeful as a young girl.

At last, the news came, via the Russian embassy in Berlin. Reading the text of the message as translated by the Japanese embassy, Itō felt a chilliness quite different from the atmosphere of a few days earlier in St. Petersburg: "Russia is free to take what actions it wishes in Manchuria." This was a decisive expression of the fact that Russia recognized no limits on its own right to invade in that area.

In exchange, Russia acknowledged "only a limited freedom of action" on Japan's part in the Korean Peninsula. The grand principle of imperialism, that a great power is always free to act while a small power is always limited in its freedom, was being taught by Russia to Japan, as a schoolmaster teaches a lesson to a primary school pupil.

"This is not what Witte said the other day," thought a somewhat dazed Itō after having put down the translated letter. "Perhaps Witte was not consulted when this was drafted." In such matters, Itō was too honest a man to understand the real situation. In fact, Witte himself had consulted with War Minister Kuropatkin while the latter was drafting the letter. In short, Witte too had caved in to the army.

The fact of the matter was that Witte had explained to the cabinet that "Japan was on the brink of bankruptcy due to its huge military budget." He went on to suggest that if Russia lent Japan the much-needed money, with appropriate collateral security, of course, Japan would no doubt feel a sense of gratitude and obligation to Russia. The army and other ministers, however, rejected this proposal as "absurd."

"If indeed Japan is on the verge of bankruptcy, that's all to the good! It can hardly wage war under such circumstances, or, if by chance it did, it would fall like a rotten tree blown down by the wind. In short, conducting diplomatic relations with Japan as our equal is totally meaningless."

This was the view of Kuropatkin and others, and, given their support for Russia's expansionist policies, this probably made a lot of sense. The Russian letter had been written on the basis of this assessment of the situation in the Far East and Russia's mood at that time. Witte had no choice but to knuckle under to the pressures of the times in Russia. Itō was greatly disappointed.

By contrast, Katsura Tarō and the other top leaders in the government felt a strange sense of relief. For this brought an end to Itō's private diplomacy—so unwelcome to the government—and meant that Japan's diplomatic course would have a single, unified direction from then on. The aim would be an alliance with Britain.

* * *

Itō had failed. When he came back to Japan, deflated, Tani Tateki, who had never liked him, went about crowing, "Itō has come back like a waterlogged rat, and, by way of contrast, the government's head has swelled to the bursting point."

The foreign minister at the time was Komura Jutarō. Prime Minister Katsura left all diplomatic decisions to him. "Itō is too simple and trusting," Komura remarked. "For Japan to take Russia's hand now would be like a young girl allowing herself to be bound hand and foot, only to be violated. And as for the promised marriage, her suitor kicks the idea aside and makes a neat escape." The Russians are a good-natured people but they are willing to tell the most incredible lies regarding affairs of state—such was the general opinion in international political circles in Europe.

Komura had no particular liking for Great Britain and knew better than almost anyone about Britain's shrewdness and cunning in diplomacy. But in choosing between an alliance with Russia or an alliance with Britain, he wanted to make his decision on the basis of the relative level of trust that could be accorded to the two countries.

When he had his subordinates investigate the diplomatic history of both Russia and Britain with respect to their alliances with other nations, he discovered to his surprise that Russia had almost made a habit of unilaterally discarding its alliances with other countries. Great Britain, on the other hand, had never done so, always faithfully maintaining its foreign alliances. Furthermore, Europeans often said that "the Russian national instinct is to plunder." For a militarily weak Japan to convince Russia to restrain its "instinct to plunder" at the negotiating table by earnest entreaties would be quite impossible.

After the Triple Intervention, when Russia, as one of the parties, took control of Manchuria, Komura Jutarō asked Yamaza Enjirō, chief of the Political Affairs Bureau at the Foreign Ministry, if he knew how the Ainu people of Hokkaido captured bears alive. The Ainu would first set out a large amount of herring roe to dry on the seashore. A bear would come. It would gobble up as much of the herring roe as possible and then, feeling terribly thirsty, would plunge its head into the incoming waves and drink its fill of sea water. The sea water would make its thirst even more intense, and the bear would go on drinking. Finally, the herring roe in its stomach would swell up, rendering the bear unable to move. The Ainu would then approach and capture the bear without difficulty.

The bear in Komura's little parable is Russia. The Ainu are Japan. The herring roe represent Manchuria, and the salty water, the Korean Peninsula. When the bear begins to drink the water of Korea, the Great Powers will not remain silent. In Komura's view, Japan should then get the aid of a Great

Power and drive the bear away. This parable proved true, and Great Britain made its appearance as the star performer in this drama.

Itō Hirobumi's failure to establish a Russo-Japanese alliance did serve some purpose. In London, Hayashi Tadasu was holding those frequent discussions about the contents of a possible alliance with Britain with Lord Lansdowne. Naturally, each side tried to make its own country's duties as light and its benefits as great as possible, and they were at a stage where neither side was prone to give in.

But here suddenly was a factor that made Britain uneasy—namely, Itō Hirobumi, who was on his way to Russia. The British thought that, as the negotiations dragged on, the Japanese may have grown impatient, and suspected that they might be "preparing the way for a Russo-Japanese alliance and thus playing a double game."

Foreign Minister Lansdowne spoke to Ambassador Hayashi about the matter. "Prince Itō's actions are hard to understand. With these important negotiations going on here in London, he ought to have come directly from Paris to London, yet he went to Russia instead. What's behind this?"

Hayashi didn't know how to reply. He could hardly say that it was just arbitrary "diplomatic play" on the part of a senior advisor to the Japanese government. Finally, he felt forced to tell a transparent lie. "It's just a matter of Prince Itō's personal health. He knows that winter is the harshest season of the year in London and wished to avoid it."

Lansdowne looked irritated. "That's strange. I'll grant that London's winters are not conducive to health, but I've never heard it said that the Russian winter is healthy either!" He went on. "I must warn you that the Russians are habitual offenders against the principles of trust and fidelity. They always treat their treaties as so much wastepaper. Please urge Prince Itō on my behalf not to immerse himself too much in the pleasures of the Russian winter."

Hayashi had already realized that the British were more eager for the alliance than were the Japanese themselves, and that was why he worked so hard at the treaty negotiations, which extended over one and a half months, doing his very best to make sure that the conditions were favorable to Japan.

But to return to Itō. Having returned to Berlin from Russia, he then went to Britain at Hayashi's urging. Itō himself could not have foreseen what happened as a result of his activities. Great Britain made major concessions regarding the contents of the treaty and hastened to conclude the alliance with Japan.

The Anglo-Japanese Alliance was formally concluded on January 30, 1902. Itō had already left London, arriving in Nagasaki on February 25. At a welcome reception given by the city of Nagasaki, he gave a speech entitled

"The Anglo-Japanese Alliance and National Preparedness," and in it he stated, "Foreign relations transcend the issues of political parties or factions. They are a matter for the whole nation. If pro-British or pro-Russian groups should emerge among us and divide us, it would lead to incalculable misfortune for our nation." Thus, he announced in the most public fashion that he had now abandoned all plans for a special relationship with Russia.

4

WINDS AND CLOUDS

Hirose Takeo, a lieutenant commander in the Japanese Navy, had only recently been relieved of his duties as a military attaché in Russia and gone back to Japan. Akiyama Saneyuki was at the time an instructor at the Naval Staff College.

One day, a sturdy-looking fellow appeared unexpectedly in Saneyuki's office. It was Hirose. His eyes were shining from a dark-complexioned face, and Saneyuki was at first not sure who it might be. The reason was that Hirose, though now so dark, was naturally fair-skinned. Also, there was something in his bearing that seemed very un-Japanese. Hirose had been stationed a long time in Russia—about five years. During that time, he had become acquainted with many Russian naval officers, and he had become the most popular foreign naval attaché.

Nor was his popularity limited to the Russian naval officers: the ladies of the Russian imperial court were also taken with him. In particular, Ariadna Kovalevskaya, said to be the most beautiful young noblewoman in St. Petersburg at the time, fell passionately in love with him. But Hirose was a confirmed bachelor and did not respond to her in that way. Finally, the order for him to return to Japan came, and he left the Russian capital. But his experiences in St. Petersburg may have changed him somewhat.

"You're surprised at my face?" he asked, taking the seat Saneyuki offered. "I got a snow tan in Siberia." Hirose had gone across freezing cold Siberia by sleigh. At first, though, he had used the Trans-Siberian Railway in order to learn about its speed and frequency so as to be able to gauge the railway's transport capacity for military use.

Hirose rode it from Moscow to Irkutsk, where he spent one week preparing for the further journey by sleigh. From his hotel in Irkutsk, he sent a last letter to Ariadna Kovalevskaya in St. Petersburg, ending with the words, "I pray that God's blessing may rest upon you, who are forever so dear to me."

He went on as far as Sretensk by train and from there began his long journey by sleigh through the snows of Siberia. Before setting out, he had bought the sleigh in Sretensk, and was given the use of three government horses and a groom by the staging post there.

Hirose said he traveled 200 kilometers per day on average. Very few Russians could have broken this record. Going to Khabarovsk via Blagoveshchensk, he had been on the sleigh for ten and a half days and nights straight. Apart from Blagoveshchensk, he never stopped for a night's rest, sleeping instead in snatches as the sleigh moved over the snow. Yet he claimed in his oral report to the Naval Ministry that he did not become too fatigued—he was a kind of superman!

"Let me talk about the state of the Russian Navy as I have observed it over the past few years," said Hirose, asking Saneyuki to prepare paper and pencils. He had made amazingly detailed observations. "They have no regard for the Japanese Navy at all." Thus, when Hirose asked to see military ports and shipyards, the Russians never refused. It seemed rather as if they thought to crush this Japanese naval officer's will to fight by showing him how impressive the Russian Navy actually was.

Russia was then in the midst of large-scale naval construction projects, with every shipyard engaged in building warships great and small. Hirose had observed the naval arsenal at St. Petersburg and the shipyards at Galerny several times; in addition, he had seen the Baltic shipyards and the naval arsenal at Sevastopol. He was also able to attend the launching of the battleship *Peresvet*, which weighed around 12,000 tons—fast but with weak defenses. "If it fought against our *Shikishima*, we would have the advantage." This was Hirose's conclusion, supported with mathematical detail. At the Baltic shipyards on the southern tip of Vasily Island, he saw the battleship *Pobeda* and the armored cruiser *Gromoboy*.

Kronstadt was a military port that served as a kind of checkpoint for St. Petersburg. The commanding officer of the naval station there was Vice Admiral Makarov. He was the most famous officer in the Russian Navy, and both Saneyuki and Hirose had read his classic *Strategy* early on. Hirose commented on Makarov in some detail. "He doesn't look like a heroic sort, but he seems as intellectual as one would imagine from his writings."

Hirose came again next day, and the topic was again the Russian Navy. This time, Saneyuki had prepared several questions, which Hirose undertook to answer. The conversation started at one o'clock in the afternoon and lasted until nine that evening.

"What about the quality of the officers?"

"Not bad at all," was Hirose's reply. "They're almost all from the nobility, so they have strong feelings of loyalty to the tsar."

"And what about the sailors?"

To this also, Hirose replied in detail. The ordinary sailors seemed to lack powers of judgment, but they faithfully carried out their orders. And they were particularly skilled at gunnery.

"Their morale is a problem, though," Hirose concluded. The sailors were from the serf class, or classes close to that. They had been drafted into the navy and had the temperament of peasants rather than soldiers. Russian peasants did not tend to take the initiative; a special kind of "resignation" seemed part of their nature.

Hirose said that this made them disinclined to think that their purpose as sailors was the sinking of enemy ships—rather, they passively awaited the enemy's fire. Hirose went on to comment on the social unrest and revolutionary movements that had been shaking the foundations of the Russian Empire for many years.

After talking in detail about the capabilities of the Russian Navy and the high performance level of its newly built warships, he added, "But there are lots of strange things about the Russian Navy as well."

First, there was the monopoly the nobility had on the officer class. Once, when Hirose was traveling by rail, the head porter, learning that his passenger was a Japanese naval officer, asked if he was a count or a marquis. Hirose answered that he was not, and explained that anyone could become an officer in Japan's army and navy if he passed the requisite examinations and that virtually all from the highest officers on down were commoners. "You must be joking, sir," the head porter had answered, incredulous.

"Japan is currently building its navy," Hirose continued to explain to Saneyuki, "with an enthusiasm that extends across the nation. Russia too is building up its navy with an energy even greater than Japan's, yet the common people of Russia are neither aware of that fact, nor would they be interested in it. The nation is owned by the nobility, so the common people regard the naval buildup as something 'their betters' have simply chosen to do, for reasons of their own. In time of war, the noncommissioned officers and sailors are taken from this indifferent commoner class, and it's questionable how much 'fight' they have in them."

The conversation shifted to the actual building of the navy. The twentieth century began with a zealous naval buildup on the part of Germany and Russia. The initial impetus came from the German kaiser, who had judged that in order to be listened to with respect in the European political world, Germany would need to have sufficient naval power to stand up to Britain. And so he started to build a large navy.

This stimulated Russia to begin a naval buildup on a scale that would surpass Germany's and would continue for twenty years. This commenced in 1901, and Hirose was able to observe its progress during the last part of his stay in Russia.

Japan had already begun its own naval buildup prior to that, but due to differences in the strength and wealth of the two countries, Japan's efforts could not be compared with Russia's massive plans. By the time news of Russia's plans of 1901 reached the Japanese Navy, Japan's defeat in the arms race seemed certain, given the scale of both sides' plans. Japan's fiscal capabilities were already almost exhausted, yet the navy would have to add several warships to its previous proposal in order to keep up with Russia.

In 1903, the year following this conversation between Hirose and Saneyuki, the new proposal was put before the eighteenth Imperial Diet and passed under the title "Third-Period Expansion Plan." According to this plan, three 15,000-ton battleships, three 10,000-ton armored cruisers, and two 5,000-ton protected cruisers were added, at a total cost of one hundred fifteen million yen over the eleven-year period from 1903 through 1913. The ships included in this proposal, of course, played no part in the Russo-Japanese War, which erupted too early for them to be of use.

After his return to Japan, Hirose Takeo started to serve on board the battleship *Asahi*, which both Saneyuki and Hirose had seen while it was under construction. Once he was actually serving on the ship, Hirose was filled with admiration for its equipment and capabilities. "This must be the best battleship in the world!" he told Saneyuki.

* * *

In early summer 1903, Akiyama Yoshifuru returned from Qing China and was appointed commander of the First Cavalry Brigade based in Narashino, Chiba Prefecture. He was forty-five years old. His rank of major general makes him sound like an old man, but Yoshifuru's physical powers were unchanged from the days of his youth. He still drank as much as ever and was if anything a more voracious reader, especially of works on military science in French, and, among these, works dealing with the cavalry and with Russia.

Yoshifuru's reassignment from China to the cavalry command in Chiba was one manifestation of the Japanese Army's shift to a war footing. Everyone agreed that, in the event of war, the only person capable of leading the Japanese cavalry against the Russian cavalry (the best in the world) was Yoshifuru.

Some months after arriving in Narashino, Yoshifuru was summoned to the Army Ministry and told that "a strange invitation has come from Russia."

It was from the Russian War Ministry, announcing that the Russian Army would be holding large-scale maneuvers in Nikolsk, Siberia, in September and requesting that observers be sent from Japan.

"We want you to go. We're planning on sending infantry major Ōba Jirō as well."

When Yoshifuru returned to his house in Yotsuya Shinanomachi, he found Saneyuki there. Saneyuki always regarded Yoshifuru as a substitute father and made a point of visiting him once a month when he was not at sea.

"Hey, Jun—I hear your drinking's become worse than ever!" said Yoshifuru with a severe look. Though he was himself the biggest drinker in the army, he was never happy to hear about his younger brother drinking.

"Look who's talking," thought Saneyuki, who answered, "You're the one who's the big drinker!"

"Drinks are like rice to me" was Yoshifuru's response. It seemed that his physiology required that he drink alcoholic beverages to avoid becoming undernourished. Thus, he continued to drink even on the battlefield and in the midst of a battle, and he kept the water jug in his office filled with some kind of liquor, drinking it in place of water.

Saneyuki, on the other hand, drank because he felt he had to. He drank to show off how much he could hold while with friends at a restaurant or while indulging in boastful talk in discussions with his colleagues.

"I hear you've been drinking with army people lately," Yoshifuru said accusingly.

Saneyuki frequently met with young staff officers of the General Staff to discuss the situation in Russia, criticizing the weak posture of the Japanese government and engaging in jingoistic boasting. Yoshifuru had heard about this.

"Since time began, talking about military matters while drinking has been regarded as the lowest sort of behavior. And shooting your mouth off about war with your drinking buddies is downright dangerous since the nation's survival is at stake. I'd say that it's a totally useless way to spend your time."

Saneyuki listened to this with a dark look on his face because, on reflection, he knew Yoshifuru's criticism had some basis in truth. "Of all the Japanese I have met," Yuan Shikai once said of Yoshifuru years later, "Mr. Akiyama is the most impressive." Yoshifuru was the sort of heroic Asian male who generally appeals to the Chinese, but toward his younger brother, he was as severely critical as any paterfamilias in Japan.

"Does he think I'm still a kid?" Saneyuki thought. Nonetheless, though often haughty toward others, he was always deferential toward his elder brother, just as he had been when a boy.

"You gambled, didn't you, on the ship from the United States to London?" No sooner had Yoshifuru returned from China than he began garnering a great many stories about his younger brother's doings. Saneyuki felt that, as a navy man, it was quite natural that he should gamble now and then, but Yoshifuru was making a different point.

Saneyuki had indeed gambled aboard ship, with some Americans who had affected the airs and graces of European gentlemen. "Aren't you a little bored?" the Americans asked disarmingly, and Saneyuki fell for their ploy. They all acted as if they were strangers to one another, but Saneyuki learned later that they were members of an Italian-American gang and in cahoots with each other. The reason they had fixed on Saneyuki was that they knew that a good many Japanese naval officers were sent to the United States and Europe to buy warships in those days, and they were usually well provided with travel expenses.

They started to play poker. At first, Saneyuki kept winning, which was part of the gang's strategy. Saneyuki didn't want to "quit right after winning," and, as the game went on, the others started to employ their tricks. Saneyuki began to lose and kept on losing. He had not only lost all the money he had on him but had begun to dip into the large amount he carried in his satchel when he realized they were swindling him. Even so, he said nothing.

Finally, when he had lost everything he had, he stood up and asked the gentleman who seemed to be the leader of the gang to come with him to his cabin, "since he had something to discuss." He locked the cabin door, shouting, "Listen, you—you don't know who you're dealing with here! I saw through your tricks some time ago, but I decided not to say anything in front of the others. Do you think a samurai's honor would allow him to be cheated of all his money that way? Return the money—all of it. If you don't, I'll use *this*!" And he drew from his waist a dagger in a plain sheath, then flashed the unsheathed blade. Saneyuki looked quite capable of killing the other man.

The gang leader was clearly afraid and, unusually for someone in his line of work, he coughed up all the money and returned it to Saneyuki.

Yoshifuru had heard the whole story from a third person. "You haven't changed a bit since your student days!" he said reproachfully, blinking his eyes with irritation.

Saneyuki looked down as he listened to his older brother. He knew that if he let Yoshifuru have his say, he would be in a good mood again very soon.

* * *

"I'm off to Siberia soon," Yoshifuru said quickly just as Saneyuki was about to leave.

Saneyuki was surprised. "Siberia" was the region that everyone was talking about, the whole world seemingly greatly heated up over Russia's occupation of eastern Siberia and Manchuria.

"To do what?"

"Official business."

"That much I know," thought Saneyuki, but if Yoshifuru didn't want to discuss the matter, he couldn't ask any further.

"Take care not to catch cold," Saneyuki said in the entranceway, by way of farewell.

A few days later, on September 4, Yoshifuru boarded a ship at Yokohama and sailed for Vladivostok. Major Ōba accompanied him, and for years afterward took pleasure in recalling this trip with Yoshifuru. "Mr. Akiyama was always smiling and drank a lot of liquor on board."

As someone responsible for planning strategy against the Russians, Ōba would dearly have liked to ask this "god of the cavalry" just how strong the Japanese cavalry really was, but it seemed a rude question, and Ōba held back. Then the night before they arrived in Vladivostok, he finally asked, "It's a very simpleminded question, but, in the event of war, what about the strength of the Japanese versus the Russian cavalry?"

"We'll go into battle intending to die. Even if all of us are lost, things will be all right so long as our total military strategy succeeds. That's the nature of the cavalry." Yoshifuru spoke as if he were talking about something unconnected with himself personally.

Ōba then asked, "And how strong is the Russian cavalry?"

Yoshifuru gazed at the infantry major with a strange look on his face and smiled. "Why, that's what we're going to see about!"

"Why do you think the Russian Army is so keen to have Japanese military officers attend these grand maneuvers?"

"They want to make us tremble with fear!" replied Yoshifuru with a laugh.

The Russians hoped to prevent the Japanese from launching a war against Russia by showing them the Russian Army, the greatest in the world, and thus convincing the Japanese that they had no chance of winning. A report had in fact come from Colonel Akashi, a military attaché stationed in Russia, saying that Russia wished to avoid conflict in Manchuria until the Trans-Siberian Railway was completed.

So the purpose of inviting the Japanese military observers to the grand maneuvers was precisely as stated above, and this was done at the direction of the Russian tsar himself. The tsar's language became, as always, abusive when he talked about the Japanese "monkeys." "How surprised the monkeys will be!"—we can imagine him murmuring this to himself.

* * *

The ship entered the port of Vladivostok on the morning of September 11. Russia had provided this military port with every possible military facility, and, in addition, the cruisers of the Vladivostok Squadron, which had been expanded in anticipation of war in the Far East, were crouched there menacingly like a group of panthers. Having seen the port and the natural setting, the Japanese felt as if the entire area were armored in steel. Everything spoke wordlessly of Russia's intentions toward the Far East.

"They say Port Arthur is even better fortified than here," whispered Major Ōba.

On the pier, a young staff officer with the rank of captain and some ten other officers stood with dignified formality to greet the Japanese visitors. The captain was named Mirsky, a staff officer in the governor general's office for the Amur region. When the Russian welcoming party saw Yoshifuru disembarking from the steamship onto the pier, they all saluted. Still more surprising was the presence behind the welcoming party of an honor guard, one platoon of soldiers all lined up.

"They must think I'm an imperial prince or something . . . " thought Yoshifuru. For truly, he was receiving imperial treatment, apparently on orders from St. Petersburg, and this continued throughout the time he was in Siberia.

The hotel was very near the pier, but a splendid carriage had been made available for the short distance. The carriage was the same sort as that in which grand dukes were driven about in St. Petersburg. The hotel was operated by the army officer corps, corresponding to the Kaikōsha Officers' Club in Japan. Not more than one hotel in Japan could compare with this Russian one in terms of the grandeur of the building itself and the gorgeous interior décor.

After a short pause to allow his guests to rest, Captain Mirsky came by, looking quite solemn. He declared that he would guide them around the city. The same carriage was again used, with a sergeant major and a sergeant mounted on the driver's seat. After a two-hour tour, the guests and their guide had lunch at the officers' club.

"What's your impression of Vladivostok, Major General?" asked Captain Mirsky in impeccable French, knowing in advance that this Japanese officer was fluent in French.

Yoshifuru, shaking himself a little, answered suddenly in Japanese. "Can't tell after just two hours!"

Mirsky was bewildered. Major Ōba translated Yoshifuru's reply into Russian.

The topic changed to France. "I understand that you studied cavalry tactics and techniques in France, Excellency."

"Cavalry . . ." mumbled Yoshifuru, as he squashed a fly that had landed on his neck.

The fly, oozing liquid, stuck to Yoshifuru's palm. Without brushing it off, he pressed his palm against the handle of his beer mug. Mirsky looked disgusted.

" . . . No, I just went to France on a pleasure trip," concluded Yoshifuru.

The Russian officers were virtually all from the nobility and had a natural courtliness of manner that was very French. So Captain Mirsky must have been amazed at this Japanese officer who didn't mind lifting his beer mug with the same hand he had just used to crush a random fly.

And yet Yoshifuru did not seem to be a coarse man. Mirsky himself had gone to France to study artillery techniques, and, as they talked, he and Yoshifuru discovered that they had several acquaintances in common. Yoshifuru spoke of these men and their various talents in a cordial way. His conversation seemed both witty and warm to an extent that was unusual even among Russian Army officers, with their grounding in French culture.

Mirsky's serene, philosophical-looking face often broke into a warm smile because he seemed to have a real liking for Yoshifuru. Sometimes, though, he would look at Yoshifuru with great seriousness and say, "During Your Excellency's stay, it is my great honor to be your servant." He said this as many as three times. Mirsky looked to be about thirty years of age and was clearly a serious young man. Yoshifuru thought him a fine military man.

The afternoon was also devoted to sightseeing. But Captain Mirsky kept showing Yoshifuru places of little importance and would go right by any military installations they happened to pass in their carriage. And so Yoshifuru began to show his high-handed side. "Oh, this is the command center . . . " he would say, stopping the carriage. "I must present my compliments!" And in he would go, leaving the flustered Mirsky behind.

He managed to view the command center for the military port as well in exactly the same fashion and stopped the carriage in front of the fortification command center too. "My compliments," he declared, leaving his calling card at the entrance desk.

"Captain Mirsky, the view from the third floor must take in both the fortifications *and* the military port, I'd guess!" And up he went, Mirsky finding it impossible to stop him.

In this way, Yoshifuru paid visits to the military governor of the Primorsky Region and the commander of the Vladivostok Squadron. He then went on to stop the carriage at a spot overlooking the port, get down himself, and have Mirsky and the other members of his escort get down as well. "How many gun emplacements are there on that promontory over there?" and "What's the range of the batteries on the hill across the way there?" Asking these and other sorts of questions that a military officer of one country ought not to ask a military officer of another, he put Captain Mirsky and the others in an increasingly difficult position. But his face was wreathed in smiles as he did this, and his attitude seemed so artless that the Russians gave him truthful answers to two or three of his questions. The Russians, of course, were nervous about all this, and so too was Major Ōba on the Japanese side.

Next morning, Yoshifuru left Vladivostok, arriving in Nikolsk by nightfall. Here too Yoshifuru was lodged in a hotel run by the officers' association, and a welcome party was held by the Russian side in the reception room of the hotel. The Russians proved to be great drinkers. Among the Russians was an officer whom Yoshifuru knew from his days in Tianjin. This Colonel Voronov had worked for the civilian agency in the Russian concession in Tianjin, but he was now the regimental commander of the hussars in Nikolsk. When he and Yoshifuru realized they were old acquaintances, they embraced one another.

"Voronov is the finest military man in Nikolsk, and the one most qualified to be a cavalry officer," Yoshifuru wrote in his journal. By "most qualified to be a cavalry officer," he meant that the other was highly observant, accurate, and quick-witted, and, in addition, bold enough to press the enemy camp during lengthy pursuits, and brave enough to plunge into the midst of a large enemy force with only a small force of his own. When he asked himself how many cavalry officers on the Japanese side had the qualities of Voronov, he couldn't help feeling a bit discouraged.

Voronov would bring many of the Russian cavalry officers to introduce to Yoshifuru, saying, "He's also a cavalryman!" Each time, Yoshifuru raised his glass of vodka. Cavalrymen had their own special character, quite different from that of infantrymen. They had a sense of comradeship with other cavalrymen that transcended national boundaries. Yoshifuru was no exception to this, and the young Russian cavalry officers showed a kind of affectionate dependence on him.

There was one young first lieutenant in particular who never left Yoshifuru's side, saying, "Your Excellency looks exactly like my father!" He said he was from St. Petersburg, and Yoshifuru later learned that his father was a count and a vice admiral in the navy.

"And how old would your father be?"

"He's sixty, sir."

"How can that be! If you say I look like him, I must be like him *before* he married your mother!" said Yoshifuru with a guffaw.

When the banquet ended, Yoshifuru went to his room on the second floor, but he was so drunk that he found it bothersome to take off his boots, so he threw himself onto the bed booted as he was. "Gloriously drunk, I am," he muttered. Never in all his years of drinking had he attended a drinking party as amusing as this one. "What fine fellows they are," he thought to himself, again and again. And yet, when at last war came, he would encounter them on the battlefield. And the Russian officers surely felt the same about Yoshifuru.

And, therefore, battle did not seem so cruel to Yoshifuru, nor would it have seemed so to the Russian officers in attendance at the banquet. The traditions of chivalry remained in Russia, as did those of *Bushidō*, the way of the warrior, in Yoshifuru's consciousness. Both the Russians and the Japanese had an aesthetic creed that saw beauty in a soldier's bravery in battle. They wished to act beautifully themselves, and they wanted their opponent to act beautifully as well—this was their constant ethical concern. Concern for such ethical matters ended with this historical period.

* * *

The inspection of the Russian forces began in the afternoon of the thirteenth, the following day. Yoshifuru borrowed a horse and rode to where the troops were encamped in barracks on the maneuver grounds some 4 kilometers from Nikolsk, and inspected both the cavalry and infantry there. That was all he did that day. He was greatly impressed with the splendid physiques of the Russian troops, finding their condition incomparably superior to that of Japanese soldiers.

Then too there was the fact that all the troops, both cavalry and infantry, wore boots. In Japan, where leather was much more expensive than other items, only the officers in the infantry wore boots. In addition, the cavalry, artillerymen, and supply corps, who all used horses, also wore boots. Yoshifuru took one of the Russian boots in hand to examine it, and found that the leather was of much higher quality and more durable than that used for Japanese boots. When he asked how much each pair cost, he was told that the Russian government bought them for the equivalent of three yen fifty sen each. Japanese government-issue boots cost as much as twelve or thirteen yen a pair.

The maneuvers began on the night of the fourteenth, ending in the afternoon of the following day, followed by a formal review of the troops on the sixteenth. Actually, the maneuvers were on a small scale, one-tenth of what had been planned.

Exercises unprecedented in their scale had been planned, with various army corps from all over Siberia assembling on the wide plains of Nikolsk. But in early September, it rained heavily throughout Siberia, and roads and railway lines became impassable. Thus, the planned army movements had to be abandoned, and the maneuvers were conducted by two brigades that were stationed in the Nikolsk area.

"The Russians must be very disappointed," Yoshifuru commented to Major Ōba.

Their plan to demonstrate the power of the greatest army in the world and thus crush the Japanese will to fight seemed to have come to nothing. Yet Yoshifuru learned a lot from the experience. The Russian cavalry was far more formidable than he had ever imagined. A Russian cavalry regiment consisted of six companies, and each company was made up of around one hundred twenty horsemen. The horses were all strong and healthy. "Far better than our cavalry's horses," wrote Yoshifuru frankly in his journal. Each company of the Russian cavalry had horses of a single color—another example of Russian richness and splendor that Japan could never hope to imitate.

In 1887, the Japanese Army purchased ninety Algerian horses and another one hundred seventy in the following year. These were used to breed more of the same type, but the rate of increase was not very great. The bulk of cavalry horses continued to be of the native variety, which seemed like close relatives of the donkey.

It was not till 1896 that Japan had breeding stations and pastures for the reproduction of cavalry horses—a first step in improving the quality of its horses. That was only seven years before Yoshifuru's visit to Nikolsk. With regard to the skill of the riders in the various equestrian exercises, Yoshifuru observed in his journal, "Well worthy of praise. Superior to our cavalry in several respects."

* * *

Yoshifuru also quietly "gave marks" to the other Russian military units in comparison with Japan's and found none of them inferior. In his notes, he gave an overall evaluation of the Russian and Japanese troops: "From what I have observed over the past few days, the Russian cavalry and artillery are somewhat superior to ours with respect to horses. There is not much difference between their infantry and our own." So he was able to give almost equal marks to the Japanese infantry, at any rate. "The officers," he went on, "are generally brave men, and the cavalry officers in particular are determined and more than willing to plunge into the midst of an enemy force." In short, they were of undeniable excellence. What would it mean for the Japanese Army to have to go into battle against such a foe?

Finally, there was the matter of the abilities of the top commanders. If they were incompetent or cowardly, no matter how fine the troops under their command might be, military victory would be difficult. It was in order to "inspect" the Russian top commanders that Yoshifuru had put so much effort into meeting the commanding officers in both Vladivostok and Nikolsk. "The top commanders, particularly the generals, are extremely able men," he wrote.

So there was nothing to criticize, and yet Yoshifuru concluded, "Nonetheless I believe it would be by no means difficult for our troops to surpass the level of the Russians if they train hard enough." This comes down to Yoshifuru consoling himself with the thought that, if Japan did its best over the coming years, it might be able to overtake the Russians. But war between Russia and Japan was to come the following year. The Japanese troops were hardly likely to have time to "train hard enough" in the hope of overtaking the enemy.

By the way, it's interesting to note that abstractions like "spiritual power" and "loyalty" that the military men of the 1930s and 1940s were so fond of invoking go entirely unmentioned in Yoshifuru's comments. He had a grasp of objective facts and discussed only the physical and material side of the military. And this is true not only of Yoshifuru but of the Japanese of the Meiji period in general. How different this is from the Japanese military of the 1930s and 1940s, who made imponderables like spiritual power and loyalty major factors in judging the relative strength of Japan's military and the enemy's, always assuming that Japan had a supreme advantage with respect to such qualities.

The maneuvers ended. By rights, Yoshifuru should have left Siberia, but he had decided to "reconnoiter" (to use the jargon of the cavalry) Russia's military facilities, including those in Manchuria. No doubt the Russian welcoming committee would be opposed to his plans, but Yoshifuru didn't care—he would make his request.

* * *

Manchuria and the adjacent region of Siberia were top-secret zones for imperial Russia at that time. Military forces were being vastly increased there, and the fortification of major centers was ongoing. Japan's General Staff was, of course, eager to learn about conditions there, but, no matter how many agents Japan employed, the Russians were so adept at counterespionage that Japan was unable to gain the most essential intelligence.

Before departing for Russia, Yoshifuru had said casually that he would "take a good look at things," much to the surprise of the staff officers.

"Sir," one of them objected, "even our most able secret agents have been unable to give us really important information from there. Please don't take any chances."

"But I'm a cavalryman," laughed Yoshifuru. One of the functions of the cavalry was to go long distances, penetrate the enemy forces, and bring back useful information. That was what Yoshifuru meant. He knew that when war came, he would be in charge of leading the cavalry into battle, and it was his duty to learn as much about the enemy as possible well in advance.

And so he said to the Russian welcoming committee, "When I was stationed in Tianjin, I often met and became good friends with General Linevich, who is now the governor general's representative in Khabarovsk. To have come this far and return without paying my respects to General Linevich would be contrary to the rules of our Bushidō code." This was said in French with a broad provincial accent, and Yoshifuru pressed his case with a look of the utmost nonchalance on his face, so the committee members were at a loss how to respond. They certainly did not want to allow a Japanese to see the new military facilities that had been established between Nikolsk and Khabarovsk.

"We are very sorry," they said, "but individual travel by persons invited to attend these maneuvers is not allowed."

"But it isn't travel, it's just paying respects to a friend."

"The paying of respects would involve travel."

"Well, of course!" said Yoshifuru, clapping the other on the shoulder.

At a loss what to say, the Russian replied, "It would require direct permission from the tsar himself." He thought this would make Yoshifuru withdraw his request.

Instead, Yoshifuru just nodded in agreement. "Do please ask for permission, then."

The Russian command in Nikolsk felt obliged to send a telegraph of inquiry to St. Petersburg. It took only a day for the reply to arrive: "Permission granted." The Russian officers were all amazed at this reply. The tsar must have judged that it would be politically advantageous to show this Japanese the might of the Russian Army, the greatest in the world, rather than trying to conceal it from him.

The telegram arrived at midnight, two hours before a train was due to leave for Khabarovsk. Yoshifuru caught that train.

* * *

Yoshifuru's "forcible reconnaissance" succeeded. He managed to get to the most vital centers in Manchuria. And the Russians seemed to be much taken with his personality, for he was popular everywhere he went.

Many cavalry regiments were stationed along the railway line from Nikolsk to Khabarovsk. The officers of those regiments would come to the station where Yoshifuru's train had arrived, take him to the station dining room, and toast him with champagne. It didn't matter whether the train arrived in the daytime or the middle of the night—the cavalry officers cared nothing for the hour of arrival. They always came. And they were all good-natured men, who viewed Yoshifuru as a fellow cavalry officer.

"The cavalry's the best!" Yoshifuru would say, pounding the table in utmost appreciation for their friendship. "Especially the Russian cavalry!" He was congenitally incapable of flattery, so this was what he really felt. And he thought to himself, "Someday I will have to meet these fine, warmhearted fellows from Siberia on the battlefield, and how will that be?"

But this military man of Meiji, a descendant of samurai, did not work himself into an emotional crisis because of such sentimental considerations. He trained himself to regard such a situation as one of the pleasures of being a man, and allowed himself no doubts about the matter. The Russian cavalry officers felt the same way. Precisely because there was a tense and sad awareness of the probability of their fighting one another, their brief time of fellowship with Yoshifuru seemed all the deeper—such was their understanding of this strange melody of the heart. This may have been the very last age in which warriors could have such feelings, cultivated ever since the Middle Ages.

In Khabarovsk, General Linevich was waiting for Yoshifuru, wearing on his chest the medal of St. George that he had won for his meritorious service during the Crimean War. Linevich was a man always mentioned together with Kuropatkin, the most brilliant officer in the Russian Army, and was even said to surpass Kuropatkin as a military strategist. He and Yoshifuru had become acquainted while he was in Beijing as commander of the occupying troops during the Boxer Rebellion. This same Linevich later aided General Kuropatkin, the commander in chief, in strategic planning during the Russo-Japanese War, and directed the fighting as commander of the First Army during the important battle of Mukden.

* * *

The night of his arrival, Yoshifuru attended a welcome banquet arranged by General Linevich at which he both spoke and drank a great deal. "Passed the time in pleasant conversation," he wrote in his journal, and he clearly had come to like the Russians more and more as people. But he also stated later, "The Russian Empire makes frequent use of deception in its foreign relations. It is a strange land, whose actions are hard to predict. Individually, though, the Russians are a very good-natured people, totally different from the policies of their nation. Particularly at a drinking party, they may well be the most pleasant companions in the world."

"What are your impressions of the Russian Army?" asked Linevich.

Yoshifuru offered sincere praise, being especially lavish in his description of the excellence of the Russian cavalry regiments. In this also he was being totally sincere.

On the day of his arrival, he had visited a preparatory school for the War Academy, the Twenty-fourth Infantry Regiment, and a government-established school for girls. He found nothing to criticize in what he saw. He thought, frankly, that in order to defeat such an enemy, fully one-third of the Japanese Army would have to die in battle.

The Russian side was very generous in its treatment of Yoshifuru during his inspection tour. The next day, he visited the Second Artillery Brigade as well.

Russia put great emphasis on firepower. The Japanese Army, emphasizing the importance of infantry battles, had no brigades made up solely of artillerymen and indeed had no conception of such a thing. And, of course, Japan did not have the economic power to emulate Russia, in any event. "Artillery brigade" here does not refer to artillerymen who directly cooperate with the infantry but is, rather, a strategic type of artillery force that can concentrate immense firepower on the necessary places at the necessary times. With economic constraints always in mind, Japan's military had no intention whatsoever of maintaining such a luxury as a strategic artillery force.

On this same day, Yoshifuru startled the Russian side by remarking how much he wanted to go to Port Arthur. This was no joking matter. A great fortification was being built at Port Arthur, and it was regarded as the most important of all Russia's secret, off-limits zones in the Far East.

"I'd like to visit Admiral Alexeyev," Yoshifuru said, "the viceroy of the Russian Far East who resides in Port Arthur, and apologize to him personally for my long silence." Yoshifuru had met Alexeyev when he had visited Beijing.

"Well, but Port Arthur . . . " murmured the welcoming committee, unable to respond to this brazen request.

But Yoshifuru, as usual, tried to coerce them, saying in Japanese, "I really must meet the admiral!" and putting the Russian side into more of a flurry. Coercing them further, he made a direct request when he was exchanging toasts with Linevich at a banquet and finally won his assent in this way.

Thus, Yoshifuru was able to enter Manchuria, go south to Port Arthur, meet with Alexeyev, and view the military facilities that were there. Prior to the beginning of the war, no one apart from Yoshifuru—not even a secret agent—had managed to view the military facilities at Port Arthur.

On October 3, 1903, when Yoshifuru returned to Tokyo from Port Arthur via Yantai, autumn was already well advanced. He had been traveling for thirty days, and his reports on the state of Russian forces in the Far East and their distribution, which he had verified with his own eyes, were sources of important information for the anti-Russian strategists at the General Staff Office.

* * *

Diplomatic relations between Japan and Russia had worsened to a degree that seemed to admit of no peaceful resolution. Some twenty days after Yoshifuru returned to Japan, his younger brother, now naval lieutenant commander Akiyama Saneyuki, was suddenly appointed as staff officer of the Standing Fleet. In time of war, he would automatically become a staff officer of the Combined Fleet.

"Jun's been made a fleet staff officer?" Yoshifuru had never shown any obvious interest in Saneyuki's promotions or the nature of his duties, but at that moment his face showed some surprise. Anyone with eyes to see could tell where the Japanese Navy was going with this appointment.

A few days later, Saneyuki came to the Akiyama home in Shinanomachi and announced his new duties with the fleet. "I'm going to sea."

Yoshifuru had already heard this from someone in the Naval Ministry, and he simply nodded.

"How's Sue doing?" he asked. Three months earlier, Saneyuki had married Sueko, the third daughter of Inō Mafumi, a commoner from Tokyo who was a general affairs official in the Imperial Household Ministry. Saneyuki was living in Kuruma-chō, in the Shiba Takanawa area of Tokyo.

"She's fine."

"You've found yourself a very good wife!" This was, from Yoshifuru, the highest form of praise for a woman.

Both of the brothers were attached to the single life, but each of them married, even if somewhat later than most men: Yoshifuru at thirty-five, when he was a major, and Saneyuki at thirty-six, as a lieutenant commander. Both of them had that very simple view of marriage, convinced somehow that marrying and having a family would weaken a man's determination. Even after their own marriages, they maintained this curious conviction.

And Saneyuki said something very similar in a letter to a friend who had written to congratulate him on his marriage. "For me, the navy is the greatest pleasure in life. I thought I'd die in battle and never thought of marrying. But as the relationship between Japan and Russia changed, with the winds and clouds gathering, I suddenly changed my mind and chose a wife. Not that I had a grand strategy for lulling the enemy by acting as if everything was peaceful. No, my marriage was just a means of dispelling low spirits while I pursued that greatest pleasure that I mentioned before. So, of course,

I haven't let anyone know about it or made an announcement of any kind. Monk that I am . . . "

For him naval strategy and maneuvers were the greatest pleasure in life, and so he calls himself a "monk," like one who has determined to follow the Buddhist way. Just why this "monk" had decided to marry, he goes on to explain in detail. Simply put, he was mocking the folly of the civilian Japanese government that, out of excessive fear of Russia, sought always to evade and escape military confrontation, much to Saneyuki's indignation. If that was to be the government's attitude, he would just as soon marry and enjoy quiet afternoon naps in his new home in Takanawa!

* * *

There was a reason for Saneyuki being transferred from the Naval Staff College to the Standing Fleet as a staff officer. The navy had already made a top-secret decision that war was inevitable, given the standstill in Russo-Japanese diplomatic relations, and it was in the process of making major personnel decisions in preparation for the war. The Personnel Division decided at once to leave all matters relating to fleet strategy in the hands of the thirty-six-year-old lieutenant commander Akiyama Saneyuki, and at the same time appointed, as commander in chief, Vice Admiral Tōgō Heihachirō, who held an easy post as commander of the Maizuru Naval Base. There was, however, one difficulty. Tōgō had had hardly any previous contact with this lieutenant commander from Iyo, Akiyama Saneyuki.

"Akiyama will handle the strategy. But if Tōgō doesn't have a really good grasp of his character and talents, they won't be able to work together well." With such considerations in mind, the Personnel Division of the Naval Ministry decided it would be better to reveal the appointments to Saneyuki in advance and have him meet Tōgō, who was then, by a lucky chance, in Tokyo. After they decided to tell Saneyuki all this, Tanaka Yasutarō and Chiaki Kyōjirō from Personnel sent someone to the Naval Staff College the day after the appointment decisions had been made to summon Saneyuki to the Naval Ministry.

Learning that Tōgō Heihachirō was to be top commander, Saneyuki was somewhat surprised. Tōgō was a quiet, unobtrusive man, and his name was hardly ever mentioned when talk turned to who might be appointed.

"You'll be the one to assist Vice Admiral Tōgō, with full responsibility for strategic planning." When Chiaki said this in a low voice, Saneyuki thought this decision entirely natural. There were many men in the navy, it was true, but none who could devise a strategy to beat the Russian fleet, apart from himself—he was sure of this.

"And yet," continued Chiaki, "Vice Admiral Tōgō and you have never served on the same ship together, and you have never worked in the same fields either. That's what we're uneasy about. And that's why we'd like you to visit Vice Admiral Tōgō and win his friendship, not tomorrow but tonight! His Excellency expects that you'll be coming."

"What odd things they say!" thought Saneyuki. Both commander of the fleet and staff officer were official positions. Why was it necessary to visit his future superior's home and win his goodwill? Full of self-confidence as he was, Saneyuki had never paid a visit to an admiral's residence. But Chiaki had a very grave look on his face, so Saneyuki nodded and said, "I'll do as you say." He then left the Naval Ministry and went back to his office at the Naval Staff College. When he sat back in his chair and considered the matter, though, it suddenly seemed ludicrous.

"Very strange," Saneyuki thought. It was inconceivable that the same genrō, government, and military leaders who had taken an extremely evasive attitude toward any war against Russia should now, all of a sudden, have decided on war and begun to make personnel decisions on that basis. "Maybe that bunch in the Personnel Division are having a little trouble thinking straight," he wondered.

What made Saneyuki interesting was that he doubted everything—even the meaning of his being summoned by two officials of the Personnel Division and being told that he had already been chosen to be fleet staff officer. He was a born strategist! The secret of strategy is the willingness to start by doubting even self-evident facts, those that would be called axioms in geometry. Saneyuki didn't believe the two Personnel Division officials. They were militarists, and, in the excess of their enthusiasm for a military confrontation, they might have called Saneyuki to their office to talk to him about a matter that had not yet been decided. In effect, they were saying to him, "We're sure you'll be made a staff officer, so you had better pay your personal respects to Vice Admiral Tōgō." It could have been a small intra-ministry tactic thought up by these militarists to create an atmosphere conducive to starting the war.

"That's all quite conceivable," Saneyuki judged.

Saneyuki shared a fault common to military men in the field of strategy, an inability to consider the future and destiny of the nation apart from purely military considerations. Saneyuki believed that the sooner war with Russia began the better, and he had had frequent discussions about that up to the summer of 1903, not only with friends in the navy but also with army men and with scholars, civilian officials, and shapers of public opinion unconnected with the military.

* * *

"Japan is now experiencing the best of times," Saneyuki wrote in a letter to a navy friend around this time, "blessed by Heaven, and enjoying geographical advantages and harmony among the people. If we let this time pass us by, Russia's military preparations will vastly increase. The best thing we can do is provoke the Russians to a quarrel right now—that's the only way. It's true that our navy's third expansion plan has been successful, and there are those, even within the navy, who look at our success and insist that peace can be maintained through a military balance of power. But think about it for a minute. It would take ten years to build eight or nine large warships. Far more effective in maintaining long-term peace would be for us to sink dozens of our enemy's large warships in perhaps one year's time instead. It's just a matter of simple arithmetic!"

A truly military way of thinking. Around this time, those who advocated starting a war with Russia were regarded by the genrō and civilian politicians as "almost akin to traitors who want to gamble with the nation's fate." This kind of judgment made Saneyuki angry. "There are too many people who act as if prudence is the only mark of loyalty. They worry about relations with this country and that country and always counsel 'prudence, prudence.' It makes me sick."

At any rate, Saneyuki was near despair at this point, regarding those in power in Japan as lacking any will to fight. So he found it very strange to be told privately that he was to be made fleet staff officer in preparation for war—he thought they were lying to him.

He was an odd sort of man. Doubting what he had been told about his imminent naval appointment, he decided to try to find out the truth. There was, of course, a way to do so. He need only ask former classmates who were working in other departments of the Naval Ministry. Fortunately, Yamaguchi Ei, a native of Shizuoka Prefecture, worked in the Military Affairs Department. Saneyuki promptly went back to the ministry, took Yamaguchi to a private room, and asked him if it was true that Tōgō Heihachirō was to be appointed commander of the Standing Fleet and that he was to be a staff officer under Tōgō, in charge of strategy.

"It would mean war, but is it true?"

Yamaguchi was surprised. "I've heard nothing about it."

"Of course not." Saneyuki nodded with a grim look on his face. This government, with its great fear of Russia, would never make the decision to start a war.

"Chiaki and Tanaka told me to go pay my respects to Vice Admiral Tōgō. I think they've lost their minds!"

Since Yamaguchi Ei of the Military Affairs Department hadn't heard anything about the matter, Saneyuki was all the more convinced it was all a lie. He had promised Chiaki and Tanaka that he would visit Tōgō, but he didn't. He felt it would be shameful to do so.

Tanaka Yasutarō and Chiaki Kyōjirō had been classmates of Saneyuki, and were both from Ishikawa Prefecture. Next morning, they heard from Tōgō Heihachirō's adjutant that Akiyama had not come the previous evening. Tōgō had apparently waited up till late that night.

"That's outrageous!" Both men were indignant and discussed how they should deal with the situation. Then suddenly Saneyuki arrived at the Naval Ministry and entered the Personnel Division.

"What the hell did you think you were doing?" yelled Chiaki Kyōjirō, pushing a chair toward Saneyuki, who reversed the chair and sat down with his arms folded on the top rung. He asked why Chiaki was so angry so early in the morning. The other accused Saneyuki of failing to go to Tōgō's residence the night before. Saneyuki explained his reasons.

"I see. You met Yamaguchi Ei from the Military Affairs Department, and you asked him about what was going on with the war . . . "

"Yes, I did." Saneyuki nodded.

"Now listen—the people in the Military Affairs Department don't know anything about these matters. We in the Personnel Division are the only ones within the ministry who know anything."

Just then someone came by and said that Vice Admiral Tōgō had come to the ministry on business.

"Fine!" Chiaki stood up and urged Saneyuki to do so as well.

This was the first time that Akiyama Saneyuki and Tōgō Heihachirō met each other one on one.

"I've taken the vice admiral to the meeting room," said the attendant.

Saneyuki and Chiaki Kyōjirō entered the spacious meeting room to find Tōgō Heihachirō sitting by himself in the middle of the room. A thin curtain covered the window behind him, and Tōgō was silhouetted against the light. There was not even a cup of tea on the table before him.

"I'm Lieutenant Commander Akiyama, sir."

Tōgō courteously rose and, in a Satsuma drawl, said, "I'm Tōgō." He was an unexpectedly small man, his hair cut short, with traces of white only at the sides. His whiskers, however, were gray, both on the chin and in his mustache, so the effect was rather strange. His features were almost too regular, so he didn't look strong and heroic.

Saneyuki knew at a glance that he was a man of character. If a large-scale combined fleet were to be organized, a man of great character would be required to lead it. Saneyuki took a seat facing the vice admiral across the long table.

"In the current matter, your help would be vital." That was all Tōgō said before falling silent. He looked at Saneyuki with the expression peculiar to Satsuma people in dealing with a guest: lips tightly closed, with a slight smile playing about them.

Saneyuki had heard that Tōgō was an extraordinarily taciturn man. He was wonderfully decisive, as shown by his sinking of the British ship that had operated in violation of international law during the First Sino-Japanese War. Neither in daily life nor in battle did he ever indulge in needless talk. Since taciturnity is one of the great conditions for leading an army, Tōgō was an extremely apt choice as supreme commander.

That was the end of the interview.

When Chiaki Kyōjirō asked afterward about his impressions of Tōgō, Saneyuki thought for a while and then replied, "That man was born to be a top leader. Under a man like that, you could do really important work."

Saneyuki believed that everyone has certain given qualities. He was sure that he did not have the kind of leadership qualities that would permit him to lead an entire massive fighting force without fostering any discontent nor the ability to make everyone do his duty even to the death. What he did have was the ability to make best use of Tōgō's leadership qualities and develop decisive strategies for him.

* * *

There are various anecdotes regarding how Tōgō Heihachirō, a man not so well known previously, became commander of the Standing Fleet during this period.

The previous commander had been Hidaka Sōnojō. He was a native of Satsuma who, during the Boshin War, joined his former domain's forces with Yamamoto Gombei's. He got on well with Gombei, so much so that after the Boshin War, he came to Tokyo and trained along with him to be a sumo wrestler.

Then, in 1870, he entered the Naval School in Tsukiji together with Gombei. Since Gombei had lied about his age and participated in the Boshin War as a boy soldier, he was classified as a "younger student" when he entered the Naval School, while Hidaka was classified as an "adult student." The younger students lived in the south dormitory, the adults in the north dormitory.

After graduation, Hidaka spent most of his time serving in the Standing Fleet, participating in every military conflict that Meiji Japan experienced. He served as an officer aboard the *Tsukuba* during the Taiwan campaign and aboard the *Nisshin* during the Satsuma Rebellion. During the First Sino-Japanese War, he moved about from battle to battle as captain of the capital ship *Hashidate*. Later, he was regularly promoted and finally became commander of the Standing Fleet, located in the naval port of Sasebo.

Among themselves, the Satsuma men referred to Hidaka as a "perfect example of a *bokkemon*." The term referred to typically hot-tempered Satsuma natives—fierce, stubborn, and unyielding.

As the clouds of conflict between Russia and Japan began to gather, it was assumed that Hidaka would become commander of the wartime Combined Fleet. Since he was the serving commander of the Standing Squadron, it was most unlikely that anyone else would be chosen. Hidaka himself had no doubt about that.

Navy Minister Yamamoto Gombei, however, decided to shift Hidaka to the less taxing position of commander of the Maizuru Naval Base and put Tōgō Heihachirō in the position of general commander of all naval forces. Informing Hidaka of these changes was a painful task for his old friend Gombei. First, he telegraphed Hidaka in Sasebo, telling him to come to Tokyo as quickly as possible. Hidaka was expecting good news, but, when he entered the residence of the navy minister, he found Gombei looking depressed.

Finding it impossible to broach the important business immediately, Gombei was silent for a while, and the short-tempered Hidaka became irritated. He leaned forward and asked, "Why did you tell me to come?"

Still, Gombei just gazed at Hidaka's face for a time in silence, then finally answered. "Actually, we want to transfer you . . ."

Hidaka's face flushed. "Give me the reason! Is there a reason?" he shouted.

Gombei answered slowly. "There's no particular reason. You've already been in that post for one year and three months, so I think a change would be good for you."

At this, Hidaka rose from his seat, gripped the table in fury, and shouted, "Shut up, Gombei! Do you think I'll be taken in by childish lies like that? Who have you chosen to replace me?"

"It's Tōgō." Gombei revealed the name of Hidaka's successor, the man who, when the war began, would lead the Combined Fleet into battle against the Russian Navy.

"Tōgō?" Hidaka Sōnojō could at first not believe his ears. Did he mean the Tōgō who was in charge of the Maizuru base? He pressed Gombei—so unexpected was the name in this context.

And it was unexpected not only to him but also to the entire Japanese Navy, no doubt—Tōgō the silent, unobtrusive man, the one who never pushed himself forward.

As a fellow Satsuma man, Hidaka felt that he knew Tōgō's level of ability. Hadn't he nearly been made a captain in the reserves just prior to the First Sino-Japanese War because he was sickly and had to take time off frequently for health reasons? But if he had been a really able man, surely he would not have been considered for the reserve list. That was what Hidaka thought.

Besides, Tōgō and Hidaka had been commissioned as sublieutenants second class almost at the same time, and both were now vice admirals. General opinion in the navy had it that Hidaka would be made an admiral, while Tōgō's last appointment would probably be his present one as commander of the Maizuru Naval Base. He would retire with the rank of vice admiral. It was no wonder then that Hidaka doubted his own ears. Me, to be replaced by Tōgō? Hidaka was a self-confident man. He had an unwavering faith in his own abilities as commander of the navy, to an excessive degree. It seemed to him a double humiliation to be replaced just before the war was to begin, and by Tōgō at that.

Hidaka lost all control. In his bitterness, he suddenly drew the short sword that hung at his waist and shouted, "Gombei! I will say nothing more. Kill me with this sword!"

A foolish display like this would have been inconceivable in the navies of advanced European countries, but in this East Asian nation, which had just recently emerged onto the world scene, even military officers of high rank retained a certain fierce savagery. Hidaka glared at Gombei, expecting a ferocious, Satsuma bokkemon-like resolution.

"Hidaka, I can understand your rage," said Gombei. "I would probably have drawn my sword as well, if I were you. But listen—you and I have walked the same road since the time of the shogunate. I have no secrets from you, and neither should you from me. That's why we know each other's strengths and weaknesses so well. Your strengths are your exceptional courage and great intelligence. I know that better than anyone. But you have your weaknesses as well. You're overconfident about everything and can never resist pushing yourself forward. And, if you once get an idea about something, you won't listen to what anyone else says about it."

Gombei did a comparison of the strengths and weaknesses of the two men while Hidaka was standing right there in front of him. "I grant that Tōgō is not as talented as you are."

"And yet you choose the less talented Tōgō—" Hidaka was still gripping his sword and becoming even more agitated.

Gombei tried to calm him down, urging him to listen to what he had to say. Gombei was convinced that the commander in chief of a great military force had to have more than a number of specific talents: he had to be the sort of man whose entire character fitted him for that role.

"In the event of a break in relations between Russia and Japan, Imperial General Headquarters will decide on a grand strategic policy and communicate it to the commander of the naval fleet. That commander will have to act as the hands and feet of General Headquarters, and, frankly, I'd worry if it were you. If you didn't like the grand strategy, you might form ideas of your own and fail to follow the orders from headquarters. Now think about it for a moment—if headquarters doesn't realize that its orders are not being followed by the fleet, headquarters will assume that they *are* being carried out and will base its next strategic moves on that assumption. And what will be the result? The strategy will fall to pieces, the naval forces will be destroyed, and in the end the nation itself will perish."

Gombei was not quite finished. "And on this point I have no worries whatsoever about Tōgō. He will be faithful to each and every policy decision made by General Headquarters and also be capable of flexible responses when necessary. If we needed heroic individuals like those who held the various provinces centuries ago during the era of Warring States, you would be a far better choice than Tōgō. But it takes very different talents to be the commander in chief of the military forces of a modern nation. That's why we chose Tōgō. My friendship for you is the same as it has always been, but the welfare of the nation has to take precedence over personal friendship."

As he listened, Hidaka began to nod in agreement and finally, with tears in his eyes, bowed his head. "I was wrong. If those were your reasons, I have no right to be angry. I'm sorry." When he raised his head, his face had a very lonely look. Gombei later said that the look on Hidaka's face then was something that he would never forget.

The truth is that Gombei had met with Tōgō the previous day to discuss the matter. Chief of the Navy General Staff Itō Sukeyuki was also in attendance. Gombei first asked about Tōgō's health. Then, shifting topics, he said very casually, "There's something we'd like you to do for us. It's not such a big thing, but we want you to take over from Hidaka. How about it?"

Tōgō listened without changing expression. He thought for a while and then with a nod said, "Fine."

Then Gombei added an important caveat. "You will have to act in accordance with directives from headquarters in all things. Is that acceptable to you?"

Tōgō nodded again. He understood, he said. He would be guided by headquarters in the essentials, but the handling of concrete problems that arose in battle would be left to him. That would be acceptable, would it not? Since that was only common sense in military terms, Gombei had no objections.

In this way, Tōgō's appointment as commander in chief was settled, but there were further reasons for the disqualification of Hidaka Sōnojō, who should have been the likeliest candidate.

As the situation between Japan and Russia worsened, Emperor Meiji once asked Gombei, who was in attendance at the palace that day, "There seems to be an active group of militarists among the populace, but if war should by any chance break out, can our navy win?"

"The relative strength of Russia's navy and our own is ten to seven," Gombei replied concisely. "If we fight the usual kind of war against such odds, I see no way we can win." He added, though, that there was a prospect of victory if the right tactics were used.

By "the right tactics," Gombei meant that Japan should take advantage of the good opportunity afforded by the fact that Russia's naval power was dispersed, rather than concentrated, among the Baltic and Black Seas and the Pacific Ocean. Japan, on the other hand, made sure to keep its single fleet together, and would use this Combined Fleet to crush the scattered power of its enemy on the seas.

It would be even better if the Russian fleet's three-part division could be made a four-part one. Fortunately perhaps, at this juncture Russia was trying to lease Masan, a port near Japan, as part of its planned invasion of Korea. The Japanese Army authorities were all in a flurry over this, but Gombei was secretly delighted. If Russia were to station part of its fleet in Masan, that would mean a further dispersal of its total power. Japan would only have to attack and destroy each of the weakened four mini-fleets.

The Japanese General Staff Office, however, in collaboration with the Foreign Ministry, dispatched businessmen to Masan to buy up in advance those areas that would be most vital for any military port, thus frustrating Russian plans. Gombei was very disappointed at this, but what he found even harder to take was that Hidaka Sōnojō had given his complete cooperation to the army's land-buying proposal without ever consulting the Naval Ministry.

"Hidaka lacks prudence and is entirely too high-handed." Gombei had known this side of Hidaka's character since they were young, but the issue of Masan was a decisive demerit.

Gombei also did not appoint Hidaka because of his inability to keep a secret. Ever since the decision to go to war against Russia was made, Gombei had done his best to keep information about the state of Japan's navy from the Russians, and had issued secrecy directives to that effect to the commanders of the fleet and of the naval bases. Then one day Hidaka entered the port of Kobe, displaying for all to see the entire fleet under his command. There were two Russian warships in the port already, and Hidaka was aware of that, but that didn't stop him—or rather, he wanted to flaunt the might of Japan's fleet in the presence of the Russian ships. He had no concern whatsoever for the policy of secrecy.

Hearing of this afterward, Gombei realized that the underside of Hidaka's fierce courage was nothing other than rashness.

5

TOWARD WAR

Around this time, in 1903, a man in a white jacket buttoned up the front presented himself at the reception desk of Shibusawa Eiichi's office in Kabutochō. He was a small man, about fifty years of age. His head was as round as a small taro, and very bald, but he had a twinkle in his eyes, which were in constant motion, like a child's.

"I'd like to see Mr. Shibusawa, please." His chin was almost resting on the top of the reception desk, and his fingertips were tapping away on its surface as he spoke. He looked as if he might be the principal of a very small primary school, at best.

"May I ask your name, please?" The young man at reception was on his guard. This fellow hardly looked the sort to come visiting Shibusawa Eiichi, the grand old man of the Japanese financial world.

"It's Kodama."

"Would you happen to have a business card with you, sir?"

"Oh, a business card!" He searched his breast pocket in a flustered way but seemed to have forgotten to bring one. "Oh, never mind. Just tell him it's Kodama, and he'll understand."

The man was Kodama Gentarō. He was a lieutenant general in the Japanese Army, but his political acumen was so highly esteemed that he was put in charge of a number of different areas. He had been appointed governor general of Taiwan in 1898 and concurrently served as army minister in 1900, a post he held until 1902. In 1903, he was named home minister and then education minister as well. The army's strategy in the Russo-Japanese War was to be in the hands of this man, who was reputed to be a strategist of unparalleled skill. He had not yet shifted to that role at the time we are describing.

The man at reception was even more doubtful, but when Kodama rested his chin on the top of the desk and smiled cheerily, he gave in and decided to deliver the message.

When he came back, he announced, "Since you have no appointment, an interview will be impossible. And, in any event, Mr. Shibusawa is about to leave the office and has no time."

Kodama looked puzzled, but the news that Shibusawa was about to leave seemed to give him hope. "When you say he's about to leave, you mean he'll pass this way, do you?"

The young receptionist nodded, with an unpleasant look on his face.

"Well then, I'll just wait here." Having said this, Kodama sat down in a nearby chair. As he crossed his legs, his small, childlike shoes came into view.

When at last Shibusawa came out, accompanied by his secretary, he saw Kodama sitting in the corridor and was amazed. "Oh, it was you, General Kodama!"

He knew why Kodama had come. He was not best pleased to see him, but, since the other had been treated with scant courtesy, he had no choice but to begin with an apology. Everything seemed to be working out for Kodama that day as if by a "natural strategy."

Shibusawa was antiwar, from a financial point of view. Kodama thought that relations with Russia had come to the point where Japan had to fight, due to the Russian side's overwhelmingly aggressive policies. He believed that both the cabinet and the military needed to make a decision. But, so long as the financial circles that would have to supply the military funding were opposed to the war, nothing could be done.

Shibusawa Eiichi could not just send away Kodama Gentarō, who had gone to the trouble of coming to see him. "I can give you an hour," he said, escorting Kodama to a meeting room and instructing his secretary to telephone the people he was going to see and explain that he would be an hour late.

No sooner were they seated facing each other than Shibusawa began, "General Kodama, as I have said so many times already, Japan does not have the money to go to war against Russia. Halfway through, the nation will go bankrupt and perish—and not from the enemy's fire." Shibusawa repeated his views: Japan's national resources were in a weakened state to begin with, and now the country was in the depths of an economic turndown. You could scrape all the bank vaults in Japan and still not turn up much money. And he had the figures to prove it.

Shibusawa was the son of a wealthy farmer from a village named Chiaraijima on the banks of the Tone River. Exceptionally for someone of peasant background, he had joined the ranks of the anti-foreign imperial loyalists toward the end of the shogunate and nearly engaged in some of the explosive attacks that were common at the time.

Later, in a destiny-changing turn of events, he was employed by the Hitotsubashi branch of the Tokugawa clan and gained the trust of Tokugawa Yoshinobu, who was to become the last shogun. In Kyoto during the mid-1860s, Shibusawa negotiated with other domains as an agent of the Hitotsubashi family, and, after Yoshinobu became shogun, he became his shogunal vassal, though of low rank. When Japan was invited to participate in the Universal Exposition in Paris, Shibusawa went to France in the entourage of the shogunal representative.

The shogunate collapsed while Shibusawa was abroad, and after his return to Japan he worked at putting the affairs of the Tokugawa clan in order. Later, he entered the new Meiji government's Ministry of Finance, but soon quit his official post to devote himself to building a Western-style financial world in Japan. He worked in many different areas, not only starting the first commercial bank in Japan but also initiating almost every variety of modern industry in the country.

In one of the interesting aspects of the new Japan, you had, facing each other across the table, on the one hand, the former shogunal vassal Shibusawa Eiichi and, on the other, Kodama Gentarō, who became a low-ranking officer in the imperial-loyalist forces as a seventeen-year-old samurai attached to the Tokuyama fief (a fief within the Chōshū domain). Kodama had participated in the Boshin War, going as far north as Mutsu, and was recognized for his services in helping smash the Tokugawa regime.

The one-hour conference did not go as Kodama had hoped. Shibusawa simply reiterated his opposition to war with Russia, and no agreement was reached. But Kodama did not give up. He met with Kondō Rempei, the next most powerful financier after Shibusawa, and urged him to travel to Manchuria and Korea to observe on the spot the great extent of Russia's military incursions there.

"After seeing that, please consider again whether the present attitudes of our financial circles are appropriate or not," Kodama insistently requested.

Kondō Rempei was a supporter of Shibusawa's view that, "given Japan's financial situation, to think of war is pure delusion," so he wasn't very enthusiastic about Kodama's plan. But since Kodama was so insistent, he acquiesced. By the time he returned to Japan in October, his views had changed 180 degrees.

* * *

After returning from his tour of Manchuria and Korea, Kondō met first of all with Shibusawa Eiichi, and reported in detail what he had seen and heard there. "How shall I put it? The great plains from Siberia to Manchuria are in process of being painted steel-gray. Large Russian forces are on the move everywhere, and Port Arthur is being fortified. On the seas, Russian warships are constantly coming and going. The map of the Far East is in the process of being totally revised. Russian military might increases month by month. In the end, Japan will be overcome and forced to commit national suicide."

Kondō's report shook Shibusawa's composure. He had no faith in the judgment of military men or the international policies they advocated, but since the report came from Kondō Rempei, Shibusawa trusted it.

A few days later, Kodama, dressed in Japanese clothing, appeared again at Shibusawa's office. He had undergone a great change himself in the short period between the two meetings. He had resigned from the positions of education minister and home minister (while remaining governor general of Taiwan) and requested appointment as vice chief of the General Staff, a lower official rank. We will have more to say about this later, but the point is that he visited Shibusawa's office for the second time on October 13, the day after he became vice chief of the General Staff. This military strategist of genius did not much care for the tight-fitting military uniforms, and so he came to the office in haori and hakama instead.

"I've heard from Kondō," Shibusawa began. He had a rosy, youthful-looking face, but that day his color was not good. "You, General Kodama, will be in charge of the war, and I'd like you to tell me what the chances of victory are."

"It won't go so far as victory. The best we can hope for is to end in a somewhat stronger position than our foes by exerting ourselves to the utmost."

"Will that be possible?"

"I think so, if we have topnotch strategies, and our officers and men give their utmost. The rest we must leave to diplomacy. And to the funding for the war. At any rate, the longer we wait, the more the advantage will be with Russia, and the weaker we will be. In two years' time, the power of the Russian Army in the Far East will be immense, and they will use that power to press Japan all the more. If we wait until then, there will be no chance of winning anything. If we act now, we have some hope. The only course of action left to Japan now is to fight against all odds."

By now, tears were streaming from Kodama's eyes. Having come so far in the thirty some years since the Meiji Restoration, Japan might lose everything. That was what Kodama himself, the man in charge of overall strategy for the Japanese Army, was saying.

Shibusawa also began to weep. "General Kodama, I'll be your good soldier. I'll do whatever it takes to raise funds for the war." This decision by Shibusawa was reflected in the agreement reached at the regular meeting of the Bank Club that was held on October 28. The members agreed to make preparations for full cooperation with the war effort.

* * *

Prior to these decisions for war, the Japanese Army had to face a grave problem: the death from illness of Tamura Iyozō, vice chief of the General Staff. He had been known as the "Takeda Shingen of our day" and had done great, authoritative research on going to war with Russia. Tamura was in the second graduating class of the Army Academy and a native of Kōshū, the present Yamanashi Prefecture, as was Takeda Shingen. No doubt it was Tamura's association with Kōshū, in addition to his military skills, that made people compare him to Takeda.

The strategies employed in the First Sino-Japanese War had been devised and carried out by Kawakami Sōroku, who was known as the "god of tactics." After that war, Kawakami threw himself into research on going to war against Russia, convinced that Russia would provide the next challenge to Japan in the area. However, he died soon, from overwork. His research had been continued and supplemented by Tamura Iyozō.

The study of the strategy to be used in a war against Russia involved unavoidable psychological stress. The odds were very much against Japan, and the stress and pain of dealing with this situation led to Kawakami's early death, and then to Tamura's. In the end, it led also to their successor Kodama Gentarō's death, but that occurred after the war had ended.

When on October 1, 1903 Tamura Iyozō died at the Japanese Red Cross Hospital, there were questions about his successor. The chief of the General Staff was Ōyama Iwao, the person with ultimate responsibility, but all the actual work was done by the vice chief—that was the custom. Tamura, the former vice chief, had been a major general.

"I'll take over," Kodama had said casually in the presence of Yamagata Aritomo and Ōyama Iwao, who were both genrō. Apparently, Kodama had already realized some time before that he would have to do the job if anything happened to Tamura. In terms of ability, Kodama was many times more capable than Tamura. Even in comparison with Kawakami Sōroku's conduct of the First Sino-Japanese War, Kodama was clearly more original in his thinking.

But Kodama had risen too high to become vice chief. He was a veteran lieutenant general who, three years earlier, had become army minister. The next year, he was due to be made a general, and at that time he was home minister as well as governor general of Taiwan. For him to become vice chief, a post held normally by a mere major general, was to accept an exceptional demotion in the military hierarchy.

Kodama, however, cared little about matters of rank in the hierarchy, and, after looking around him, he came to the conclusion that there was no one in the whole army better qualified than he to devise a strategy against Russia. That is why he immediately decided to ask for the vice chief position. Yamagata and Ōyama were both delighted.

"If it's all right with you, General Ōyama," Yamagata Aritomo said, "I'd be happy to take over as chief!"

But Kodama broke in. "No, I couldn't accept that." He treated Yamagata's offer as a joke and got him to withdraw it. Yamagata would have been unsuited to the post of a top leader. He had his own views and tastes regarding everything, and tended to enforce these on those below him. Kodama was a Chōshū man, and Yamagata was the kingpin in the Chōshū military clique, but Kodama felt he would never have freedom of action if he worked under him.

By contrast, Ōyama Iwao from Satsuma was a natural as top leader, ready to leave everything to his able subordinates. Kodama was sure that, with Ōyama at the top, he could do his work as he saw fit. And indeed that was what happened.

* * *

Sometimes an academic education may be unnecessary for a true genius. Kodama Gentarō had never graduated from a military academy, any more than had the military leaders of the era of Warring States in Japan or the generals selected from among the ranks by Napoleon. Kodama had participated in the Boshin War as a seventeen-year-old "boy soldier," being shifted from Mutsu in northern Honshu to Hakodate in Hokkaido. His only schooling was three months in the "military school" temporarily set up in Tamatsukuri in Osaka.

Then he was made a low-ranking officer of the sixth grade and next promoted to sergeant in 1870, when he was nineteen. Thus, he had to work his way up from being a "boy sergeant." When one considers how Nogi Maresuke, also from Chōshū, was appointed as major immediately after the Boshin War, Kodama's beginnings do not seem so fortunate. Around the time of the Satsuma Rebellion of 1877, however, he rose to the same rank of major as Nogi. His ability had been recognized and, from then on, Kodama's career kept pace with the stages of development of the Japanese Army. He mastered the science of warfare on his own.

Kodama Gentarō could not benefit from the education offered at the new Army Staff College because he was too old, already a thirty-four-year-old colonel and chief of the First Section of the General Staff when it opened. The following year, when he also assumed the post of head of the college, he listened to Meckel's lectures. He had received his primary and secondary education in the domain school of his childhood, and so this was the only time in his life that he had the experience of being formally taught. Kodama listened to Meckel's lectures not as a student but as an auditor.

Meckel was frequently astonished at Kodama's brilliance, and, when his time in Japan came to an end, he was asked, "Who is the most impressive of all the Japanese you have taught?"

He is said to have immediately replied, "Kodama."

Kodama had the exceedingly rare ability to make and retain ten or twenty associations on the basis of one remark of Meckel's. He had a sunny, carefree character, and, in addition to his genius as a strategist, he was skilled at statecraft. Since he was without personal greed or desire, his political skills surpassed everyone else's of the same period. Precisely due to those skills, he was put into various posts at others' convenience, being made to serve frequently as minister in areas other than the military. And this man willingly became vice chief of the General Staff as successor to Tamura Iyozō, who was very much his junior, thus returning to his chosen field of strategy.

Kodama was already well known as a strategist among the military attachés of various foreign countries, so, when his appointment was announced, telegrams went from the various embassies in Japan to their home countries to the effect that "Japan has decided on war with Russia."

* * *

The Japanese government entered into final negotiations with Russia in the summer of 1903, while hiding its resolve to launch a war. A proposal for an understanding, or entente, with Russia was agreed upon at a cabinet meeting held in the presence of the emperor on June 23, and this was presented to the Russian government through Kurino Shin'ichirō, the ambassador in St. Petersburg, on August 12.

The main points of the proposal were: "The independence and territorial integrity of the Qing and Korean empires shall be respected." "Russia shall acknowledge Japan's predominant interests in Korea. In turn, Japan shall acknowledge Russia's special interests regarding the administration of the railways in Manchuria."

In other words, Japan would have special rights and interests in Korea, while Russia would have special rights and interests in Manchuria, and neither power would attack the other.

Today, at a different stage of history, Japan's fixation on Korea seems completely unreasonable, or even ludicrous. Japanese and Russian imperialism had locked horns with each other there, because each empire wished to become a modern industrial nation, on the model of Great Britain, and, for that, colonies were absolutely necessary. Therefore, Russia wanted Manchuria, and Japan, which had no colonies, hung on to Korea for dear life.

From the nineteenth century to the beginning of the twentieth, the world's countries and regions had only two paths open to them: to be colonized by another nation, or, if that was unacceptable, to create industries, gain the necessary military strength, and join the ranks of the imperialist powers. Now in a later age, we fantasize that the nations of that time should have adopted a policy of "neither invade nor be invaded" and should have focused only on the peace of mankind. We attempt to impose this fictive standard followed by these fantasy countries on the actual nations and international society of an earlier age, and then we use this fictive standard to judge the rights or wrongs of a nation's policy. This kind of thinking turns history into nothing more than clay to be used for making clay figurines in whatever shape one likes.

The world was at a different stage then. Having once chosen the path of autonomy through the Restoration, Japan had to preserve that autonomy, even if it was to the detriment of another country (Korea). At that historical stage, Japan had to fixate on Korea. If it had not done so, then not only Korea but Japan itself might have been swallowed up by imperial Russia. Such was the nature of national autonomy during this period.

The Japanese proposal, at any rate, was handed to the Russian side. Russia's reply was: "Our government here in St. Petersburg will not deal with this issue. Foreign policy concerning the Far East is entirely in the hands of Alexeyev, viceroy of the Far East, who resides in Port Arthur. Therefore, we would like negotiations to be conducted not in the Russian capital, but in Tokyo."

Japan agreed to this, and negotiations between Foreign Minister Komura Jutarō and the Russian ambassador Rozen began on October 6 in Tokyo. Russia ignored the Japanese proposal and stated that it wanted "the portions of Korea north of the thirty-ninth parallel to be a neutral zone." This neutrality was to be in name only, of course, with everything north of the line from Pyongyang to Wŏnsan falling under Russia's control. To be blunt, Russia wanted the northern half of the Korean Peninsula.

This demand from the Russian side made the Japanese side shudder with apprehension. Russia had already taken Manchuria, and, from the Manchurian border, Russia's development projects, which were backed by Russian military power, controlled the north of Korea. What would happen, then, if the Korean Peninsula were divided in half between north and south, as the Russians were proposing? The Russian military was powerful. The Russian desire to move southward was the strongest of any since the beginnings of the history of imperialism in Europe. Sooner or later, Russia would move its army southward and attempt to absorb "the south." Japan, as supporter of "the south," would have to engage in a defensive war at the thirty-ninth parallel. If it failed to do so, the Japanese archipelago itself would ultimately fall victim to the energy of Russia's southward expansion, and Tsushima Island and Hokkaido at the very least would surely become Russian possessions.

Within the Russian government, the pro-invasion party already had control of the court, and even Home Minister Plehve, who was regarded as a moderate man, was saying, "It is due to the power of our military, not our diplomats, that the Russian Empire is able to pride itself on its current flourishing state. Problems like those in the Far East ought to be solved not by the pens of diplomats, but by the bayonets of our soldiers."

So long as the idea of solutions by bayonets lay at the heart of Russia's attitude, that empire naturally responded to Japan's proposals with a total lack of compromise. Russia was intent, rather, on challenging Japan. But powerful Russia could not imagine that weak Japan would determine to fight, unless it was completely out of its mind. When Tsar Nicholas II said, "So long as I do not want war, there can be no war between Russia and Japan," he was not really boasting. That was the commonsense judgment of the Russians. If Russia was strengthening the fortifications at Port Arthur and pouring troops into Manchuria via the Trans-Siberian Railway, this was to heighten the impressiveness of its "bayonet diplomacy," not necessarily because it anticipated war with Japan. Both politicians and military men felt that such anticipation would itself be foolish.

In the face of Russia's strong response, Japan could not but bend. Foreign Minister Komura presented Ambassador Rozen with a compromise proposal that went as far as Japan could possibly go. It was in essence a proposal to trade Manchuria for Korea. Russia could do as it liked in Manchuria but it must not interfere at all in Korea's affairs.

* * *

In summary, no matter what explanations later historians may attempt to make, Russia did have an all-too-strong intention to invade the Far East. The Japanese government was at that time attempting to promote an entente with an almost supplicatory attitude, and the Russian government at first responded in a serious way but then as time went on began to intentionally delay its responses. During this time, Russia expended tremendous energy in greatly increasing its military power in the Far East.

Not only did Russia send increasing numbers of warships from European Russia to the Far East, it also sent the materials for making smaller ships like cruisers as far as Port Arthur by the Trans-Siberian Railway and its extensions, and then managed the feat of assembling them on the spot. There were already as many as seven ships that had been built in this way within Port Arthur, and the longer the negotiations lasted, the more ships would be built.

In addition, during the negotiations, in the name of "testing the transportation capacities of the Trans-Siberian Railway," two infantry brigades, two artillery battalions, and a small number of cavalry were sent during the "test period." The construction of fortifications at Port Arthur and Vladivostok was ongoing even at night, with the aid of searchlights. And in mid-October, as the negotiations continued, a fourteen-car train loaded with a complete field hospital departed from Russia for the Far East.

"Our reply to Japan should be delayed as long as possible"—this appears to have been the Russian military's request to the civilian government.

Alexeyev, viceroy of the Far East in Port Arthur, served as the representative of the tsar. He was one of the spearheads of the invasion policy, more so even than other court officials. When he sent the Japanese proposal for an entente to the tsar, he appended his own opinion: "Japan is a small country. Its troops are few, and its finances inadequate. That this small country should try to make a false show of power in the face of a great nation like Russia is the result of agitation by the United States and Britain—particularly the latter. That is the cause of it all. Moreover, in the unlikely event of war, Britain does not have the determination to rouse itself to come to Japan's assistance. Even if it did have such determination, Britain would not have enough actual strength to fight against our great Russian Empire in the Far East. Japan is well aware of these facts regarding Britain and thus will never resort to war as the final means of pursuing its policies. Russia, therefore, should continue to take a hard line in negotiations. If we are firm, Japan will be sure to do as Russia wishes."

The very much delayed Russian answer finally was handed to the Japanese Foreign Ministry on December 11. Foreign Minister Komura groaned when he read it. "There can hardly have been in all history a diplomatic reply as arrogant in tone as this!" There was no hint of compromise. Indeed, the response was harder in its attitudes than the first Russian reply had been. It did not even touch upon the issue of Manchuria, which Russia was already occupying, and repeated the demand that, in effect, half of Korea, where Japan had such strong interests, be handed over to Russia.

Japan could only despair of the negotiations.

* * *

Even looking at the matter in the present, when things have cooled down, there is nothing in Russia's attitude that can be defended. Russia was consciously trying to drive Japan to its death. Russia drove Japan into a corner, like a cat with a mouse. All Japan could do was bite the cat with every last bit of energy it could summon.

If we examine the diplomatic history of the various countries in Europe, we can find no example of such a cruel, sadistic policy on the part of a Great Power toward another nation. Diplomatic moves that would be unacceptable among Caucasian powers could be employed without a second thought if the other country was composed of heathens and, more especially, of the yellow race, which was regarded as racially inferior. This is what was so painful to the Japanese.

Let us digress a little at this point. We personally find the stupidity of the Japanese political leadership during the run-up to the Pacific War absolutely unforgivable. But we also think that the statements of Justice Radhabinod Pal, the Indian representative at the Tokyo War Crimes Tribunal, reflect his profound wisdom and keen powers of observation with regard to history. Pal argued that the United States hounded Japan into a corner; even a small country without any weapons would have risen up to resist.

The harshness of the United States at that time would not have had that odor of sadism if those same diplomatic policies had been used, not against Japan, but against some Caucasian, European country. A yellow race taking its place in civilized international society looks like cheeky behavior only to Caucasian nations. On August 6, 1945, an atomic bomb was dropped on Hiroshima. Even if dropping the bomb seemed like a necessary wartime strategy to the Americans, we suspect that they would have hesitated to drop it on a Caucasian, European city if a European nation had been in the same situation as Japan. Racial issues among nations do not surface in normal times, but in wartime, when governments are under extreme psychological stress, racial principles tend to be neglected. So it is easier to say, "Since they're Asians, why not do it?"

On August 8, 1945, the Soviet Union, trampling on its non-aggression pact with Japan, poured a large army into Manchuria. The Soviet Union broke the terms of the pact without a second thought, in a way that we might be tempted to call typically Russian. But perhaps it was because the treaty partner was an Asian nation that the Russians could, without mercy or consideration, break the terms of the pact and not feel much ethical remorse.

At any rate, Russia's attitude prior to the beginning of the Russo-Japanese War was so harsh as hardly to be worthy of the name "diplomacy," as Finance Minister Witte himself acknowledged in his memoirs.

* * *

The Japanese government feared war. Fear of Russia had the effect of slowing the tempo of negotiations with that country, and it seemed to ordinary Japanese as if their government had adopted a low, pleading posture toward Russia. Popular opinion was pro-war. Most of the newspapers fanned the flames of war throughout their pages, with only the *Heimin News*, which was antiwar, opposing war with Russia. Apart from that, there were only two newspapers, known for always supporting the government, that urged a more careful, prudent policy.

Around this time, people representing various spheres of Japanese society frequently came to see Prime Minister Katsura Tarō, Ōyama Iwao, and Itō Hirobumi to urge a quick decision to start war against Russia.

"Today there were seven fools who came to see me!" Ōyama Iwao revealed to his second son, Ōyama Kashiwa.

"What I want right now are not your esteemed views and opinions, gentlemen. We're consulting on the state of our finances and our armaments at the moment" was Itō Hirobumi's reply.

To the seven professors from Tokyo Imperial University who came to press him for a decision by the government, Prime Minister Katsura said, "Forgive me, gentlemen, but I do not intend to seek your advice on military matters. Remember, please, I was originally a soldier."

People outside the government were seething with pro-war feeling, and meetings to promote the war were held all over the country.

On the other hand, even ranking officers in the Naval Ministry could not say for sure whether Navy Minister Yamamoto Gombei really wanted war or not. "What about the sailboat?" they asked, dividing into groups to try to find the answer, but they reached no conclusion. The reference to a sailboat referred to Yamamoto Gombei's habit of signing policy papers, not with his seal but his signature, which somewhat resembled a sailboat.

Someone had an idea. If war came, a great deal of coal would be needed as fuel for the warships. The coal would have to be of good quality, emitting little or no smoke. British coal would be the best. The naval officers proposed buying 900,000 tons of such British coal. If Yamamoto Gombei affixed his "sailboat" signature to that proposal, it would mean that he was ready for war.

Vice Minister Saitō Makoto put the request in the form of a document and took it to Gombei, who took a good look at it and then asked, "Do we have the money for this?"

"Right now, we don't," Saitō answered. "But the British company concerned said that it would accept payment in the new fiscal year."

Gombei silently picked up his brush and wrote a nice round sailboat on the document. With this, the people in the Naval Ministry at last understood

Gombei's intentions. This massive order for British coal, however, made the price of coal shoot up, which not only caused consternation in the kitchens of London, but also let the various nations know of Japan's intention to wage war.

* * *

The Russo-Japanese War was, without question, one phenomenon born from the period of imperialism in world history. But it is also unquestionably true that, in this context, Japan was under severe pressure and forced to fight a defensive war with all the resources it could summon.

And now we want to turn to a quite different topic. We want to ask how much confidence the major figures in Japan's government had in Japan's ability to win the war. To answer this question, we must turn to a person who was not quite as much of a major figure of the time as the others. This was Kaneko Kentarō, who had already served as justice minister. He was from Fukuoka Prefecture and, shortly after the Restoration, came to Tokyo under the patronage of Hiraga Yoshitada, an older government official who was also from Fukuoka. While Kaneko was a student, he lived in Hiraga's house and had to do work there too—a typically Meiji period sort of arrangement.

The officials of early Meiji for the most part had no sense that the four traditional classes (samurai, farmer, artisan, and merchant) had become equal. This was certainly true of Hiraga Yoshitada of the Ministry of Justice, who treated the live-in student Kaneko like a lackey of the Tokugawa period. When Hiraga went to his office, he was accompanied by Kaneko, who carried a lacquered box of Hiraga's things on the end of a pole, as if Hiraga were a Tokugawa daimyo. At day's end, Kaneko was forced to kneel before Hiraga at the building's entranceway and prostrate himself. This was unbearable to Kaneko, whose way of thinking was already quite modern and enlightened.

When in 1900 Kaneko became justice minister in Itō Hirobumi's cabinet, he stood in the entranceway of the ministry, turned to gaze calmly at his subordinates and said, "When I was young, I knelt and prostrated myself here, and looked after people's footwear. When I consider that I have now become the minister here, I look back on the past and also think of the present, and find my heart full of so many emotions." The words "find my heart full of so many emotions" express in poetic form the intention to succeed in the world that the men of Meiji so unwaveringly embraced. This is a good illustration of such feelings.

Kaneko had the opportunity to study overseas in his student days and traveled to the United States, reading law at Harvard. One of his classmates, Theodore Roosevelt, became president of the United States.

The Japanese government decided on war against Russia at a final meeting in the presence of the emperor, held on February 4, 1904. After this meeting, Itō Hirobumi, the president of the Privy Council, summoned Kaneko Kentarō and revealed, "We've just decided on war." Kaneko said later that Itō's eyes were red as if from weeping.

Itō, who could scarcely believe that Japan would win the war, must have had powerful emotions to deal with when the decision was made. He said to Kaneko, "I want you to go to the United States. Rouse sympathy for Japan in the American president and people so that at the right moment, through the good offices of the United States, we can move toward an armistice and peace agreement. I want you to work toward that end."

Kaneko Kentarō had no confidence he could succeed in that. "If Japan and Russia fought, surely Russia would win," he thought. The imbalance of power between Russia and Japan was too great. If Japan lost at Russia's first blow, the good offices of the United States could not even come into play. Such beliefs made Kaneko hesitate to respond either way to this self-serving mission that Itō Hirobumi was trying to push onto him.

Itō guessed what Kaneko was thinking. "You hesitate to give an answer because you're worried about the success or failure of this mission—isn't that so?"

When Kaneko admitted that it was, Itō drew his chair closer. "Well, let me tell you that when it comes to this war, not only the Ministry of Finance, which deals with money matters, but the army and navy, which will do the actual fighting, have no certainty at all that Japan will win." He spoke in his characteristically candid, straightforward way. "I myself asked the responsible people in the army and navy before we made the decision for war, and there was not one person who was sure that we could win."

But, on the other hand, if Japan did nothing, then Russia's aggression would not stop at Manchuria and Korea—it would extend to Japan itself. "When things have come this far, we have no choice but to fight, staking our national survival on it. We don't have the luxury of arguing whether we will succeed or fail." And the person uttering these words was Itō, who had always pushed for Russo-Japanese cooperation.

"If the Japanese Army is annihilated on the plains of Manchuria, and all the Japanese Navy's ships are sunk in the Tsushima Strait, and the Russian forces attack this nation by land and sea, then I will recall how, many years ago, I led a unit of sumo wrestlers into battle against the shogunate. I will pick up a rifle and become a common soldier, fending off a Russian landing anywhere between San'in in western Honshu and the west coast of Kyushu. I intend to die in a hail of gunfire."

Kaneko was amazed. If Itō was that determined, he ought not to be complaining about the disadvantages of the job he was being assigned. He felt forced to accept it. But as to whether the United States would really mediate the conflict at a time advantageous to the Japanese side, he could not say. Deciding to seek the opinion of a military specialist on how the Russo-Japanese War was likely to go, he went to see Vice Chief of the General Staff Kodama Gentarō, who was in charge of all army strategy.

Kaneko revealed the nature of his assignment. "I'd like you to tell me frankly whether we really have a chance at winning this war."

Kodama let out a great puff of smoke from his cigarette and started to speak. "For these past thirty days, I've stayed in this room, sleeping in my uniform with a blanket thrown over me at night. No matter how I rework our strategy, even a fifty–fifty chance seems the best we could do."

"But fifty–fifty won't solve anything, will it?" asked Kaneko, and Kodama nodded.

"Right. At fifty–fifty, there'd be no point to the war. I want to make it at least sixty–forty and have been trying to figure out how to do that. That's what's been worrying me these last two or three days."

"Fifty–fifty seems the best we could do." This estimate by Kodama sounded somehow untroubled from the lips of such an optimist as he. From the lips of someone else, however, nothing could sound darker or more severe.

"I want to reach sixty–forty somehow or other," Kodama repeated. "Win six times and lose four. Then a peacemaker should appear—the United States would be best. I feel like begging you on bended knee to do your absolute best there in the United States." These were the words of the man in charge of army strategy in the coming war.

Kaneko Kentarō, a bit stunned, responded, "I'm willing to give my life for the success of my mission in the United States. But I hope you can manage to make it to sixty–forty."

Kodama brought out a map of Manchuria and Korea. "First we'll land troops at key points in Korea and chase the Russian troops in northern Korea north of the Yalu River. This is our first-stage strategy, our first real battle. If we lose this first battle, our troops' morale will be broken, and the war is lost. If Russia brings ten thousand troops, we will bring twenty thousand in order to win this battle. If they bring thirty thousand, we'll bring sixty thousand. We intend to fight outnumbering them two to one. If we do win this first battle, the enemy's morale will be weakened, and we may be able to bring our chances up to sixty–forty.

Both Kodama's strategy and his explanation of it were very reasonable, and Kaneko understood exactly what he meant. Then, wanting to know what the situation in the navy was, he went at once to the Naval Ministry to see Minister Yamamoto Gombei.

As with Kodama, he explained the nature of his mission in the United States, and Gombei, who was already aware of it, repeated what Kodama had said. "Please do your best. The fate of our country depends on your struggle there."

Kaneko later said that, hearing these words, he felt "very disheartened." But the outlook for the navy, as explained by Yamamoto Gombei, was somewhat brighter than Kodama's view of the army's chances. "First off, half of Japan's warships will be sunk, and half of our men killed. But with the half that remain, we will destroy the Russian fleet."

Kaneko then investigated the financial situation. It was not good. There was no way to raise all the funds that would be needed for the war. The scarcity of funds was such that after the final meeting in the presence of the emperor, Finance Minister Sone Arasuke tendered his resignation, saying he was not up to the task at hand. Prime Minister Katsura anxiously went to see the genrō Matsukata Masayoshi to ask his advice, and Matsukata told him that he absolutely must dissuade Sone from resigning.

Of course. If the finance minister resigned just when the decision to go to war was made, foreign powers would lose confidence in Japan's financial state, and its prestige would fall drastically even before the fighting began. Matsukata promised to help Sone with any difficulties he faced so as to get through the present crisis, and Katsura, on that basis, decided to dissuade Sone from resigning. Sone felt he had no other choice but to withdraw his earlier resignation.

6

SHELLFIRE

Japan informed Russia of the cessation of diplomatic relations on February 6, 1904. Russia announced a state of war with Japan on February 9, and Japan on February 10. Fighting had begun prior to those dates.

We must go back a little in time and give an account of both the Japanese and the Russian strategies. "As I've said many times, we can't fight a long war," Ōyama Iwao, the chief of the General Staff told his vice chief Kodama Gentarō, who was doing the strategic planning.

Kodama was in complete agreement. If the war was prolonged, Japan's ability to fight would dissipate, and the nation would destroy itself. Every member of the government knew that the war would be absolutely pointless if Japan failed in its strategy of winning battles as impressively as possible at the beginning, and then seizing the psychological moment to deploy diplomacy and bring about peace. Therefore, it was necessary to send a larger number of troops to the prospective battlefield and more quickly than the enemy, mass them there, and begin the attack. The enemy would not be fully prepared. Japan could, of course, win, and Japan's victory would be highly impressive both domestically and abroad. This was the hoped-for result at, for example, the battle to be fought at the Yalu River.

But it took great national power to assemble a large fighting force on a distant battlefield more quickly than the enemy. What was needed was the power to transport men and matériel by land and sea. In Japan, where only some thirty years had passed since the Restoration, only fourteen trains per day could be moved along those domestic railway trunk lines available for military transport. As for sea transport, the steamship tonnage that could be used for military purposes amounted to no more than three to four hundred thousand tons. Japan's strategy turned on whether it could win a competition with Russia that depended in large part on speed, even though Japan was saddled with such a feeble transport system. Moreover, when Japan transported its ground troops by sea, the powerful Russian Pacific Fleet (based at Port Arthur and Vladivostok) would not fail to act. It goes without saying that there would be a battle for control of the seas between the Russian and Japanese fleets. The question was: could the Japanese Navy win this battle?

Assuming the Japanese Navy did win, Japan's First Army, which had landed in Korea, would be fighting the first battle of the Russo-Japanese War near the Yalu River. The Second Army would land in southern Manchuria, advance to the area of Liaoyang, where General Linevich's corps was based, and attack and destroy it.

At this point, the plan to launch an immediate attack on the fortifications of Port Arthur had been put on hold, so the campaign was a two-pronged one, as explained above.

"At any rate, if we don't amaze the world by winning battles at an early stage of the war, we won't be able to get enough funds from abroad to carry on." As Kodama Gentarō often said, the grave problem of the wartime economy hung upon Japan's early-stage victories.

* * *

In comparison with Japan's carefully calculated war strategy, Russia's was casual and crude to an unfortunate degree. Certainly, it was not the case that Russia's strategic planning for the war had begun later than Japan's. On October 24, 1903, while Russia and Japan were still engaged in negotiations, Alexeyev, the tsar's viceroy in the Far East, presented to his government a plan for a strategy aimed at Japan, and, on October 31, the tsar approved it. Then, on November 18, a more detailed proposal was presented that was finalized on January 1 of the following year, under War Minister Kuropatkin's direction, and approved by the tsar.

The British Foreign Office was the first to get the news that the Russian Army's strategic plan against Japan had been approved. Britain immediately notified the Japanese government of this, as it was obliged to do under the Anglo-Japanese Alliance. Japan had heard the same news from a different source, and, since the information was regarded as highly reliable, it became one important factor behind the Japanese government's decision to go to war against Russia.

Thus, Russia did not lack the time to devise a plan. On the contrary, Russia's large military buildup in Manchuria even prior to the plan shows that it was always ahead of the game.

And yet its strategic planning was so crude! Russia's center of operations for political and military strategy in the Far East was the viceregal headquarters for the Far East newly established in Port Arthur. In October 1903, the Army Department within the viceregal headquarters sent the chief of the Naval Department an important query about making plans to counter Japan. "We think that even after a full month of war, the Japanese Army will be blocked by the Russian Navy and unable to land at Yingkou"—the port for Liaodong Bay. "Do we have reason to be confident about this line of thinking?"

Another question concerned the defense of the northern part of Korea. "The Japanese Army will try to land on the coast of Korea. At that juncture, the Russian fleet will act to block them and will have to engage in battle with the Japanese fleet several times. Even granting that the Russian Navy will not be able to completely block the Japanese Army's landing in Korea, we want to know how long our navy will be able to delay it."

The responses of the chief of the Naval Department were very clear. "So long as our Russian fleet is not totally destroyed, landings by the Japanese Army at Yingkou in Liaodong Bay and on the coast of northern Korea will be impossible. A comparison of the Japanese and Russian fleets make it inconceivable that our fleet would be destroyed in the Yellow Sea and Korean coastal waters."

In other words, the Russian fleet in the Far East was indestructible, and the Japanese Army would either be unable to land in Korea or Manchuria, or would be greatly delayed in doing so. The Army Department made its plans for a land strategy on the basis of this reply. This was its fundamental mistake.

* * *

The Russian Army and Navy came up with such crude plans because they judged the military strength of Japan solely by the numbers, paying no attention at all to their potential enemy's abilities. From the start, the Russian generals looked upon the Japanese Army and Navy as of no real account and therefore made no serious attempt to investigate their true state and strength.

For example, on the day that the Russian tsar issued a declaration of war against Japan, two major figures in the Russian Army met to discuss how to lead their forces. The two were Vannovsky, the former war minister, and Kuropatkin, the present holder of that post. Judging from the results, the substance of this meeting could hardly have been more foolish. The question was how the military power of the two nations would compare.

Kuropatkin's view was: "We should allot Russian soldiers against Japanese at a ratio of one to one and a half."

"You are overestimating the Japanese soldiers. One Russian soldier to every two Japanese will be quite sufficient," Vannovsky replied.

Witte, who had already been dismissed as minister of finance, heard of this later and sarcastically remarked, "This was the opinion of the former and present war ministers, supposedly the most knowledgeable about the military strengths of both enemy and their own forces!"

Still, Witte relied somewhat upon the abilities and thought processes of Kuropatkin. Soon after the declaration of war, Kuropatkin left his post as chief of military administration to head for the battlefields in the Far East as commander of the army at the front. He visited Witte's residence to say farewell. The tactics and strategy he discussed with Witte at this time were different from the careless views described above. "The Japanese Army's strategic planning and preparations are better than we anticipated. As a result, we must make changes in the approach we've followed up to now," he said.

"The approach we've followed up to now" refers to the overly optimistic view that Russia could scatter the Japanese with "one touch of its armored sleeve." The new view required that very large forces be sent to the Far East, but the transport capacity of the Trans-Siberian Railway was limited, and it would be impossible to send such forces all at once. They would be sent gradually, and that would take time. "Buying that amount of time is the key to victory," concluded Kuropatkin.

Buying time was Kuropatkin's basic strategic policy. He would wait for the buildup of a great military force several times the size of Japan's army and then plan the final decisive battle. In the battles up to that point, he wanted to avoid the loss of his forces as much as possible. The Russians would retreat gradually, in several stages, while forcing the Japanese Army to suffer a fair amount of attrition. Kuropatkin said that the line for the "final decisive battle" would be drawn at Harbin. He was known as the finest general in the Russian Army, and he did indeed have a mind that could correctly grasp the nature of the coming war on the plains of Manchuria. The tactic of "attack and then withdraw" might appear strange but was a traditional one in the Russian Army. The aim was to make the enemy extend their supply lines as far as possible and then, when their supplies were cut off, to launch a massive counterattack. Napoleon had been defeated by this tactic in the past, and Hitler would be defeated in the same way in the future.

* * *

Excellent tactics and strategy are largely a matter of arithmetic and have a clarity about them that an amateur can fully understand. Or, to look at it the opposite way, obscure tactics with philosophical touches and strategy comprehensible only to a professional exist only rarely, and, if they do exist, belong to the losing side.

A good example of the latter would be the tactical and strategic thought of the leaders of the Japanese Army in charge of the Pacific War. They forgot about the arithmetical aspect fundamental to strategy and made great use of philosophical and mystical elements, to an extent rarely seen in world history. Indeed, they introduced philosophical elements as a substitute for the arithmetical ones lacking in their strategic thinking. The thinking of these uniformed war leaders was, to an incredible degree, a kind of mystical philosophy advocating "faith in certain victory," without a strategic or economic basis. It promoted the idea of "the indestructible divine land of Japan," and the glorification of and fixation on suicidal tactics.

An analysis of the strangeness of these attitudes is not the aim of this work. Only, the group of top leaders and devisers of the political and military strategy at the time of the Russo-Japanese War, who were so firm in their commitment to rationally planned policies, seem to have been an entirely different breed of men from their successors some thirty years later. Perhaps this is due in part to the influence of the orthodox Zhu Xi school of Tokugawa Confucianism, which had led to a universal culture of rational thinking among educated Japanese who were forty or older at the period we are discussing. The Zhu Xi school's position was strictly rationalistic and very much opposed to any kind of mystical tendency. Its teachings had penetrated to the very marrow of the bones of Japanese intellectuals from the mid-Tokugawa through mid-Meiji periods.

There was no mysticism in the tactics and strategy devised by Kuropatkin, the commander of the Russian Army at the front. Kuropatkin knew that the Japanese Army did not want to keep endlessly advancing northward. Their supply lines would be lengthened, and the transport of munitions and foodstuffs would be delayed. Moreover, they would lose some of their forces in every battle, and, when they had advanced as far north as they could, they would be very much weakened. Kuropatkin also knew that Japan had very limited resources and would not be able to fight a protracted war. Finally, at the "Harbin line," Russia, with its huge forces, would strike an annihilating blow at the weakened Japanese Army and thus win the war.

If Russia had given Kuropatkin its support with steely determination from beginning to end and managed its domestic and external affairs so as to make it easy to carry out his strategy, no doubt the positions of victor and loser in the Russo-Japanese War would have been reversed. But Russia did not do so. And the Japanese had a firm grasp of the problems both sides were facing and kept to its plan for a short war. This made both internal and external affairs function in ways that were ideal for its war effort. So we can conclude that as far as the outcome of the Russo-Japanese War was concerned, the skill or lack of skill of a given general was a matter of minor importance.

* * *

When General Kuropatkin visited the home of Witte, who was said to be the wisest politician in Russia, it was February, and still cold and snowy. Witte kept urging brandy on his visitor, and Kuropatkin became pleasantly drunk. Kuropatkin's mood was buoyed by the fact that the tactics and strategy he described to Witte met with the full approval of his sagacious listener.

"I am in complete agreement with your strategy," said Witte. He was an amateur when it came to war, but he knew a lot about tactics and strategy. And to repeat, tactics and strategy need to be made understandable even to an amateur.

Kuropatkin showed his acceptance of this essential truth when he asked Witte on parting, "If you have some better ideas, please share them with me now." The complacency so common among military men seems to have formed no part of Kuropatkin's makeup, or, at any rate, very little.

"Thank you for asking. I do have one suggestion," replied Witte. But, before revealing his secret strategy, he asked Kuropatkin what kind of men he was taking with him to the Far East.

"Several staff officers and aides."

"Are they men worthy of trust?"

"Yes, of course."

"Well then, I'll tell you what I think. It concerns Viceroy Alexeyev. He has authority over military, internal, and external affairs in the Far East. You will be going as commander of the army in the field, but Alexeyev will take advantage of his greater authority to issue his own orders to the army under your command. Our army will be caught between the orders from you and from Alexeyev, which will cause great confusion and ultimately lead perhaps to defeat."

"That is possible." Kuropatkin too had been worried about the same thing.

"Alexeyev is in Mukden now. You will, of course, be going directly there to offer him greetings after your appointment. Now, if I were you, I would send several of your officers to arrest him. Restrain him, set a strict guard on him, throw him onto the train you yourself arrived on, and send him back to Russia! At the same time, send a telegram to His Majesty the tsar. Write something like 'In order to perfectly carry out the grave mission Your Majesty has entrusted to me, I arrested the viceroy immediately after arriving here. I did this because victory in this war is inconceivable without taking such an action. If Your Majesty wishes to punish me for overstepping my command, please issue an order that I be shot. But, if not, I beg you to bear with me for a time, for the sake of the nation.' That's the kind of telegram to send," Witte concluded.

Witte knew better than anyone that Viceroy Alexeyev, who held supreme power over military and political affairs in the Far East, was a kind of cancer in the body of Russia. He was the tsar's trusted minister and discussed the gravest matters concerning the Far East directly with the sovereign—even the foreign minister often did not know the contents of these conversations. Furthermore, the staunchest imperialists had grouped themselves around Alexeyev, and these people made him the driving force for the Russian invasion of the Far East.

Now war had come, just as Alexeyev had hoped, and the viceroy held supreme power over military affairs in the Far East with authority over Kuropatkin. "Incredible really," Witte had often said, "to put that man in charge of a great army numbering hundreds of thousands." (In fact, it grew to nearly one million troops eventually.) And all the more conscientious elements in the Russian government had the same doubts.

For example, this Alexeyev, who may have had less knowledge of army matters than any newly appointed second lieutenant, could not even ride a horse! At the review of the troops at Port Arthur, when he should by rights have made a splendid appearance on horseback, he came on foot. It was not only a matter of coming mounted or not—Alexeyev was actually terrified of horses.

He was a navy admiral. Yet even his knowledge of naval matters was questionable, and he was in addition a mediocre politician. "He is merely cunning," Witte said. "He has no natural talent or feel for politics whatsoever." How strange that such a person should be in a position to direct the destiny of the Russian nation. But because absolute despotism determined the course of politics in Russia, even a monkey could serve as archbishop if only it won the favor of the tsar.

Thus, Witte advised Kuropatkin to arrest Alexeyev and send him back to Russia at the earliest opportunity. But to arrest his own superior was unthinkable to a man like Kuropatkin, bureaucratic and prone to compromise as he was.

"Surely you're joking!" he said with a rueful smile.

"I'm not joking," Witte answered, shaking his head. "It's the only way to avoid defeat."

"You may be right, but . . . " Kuropatkin nodded with a noncommittal look on his face and then took his leave.

In the end, Witte's fears proved well founded.

When Kuropatkin arrived in Manchuria, he set up separate headquarters and tried to keep his distance from Alexeyev as much as possible, but Alexeyev was aggressive about putting a brake on Kuropatkin's ideas and plans. Alexeyev's whole strategy was one of aggression. "The Japanese are monkeys!" he constantly said, in line with the tsar's comments; as such, they could easily be defeated. What need was there for so much caution on the Russians' part? And so the high command of the Russian Army was divided and in disarray during the first half of the war. (Though eventually Alexeyev was recalled to Russia, and Kuropatkin was able to have complete command of the Russian forces in Manchuria.)

* * *

Now we must touch on naval strategy.

"The navy's Gombei is too timid." This was what the young, optimistic militarists kept saying. Yamamoto Gombei, with his capacity for careful planning, almost godlike creativity, and power to command, was indeed prudence itself until almost the outbreak of the war. For the previous ten years, he had been focused on the Russian Navy, building up Japan's naval forces with Russia as the hypothetical enemy. He had created a fully equipped fleet, its principal ships recent products of Britain's great shipyards, better in performance than the Russians' own. Gombei was a firm believer in the importance of quality performance in weaponry. In his realization that victory or defeat in war would be determined by superior weaponry, he was more "modern" than the leaders of the navies of the more advanced nations. Like most of the leaders of Japan at that time, he never once in his life made senseless pronouncements in an attempt to rally the spiritual force of the nation. He felt that his duty was to ensure the material and organizational resources necessary to prevent defeat in the event of war against the hypothetical enemy. He had devoted himself to that alone over the past ten years.

While Japan had only a single naval fleet, Russia had two: the Pacific Fleet in the Far East and the Baltic Fleet at home. If these two combined, the Japanese Navy had no chance of winning. The Japanese naval strategy directed by Yamamoto Gombei was to sink the Pacific Fleet before the Baltic Fleet arrived to join it, and then to sink that fleet too. Each would be destroyed one at a time.

Russia's Pacific Fleet and Japan's one and only fleet were roughly equal in strength. Gombei wanted to ensure that the number of ships and the ratio of total tonnage would be brought to a level at least slightly to Japan's advantage. In naval battles, numbers and quality performance count. With numerical superiority, not only would the military gains be great, but the losses to one's own side would also be minimized.

In what he regarded as the initial round in the war, Gombei aimed at keeping Japan's losses to the minimum in confrontations with Russia's Pacific Fleet. If he failed to do so, there was little chance of success in the second round against the Baltic Fleet. For this reason, the Japanese Navy purchased two additional light armored cruisers just prior to the start of the war. They were of the most up-to-date type, ordered from the Genoa shipyards by Argentina and almost completed before Japan actually bought them. Though they were classed as cruisers, one had 10-inch guns with a range of 20,000 meters, the longest in the world. Russia had hoped to purchase both ships, but Japan beat the Russians to them. They were named the *Nisshin* and the *Kasuga*. They sailed to Japan before the outbreak of hostilities, successfully evading the Russian naval cordon.

In short, Japan's aim was to strengthen its single fleet and use it to strike at the slightly weaker Russian Pacific Fleet.

* * *

Next we must consider Japan's strategy regarding the fleet in Port Arthur. Japan knew that the hills, islands, and entrance to the bay near the military port were armed with so many artillery emplacements as to be almost covered in steel and concrete. This was home to the Russian fleet. Entering it to attack would be impossible. The idea from the beginning was to lure the fleet to the waters outside the port and attack it there. But would the Russian fleet be willing to leave the safety of the port and venture out into the open seas? That would determine which of the two navies would be victorious and which defeated.

Some in the military command feared that the Russians might not come out. Their fleet might avoid battle by remaining hidden deep within the bay of Port Arthur and waiting until the arrival of the Baltic Fleet. Then the two fleets would join together in battle against the Japanese, whose fleet would be only half the combined Russian force's size. In such a situation, the Japanese would surely lose.

Akiyama Saneyuki, who had witnessed the blocking of the port of Santiago in the Spanish–American War, suggested that the army attack the fortifications of Port Arthur, and at the same time the navy would sink steamers at the mouth of the bay to block it. This plan was not, however, formally considered until after the start of hostilities. An attack on the fortifications of Port Arthur was not initially part of the army's strategy. At any rate, if the Russian fleet came out into the open seas, there would be no need for such actions.

The Japanese government, despairing of progress in diplomatic negotiations with Russia, attempted to break them off several times, only to be stopped by Emperor Meiji. Japanese court circles preserved the old, aristocratic tradition and were very unmilitary in character; Emperor Meiji was no exception. When, however, information came by telegram on February 1 that the tsar had given permission to plan war against Japan, the army felt it had to press for the breaking off of negotiations. On that same day, Ōyama Iwao rushed to the palace and advised the emperor that the time had come to open hostilities against Russia.

In the navy, Yamamoto Gombei's decision came on February 3, with the news that the Russian fleet at Port Arthur had sailed from port. The information was correct. The Russian fleet left Port Arthur on the third, arriving that same night at Dalian, and returning to Port Arthur on the fourth, anchoring in the outer harbor. The original news report, however, stated that the Russian fleet's destination was unclear. Nothing could have been better from the standpoint of Gombei's strategy. Japan needed to catch the Russians on the open seas and deal a crushing blow.

The decision to break off negotiations was made on the fourth, the day after the Russian fleet left Port Arthur.

* * *

The Japanese Combined Fleet was assembled in Sasebo. The orders for the attack would come from the Navy General Staff in Tokyo, but Tokyo dispatched not a telegram but a personal messenger. He left Tokyo by train on the night of February 4 and proceeded south on the Tōkaidō line. The messenger chosen for this mission was a staff officer, Captain Yamashita Gentarō. The order was no doubt sent in this leisurely way because maintaining secrecy by telegram was difficult. But it wasn't so much a matter of worry about information getting into the wrong hands as the feeling that they weren't in any great rush.

Amazingly, Russia exerted great pressure on Japan but was convinced that Japan lacked the ability to fight a war against Russia and would not initiate hostilities. Russia thought the war would come in perhaps one or two years. Ideally, this would give Russia two years to prepare for its crushing defeat of Japan. This sort of thinking was typical of a Great Power.

On February 4 at six o'clock in the evening, the cabinet met in the presence of Emperor Meiji, and Japan decided to break relations with Russia. On the fifth, the Foreign Ministry cabled Ambassador Kurino Shin'ichiro in St. Petersburg, ordering him to officially inform the Russian government of this. On the sixth in Tokyo, Foreign Minister Komura Jutarō summoned Ambassador Rozen to the Foreign Ministry and announced the severance of diplomatic relations.

"What does this cutting of relations mean?" Rozen asked with a clearly disconcerted look on his face. "Does it mean war?"

The severance of diplomatic relations means specifically the withdrawal of diplomatic envoys present in the respective countries in peacetime and the departure of each country's nationals from the other's territory. And, of course, after the cutting of relations, diplomatic negotiations in accordance with normal peacetime rules become impossible no matter what occurs. This "no matter what" can naturally include a state of war, so Ambassador Rozen's question was a foolish one. Or rather, even Rozen himself underestimated Japan, assuming that it would never cut off relations and then launch a war.

"Severing relations is not war," Komura replied like a professor at a law school being questioned by a student.

To reply thus to Rozen's question was to be completely faithful to the meaning of the words. And, of course, Komura's statement included diplomatic maneuvering. He knew all about the Japanese Army and Navy's strategic plans for a first strike at the earliest opportunity after the breaking off of relations.

The Russian viceroy Alexeyev also took too light a view of the meaning of "severance of relations." It was he who had spearheaded the policy of pressuring Japan, yet he had kept saying, "Can the monkeys make war?" Now too he said, "The breaking off of relations doesn't mean war. Japan is hardly ready to start a war with us—as a nation, it is simply not powerful enough. Of that, I am sure." As he conveyed this opinion to his government in St. Petersburg on the night of February 4, Yamashita Gentarō was on board the Tōkaidō line train going south.

* * *

Yamashita Gentarō was a native of Yonezawa from a samurai family formerly attached to the ruling Uesugi clan. When he was studying at the private Yonezawa Middle School, a British teacher there spoke of the strength of the British Navy. "By contrast, there has never been a great naval commander in the whole history of Japan. The Japanese Navy is very weak indeed." As Yamashita often said in later years, that was why he determined to join the navy. He entered the Naval Academy in Tsukiji in 1879 as one of twenty-nine cadets.

During the First Sino-Japanese War, he was a lieutenant staff officer at the Yokosuka Naval Base and very dissatisfied with the central command. The Naval Ministry's basic strategy at this point was not to allow the fleet to make any sorties from the harbor at Sasebo out of an excess of fear of the Qing navy's *Zhenyuan* and *Dingyuan* battleships.

Yamashita was convinced that "not to attack was not to gain a victory" and argued that point with Itō Sukeyuki, the fleet commander. Having won Itō's assent, he proceeded to Tokyo where he tried to make Navy Minister Saigō Tsugumichi abandon the passive, conservative policy then in force. This policy had been adopted by Nakamuta Kuranosuke, then chief of the Navy General Staff, who had served in the Saga domain's navy. Saigō removed Nakamuta from his post prior to the outbreak of the war and appointed as his successor Kabayama Sukenori, originally from Satsuma and a bit of a daredevil. Nakamuta's passive strategy was thus abandoned.

Ten years had passed since then, and now Yamashita as a captain in the Navy General Staff was on his way from Tokyo to the Combined Fleet in Sasebo to transmit the order to begin hostilities. How great had been the progress of the Japanese Navy as compared with the days when, out of fear of merely two ships in the Beiyang Fleet—the *Zhenyuan* and the *Dingyuan*—it had adopted a policy of remaining passively in Sasebo Harbor just prior to the outbreak of the First Sino-Japanese War!

"Every time I think about that, I am amazed," Yamashita recollected later. Even he who had been so deeply involved in it all could hardly believe the changes that had taken place in a matter of only ten years.

The trains at that time were slow. Yamashita left Tokyo at night and arrived in Sasebo the next day—February 5—at half past six in the evening. In his briefcase were what naval parlance termed "sealed orders." These were orders to Commander in Chief of the Combined Fleet Tōgō Heihachirō, and, as the literal meaning of the words suggests, they were to be unsealed at a specified time and place. Actually, there were two sealed documents, one the actual orders and the other an imperial rescript. After recounting the situation that had made cutting off negotiations with the Russian government necessary, the rescript went on to state, "We have decided to order our government to cease negotiations with Russia and to act freely in order to safeguard Japan's independence and defenses. We have confidence in the loyalty and valor of you all, and trust that you will accomplish our aims and thus bring to perfection the glory of our empire."

Yamashita left the coast by launch, and, when he finally boarded the flagship *Mikasa*, it was seven o'clock. The *Mikasa* was then the largest, most powerful battleship in the world, capable of a speed of 18 knots per hour, with a displacement of 15,362 tons of water. Its principal armaments included four 12-inch guns, fourteen 6-inch canons, twenty 3.1-inch guns, and four torpedo launchers.

When Yamashita entered the office of the commander in chief of the Combined Fleet, Tōgō Heihachirō was waiting for him together with his staff officers, who had been previously notified of Yamashita's arrival.

Among the staff officers, the youngest by far was Lieutenant Commander Akiyama Saneyuki.

"Ah, Akiyama's here," the rather tense Yamashita thought. Then, oddly, he noticed that Saneyuki had some stubble on his chin. "I'll have to make him get a good shave," he thought, as he moved forward to present the two sealed documents to Tōgō.

Lieutenant Commander Nagata Yasujirō, Tōgō's adjutant, took out a pair of scissors and handed them to Tōgō, who bowed, cut the seals himself, took out the imperial rescript, and read it silently. The next document to be opened contained the orders from Navy Minister Yamamoto Gombei: "The commander in chief of the Combined Fleet and the Commander of the Third Squadron Kataoka Shichirō are to aim for the total destruction of the Russian Pacific Fleet . . . The commander in chief of the Combined Fleet shall immediately advance and destroy the Russian fleet in the area of the Yellow Sea . . . The commander of the Third Squadron shall immediately occupy Chinhae Bay and guard the Korea Strait."

The date of this sealed order was given as "7:15 p.m., February 5, 1904."

Akiyama Saneyuki took out his pocket watch and observed that it was precisely that time. Shortly afterward, a meeting was held, and the hour grew late. At one o'clock on the morning of the sixth, a light appeared on the mast of the *Mikasa* and immediately began to blink on and off. It was a signal to the entire fleet at anchor in Sasebo: "The commanders and captains of all vessels are to assemble on the flagship." Suddenly, there were many waves breaking the surface of the harbor's waters. Launches were lowered from all the ships and moved toward the *Mikasa*.

The orders concerning the opening of hostilities and naval attacks were transmitted in the office of the commander in chief of the *Mikasa*. There were about forty or fifty commanders and captains of the various ships assembled when Tōgō entered the room with his staff officers. He proceeded to the central seat at the table.

"The imperial command has been issued," he declared, informing them of the contents of the rescript and of the orders from Navy Minister Yamamoto. Then he issued his first order to the Combined Fleet. "Our Combined Fleet will immediately proceed to the Yellow Sea and destroy the enemy fleet at Port Arthur and Inch'ŏn."

* * *

The chief of staff of the Combined Fleet was Shimamura Hayao. He was from Tosa and had entered the Naval School in 1874. He later was promoted to admiral of the fleet and died in 1923. He was a brilliant strategist, yet, unusually for a military man, he was not concerned with making a great name for himself. All his life he gave credit to others—a person with a naturally magnanimous character.

Yamamoto Gombei decided "it would be best to have Shimamura work under Tōgō." Tōgō was to have general command, while Shimamura's wise stratagems would direct the fleet's movements. But Shimamura himself was delighted when Saneyuki joined the staff officers, and he privately informed Saneyuki, "I'll leave everything to you." And that is just what he did. Shimamura believed that the campaign should be directed by a man of genius and that the mere fact of his being senior in rank did not mean that he should use his lesser talents to interfere. That was the sort of man he was.

One anecdote about him from the Russo-Japanese War recounts how the journalists assigned to Imperial Headquarters in Tokyo began to notice the excellent writing style of the reports from the Combined Fleet. At one point, the newspaper *Yomiuri Shimbun*, believing them to be written by Chief of Staff Shimamura, published an article praising him to the skies. Shimamura was amazed to see that and made a point of writing while still at sea to Ogasawara Naganari, who was in charge of the press section at Imperial Headquarters. "I was stunned and embarrassed to read the article. As you are aware, I have a subordinate, and it was he who wrote the reports in question." Thus, he identified Saneyuki as the author and asked that the *Yomiuri* be informed of the mistake in its article. Shimamura was that kind of man.

After the Russo-Japanese War, he became famous for having been the chief of staff of the Combined Fleet, but he kept denying that he deserved such credit. "From the start of the Russo-Japanese War until the fall of Port Arthur," he stated at a public meeting, "I served as chief of staff of the Combined Fleet. It is often said that I continued in that position until the battle of Tsushima, but by then I had been transferred to another post and was no longer chief of staff. The fact is that the activities of our fleet during the Russo-Japanese War were directed by Akiyama Saneyuki. The surprise attack outside the entrance to Port Arthur, the battle of Inch'ŏn, the three blockades of Port Arthur, the large-scale transport of the Second Army, the strategic planning and implementation of the battle of Tsushima—all were conceived by Akiyama and proposed by him in writing, and his proposals were almost always approved immediately by Admiral Tōgō."

We might mention again that Commander Arima Ryōkitsu served as vice chief of staff under Shimamura. When, after the blockading of Port Arthur, Arima left the fleet to take up duties at Imperial Headquarters in Tokyo, Tōgō and Shimamura decided that they would not appoint a new man as his successor but instead promote Saneyuki and make him the vice chief of staff—an exceptional measure. Thus, a thirty-seven-year-old man came to bear, virtually on his own, the burden of devising the naval campaign that was to determine the destiny of Japan.

* * *

Moriyama Keizaburō was a former classmate of Saneyuki's and a lifelong friend. He was at the time a lieutenant commander and staff officer of Rear Admiral Uryū Sotokichi's division (the Fourth Division) in the Second Squadron aboard the cruiser *Naniwa*. He was one of those who gathered in the office of the commander in chief on the *Mikasa*, and he describes how things appeared when Tōgō Heihachirō relayed the order to attack. "I stood there silently, looking down. I couldn't stop my tears from flowing. Not one of those present raised his head. No one spoke—it was as if we were in some mountain fastness."

Moriyama recollects thinking at the time that Japan might lose to Russia. He had gone to Europe on official business two years before and passed through Poland, observing its utter ruin. He saw in each town how mercilessly the Russian victors treated the Poles as if they, the Russians, were their absolute masters, and he couldn't help recalling those scenes. The fear that Japan might meet the same fate made him lose control and reduced him to tears. "No doubt not everyone in the room was as weak-spirited as I was, but, judging from the dead silence, I think everyone had similar feelings. It felt as if we were standing on the edge of a precipice, and our next move meant life or death to Japan."

When at last the orders had all been read out, champagne was handed around and Tōgō raised his glass. "I trust you will all fight with the utmost valor and look forward to the success that lies ahead—a toast!" He emptied his glass.

When everyone had done the same, the feeling of tension vanished and, as Moriyama states, "The atmosphere changed to one of celebration." The captains of the various ships started to leave the commander's office, but Moriyama heard someone say that orders would be handed to the staff officers so they should remain, and he attempted to do so. But he was pushed along by the crowd and passed down the corridor until he came to the chief of staff's room, where he found the door open. The spacious office was brightly lit, and in the center of the room was a large table with a naval map spread out on top.

Two men were having an intense discussion—Shimamura Hayao and Akiyama Saneyuki. For his entire life, Moriyama revered his classmate Akiyama Saneyuki almost like a god, and he often recounted this scene in later years. "It was moving to see these two extraordinarily gifted military men devoting themselves heart and soul to planning the coming campaign."

He then goes on to describe what the two men were doing. Saneyuki had a compass in his right hand and a ruler in his left, and moved them about, indicating the routes of the ships on the map. On the other side of the table, Shimamura had bent his large body over the map and gazed at the routes Saneyuki was tracing on it.

Eventually, Saneyuki noticed Moriyama standing in the doorway and called out to him, "Your division is going to go to Inch'ŏn. We'll supply you with the *Asama* and some torpedo boats." Then he returned to looking at the naval map.

* * *

At the beginning of the war, the navy was responsible for attacking the Russian fleet at Port Arthur, gaining control of the seas, and landing army troops at Inch'ŏn in Korea. The main force was to go to Port Arthur.

At nine o'clock in the morning on February 6, the main force of the Combined Fleet left the port of Sasebo. The first to leave was the Third Division (of the First Squadron) with *Chitose* (a protected cruiser) as its flagship. The *Chitose* was followed by the *Takasago*, *Kasagi*, and *Yoshino*. The ships at anchor sent them off by manning the side rails and shouting, "Banzai!" Then the First through the Fifth Destroyer divisions and the Ninth and Fourteenth Torpedo Boat divisions followed, cutting through the waves. Next came the Second Division (of the Second Squadron) under the command of Vice Admiral Kamimura Hikonojō, with its flagship *Izumo* (an armored cruiser) in the lead, followed by the *Azuma*, *Yakumo*, *Tokiwa*, and *Iwate*. Finally came the First Division (of the First Squadron), which was the core of the Combined Fleet, with its flagship the *Mikasa* (a first-class battleship) in the lead, followed by the *Asahi*, *Fuji*, *Yashima*, *Shikishima*, and *Hatsuse*. The last was a torpedo boat division. Captain Yamashita Gentarō, who had come from Imperial Headquarters in Tokyo, saw them off as a representative of the entire navy.

By around noon, the harbor at Sasebo, which had been so crowded with ships of various types until the day before, was almost empty. Only a few middle-sized ships remained: the protected cruisers *Naniwa* and *Takachiho* and the small protected cruisers *Akashi* and *Niitaka*. The only large ship was the armored cruiser *Asama*, at 9,750 tons. These ships were known as Uryū's division (of the Second Squadron) and were responsible for landing army troops at Inch'ŏn as security forces.

Uryū's division left port at two o'clock in the afternoon. Already a landing force of two thousand two hundred army troops (four battalions from Kokura, Fukuoka, and Ōmura) had been loaded on three transport ships and were speeding in the same direction as the naval squadrons.

"When did the army get here?" the sailors asked each other in surprise.

"The three transport ships were hiding in some inlet near the outer harbor of Sasebo," Moriyama Keizaburō of Uryū's division later said. "Even though I'm a staff officer, I didn't know of their existence until the orders came. The coordination between the army and the navy was superb."

All the squadrons moved toward their target, and there was just one warship in the Japanese Navy that was placed in a painful position—the small armored cruiser *Chiyoda* (2,450 tons). The only ship not among the others at this time, it was in the foreign waters of Inch'ŏn, Korea, which served as the port for the city of Hansŏng (present-day Seoul) some distance away. Many foreign vessels were at anchor there, including two Russian warships. The *Chiyoda*'s misfortune was that it served as a decoy. News of the breaking of relations with Russia had of course been cabled to the *Chiyoda*, but it had been left in Inch'ŏn Harbor as part of a strategy not to let Russia or other countries know about the secret activities of the Combined Fleet at the start of the war. It was only to be expected that the first battle of the Russo-Japanese War would take place, therefore, in the harbor of Inch'ŏn.

* * *

The port of Inch'ŏn's role in relation to Hansŏng corresponded to Yokohama's role in relation to Tokyo. Just as Yokohama had been only a fishing village until the opening of the treaty ports under the Tokugawa shogunate, so Inch'ŏn had been just a fishing village called Chemulpo until the opening of the port to foreigners in 1883. And, just as the first railway in Japan was built between Tokyo and Yokohama, so the first railway in Korea was built in 1900 linking Hansŏng and Inch'ŏn. Apart from the extreme difference in water level between high and low tides, the port of Inch'ŏn was easy to use because of its large size and ability to handle a great number of ships.

At the time we are describing, there were many ships in the harbor. Taking warships alone, the British *Talbot*, the Italian *Elba*, and the French *Pascal* were all at anchor there. In addition, there were the Russian protected cruiser *Varyag* (6,500 tons) and the gunship *Koriets* (1,213 tons). The small armored cruiser *Chiyoda* was anchored among them as the only Japanese ship.

"No warship has met a sadder fate than the *Chiyoda*," recalled Moriyama Keizaburō with great sympathy even many years later. He had been part of Uryū's division that went to save the isolated Japanese cruiser. The *Chiyoda* had gone to Inch'ŏn in December of the previous year in order to protect Japanese civilians there.

The two Russian ships anchored in the harbor were charged with a similar mission. The *Varyag* was the largest of the warships at Inch'ŏn, and, if hostilities broke out, the small *Chiyoda* would have been pulverized immediately. And, to make matters worse, the *Chiyoda* was in the closest position to the *Varyag*. Also, there were no other ships between it and the *Koriets*.

In charge of the *Chiyoda* was Captain Murakami Kakuichi, a calm man who ordered the crew to be on the alert and made them understand that they might all die if there was, unavoidably, a military clash with the *Varyag*. When night fell, the *Chiyoda* secretly uncapped its torpedo launchers and aimed them at the *Varyag*; when day dawned, they were capped again as if nothing was amiss. The Russian ship became aware of what was happening and lodged a bitter complaint via the captain of the British ship, who had seniority among all the ships' commanders.

At last, on the third, the eve of the decision to break relations with Russia, Captain Murakami intuited that an emergency might be imminent. Taking advantage of the darkness, he quietly shifted his ship to a position near the British warship and anchored there. On the seventh, learning by telegraph that a Japanese squadron had captured a Russian steamer near Pusan, Murakami realized that war had begun. Fortunately, the *Varyag* seemed not to be aware of the situation as yet.

At eleven o'clock that night, the *Chiyoda* decided on making its escape and began to move quietly at slow speed toward the harbor entrance. As it did so, the bow of the *Varyag*, which had been monitoring the Japanese ship, suddenly hove into view at a narrow spot near the harbor entrance, and it seemed that the two ships would actually scrape against each other. The nearby British warship, however, shifted position, and a way was opened for the *Chiyoda* to move out of the harbor.

Having escaped from Inch'ŏn Harbor, the *Chiyoda* moved southward, seeking other Japanese ships. It kept moving south as the new day dawned, and, at half past eight on the morning of the eighth, it saw a great amount of smoke on the horizon, which turned out to be Uryū's division. Captain Murakami Kakuichi immediately went by launch to the flagship *Naniwa* to meet the commander of Uryū's division, who urgently asked, "Surely the *Varyag* and the *Koriets* have not left Inch'ŏn Harbor, have they?"

If these two ships were allowed to escape to Port Arthur, they would greatly strengthen the Russian fleet there. They needed to be attacked and defeated, but the harbor at Inch'ŏn belonged to a neutral nation, and many warships of European powers were anchored there. It would be impossible to fight a battle there. Imperial General Headquarters was nervous about any action that might cause an international outcry and had telegraphed Uryū's division ordering it to exercise utmost care: "We must not launch an attack in Inch'ŏn Harbor unless the Russian ship opens fire on us."

The foreign warships in Inch'ŏn Harbor were surprised to see the *Chiyoda*, which had slipped away the night before, now return at the head of a Japanese fleet. Uryū's division anchored in the harbor where the two Russian warships still were. Thus, allies and foes were side by side, and it was hard to tell when a battle might break out inside the harbor. The foreign warships could hardly overlook this danger, so at nine o'clock on the evening of the eighth, the captain of the British ship came to the *Takachiho*. "This is a neutral country's harbor," he said, "so you mustn't fire on any foreign warships or take any other action that might damage them."

"Our orders are only to get our army troops ashore," Mōri Ichibei, the captain of the *Takachiho*, responded. "We haven't been ordered to make war."

It was after midnight on the ninth. When it was clear that the disembarkation of the army troops would be over by four in the morning, Uryū's division sent a letter of challenge in English to Captain Vsevolod Rudnev of the *Varyag*: "As you know, Japan and Russia are already in a state of war. I therefore demand that you withdraw your forces from Inch'ŏn Harbor by noon of February 9. If you do not respond to this demand, we will be forced to take military action against your nation's warships inside the harbor." This was sent to the Russians via a military envoy, who also went to the various foreign warships with the request that they move to anchorage where they would be out of any danger. This was done at seven o'clock on the morning of the ninth.

At five minutes before noon, the *Varyag* and the *Koriets* raised anchor and began to move, soon making for the sea outside the harbor full steam ahead. The Japanese had been hoping the Russians would do just this and had the *Asama* lying in wait outside the harbor.

The protected cruiser *Varyag* (6,500 tons) had four funnels and was capable of great speed, but the gunboat *Koriets* (1,213 tons) that followed it was much slower and lacked the speed necessary for an escape. The Japanese armored cruiser *Asama* (9,750 tons) lay in wait with other smaller ships outside the harbor. Captain Yashiro Rokurō, well known for his bravery, was in command.

"The enemy ship has left the harbor!" shouted the signalman from high on the mast, and immediately the entire group of ships was battle ready. But the small armored cruiser *Chiyoda* alongside had no time to raise anchor and had to cut the anchor chain to free itself, so sudden had been the appearance of the Russian ships.

On Japan's side, Uryū's division was composed chiefly of older and smaller cruisers, each of about 3,000 tons. Though they were rather dilapidated, if all of them joined together, they could put up a good fight against the *Varyag*. The *Asama* had been added to their group so that the *Varyag* could be made to surrender without damage to the Japanese side. The *Asama* increased its speed.

The *Varyag* and the *Koriets* sailed toward Palmi Island near the entrance to the harbor. Both had raised their battle flags. The *Asama*, which had been lying in wait, then ran up its battle flag and drew closer to the Russian ships. When the distance between the Japanese and Russian ships had shrunk from 6 to 7 kilometers, the *Asama* test-fired its 8-inch guns and then began to fire from its portside. Shells from the aft 8-inch guns struck the fore bridge of the *Varyag* with violent explosions.

Torpedo battles had already taken place that day in the vicinity of Port Arthur as well, but if we are to speak only of the firing of shipboard artillery, then the first round from the Japanese side in the Russo-Japanese War was probably from these 8-inch guns on the *Asama*. This gun's firepower was the greatest in the Japanese Navy. Shells from the fore 8-inch guns next hit the enemy ship in approximately the same area as the previous ones had. As a result, the *Varyag*'s fore bridge was smashed to pieces, and the area around its funnel was hit as well. Then several shells hit the central area of the vessel and its aft bridge, causing a conflagration.

Yet still the *Varyag* did not give up. It retreated behind Palmi Island to attempt to put out the fire. The Japanese could not pursue that far because it was within Inch'ŏn Harbor. After about fifteen minutes, the *Varyag* reappeared, firing powerful broadsides from its guns.

The small *Chiyoda* raced around the area. During this period, a warship was painted gray in wartime and black in peacetime. The ships of Uryū's division had all been painted gray, but the *Chiyoda*, having been left anchored in Inch'ŏn Harbor for so long, was still painted black. And, though the entire fleet had been supplied with British coal for fuel, the *Chiyoda* alone was still using Japanese coal, as in peacetime.

Thus, this small vessel was belching forth great clouds of black smoke from its funnel.

The *Varyag* was listing to the left. The *Koriets* was still undamaged. The only way these two vessels could survive was by retreating once again into the neutral Inch'ŏn Harbor. The *Asama*, fearing an international incident, stopped firing and returned to the harbor entrance.

The state of the *Varyag* was pitiful to behold. It was listing sharply to the left, and almost all of its large guns had been destroyed. Ordinarily, its only recourse would have been to surrender, but Commander Rudnev tried to avoid the dishonor of having a warship of the Russian Navy surrender at the very start of the war. He asked the warships of the various other countries to help deal with his men. The wounded were taken on board the Italian,

French, and British ships, and the French warship *Pascal*, as an act of friendship from an allied nation, took on board the other, uninjured personnel as well. It was decided to transport them to Shanghai so long as it was guaranteed that they would not leave Shanghai until the war's end. This was in keeping with international law.

After all this had been done, the *Varyag* opened its Kingston valves—sea cocks at the bottom of a ship—and sank itself. The *Koriets* ignited its powder magazine and, after the captain and crew had safely disembarked, sank as a result of the explosion.

This naval battle, though small in scale, was the first to be fought between Japanese and Europeans. Precisely because this first engagement had gone so well, it gave a great boost to the self-confidence of the Japanese.

The Japanese consul Katō Motoshirō at Inch'ŏn, who thought that Japan would suffer considerable casualties, actually had built an emergency Red Cross hospital on the grounds of the consulate to care for the wounded. After the victory at Inch'ŏn, Lieutenant Commander Moriyama Keizaburō came ashore and visited the consulate. Consul Katō asked him about Japanese casualties.

"There were none" was Moriyama's reply.

Katō didn't believe him. "Judging from the great damage done to the Russian side," he said, inviting Moriyama into his office, "there must have been some Japanese casualties as well. There are no outsiders here, so please tell me the truth."

Moriyama assured Katō that he was telling the truth. Not even a rope on the Japanese ship had been cut through. Katō was stupefied and then began to cry. Could it really be that the Japanese had defeated Caucasians? As an official in the Foreign Ministry, Katō must have indeed felt great surprise and joy.

"There's nothing to be surprised about. We went to the trouble of bringing along a great ship like the *Asama*. We ought to have won, and we did!" Moriyama attributed the victory to Saneyuki's strategy of building up massive matériel.

But even if Japan's victory was natural and appropriate under the circumstances, still, the Japanese were amazed at how very weak the firepower was on the Russian side. The *Varyag* had fired a huge quantity of shells during the battle—1,530 rounds, but not one of them had hit the Japanese. Dead and wounded on the Russian side numbered 223 men. There were no casualties on the Japanese side. It was not so much a miracle as it was proof of the poor quality of the Russian gunnery.

7

PORT ARTHUR

The Combined Fleet considered the attack on Inch'ŏn the responsibility of a separate naval unit, but they saw attacking Port Arthur as the job of the main force. Almost the entire main force of the 190,000-ton Russian Pacific Fleet was in Port Arthur, since the port of Vladivostok had iced over. These ships had to be destroyed, but unless the enemy squadron came out onto the open seas, the artillery emplacements that guarded the harbor would keep the Japanese fleet from coming near.

And so torpedo tactics seemed vital. The idea of sending destroyers loaded with torpedoes against the enemy was a naval tactic that had been planned by the Navy General Staff for a long time. But the state of Port Arthur's artillery emplacements and of its naval squadron remained a mystery to the Japanese side.

"Port Arthur is not going to be an easy place to attack!" declared Yamashita Gentarō, the Navy General Staff's chief of operations. He had been sent to Yantai in September of the year before the war began and made this point very forcefully after his return. He had gone to Yantai to find out about conditions in Port Arthur. At the time, the most he could do was observe Port Arthur from across the Bohai Gulf at Yantai on the Shandong Peninsula. Even so, he could learn something about the conditions at sea.

"People who talk of sending destroyers into the narrow sea entrance to Port Arthur," he observed, "don't understand the sea conditions in winter. There's the well-known cycle of three cold days and four warm ones, and, when the north wind is blowing strongly during a cold spell, the sea becomes very rough, and a small destroyer would lose speed and stability. If attacked at a time like that, it would be lost. The Russian authorities at Port Arthur are very vigilant. The *Novik*"—a small protected cruiser—"goes out every day as far as Gaojiao Cape, at the tip of the Shandong Peninsula. If our ships fell into the *Novik*'s clutches, there'd be no way to help them."

So said Yamashita, and he had been saying the same things to Tōgō, Shimamura, and Akiyama before the war began. These observations of Yamashita were all that was known about the situation in Port Arthur.

The conclusion was that a considerable defensive force should be sent to a point not quite within the range of Port Arthur's artillery emplacements. This plan was centered on the main force of the Combined Fleet, which would form that defensive force. Akiyama Saneyuki intended to employ the extraordinary dual strategy of having the destroyers attack the harbor while at the same time blocking the entrance to the harbor by sinking dilapidated ships there. Even Tōgō, however, who usually agreed with all of Saneyuki's plans, crushed this idea of blocking the harbor entrance. "The group who carried out this plan would almost certainly not survive. We shouldn't do it." And so an attack by destroyers alone became the plan.

* * *

The Combined Fleet's main force that had left Sasebo on the morning of February 6 reached the waters near Yuandao—"Round Island"—44 nautical miles to the east of Port Arthur, at six o'clock on the evening of the eighth. The waves were low with a slight wind blowing from the northwest; the sky was cloudless, with a reddish evening afterglow. Saneyuki had chosen this area as the place to launch the destroyer group against Port Arthur.

"This is the spot," he said to Shimamura, who then turned to Tōgō and repeated the same words. Tōgō nodded.

In time, a signal flag fluttered from the mast of the *Mikasa* with the message: "Attack as planned. We pray for your success."

Saneyuki had planned to throw the Combined Fleet's entire destroyer force into this attack, and that is what he did. He sent the First, Second, and Third Destroyer divisions to Port Arthur and the Fourth and Fifth Destroyer divisions to Dalian Bay (though it turned out that there were in fact no enemy forces in Dalian Bay).

"We are confident of success" was the reply signal sent by Captain Asai Shōjirō, commander of the First Destroyer Division on board the *Shirakumo* (372 tons), as representative of the attack group, which then moved away from the Combined Fleet, leaving an arc of white foam in its wake. When at last the destroyers had disappeared beyond the darkening horizon, the Combined Fleet moved on its set course. Later, it too would head for Port Arthur, but only after first spending some more time at sea.

"What do you think? Will it succeed?" Shimamura asked.

"All we can do is pray for Heaven's help," Saneyuki answered rather brusquely.

He hoped to be able to sink five Russian warships in this surprise attack by the group of destroyers. If Japan didn't reduce the number of enemy warships, it would be at a great disadvantage in the coming sea battle between the two countries' main forces. The whole point of the surprise attack strategy was to weaken the enemy in advance.

The results, however, were not as Saneyuki hoped. Not a single Russian warship was sunk, and only two battleships and one cruiser suffered fairly extensive damage. It was Saneyuki's very first chance to carry out a strategic plan of his own, so naturally he had hoped and prayed for success. A strategist has some time on his own after the group that is to carry out his plans has left. Saneyuki wanted to use this time to sleep. In the military, there's a set time to go to bed, but Saneyuki didn't care much about such military regulations.

"Chief of Staff, I'm going to get some sleep now," he declared, going to his cabin and lying down on his bed still in his military uniform.

Shimamura had no objections to this, but Tōgō always looked unhappy about such actions on Saneyuki's part. Shimamura did not go so far as to excuse Saneyuki by saying out loud, "He's a kind of genius, after all," but by the expression on his face he did manage to convey his wish that Tōgō too say nothing about it. And, in fact, Tōgō never did rebuke Saneyuki for his behavior.

* * *

It was unfortunate for the Russian fleet in Port Arthur that they were unaware even that war with Japan had begun, much less that a sudden attack force was on its way that very night. They were not even patrolling the seas in an extensive way. And yet a crucially important telegram from the tsar had already arrived, addressed to Viceroy Alexeyev. "Japan may be about to start hostilities. If the Japanese fleet appears off the west coast of Korea moving northward, do not wait for them to fire on you. Attack them at once."

But, on this night, Port Arthur was so calm that it seemed foolish to imagine any danger approaching. Unfortunate too was the fact that it was a feast day of the Blessed Virgin in the Russian Church. It was the custom to congratulate women with the name Maria on this day. A group of army officers went to the quarters of the head army doctor in Port Arthur in formal dress and held a party complete with dancing in honor of the doctor's wife, who was named Maria. Most unfortunate of all was the fact that the wife of Vice Admiral Oskar Stark, the commander in chief of the Russian fleet, was also named Maria. She had invited many officers under her husband's command to the official residence for a festive dinner. With witty conversation and graceful dancing, this gathering was reminiscent of aristocratic dinners in the capital of St. Petersburg, though on a smaller scale. The party went on far into the night. No one suspected that all the while the "uncivilized monkeys," as they termed the Japanese, were stealing into the entrance to the harbor.

Suddenly, thirty minutes after midnight, the assembled party heard an explosion that rocked the floor, followed by several more.

"What was that?" asked Vice Admiral Stark of the officer next to him, in as calm a manner as possible so as not to disturb the pleasure of the guests by his own surprise.

Several of the officers left the hall and contacted army staff headquarters in the fort. The response was reassuring. "We think the battleship *Retvizan* has been doing nighttime firing exercises."

Everyone felt relieved and the party continued, but thirty minutes later a tremendous artillery blast made the window glass shake. Now everyone looked rather anxious, but still no one left the party. They had full confidence in the immense size and power of their nation's fleet. Very shortly after, a siren sounded a warning. Now they knew for the first time of the Japanese attack. Panic-stricken and with no time to change into battle dress, they rushed, dressed in their formal clothes, to their various posts. The command headquarters, the fleet, and the fortifications were all in turmoil, with people running about—it is hard to describe the degree of confusion.

* * *

The Russian fleet at Port Arthur had been totally unprepared. Not only had the various ships not bothered to set up protective nets against torpedoes, but the Russian fleet's ships were lined up together near the entrance to the harbor, like so many sitting ducks taking an afternoon nap. The battleships were anchored near the coast of the port while the group of cruisers was a bit further out in the offing.

The Japanese destroyers neared the harbor entrance around half past ten at night on February 8, but they didn't immediately enter, spending some two hours outside the harbor in order to assess the enemy's situation. During that time, the Russians' searchlights were busily sweeping over the surface of the water. In time, two destroyers charged with sounding any necessary alarm to the Russian side approached, shining their searchlights. This threw the Japanese side's plan of action into confusion. The ten Japanese destroyers of the First through Third Destroyer divisions were at the time proceeding side by side. This lead group became alarmed and, in order to avoid being discovered by the Russian ships, immediately slowed down and indeed began to reverse direction. This threw the ships that were following into confusion. It was night, and there were no lights. The attack group's formation fell apart, and there were some ships that were not even sure of their own present position.

Thus, it became necessary for the ships to launch separate attacks. Each ship proceeded blindly through the darkness. This disorder was the reason for the Japanese side's relatively small gains, despite the Russians' lack of preparation.

On the Russian side too, there was an incredibly great mistake. Though the two Russian warning vessels had discovered the Japanese surprise attack, they did not fire on the Japanese. And not only did they fail to open fire, but they left the scene and returned to the harbor entrance in order to report to headquarters. Because of this failure to open fire, the Russian ships anchored in the harbor slept on undisturbed. The Japanese destroyers then moved in on them with their torpedoes.

The actions of the two Russian warning vessels were unbelievably stupid, but they had their reasons for what they did. They had already been issued orders by Commander in Chief Stark that flew in the face of common sense. Captain Aleksandr Bubnov, the commander of the gunboat *Bobr* (950 tons), which was in the harbor at the time, described this later in his memoir, *Port Arthur*:

> On the night in question the two warning vessels had received orders from Commander in Chief Stark not under any circumstances to fire even if they discovered a surprise attack being carried on by the enemy. If they discovered something suspicious, they were to return and report directly to the commander in chief. When they finally discovered the Japanese destroyers, they were amazed, but the commanders of the two ships obeyed their orders. They did not fire but returned quietly and, wanting to report to the commander in chief, approached his flagship.

By that time, the cruiser *Pallada* was sending up great columns of fire in the darkness far behind them.

The Japanese attack had begun.

* * *

The destroyers of this period were small ships, barely large enough to be termed "ships," in fact, 200–300 tons at most. They carried only two torpedoes. The rule was "Fire, then flee."

They were sailing in the dead of night. If, for example, the enemy ship that was their target was 2,000 meters away, a ship would need to carefully regulate its engines and cut through the waves at a speed of 12 knots. Time had to be measured using that fixed speed, and the distance to the enemy ship calculated minute by minute. When within 1,000 meters or so, a shape that might be the enemy vessel would be dimly seen through binoculars, even in the dead of night.

The cruiser *Pallada* (6,731 tons) had been torpedoed in the night attack on Port Arthur. No precautions had been taken before the attack that night. This was despite the fact that the ship had been ordered to leave port at dawn and go to the Tsushima Strait as a precautionary measure, since war seemed to be near. The evening before that planned departure, the *Pallada* was fully loaded with coal for fuel. Scheduled to leave port early the next day, it must have been somewhat on alert.

Several high-ranking officers of the ship were on land that night. One of the officers on duty on board was a young sublieutenant second class, just recently appointed; it was he who first saw the approaching group of Japanese destroyers. There were four in all. He didn't think they could possibly be Japanese vessels. Each had four smokestacks. They looked very like the destroyers built at the Nevsky Shipyard in Russia.

"What are those destroyers?" he asked, turning toward the signalman. Just then, there was a flash of light from one of the unknown ships. Even this inexperienced sublieutenant second class realized that it was the flash that occurs when a torpedo is fired. He could also see the white wake left by the speeding torpedo.

"Torpedo to portside!" he shouted, but since the ship was at anchor, it could take no evasive action. Immediately, there was a great roar as if heaven and earth had been split apart, and the 6,731-ton *Pallada* was violently shaken, with its deck suddenly sloping upward. The ship listed to the right. The explosion raised a great column of seawater, which then collapsed and fell on the deck like a waterfall.

The ship was in tumult. Sailors and low-ranking officers raced about, and the gunners ran to their posts heedless of their officers' orders, starting to fire haphazardly at the dark surface of the sea.

The scenes on the battleships *Tsesarevich* and *Retvizan* were much the same.

Gunfire came from all the ships in the harbor entrance, and the glare from over twenty searchlights began to sweep crazily over the surface of the water. But the Japanese destroyers had already scurried away, like so many mice.

However, the Japanese torpedo attack group too had proved itself very unskillful. It had fired twenty torpedoes in all, yet only inflicted heavy damage on two battleships and one cruiser, and even these three were able to return to service after two months' repair. Given the excellent conditions that the Japanese ships were working under, this was an almost unthinkably poor showing.

* * *

The Russian viceroy for the Far East, Alexeyev, was at the time in Port Arthur. Wearing the formal uniform of an admiral, he was giving a party for his staff officers and civilian officials in a large room in Navy Hall. Even after the sound of firing came from the harbor entrance, he remained undisturbed, until the report on it came to him. And, when he learned that there had been a surprise torpedo attack by a group of Japanese destroyers, he continued to drink on in a quite relaxed way. Indeed, he asked the man who had brought the report, "Did the Japanese really attack, then?" with a dubious look. The messenger had to repeat that it had certainly been an attack by Japanese destroyers. No one was as completely certain of Russia's greatness as Alexeyev. He had received a lot of information to the effect that Japan might be about to launch a war, yet he had neglected even to have the ships at the harbor entrance set up anti-torpedo nets. When his Naval Department suggested doing so, he had actually replied, "It's too early for that, I'd say."

Alexeyev had no reputation whatsoever as an able admiral of the navy, but he may have been very able as viceroy for the Far East, a political post. Even after learning of the Japanese surprise attack, he kept the party going. This may have partly been out of his utter contempt for the enemy—mere Japanese, after all; but it may largely have been out of concern not to upset his subordinates and injure their morale over the simple fact that destroyers from the Japanese fleet had intruded into the harbor entrance.

The highest-ranking officer of the Russian Army in Port Arthur was the commander of the fortifications, Lieutenant General Anatoly Mikhailovich Stoessel. He was in his official residence at the time of the sudden outburst of firing at the harbor entrance. Surprised, he merely asked about what had happened.

He took seriously the report that it was a naval exercise and, giving no orders regarding the fortifications, simply went to bed that night in his usual way. That night would be the last peaceful one he would know for some time. Incredibly, over an hour passed before the news of the first outbreak of firing was brought to Stoessel's official residence by a most reliable messenger—Captain Dmitriyevsky, a high-ranking adjutant to Stoessel, who had received word of the attack from the viceroy's staff. He told the orderly at the official residence to wake General Stoessel, but the orderly asked the captain himself to do this. And so the captain had to knock on the general's bedroom door. Stoessel's wife Vera Alekseyevna emerged.

"The Japanese have come to the harbor entrance," the captain said, relaying to Madame Stoessel all the information he was sure of. At last, Stoessel roused himself and went to headquarters at two o'clock in the morning. His staff officers were already there.

Some of the greatest fortifications in the world were under Stoessel's command, but there were as yet no plans for the efficient mobilization and movement of the forces inside if war broke out. This fact alone shows that Russia did not believe that Japan would ever rise up in an offensive assault.

* * *

The night Japan attacked Port Arthur, a telegram relaying the news was sent to St. Petersburg. Though the news came late at night, Nicholas II was not in a bad mood. The tsar, who longed for heroic ventures, had exactly the same attitude toward Asia and Japan as Viceroy Alexeyev. In fact, having heard so much positive propaganda regarding Russia's great chances for expansion from his trusted minister Alexeyev, Nicholas must have thought that the war that the "monkeys" had launched would provide a brilliant start for the control of Asia that Russia had already embarked on. He never dreamed that the war would ultimately lead to a revolution ending in the cruel death of himself and his whole family.

In fact, the tsar must have been listening to Home Minister Plehve's very particular "theories" about war and revolution. Plehve was one of the ministers who ingratiated himself with the military and was in charge of the domestic police force. His view was that "a small-scale war was absolutely necessary to sweep away the revolutionary feelings stirring in the hearts of the people at present. Of course we must win that war and show the trustworthiness of the imperial government."

This view was not Plehve's alone. Rather, it was a theory held in common by the political adventurers who were in cahoots with Plehve. The tsar was insensitive to the latent revolutionary feelings that Plehve was speaking of, but he must have listened to Plehve's adventurist notions and surely thought that war would be advantageous to Russia, on both domestic and foreign fronts.

However, the pro-war "political adventurist group," as Witte had called them, was represented in the cabinet by Plehve alone—they were not numerous. Even War Minister Kuropatkin was critical of Plehve and by no means wanted to hasten the war with Japan. The tsar, in short, was being pulled along by what was a minority opinion.

At dawn on February 9, the tsar issued a declaration of war, and a great prayer service was held in the Winter Palace. The Eastern Orthodox Church, which was the state religion of Russia, is richer in solemn liturgical forms than any other religion on earth, and the prayer service on this day was especially so. But, according to Witte, who attended the service, "The chapel was somehow wrapped in gloom, and people's spirits were not raised by the service at all."

But as the tsar was retiring after the service, General Bogdanovich, thinking perhaps to relieve the gloom, shouted "Hurrah!" in a loud voice. Witte says, however, that only a few people present shouted along with him. Even the aristocracy was either indifferent to this war in the distant Far East or was very nearly opposed to it. Moreover, among the general populace, it was clearly unpopular and cursed in many quarters. In order to improve popular morale, the Home Ministry gathered people together for meetings and parades of support, but still this did not raise people's spirits in the least.

* * *

At nearly the same time, Tōgō was aboard ship on the Yellow Sea. Having learned the results of the previous night's torpedo attack by the Japanese destroyer group, he telegraphed Tokyo: "Damage was inflicted on three large enemy vessels." He was disappointed that none had been sunk.

At any rate, Tōgō approached Port Arthur at the head of the main naval force.

"I think that once or twice should do it," Saneyuki said to Shimamura Hayao during the voyage. He was talking about how to carry out the attack on Port Arthur. Tōgō wanted desperately to destroy the fleet at Port Arthur prior to the Baltic Fleet's arrival from Russia. Yet, if, in an excess of enthusiasm for the battle at Port Arthur, the Japanese side suffered major damage, it would be unable to fight the Baltic Fleet. Tōgō's very difficult problem was how to sink the whole of the enemy fleet at Port Arthur while suffering no damage to his own ships.

The Russian fleet at Port Arthur did its best not to fall into this trap. Even though equipped with roughly the same naval strength as the Japanese side, it adopted a policy that might be termed "making the fleet a fortress." This meant that the Russian fleet withdrew deep inside the harbor and, protected by the fortifications on land, took a passive posture. The artillery battles meant to drive Tōgō off were left entirely to the fortifications' guns, while the fleet itself waited inside the harbor until the appearance of the Baltic Fleet, which the Russians knew would be coming at some point. If by any chance ships did venture from the harbor, they had all been ordered by Commander in Chief Stark to "stay within range of the fortifications' artillery fire." Stark's strategy was arithmetically correct, but he failed to take into account morale, that very important element in warfare. His policy greatly diminished the morale of the fleet in Port Arthur.

Tōgō was on his way. His forces sailed in single-line formation with the *Mikasa* in the lead. The *Asahi* came next; then the *Fuji*, *Yashima*, *Shikishima*, and *Hatsuse*. Then came, from the Second Division, the *Izumo*, *Azuma*, *Yakumo*, *Tokiwa*, and *Iwate*; and, from the Third Division, the *Chitose*, *Takasago*, *Kasagi*, and *Yoshino*.

When the fleet neared the entrance to Port Arthur's harbor, the protected cruiser *Diana* (6,731 tons), which happened to have ventured into the waters outside the harbor just then, discovered the Japanese fleet. Immediately, the *Diana* made a bold and provocative approach. It was a feint aimed at drawing the Japanese side within range of the fortifications' artillery. Eventually, the *Diana* turned around and started to withdraw but fired its tail guns at the *Mikasa* as it fled. The *Diana* fired three times. Spray fell around the *Mikasa*, but none of the shells scored a hit. Tōgō was standing on the fore bridge. He had the crew raise the battle flag—the first time the flagship had done so. Then Tōgō ordered Saneyuki to have a line of signal flags raised as well. Soon the mast bore this message to the fleet: "Victory or defeat will be decided in this battle. Everyone, do your best!"

* * *

This naval engagement later came to be called "the battle outside Port Arthur Harbor." It cannot be regarded as a real success for the Japanese side.

Tōgō was standing on the fore bridge, and he first caught sight of the enemy ships at the entrance to the harbor through his binoculars. These binoculars of his were the latest "8 magnification" model made by Zeiss—the only ones of this type in the whole Japanese Navy. Shimamura and Saneyuki, standing beside him, both had only old-fashioned "2 magnification" binoculars. So, of the three, Tōgō was always the first to sight the enemy.

"Ah, you can see them?" Perhaps the innate good nature of the large, sturdily built Shimamura caused him to put a note of admiration in this comment, which made all the staff officers relax a bit.

The Russians' casual attitude was evident in the way their ships remained concentrated near the harbor entrance, just as they had been when attacked by Japanese torpedoes the previous night. It may have been inevitable that the three damaged vessels should remain stranded there, but most of the other ships also were still at anchor there. Seven battleships, seven cruisers, and a number of destroyers and gunboats were grouped there together.

Tōgō continued to observe them through his binoculars, but when the Japanese flagship came within 8,500 meters of the enemy ships, he had it change course. The ship was now moving from east to west so as to pass directly in front of the enemy. It was an intentional provocation. The enemy finally panicked. Some vessels rushed to raise anchor, while others tried to turn to the right, belching forth clouds of black smoke, and still others to the left, attempting to flee into the safety of the harbor. There was utter disorder and confusion.

Captain Bubnov of the Russian side left notes on what happened. A bit earlier, when four cruisers acting as a Japanese scouting party came to investigate the situation at the harbor entrance, the Russian small protected cruiser *Boyarin* (3,020 tons) suddenly appeared, sometimes pursuing and sometimes withdrawing. Captain Bubnov writes that "on the Russian side, the all-important commander in chief himself was not with the fleet." Stark had been on board the flagship, but in the midst of it all, he was, oddly, summoned to attend on Viceroy Alexeyev, who wanted "a report on what is happening." Alexeyev was, of course, in his official residence in the town of Port Arthur at the time. It would take a full hour for Vice Admiral Stark to make the round trip from the flagship. Stark left the ship, boarded a launch, and raced to the viceroy's residence after landing in Port Arthur.

Meanwhile, Tōgō raised the battle flag over the *Mikasa*, fired test rounds from the ship's forward 12-inch guns at a distance of 8,000 meters, and landed them all around the group of enemy ships. Then, at a distance of 7,500 meters, Tōgō ordered his entire fleet to fire an artillery barrage. It was nine minutes after noon.

The various gun emplacements that defended Port Arthur like a many-spined porcupine began to roar out their fire, and the Russian fleet in the harbor entrance started to shoot wildly. Among all these, the Dianqi Reef artillery was especially effective in its firing, and the *Mikasa* was immediately hit by three large shells, one of which scraped its mainmast, cutting the flag lines. The other shells injured seven men including a staff officer.

The warships at sea could exchange fire with the artillery in the land fortifications but were ultimately no match for them. That is an iron rule of combat. Tōgō did not want to fight against the fortifications at Port Arthur. Yet, without coming within range of the fortifications' artillery, he could not fire shells against the Russian fleet inside the harbor.

"It's a real problem for us," Chief of Staff Shimamura was always complaining to Saneyuki.

"The enemy fleet will at some point go far into the harbor," Saneyuki always replied. "At that point, we may have to blockade the harbor entrance."

Tōgō, however, would not permit that. A strategy that forced one's men to die showed the incompetence of the strategist; it was not, in fact, a strategy in the real sense. That seemed to be Tōgō's point of view.

The naval battles continued. The Russians' coastal artillery all blasted away, and their fleet too became more active. The Russian land and sea artillery together wrapped Tōgō's fleet in fire and smoke and jets of water; the Japanese side too sent forth clouds of smoke as it fired away. The sea and sky darkened until the fleets of friend and foe became indistinguishable.

The first battle flag that the *Mikasa* raised was soon shot down, but it ran up a new flag at once. That too was torn away by a shell that came in rather high. The battleship *Fuji*, the third vessel in line, also received two hits, and its chief gunner died on the spot. In all, there were twelve dead and wounded on the *Fuji*. The *Shikishima*, the fifth battleship, was hit by one shell that wounded seventeen crewmen, including the chief navigator. The battleship *Hatsuse*, which was bringing up the rear, received two hits, and sixteen men, including its chief navigator, were killed or wounded. Human flesh was stuck to the mast, and the decks were awash with blood. Every ship was in a terrible state.

Nonetheless, Tōgō was unruffled. He led the fleet in a very long single file right past the entrance to the harbor, heading west. After passing just in front of the enemy, each of the ships changed direction one by one and moved southward. By the time the *Mikasa*, in the lead, had moved beyond the range of the enemy's guns, the Combined Fleet's Second Division (made up of armored cruisers), which belonged to the Second Squadron led by Kamimura Hikonojō, was passing just in front of the enemy and began an artillery barrage.

The Russian side too had its brave commanders. Nikolai von Essen, a young commander of German-Russian descent in charge of the small protected cruiser *Novik* (3,080 tons), was known on both sides for his valor and seamanship throughout the war. The seamen serving under him were a group of wild men whom the various ships in the Port Arthur Squadron had found too hard to handle. Von Essen knew how to control these crew members, and the morale on his ship was exceptionally high.

When the *Novik* with von Essen in command left the Russian ranks and suddenly moved in the direction of the Japanese Second Division, the Japanese side was surprised. A small protected cruiser's armor plating was as thin as tin, and it had far more wooden sections than did a protected cruiser. One hit from an enemy shell would put paid to it. Von Essen seemed to have decided to attack in the manner of a Japanese warrior, without helmet or armor, clad only a *fundoshi* loincloth.

Von Essen's aim was accurate, and the Second Division on the Japanese side suffered several severe hits.

"It's like a falcon!" said Matsumoto Arinobu, the captain of the *Yakumo*, the third ship in the Second Division. He was stunned at the ferocity of the *Novik*'s solitary sally.

Though, of course, the *Novik* had the aid of the artillery from the fortifications to the rear, it was no more than a small protected cruiser just over 3,000 tons, while Japan's Second Division, though consisting of cruisers only, was made up of large ships, all close to 10,000 tons. Moreover, there were five ships in all: the flagship *Izumo* in the lead, followed by the *Azuma*, *Yakumo*, *Tokiwa*, and *Iwate*. There was no way the *Novik* could win, and indeed the ships on the Japanese side ignored it and kept lobbing shells at the larger ships that were hiding far beyond the *Novik*.

Only the *Yakumo* decided to attack the *Novik*, ignored by all the others. Its main guns fired away, and the first shell hit the *Novik*'s central section, blowing away the structures on deck, yet, amazingly, the *Novik* didn't falter but continued moving, firing its own guns.

The *Yakumo* grew stubborn, this large ship going after the small Russian ship, which was moving about like a hunting dog, and blasting away at it. But the more stubbornly the *Yakumo* attacked, the fewer hits it scored against the smaller ship. And soon the *Yakumo* slipped past the harbor entrance and moved out of firing range.

Kamimura, commander in chief of the Second Squadron, made the ships under his command turn, following the First Division under the direct command of Tōgō. The ships slowed as they turned, and this gave the Russians an opening. All the fortifications' artillery roared out, and the ships of the Port Arthur Squadron near the harbor entrance increased the rate of their artillery fire as well. The *Yakumo* was hit by one shell and suffered one wounded. Another shell hit the *Azuma*, and its flag was torn away. The *Iwate* was hit by two shells, and ten men, including the chief gunner, were wounded. The Japanese Navy learned from bitter experience the terrible power of Port Arthur's fortifications.

Far to the left, Laotie Hill at the tip of the Liaodong Peninsula showed white against the sky, with no fire from artillery to mar it, but all of the other peaks and shore reefs kept belching forth so much fire that they seemed to turn deep red. In particular, the artillery on Golden Hill and Dianqi Reef inflicted terrible damage.

"In comparison with Port Arthur, taking the fortifications at Santiago blockaded by the American forces was mere child's play," thought a surprised Saneyuki, who was the main strategist for the Japanese side.

In the midst of all this, only the *Novik* continued to dash about. After the Second Division had left, the Third Division next appeared on the scene. It was comprised of the *Chitose* (4,760 tons) as flagship and four protected cruisers. The *Novik* proceeded to attack these as well, joined by the protected cruiser *Askold* (5,905 tons). The joint attack was fierce, and the Third Division faced a crisis: fighting on meant the possible loss of one of its ships.

Tōgō, watching from afar, gave the order to escape. "The Third Division is to move beyond artillery range." Tōgō was always thinking about the coming battle with the Baltic Fleet, and he did not want to lose even one ship until then. The Third Division hurried to escape, and eventually the entire Combined Fleet left the area.

Neither side lost a single ship in this first battle between the main forces of the Japanese and Russian fleets just outside the harbor of Port Arthur. The two sides were too far apart for the artillery to be used to good effect. Also, only when the Japanese fleet passed by the harbor entrance could the battle be joined, and that was only for about one hour. The brevity of the battle reduced the damage to both sides.

More Japanese shells had actually hit their target, but this could not be taken as proof of their superior artillery skills. The Japanese had attacked when the Russian ships were at anchor and not on alert. The Russians could not shift position until they finished lifting anchor and thus provided the Japanese with stable targets, easy to hit.

If we are to grade the Russian side, we have to say that one or two of the cruisers performed very well, while the battleships were all clumsily handled, perhaps because they were commanded by mostly elderly officers. The Russian naval forces did not in general respond forcefully; the army's artillery barrage from the land fortifications was far better. Stoessel had reason to be proud of himself.

"Well, we failed," Akiyama Saneyuki frankly told Shimamura as they sailed away from Port Arthur. The goal of the strategy had been to lure the enemy out, but that had not happened.

The Russians, however, saw that this battle had a remarkably bad effect on their Russian sailors' morale. Viceroy Alexeyev had ordered them "not to go beyond the range of our land artillery." That was why, even though the Russian sailors had fired so many shells, they could not escape the feeling that they had been helplessly pounded by the Japanese side. When the Japanese fleet turned tail and fled, the Russian forces were not able to give chase. This was very damaging to the Russian sailors psychologically.

Pavel Stepanovich Nakhimov, whose name has gone down in Russian naval history as a great admiral, led the Black Sea Fleet in fighting the Turkish fleet during the Crimean War in 1853 and won. Later, he was to be mortally wounded, but the advice he left is famous: "Whenever you find the enemy, you should attack. You should not stop to compare your relative strength and the enemy's." The head of the Russian Navy at Port Arthur forgot this, and, from an excess of prudence in preserving his fleet, forgot too that to cause a loss of morale in one's own men is a far graver matter and inflicts far greater damage than the loss of two or three warships.

Tōgō made the area just outside Inch'ŏn Harbor in Korea his base and took his fleet there. "Since you're faced with an enemy that doesn't want to move," he instructed the assembled commanders of the various divisions, "you're going to need great patience to get them out onto the open seas. You'll also have to bombard them constantly and fiercely."

Two days later, the weather grew worse. Great waves roiled over the ocean. The winds were strong, and it even snowed. In spite of this, the small 375-ton destroyers *Hayatori* and *Asagiri* set out on a difficult voyage through the rough seas, pushing through the Yellow Sea until they reached Port Arthur Harbor. Immediately, they fired torpedoes and then fled back across the Yellow Sea. Later, the Japanese learned that the flagship *Petropavlosk* had been severely damaged, which again weakened the morale of the Russian squadron sitting there in the harbor.

* * *

It had not, in fact, been Akiyama Saneyuki who first strongly suggested the emergency strategy of "blockading Port Arthur," even though he had been a careful witness of the American blockade of Santiago Harbor and had written the scientific report that had amazed the Naval Ministry. He was, in that sense, the only authority in Japan on the special strategy that the Americans had planned and executed at Santiago. The view that "Akiyama really knows about blockades" may have been one small reason for his being selected to be one of the fleet's staff officers. In the event of war with Russia, the navy's first-stage strategy would of course have been a battle over Port Arthur Harbor. There had been talk of plans for "a blocking operation" at the Navy General Staff from early on. This meant sinking several decrepit ships at the entrance to the harbor and physically penning the enemy fleet inside by capping the "mouth of the bottle."

The entrance to the harbor at Port Arthur was very narrow. It was only 273 meters wide, and, since there were shallows on both sides of this channel, a large ship could only leave or enter at the channel's very center, with a width of only 91 meters. The idea was to block that area by sinking five or six old ships side by side there.

Tōgō's vice chief of staff Arima Ryōkitsu and Lieutenant Commander Hirose Takeo, in charge of torpedoes on the battleship *Asahi*, had been insisting since before the war began that "a blockade is the only way to go."

Arima took the lead; he was very good at getting things done. "Stop arguing and start preparing!" he said, and prior to the war, while the fleet was still at Sasebo, he had been making preparations in a semi-official way. Tōgō's attitude to this was always noncommittal. Arima even chose five steamships, prepared the explosives, and packed them on board. He was helped in all this by one of Tōgō's other staff officers, Lieutenant Matsumura Kikuo. Though staff officers, these two intended to command the task force assigned to the mission. Tōgō wasn't happy about that either.

On February 9, Matsumura was wounded on the aft bridge of the *Mikasa* during the first attack on Port Arthur by the Combined Fleet and sent to the naval hospital at Sasebo. Arima, therefore, was in need of an officer to take Matsumura's place. He raised the matter with Hirose, who had been thinking of the same thing for some time and now agreed without raising a single objection.

Saneyuki, however, the sole "authority" on blockades, was doubtful about the idea. Once he understood the full extent of Port Arthur's fortifications, he raised objections. "A blockade was possible at the port of Santiago, but Port Arthur is a different story. It has a thousand times the firing power of Santiago, and, first and foremost, we're dealing with a major Russian fleet, not a Spanish one. If we go ahead with this blockade, some of our men will certainly die." Saneyuki always said that "the best strategy is the least bloody one." So he was cold to the idea of a blockade, but, doubtful though he was, he could not directly oppose a plan that Arima, a staff officer senior to him, was so eager to carry out.

* * *

And yet Saneyuki's ideas seemed to swing back and forth like a pendulum. At times, he thought, "Perhaps a blockade *is* the only thing to do." His indecisiveness on this matter is rather strange, given his resolute character. The staff officers are regarded as the principal planners of wars and battles. They must change their plans moment by moment according to how the fight is going, which changes moment by moment. The task force then has to carry out the plans moment by moment. A good or a bad plan determines the number of men who die carrying it out.

"Strategy is the most terrifying thing of all," Saneyuki often said. He hated bloodshed to a degree that may have made him a bit unsuitable as a military man, and, after the Russo-Japanese War had ended, he declared, "I want to leave the military." He thought of becoming a Buddhist priest so he could devote himself to prayer for the souls of those who had been killed as a result of his strategies. The Naval Ministry hurried to mobilize people who were close to Saneyuki to convince him to stay on, but he wouldn't listen, and some people thought for a time that he had gone mad. At any rate, it would have meant trouble for the Naval Ministry had Saneyuki actually become a priest. If they had gone along with his reasoning on this point, then, every time a war ended, there would be a great rush to the clergy.

Given his dislike of bloodshed, he was not in favor of the blockade strategy, even though he was uniquely expert in that field. "If you want a strategy that depends on luck and the deaths of a large number of your men," he occasionally said outright, "then there's no real need for a strategist."

As an advocate of the blockade strategy from the very beginning, Arima argued, "There is nothing wrong with such a plan if I, as the planner, am willing to put myself in mortal danger by leading the mission—what you could call acting on 'a reason beyond reason.'"

The blockade was finally ordered on February 18, and very careful preparations were made for the operation. As part of these, the commanders of the various task force squads were assembled on board the *Mikasa*.

At the meeting, Saneyuki had some very discouraging things to say. "If midway the Russians discover what we're doing, and heavy shelling begins, I suggest that the squads withdraw and put the mission off till another time."

"Don't talk like that!" Hirose Takeo, who would be leading the task force, stood up to object. "We can't adopt such a weak and negative attitude in this operation. 'If one acts with resolve, even the demons will give way'— that's the attitude to take. Of course the Russians will start heavy shelling. The only way to succeed in this is to push on and push on to the death. If we follow your advice, we'll never make it, no matter how often we try."

In the end, Tōgō made the decision—a compromise. "We'll leave the decision as to whether to come back to base or proceed with the mission to the commanders on the spot." Next was the problem of how to evacuate the task force, and in this Tōgō took the safest course. Each steamship would be accompanied by a torpedo boat that would wait just outside the entrance to the harbor until the mission was completed and then evacuate the task force members. The actual planning of the blockade was assigned to Arima Ryōkitsu and Hirose Takeo.

Five steamships were to be sunk at the harbor entrance: the *Tenshin Maru*, *Hōkoku Maru*, *Jinsen Maru*, *Buyō Maru*, and *Bushū Maru*. Fourteen or fifteen men would be aboard each of these ships. Leaving aside the commanders and chief engineers, a total of sixty-seven men would be needed. Petty officers and below would be recruited from the whole Combined Fleet. In the event, Arima and Hirose were amazed to find that two thousand men applied immediately. Some of them had written their requests to join the task force in their own blood.

"We'll win this war," Hirose told Saneyuki. He pointed out that the officers had put themselves forward for the military when still very young, received excellent treatment, and trained themselves to die in battle, whereas the ordinary sailors had come from purely civilian backgrounds, to use the term commonly employed abroad. They too had volunteered with much enthusiasm, proving that this was a "people's war." Hirose could say this because he knew so much about Russia. He had returned to Japan before the war began, so he didn't know exactly what was happening in Russia now that the war had begun, but he had some idea of how things must be. The people of imperial Russia were not so simpleminded as to rejoice at this foreign invasion, carried out to preserve the tsar's new properties in China. In the cities of Russia, there was already some revolutionary feeling, and the imperial regime itself was in danger. Hirose was aware of all this.

From the two thousand volunteers, sixty-seven men were chosen on the basis of who had the fewest living relatives. At six o'clock in the evening on February 19, Tōgō invited the officers of the blockade task force on board the *Mikasa* for a farewell banquet. Hirose was of course one of the honored guests, and Saneyuki attended as one of those saying farewell.

"Your task will be a hard one." Tōgō rose slowly to his feet and raised a glass of champagne after everyone was seated at the table. He spoke in a low voice. "I am hoping for your complete success." It was quite a long speech for so reticent a man as Tōgō. "I am hoping for your complete success," he had said, but it is doubtful how confident he was in his heart of the chances of success. Even Arima Ryōkitsu concealed strong doubts inside.

The blockade plan was to be carried out at night, and, since they would be working in the dark, their intuitive feel for the situation would determine whether things went well or not. Arima's plan had been to make their approach quickly just before dawn and begin the actual work as the darkness gradually lifted. This meant that they would carry on their mission in sunlight, and every member of the task force would probably die under enemy shelling. But Tōgō had the time of the operation changed so it would be carried out at night. After the job was done, everyone could be picked up safely under cover of darkness. This meant that the chances of the men returning alive from their mission were greatly increased, but the likelihood of success in blowing up the old steamships and blocking the channel was reduced to that same degree.

* * *

It had been decided that Hirose Takeo would command the *Hōkoku Maru* (2,400 tons). The chief engineer would be Kurita Tomitarō, and the crew members would number fourteen in all. This old steamship had already been loaded with rocks and concrete to make sure it would sink. The explosive devices had already been set by another technical expert.

Yashiro Rokurō, whom Hirose and Saneyuki both looked up to as an elder brother figure, commanded the armored cruiser *Asama*, the ship that had attacked the *Varyag* and the *Koriets*.

Yashiro was fond of Hirose. When he learned that Hirose was one of the five commanders of the blockade task force, he immediately dispatched a letter by courier boat to Hirose on the battleship *Asahi*. When Hirose opened the letter, he found this message: "If you should die in this action, you would exemplify the saying, 'He who seeks virtue finds virtue.' The future of our nation will be glorious, without question. You need have no worries; you can die with an easy mind." Yashiro, who was known as "the brave hero of the Japanese Navy," had a fine epistolary style, and after his death a book entitled *Collected Letters of Navy Admiral Yashiro Rokurō* was published, in 1941.

The message to Hirose is simple but has a meaningful background. After the Meiji Restoration, the clan domains were dissolved, the privileges of the samurai class were abolished, and a conscription system was introduced. Thus, men of both samurai and commoner origins entered the military, and for the first time in Japanese history a popular nation-state came to exist, at least formally. Yet in reality the consciousness of being a member of such a nation-state was still amorphous. As a result of the First Sino-Japanese War, such feelings became stronger, but even then soldiers of commoner origin still only faintly sensed a duty to volunteer to serve their country in its time of need.

Then ten years later, the Russo-Japanese War began, and at the very start there was the call for volunteers for the blockade task force. Yashiro assumed there would be no more than about one hundred volunteers, yet some two thousand men came forward. For the first time in post-Restoration Japan, a truly national feeling had emerged as a result of this undertaking—that was Yashiro Rokurō's view.

That was why he wrote, "The future of our nation will be glorious, without question."

Yashiro and Hirose had originally been brought together by their shared love of judo. Later, their mutual study of the Russian language deepened their friendship, and, when both of them were posted to St. Petersburg as military attachés around the same time, they came to regard themselves as closer than brothers. They were similar in temperament, and their shared interest in classical Chinese poetry also must have drawn them together. One day, as they were on their way to the Japanese embassy in St. Petersburg, Yashiro suddenly chanted a line of Chinese poetry rendered into Japanese: "The Great Wall did not keep out the Huns . . . " He then demanded that Hirose turn it into a haiku as they took the next thirty steps. They had not taken more than five or six steps when Hirose turned to Yashiro and recited: "They built a hedge/ not knowing that the robber/ was among their sons." Yashiro was filled with admiration.

While in Russia, Hirose had translated several poems of Pushkin into classical Chinese and had devoted himself to reading Nikolai Gogol's *Taras Bulba*, as well as all the works of A. K. Tolstoy. He was one of the first Japanese to be able to read Russian literature in the original.

Hirose Takeo remained single all his life. When not at sea, he spent most of his time on judo practice. There is no evidence that he played around with geisha or the like while in Kure and Sasebo. It may well be that in the thirty-seven years of his life he never had intimate relations with a woman.

"He was a happy, good-natured man," said Takeshita Yūjirō, his onetime classmate at the Navy Academy, "and very kind to his subordinates, so the ships he was on all had a bright, cheery sort of atmosphere. They performed well too."

Even if Hirose himself made a point of not getting too close to women, he was popular in their circles as is evidenced by the beautiful Ariadna Kovalevskaya's great love for him. She was the daughter of Rear Admiral Count Vladimir Kovalevsky, who had accepted Hirose as one of his closest family friends. Ariadna was a highly literate young woman of St. Petersburg, famed for her intelligence and beauty among the single officers of the Russian Navy. During the nearly five years of Hirose's stay in St. Petersburg, she was unable to think of any man but him. The letters they exchanged show that Hirose too became extraordinarily fond of her. Ariadna would send him poems she had written in Russian, and he would respond with classical Chinese poems, with a Russian translation attached. This exchange of letters, reminiscent of love poems received and sent by ancient Japanese in the eighth-century *Man'yōshū* anthology, has been examined by Shimada Kinji in his *Hirose Takeo in Russia*.

This romantic relationship ended with Hirose's return to Japan, but before noon on the day he set out for Port Arthur on the *Hōkoku Maru* blockade mission, he sat in the commander's room and first wrote a final letter to his beloved Ariadna, whom he thought he would never meet again on this earth. We have no way of knowing what he actually wrote to her. Sent by courier boat to the Combined Fleet and then on via a neutral country's post, it would eventually arrive in St. Petersburg.

Hirose was also much loved by Dr. Pavlov and his family in St. Petersburg. Boris Vilkitsky, a young cadet just graduated from the Naval Academy, was a frequent guest at the Pavlovs', and he looked up to Hirose as an elder brother, calling him "Take-niisan"—Older Brother Take. When the time came for Hirose to return to Japan, he made the following promise to the Russian youth at a farewell party at the Pavlov home: "It might happen at some point in the future that Russia and Japan will have the misfortune to fight each other. Each of us will want to fight to the end with all his strength for his own fatherland, but I want us to remain friends for life, whatever happens. Even if it comes to war, let's keep in touch and make sure we know each other's whereabouts."

And, in fact, Hirose knew what became of young Boris Vilkitsky and where he was. He was later commissioned as a sublieutenant second class and assigned to a battleship. Leaving aside the matter of whether it was Vilkitsky's good fortune or bad, that battleship was the newest and largest in the Russian Navy, the *Tsesarevich* (12,912 tons). Shortly after the sublieutenant second class joined it, the battleship was sent to the Far East and entered the harbor of Port Arthur. This was at the end of the year before the war began. Vilkitsky kept his promise to Hirose and immediately sent a letter to Sasebo, where he thought Hirose was likely to be: "I am in Port Arthur, on board the battleship *Tsesarevich*."

Hirose had read this letter in the torpedo section chief's office aboard the battleship *Asahi*, which was at anchor in Sasebo. With intense emotion, he recalled all those who had been so kind to him when he was in St. Petersburg. He thought particularly of Ariadna, who had been the only woman in his life. Hirose had an excellent memory, and he could recite by heart all of the love poems that Ariadna had sent him. He had been very busy at that time, and he couldn't reply to Sublieutenant Second Class Vilkitsky in Port Arthur just then. Very shortly after that, the war began.

Because the *Tsesarevich* had its hull damaged during that nighttime torpedo attack launched by the Japanese Navy at the very start of the war, it was left stranded in the harbor. Hirose's *Asahi* had participated when, on the ninth, the day after the torpedo attack, the Japanese Combined Fleet had approached the waters outside Port Arthur and, from the great distance of 6,000 meters, fired the massive artillery of its battleships on the Russian fleet near the harbor entrance. He had looked for the *Tsesarevich*, but the battleship *Retvizan*, heavily damaged and listing stranded in front of him, blocked his sight.

Vilkitsky was aboard the newly constructed ship that now sat stranded in the harbor shoals. When the Japanese Combined Fleet approached, the *Tsesarevich*, though run aground, kept up ceaseless fire from its 6-inch guns. What Hirose and Vilkitsky had secretly feared that night in St. Petersburg had now become a reality.

Aboard the *Hōkoku Maru*, Hirose also wrote to Boris Vilkitsky in Port Arthur, and we know the contents of this letter. As Hirose was writing it, Lieutenant Commander Katō Hiroharu of the *Asahi*, who had been with Hirose for a time in Russia, came by, and Hirose told him what he was writing. "I truly regret that we are now engaged in hostilities with your country. Yet, even as each of us does his utmost on behalf of his own nation, there is no change in our personal friendship. I was on board the warship *Asahi* on the ninth and engaged in intense shelling of your country's fleet. Even that seems extraordinary, given our friendship, and now I am in command of the *Hōkoku Maru*, which we plan to use to blockade your harbor. Dear friend, be well!"

This letter too was sent off by courier boat and reached Vilkitsky some months later, via a neutral country.

* * *

The five ships of the blockade task force assembled 20 nautical miles southeast of Round Island at the twilight of February 23. They would all leave from here but pursue their own courses to Port Arthur. The Combined Fleet was also gathered there to see them off. When the time for departure came, a band aboard the *Mikasa* played music, and the crew members aboard each ship of the Combined Fleet gathered on deck to salute and give three cheers of "Banzai!"

The First Destroyer Division, which would act as defense for the five steamships, took the lead, while the Fourteenth Torpedo Boat Division, comprised of four torpedo boats including the *Chidori*, served as a defensive group to the right of the five steamers, and the Ninth Torpedo Boat Division followed. The sun went down and the moon, waxing, rose. Compared to the previous day, which had been so rough and windy, the sea was calm. With Arima Ryōkitsu on board, the *Tenshin Maru* was the first of the five ships, followed by Hirose's *Hōkoku Maru*, the *Jinsen Maru*, the *Buyō Maru*, and the *Bushū Maru*.

Hirose had his evening meal on the bridge. The secret ocean charts and other important documents had already been burned, and there was nothing particular to do after dinner.

"What do you think, Kurita?" asked Hirose. "I'd like to write something to commemorate this . . . " Only Hirose himself, however, knew what he really meant. He wanted to wrap a large piece of cloth over the bridge and paint some words on it.

"What is there to commemorate?" wondered Kurita, but he helped Hirose to do what he wanted. What Hirose wrote in large letters on the cloth was a line in Russian, which the two of them wrapped around the bridge. When the ship was sunk at the harbor entrance, probably only the bridge would appear above the waterline, and the Russians would read it.

"What did you write?" asked Senior Engineer Kurita. As Kurita recalled in later years, the expression on Hirose's face was a mixture of pleasure and a strange embarrassment. The original is of course no longer extant, but, according to what Hirose said to Kurita at the time, the meaning was "This is Hirose Takeo of Japan. I've come to blockade your harbor. But this is only the first time—I may be back many times after this."

After the *Hōkoku Maru* sank, the Russians read this message. Captain Bubnov recorded the message as follows: "Respected Gentlemen of the Russian Navy, please remember me—Lieutenant Hirose Takeo of the Japanese Navy. I have come here aboard the *Hōkoku Maru*. I intend to come several times again!"

Hirose wrote this because he assumed that many of his acquaintances from St. Petersburg would see it. Moreover, he probably assumed that the news of this inscription, making its way to St. Petersburg, would serve as a final word of farewell to his Ariadna as well.

* * *

This came to be called the first blocking operation. It didn't produce much in the way of results. The moon had set at about thirty minutes after midnight, and the sea was very dark. In place of the moonlight, the searchlights of the enemy began to flash here and there. The searchlights from the gun emplacements on Golden, Chengtou, and Baiyin hills swept over the surface of the water outside the harbor entrance, denying access to even the tiniest thing.

"When the glare of the many searchlights that had been sweeping the waters suddenly focused on one spot," Aleksandr Stepanov wrote in *Port Arthur*, "our side discovered a large steamship there. It was creeping along the coast just under Laotie Hill, making for the harbor entrance." This steamship was the *Tenshin Maru*. The beams from numerous searchlights fastened on the *Tenshin Maru*, and shells rained down on the helpless victim from all the gun emplacements. The steamship's decks became a living hell, with shells bursting all around and explosions on board from direct hits. The glare from the searchlights blinded the pilots of the ship, and they didn't know where they should be heading. Thus, they were unable to reach the harbor entrance, with the prow of the steamship running up against the rocky reef beneath Laotie Hill, still far from their goal. They became stranded there. Arima believed that their situation was hopeless. It was rather pointless, but he decided to blow the ship up then and there.

Then the other steamships started to arrive. "To starboard, to starboard!" Arima shouted to them from the *Tenshin Maru*'s deck. Hirose's *Hōkoku Maru* turned sharply to the right, and the *Jinsen Maru* did so as well. The gun emplacements roared out and concentrated their fire on both the *Hōkoku Maru* and the *Jinsen Maru*. The *Hōkoku Maru* alone succeeded in getting just below the lighthouse at the harbor entrance, where it ran aground but was far from being able to block the channel. The *Jinsen Maru*, which was following Hirose's ship, turned too sharply to the right and lost its way for a time, ultimately sinking at a point rather distant from the harbor entrance.

Next came the *Buyō Maru* under the command of Lieutenant Masaki Yoshimoto. It struggled forward under a hail of shells until it saw a ship that had run aground just ahead. This was the lead ship the *Tenshin Maru*. The commander thought, mistakenly, that they may have arrived at the entrance to the harbor. Soon he realized his error and that the *Tenshin Maru* had become stranded while attempting to move forward. As the *Buyō Maru* moved past the other ship, the final ship in the convoy, the *Bushū Maru*, came up very unsteadily from behind. Helm broken by an enemy shell, it could no longer control its course. But Masaki was unaware of his sister ship's true condition. The *Bushū Maru* could no longer keep to a course, so it blew itself up near the western entrance of the harbor.

"That must be the entrance to the harbor proper," Masaki wrongly concluded. Apart from this misapprehension, his management of the situation was very cool and composed. He brought his ship up alongside the *Bushū Maru* and halted there. Then he opened the Kingston valves and sank his own ship.

"To prepare five unarmed steamships and send them to blockade an enemy port is an unprecedented measure. Its effectiveness is of course not to be judged solely on what was achieved." Chief of the Navy General Staff Itō Sukeyuki sent this telegram of congratulations to Tōgō after the event.

* * *

This first attempt at blockade ended essentially in failure, but the injuries among the crew were unexpectedly light. Tōgō was pleased at this. He accepted Arima Ryōkitsu's request via Chief of Staff Shimamura to "continue the attempts." Imperial General Headquarters in Tokyo also took concrete steps to support this decision and immediately began preparing more steamships for the blockade. The vessels were dilapidated and so cost very little. What did cost money was loading them with rocks and cement, and fitting them with explosive devices. Even this represented a notable financial burden given Japan's wartime fiscal conditions.

Four ships were chosen for the second attempt. The commanders were the same as the first time. The policy was not to permit ordinary crew members to take such a risk a second time, whereas officers could go any number of times. The commander in chief of the squad was Arima Ryōkitsu; the other commanders were Hirose Takeo, Saitō Shichigorō, and Masaki Yoshimoto.

"The enemy will be prepared this time," Saneyuki said to Hirose, who was visiting the *Mikasa*. It wouldn't be like the first time, when the other side was caught unawares. "And Vice Admiral Makarov should soon be taking charge at Port Arthur. The morale of the men there will have received a tremendous boost."

Vice Admiral Stepan Osipovich Makarov could be called the greatest treasure of the Russian Navy. He was a true Slav, and what made him so exceptional a figure in the Russian Navy was that he was not of aristocratic background but a commoner. He rose from the ranks of sailors during the navy's sailing ship days but he was not a simple, practical man of the sort that is often seen among those who rise from the ranks. On the contrary, no other European navy could boast so great a theorist as he. His method was to abstract a theory from reality, then return to the reality to rework the theory, and to repeat this process over and over until an appropriate system could be evolved. His *On Strategy* was world famous, and Saneyuki had read it thoroughly in his student days. Makarov's works were not limited to naval strategy, by the way; he wrote on oceanography and the science of shipbuilding as well. He may well be termed the most able scholar that Russia had at the time.

In addition, this scholar was exceedingly muscular in build, quicker than anyone in climbing a mast when he was young. He was the type of man who, if asked, could handle every kind of work aboard ship, from stoker to commander in chief. Due to this and to his commoner origins, he was immensely popular with the petty officers and seamen. He assumed command at Port Arthur on March 8, replacing Commander Stark. He was an extremely dynamic head of command, and the morale of the Port Arthur Squadron rose to an astonishing degree with his appointment.

Hirose had met Makarov, then serving as chief of the naval station at Kronstadt. "He was a very energetic old man," Hirose told Saneyuki. That Hirose should now be taking the blockships to Port Arthur, which was being guarded by Vice Admiral Makarov, a man he knew, was in itself a strange twist of fate. Still more strange was the fact that Makarov knew exactly the day Hirose would come, and how many ships he would bring with him for the second blockade.

The term, *Ro-tan*, "Russian spy," was often heard in Japan at that time. Russian spies were apparently very active in Tokyo and Sasebo, though there was little concrete evidence even after the war. Such information networks had kept Port Arthur informed about the attempt at a second blockade. All the Port Arthur authorities had to do was lie in wait for it. Makarov did everything possible to prepare. For example, in order to prevent the blockships from approaching the harbor entrance, the Russians themselves sank steamships in the area where the Japanese ships seemed likely to come. Makarov himself oversaw the operation on the spot, and the *Hailar* and

Harbin were sunk there. Mines were also laid, and two destroyer divisions were put in place to prevent any blockade.

The Japanese side, learning from its earlier failure, installed two machine guns on the foredecks of each blockship to offer resistance to any enemy destroyers that might obstruct the Japanese vessels around the harbor entrance.

March 24 was set as the date of departure from the Japanese fleet's base area, but the whole area was engulfed in thick fog, the wind was fierce, and the waves high on that day, so the departure was postponed. Saneyuki went to see Hirose on board the *Fukui Maru* that day. Hirose was waiting for him in the ship's "saloon," by the stove.

"If you're overwhelmed by enemy fire, come right back." Saneyuki warmed himself by the stove and repeated what he had already advised Hirose.

"That's what you keep telling me," Hirose answered. "A strike force is different from a strategic planner—we mustn't expect to come back alive. The key to victory is to press on, no matter what."

At half past six in the evening on March 26, the four blockships left the base area. At two in the morning on the twenty-seventh, they went into a single-line formation as soon as they came just south of Laotie Hill, with the *Chiyo Maru* in the lead, followed by the *Fukui Maru*, *Yahiko Maru*, and *Yoneyama Maru*. They then proceeded toward the Port Arthur Harbor entrance. The night fog was rather heavy and made the moonlight hazy. Conditions were good for setting up the blockade. Each of the ships "pressed on," to use Hirose's words.

At half past three in the morning, the searchlights of the Port Arthur fortifications discovered the *Chiyo Maru* in the lead. The sky and sea were enveloped in flashes of light and the roar of artillery.

"We knew of this enemy attack several days beforehand," a Russian history of the war relates. "Two sentry ships were watching the sea, while maintaining constant contact with the artillery on land. At ten minutes after two in the morning"—a time different from that given by the Japanese side—"our artillery's searchlights discovered ships approaching, raising waves as they moved over the dark sea. The *Chiyo Maru* was in the lead, followed at some distance by the other three vessels in a single-line formation. The enemy ships were able to establish a formation and maintain their progress in the correct direction despite the darkness of the night. Our land artillery and the various ships all rained intense fire on the Japanese, but the damage was slight, and the enemy ships kept coming on, maintaining the same course."

The first ship, under Arima's command, was blinded by the constant glare of the Russian searchlights, as it had been on the first attempt, and once again lost its sense of where the harbor entrance actually was. Arima's ship veered too far to the right of the harbor entrance, entering a channel near the shore beneath Golden Hill. His ship cast anchor with its prow landward, then blew itself up, and sank.

Hirose, watching this from the second ship, the *Fukui Maru*, believed that this had occurred at the harbor entrance. He moved his ship up to the left of the *Chiyo Maru* and was trying to cast anchor when a Russian destroyer approached and launched a torpedo. It made a direct hit on the Japanese ship's prow, causing a huge explosion and ripping open the hull. At once, water poured in, and the *Fukui Maru* began to sink.

Nonetheless, the Japanese crew was able to escape in time. They lowered a lifeboat, as had been planned. The crew had been told to assemble on the aft deck after the operation was finished, and they did so. According to Senior Engineer Kurita Tomitarō's later account, Hirose went around checking all relevant areas of the ship and then, arriving at the assembly point last of all, shouted in his lively, rather high-pitched voice, "Okay, okay—is everyone here?" and ordered them to call out their numbers. Some men were already in the lifeboat. Checking their numbers, it became clear that Superior Petty Officer Sugino was missing. He had been working on the foredeck when the explosion occurred.

"Sugino! Sugino!" shouted Hirose as he ran about the upper deck with the sailors who had not yet evacuated.

Shells large and small were exploding around them, and the enemy searchlights revealed everything. It was a horrific sight, not of this world.

Everyone returned to the aft deck and started to search again. Hirose asked each of the crewmen, but none had seen Sugino in the course of the mission.

"Superior Petty Officer Sugino must have been blown off the ship when the enemy torpedo hit us." Only Petty Officer Iimure Nakanosuke ventured to speculate. But that was merely a surmise.

"Sugino! Sugino!" Shouting, Hirose set off on a third search for Sugino. He ran toward the foredeck. As Hirose's voice grew distant, there seemed less and less hope, Kurita said later. Hirose did not return for a long time. It seems he went into the hull to look for the missing petty officer. By the time he came back, the water was at everyone's feet.

"We're sinking!" Kurita could not stop himself from exclaiming.

Hirose at last gave up on Sugino and ordered the explosives to be prepared. The whole crew shifted to the lifeboats. The long explosive fuse extended far, even to the lifeboat. The lifeboat moved away from the ship, and, when it was about four or five boat-lengths away, Hirose himself pressed the switch. The aft portion of the ship was blown up splendidly.

All that was left to them was to keep rowing the lifeboat. Hirose sat on the rearmost portion of the right gunwale wearing a mantle on top of his overcoat, shouting encouragement to the crew members, some nearly immobilized by sheer terror. "Look me in the face, all of you! Look at me, and row!" The enemy searchlights continued to fix on the lifeboat. Both shells and bullets fell all around them, seeming to bring the waters to a boil.

Just then Hirose vanished. A huge shell flew across the lifeboat, sweeping him away. It happened so quickly that even Iimure, who was sitting next to him, holding the tiller, didn't notice.

When news of Hirose's death reached St. Petersburg, his beloved Ariadna, though the daughter of a count and rear admiral in the Russian Navy, went into deep mourning, wearing black for the Japanese naval officer whom she had hoped to marry.

8

THE ARMY

Meanwhile, the Japanese Army had been inactive. Only Kigoshi's brigade, which left Sasebo at the beginning of the war, had landed at Inch'ŏn under the protection of one part of the Combined Fleet and then advanced to Hansŏng. This ought properly to be called the "Korea garrison" and was more for diplomatic use than a fighting force. The diplomatic "other" in this case was Korea.

The Korean government had seen the massive military force of the Russian Army stationed on the Manchurian–Korean border and felt it had to show as much goodwill toward Russia as possible. Yet Korea could not cold shoulder Japan either and therefore declared an attitude of "neutrality" toward the war that was just beginning. Japan, however, had determined on a strategy of forming a Japanese-Korean alliance, even through forceful pressure, so as to move the war against Russia in a direction beneficial to itself. Japan thus tried to exert pressure on the Korean government through military force and so at the very beginning of the war had undertaken this risky sea transport of the brigade, headed by Major General Kigoshi Yasutsuna, which advanced on Hansŏng.

Korea was in a position where it could not but agree to a Japanese-Korean alliance when the Japanese Army advanced. Then the main force of the Twelfth Division (from Kokura) landed in Korea. This too could be said to have been a diplomatic ploy on Japan's part.

In other words, the main force of the Japanese Army as a whole was still not active. Sending a large force would require a massive number of transport ships, and such a massive sea transport would be very risky. That was why the navy was desperately trying to hammer away at the Russian fleet inside Port Arthur.

The army's strategy was as follows: first, two "armies" would be formed. The First Army would land in Korea and would mount as strong an attack as possible on the Russian Army that was encamped on the border between Korea and Manchuria. Then the Second Army would land on the Liaodong Peninsula and immediately proceed north toward central Manchuria. Teaming up with the First Army coming from Korea, it would defeat the Russian main force in a great battle on the Liaoyang plain. That was the strategy. Kodama Gentarō, who had created this plan, insisted it was the only way forward.

The enemy's main force was at Liaoyang. This was the First Siberian Army Corps, led by General Linevich, by itself equal in military power to the combined First and Second armies that formed the main force of Japan's field army. Russia was also in the process of enlarging the Second Siberian Army Corps, a newly established army headed by General Aleksandr Bilderling in Harbin in northern Manchuria. In order to complete this army's enlargement, the Trans-Siberian Railway was used to full capacity, sending troops, guns, and munitions to Manchuria.

Kodama knew that if he did not quickly advance on Liaoyang and smash Linevich's army there, he would have to face the enemy's two huge armies with a force half their size. The battle at Liaoyang would thus decide the outcome of the Russo-Japanese War itself.

* * *

Japan's First Army, heading for the Yalu River, fought the first land battle of the Russo-Japanese War. Since the view was that "a very bold commander would be best," General Kuroki Tamemoto was selected. He was originally from the Satsuma domain and had participated in the Boshin War from the opening battle of Fushimi in Kyoto to the fighting in northern Honshu. He had never attended any military college, but he had the qualities typical of a canny leader. In biding his time during a war, he was like an experienced boatman who can judge the weather from the ebb and flow of the tides— he had exceptional talent of that sort. He was reticent in speech, and his ruddy face showed little emotion; he was never excitable, even in wartime.

Kuroki's First Army came together in Hiroshima at the beginning of March. When they were about to leave port, Kuroki called the officers together and made a speech, something unusual for him. "Gentlemen, you and I are now the spearhead of the Japanese Army . . . The soldiers of the Yamato race are moving into a struggle against a Slavic people. This is an unprecedented action, an epoch-making event. The nations of the world are pricking up their ears, eager to hear what will happen. Gentlemen, let not a single act of ours be base or mean!"

The Meiji Restoration was the result of external pressure from the Great Powers. Kuroki Tamemoto had rallied to the cry "Expel the Barbarians!" toward the end of the shogunate and had then passed through the battles that led to the Restoration. He could not but have felt strong emotion when he spoke those words.

Ōyama and Kodama's choice of leaders in the war against the Russians could hardly have been better. As chief of staff for Kuroki, the former samurai who had become a "skilled craftsman of war," they appointed Major General Fujii Shigeta, a native of Hyōgo Prefecture, who was in the first graduating class at the Army Staff College and had studied under Meckel. They, thus made sure that there would be the best possible combination of leaders for waging a modern war.

As their assignment, Kuroki's army was to "beat the enemy at the Yalu River and then enter Manchuria." It was essential, as Kuroki said in his speech, to smash the enemy as thoroughly as possible in this, the first land battle of the war, and thus establish Japan's credibility among other nations. The Japanese government was selling bonds in London at the time, to raise funds for the war. But since almost everyone believed that Japan would lose to Russia, there were very few buyers. In order to make the bonds more attractive, Japan had to win this first battle. In that sense, Kuroki's army had to play not only a military but also a major diplomatic and fiscal role in this war.

Because of this, Imperial General Headquarters not only took the greatest care with the strategic planning for Kuroki's army but also supplied it with more than enough artillery and shells, most unusually for the Japanese Army at the time. Throughout the Russo-Japanese War, there were too few troops available on the Japanese side in virtually every battle, so that "the few had to fight against the many." But in the case of Kuroki's First Army in the battle over the crossing of the Yalu River, General Headquarters managed to supply a force of forty thousand Japanese troops against the Russian force of twenty thousand. Kuroki's army left the port of Hiroshima in good order beginning on March 8, heading for the various landing points in western Korea. Since the Combined Fleet was using all its resources to block the harbor at Port Arthur, the Russian fleet never made an appearance on the high seas, and the troop transports were carried out without any problems.

* * *

The Yalu River flows along the border of Manchuria and Korea for a distance of 900 kilometers. Known in ancient Japan as the "Arinare River," it has played an important part in the history of East Asia since ancient times.

Kuroki's First Army, while repelling small enemy units on the way, moved into position on the left bank of the Yalu River (the Korean side) by around April 20.

"I realized there would be at least two or three fierce battles in northern Korea, but I did not expect what actually happened," Kuroki later recalled.

The Russian policy was to retreat and then guard their new positions. All the troops that had been stationed in northern Korea were withdrawn and concentrated in encampments on the right bank of the Yalu River (the Manchurian side). Only cavalry patrols were left to scout the area in the north of Korea. They belonged to the cavalry brigade headed by the famous Major General Pavel Ivanovich Mishchenko. Their movements were swift and deft, as befitted the Russian cavalry, said to be the best in the world. The Japanese Army felt as if they were watching birds in flight and could not lay a finger on them.

Mishchenko, however, had been warned by General Kuropatkin, the commander in chief of the Manchurian Army: "Don't take any chances and don't go too deeply into Japanese-held territory." In addition, Mishchenko had been put under other restrictions by General Linevich, who was his immediate superior.

But then a reprimand came from Viceroy Alexeyev in Port Arthur, who was at the time engaged in a power struggle with Kuropatkin. "Running away is all you know how to do! Why don't you strike a blow against the Japanese cavalry?"

Mishchenko was thrown into utter confusion. In the end, he withdrew to the Manchurian side of the Yalu River, having accomplished at least one thing: extremely swift and accurate observations of the Japanese Army's situation. The Russian encampment on the Manchurian bank of the Yalu centered on an artillery emplacement at Jiuliancheng, extending to the left all the way to Shuikouzhen and to the right as far as the river mouth in Andong County. Their aim was to prevent Kuroki's army from crossing the Yalu. Probably the first decisive battle of the Russo-Japanese War would be fought over this attempted crossing.

There was no bridge over the Yalu River. The Japanese would have to build one, employing their engineering corps. Steel pontoon boats, which Captain Meckel had taught them about back in 1886, were now used for the first time. The Twelfth Engineer Battalion was to build a 500-meter-long bridge within five hours at night, right in front of the enemy. First, they had to measure the width of the river, and their way of doing so was very primitive indeed.

Sergeant Koga and the two superior privates who were his assistants, attached a narrow piece of rope to their waists, jumped into the icy stream formed by the melted mountain snow from Paektusan, and swam across to the opposite bank, where the enemy was. This was how they planned to measure the width of the river! But the water was so icy cold that Sergeant Koga fainted, his body floating to the surface in full sight of the enemy. Measurement became impossible. The military observers from other countries who were on the spot were amazed and disgusted by the "barbarity" of the Japanese, seeing no bravery in such acts.

On April 30, the Twelfth Division started to cross the river. Kuroki's army aided the embattled crossing by shelling the enemy encampment with the largest artillery pieces it had, and, by the time the division had reached the other bank, the Russian Army had fled.

* * *

A cardinal rule of strategy is not to use deceitful tricks and wiles. The Japanese have always preferred a strategy that has a small force making free use of various ingenious methods to fool and ultimately destroy a large army, and a master of that sort of strategy would gain a name as a great general. Minamoto no Yoshitsune's sudden attack at Hiyodorigoe and Kusunoki Masashige's holing-up in the Chihaya Castle are typical examples of the kinds of strategy Japanese tend to prefer.

However, gathering troops and firepower double that of the enemy forces on the planned battlefield and thus overwhelming them, as Oda Nobunaga and Napoleon Bonaparte both did, is the basic grand principle of strategy. Even when faced with the difficult problem of gathering a limited amount of forces and firepower for a major, decisive battle, a great general can carry on all sorts of negotiations, internally and externally, and obtain enough forces and firepower in amazing ways. For the rest, there is the well-known adage "A great army needs no set strategy." One must just carry on the battle.

The historians and the common people of the Tokugawa period preferred the ways of Kusunoki Masashige and Minamoto no Yoshitsune, and that tradition was maintained for a very long time. Even the military leaders of the Shōwa period were ruled by this sort of "amateurs' taste," though they themselves were specialists in military matters. They created a strange, peculiarly Japanese philosophy of the military, which they themselves believed in and which formed the basis of the war against the United States.

Japan's military philosophy at the time of the Russo-Japanese War, however, was utterly different from those later attitudes. Throughout the war, Japan had to struggle very hard, hampered by a lack of troops and munitions. Even so, in principle, it always tried to be equal or superior to the enemy in numbers. In the case of the navy, Japan attempted to surpass the enemy in both quantity and quality, and did in fact succeed in doing so.

The battle over the crossing of the Yalu River, the first land battle of the Russo-Japanese War, was fought on the basis of an extremely orthodox type of strategic thinking, for the reasons mentioned above. Kuroki's army was very amply supplied with everything it needed and was able to crush the Russian Army, for the most part because of superior artillery. The attack on Jiuliancheng saw them making use of these strengths. This Russian Army encampment in defense of the Yalu River could not perhaps be termed a fort, but it had a large-scale artillery force. Kuroki's army, however, had prepared twenty huge 12-centimeter howitzers. Advancing quietly during the night, it lobbed an almost infinite number of shells at the Russian camp for several hours starting at dawn, smashing both the enemy's artillery and their will to fight. The Russian Army then abandoned Jiuliancheng.

The news that the Japanese "had in a single day pushed across the Yalu River and also smashed the Russian camp at Jiuliancheng" flashed around the world, resulting in an obvious improvement in sales of Japan's bonds to foreign countries, which the government had been counting on. The view that "You won't lose by buying Japanese government bonds" spread as a result of this overwhelming victory in the first land battle.

"It's not only our forces," said Fujii Shigeta, chief of staff of Kuroki's army. "Good fortune is with us too. During the crossing of the Yalu, it looked as if it was about to rain. If that had happened, the river's water level would have risen, the speed of the current would have increased, and that flimsy bridge we built would have been washed away. Our whole battle plan would have been ruined. Fortunately for us, it didn't rain during our crossing, but when we'd finished crossing over, a very heavy rain started to fall."

* * *

At the start of the war, Akiyama Yoshifuru was forty-six and the head of the First Cavalry Brigade at Narashino in Chiba Prefecture. He was a major general in the Japanese Army. The war began with the navy's struggle for control of the seas; the army had to wait for a while. When Kuroki's First Army landed on the Korean Peninsula, Yoshifuru's cavalry brigade played no part in that. They continued to wait out wintry days at Narashino. His brigade expected to be attached to the Second Army in preparation for a decisive battle on the Manchurian plains.

"We'll be mobilized in early summer, most likely," thought Yoshifuru.

On February 20, he sent a letter to his younger brother Saneyuki on the *Mikasa*, now in a combat area on the high seas. It was a letter of encouragement, almost like a last will and testament, which opened with the following words: "The navy's successive victories have driven the people mad with joy. The army's advance has been delayed by icy conditions, but there will be a gradual deployment, and after a few months there should be a great, decisive battle. The date of my departure has not yet been set, but since I expect to participate in the battles north of the Liaodong Peninsula, it should be around May."

Yoshifuru also gives advice to Saneyuki, who was one of Tōgō Heihachirō's staff officers, as to what a staff officer should remember. Yoshifuru's unsparingly preachy tone here is exactly the same as the one he adopted when Saneyuki came to Tokyo from Matsuyama to enter the Preparatory School. Saneyuki, who tended to ignore the opinions of others, may have needed a brother like Yoshifuru, who would admonish him in this way. And, in fact, Saneyuki would listen with childlike meekness to Yoshifuru and to him alone.

"It's the duty of a staff officer," Yoshifuru continued, "to act adroitly as a kind of lubricant between those above and those below, so that everything goes smoothly. You must never try to stand out."

If we look at Saneyuki's future career, it is obvious that he took to heart his brother's warning against taking credit for himself. Others within the navy were always the ones who said that Akiyama Saneyuki had managed the battle of Tsushima. Saneyuki himself never made such a claim.

Continuing in the manner of a last will and testament, Yoshifuru writes something very important: "A nation's decline always starts with the corruption of its upper classes." Leaving aside the question of how to define "upper classes," we may say that in the Japan of those days, the families of majors in the army and lieutenant commanders in the navy and above belonged to the upper classes. This is particularly true if we ignore the issue of salary, since sometimes officers got less money but still were of the upper classes. Yoshifuru writes on the assumption that he and Saneyuki belong to those privileged classes. "I have felt for a long time that I ought soon to withdraw from this society and retire." In other words, becoming a major general was a considerable honor, and he ought not to aim for something greater than this. This would seem to be his meaning. To quote his original wording: "Our family and clan have brought benefit to the nation. Casting aside thoughts of fame and profit, I should quickly begin a life of retirement." Yoshifuru was saying that the whole family should try to benefit the nation and not seek fame or profit as a result of what they have done—a most romantic view in an age when the nation was the highest good and the very font of romantic ideas. "My wish to retire cannot be acted on because of the present war."

He concluded with the words: "To achieve death with honor on the battlefield is the highest happiness for a man."

* * *

Yoshifuru belonged to the Second Army, and, on March 15, over a month after the war began, its command structure became clear. The army's commander in chief Oku Yasukata had been a retainer of the former Kokura domain. Like the commander of the Eighth Division Tatsumi Naobumi (from the Kuwana domain), Oku had fought on the side of the shogunate, since his domain had remained loyal to the Tokugawa regime at the end of the Tokugawa period. Both Oku and Tatsumi were peerless masters of the art of war, which was no doubt the reason they were able to associate themselves with the Satsuma-Chōshū group that took control of the new government in Tokyo, even though they were from domains that had fought for the old regime.

From his youth, when Oku had been a major in the Meiji government army during the Satsuma Rebellion, he had shown a remarkable passion for keeping his own accomplishments hidden, even in official documents. Thus, people in the army itself knew almost nothing about the details of what he had done. Still, "everything will go well if Oku is there" became a widely accepted notion on any given battlefield. In his refusal to dramatize his own words, actions, and his very self, he stood in contrast to Nogi Maresuke, the commander in chief of the Third Army, who was a native of Chōshū. Nogi was not self-promoting, but everything he did became somehow dramatic, while Oku rendered his own accomplishments invisible, like smoke that drifts away unnoticed. The army employed Oku for the sudden advance into Manchuria—the most orthodox aspect of its strategy—because it had high regard for his orthodox mastery of warfare and also for his temperament, which was smoother and less difficult than either Kuroki's or Nogi's.

Three divisions and two brigades belonged to the Second Army: the First Division (Tokyo), the Third Division (Nagoya), the Fourth Division (Osaka), the First Field Artillery Brigade, and the First Cavalry Brigade. To complete the transport and landing of this great military force would perhaps take more than forty days.

Although included among these sections, Yoshifuru's First Cavalry Brigade was mobilized slightly later than the others, for transport and other reasons. That was why Yoshifuru and his men were still in Narashino, as the Second Army began to assemble in Hiroshima, the port chosen for dispatch of the troops going to the front.

Around this time, reports from the First Army, which had battled its way across the Yalu River, began to pour in. "What about the cavalry?" was the matter of greatest interest to the cavalry officers at Narashino. They knew that Mishchenko's cavalry brigade had divided into smaller units directly in front of the First Army and shown great skill and deftness in their performance as a cavalry. The First Army had been passive in its use of its own cavalry, ignoring Yoshifuru's constant urgings to "use the cavalry as a single unit under the direct supervision of the army." To the contrary, the First Army divided the cavalry among the several divisions, employing sections of it separately. Moreover, neither the army nor the divisions were accustomed to using the cavalry and so were incapable of taking advantage of its particular strengths. Thus, the brilliant work of the enemy's Cossack cavalry under Mishchenko stood out all the more.

* * *

After pushing across the Yalu, the First Army encountered the Russian Cossacks for the first time. It seemed that whenever the Japanese cavalry came up against the Russian cavalry, the Japanese side was driven back and scattered. Of course, at this stage, we are speaking of skirmishes between small scouting parties; a major cavalry battle was yet to come.

Major General Shibuya Ariaki headed the Quartermaster Corps of the First Army and was quite a senior officer in comparison with Yoshifuru and his colleagues. He knew a little about the cavalry, so he sent critical comments from the front line on the Japanese cavalry's perceived "weakness." "The Japanese cavalry scouts are always driven back by the Russian scouts because the Russian cavalry scouts are a stronger military force than ours. Taking a lesson in tactics from this, our scouts too ought to greatly increase their strength."

Yoshifuru went to the General Staff Office to point out the mistakes in Shibuya's idea. "You absolutely must not take this as a lesson in tactics," he also told the officers under his command and then went on to describe how the Japanese cavalry should conduct themselves in battle against the Russians. "If you compare their cavalry's military strength with ours, of course we are far weaker. That's why it's pointless to try to increase the strength of our scouting parties to compete with the enemy. The real job of a scouting party is to find out about the enemy's situation, not to fight. Scouts should avoid pointless battles. If they encounter a superior enemy, they should take evasive action at once. Therefore, it's actually better if our scouting parties are weaker than the enemy's. The Russians, taking advantage of their cavalry's abundant strength, are building up separate scouting parties. That's actually to our advantage! They are scattering their forces while hardly being aware of doing so, and this is their great weakness. We ought to limit the strength of our scouting parties and have them do nothing but surveillance. At the same time, we should strengthen the main force of our cavalry as much as possible. Then, when it comes to a battle of the two cavalries' main forces, we will be sure to gain the victory."

This view of Yoshifuru's became the basic way of thinking about the use of Japan's cavalry in the Russo-Japanese War.

The mobilization order for Yoshifuru's First Cavalry Brigade came on April 9. The brigade left Narashino on the twenty-ninth and thirtieth. Yoshifuru did not take his army sword with him, just as he had not during the First Sino-Japanese War. He wore only a ceremonial sword, used for training exercises. Also hanging from his waist was a map pouch, but all it contained was a pencil, two or three maps, and a sake cup, the same as when he went on ordinary military exercises. An adjutant asked him why he didn't have his army sword with him, and Yoshifuru responded with only a laugh. "My army sword is the Japanese cavalry that I have worked so hard at polishing!" he would probably have replied if pressed.

The brigade gathered at Hiroshima and embarked from the port of Ujina on May 18.

* * *

The Second Army's mission was to occupy the area around Jinzhou and Dalian. They were to let be Port Arthur, and take the area around Dalian Harbor, midway along. They were to build a major base there for future advances, securing a place where supplies could be unloaded, and then proceed northward for a decisive battle with the enemy army on the Manchurian plains. That was the strategic plan.

The landing was carried off easily. The key people formulating the Russian strategy had sensed early on that "the Japanese Army would land on the Liaodong Peninsula." Of course, the Russian Army should have built a beachhead defense to prevent the Japanese Army's landing. It would only be common sense strategically to try to kill at least half of the landing army right there on the shore. At the time we are describing, however, the strategy of "annihilation on the shore" was unknown, and it did not occur to the Russians to attempt such a thing. The Russian Army's strong points were defensive action relying on fortifications and very large-scale battles on broad plains.

Yet another reason the Russian Army in Manchuria did not think of this strategy was the notion that such things should be left to the Port Arthur Squadron. The point of stationing such a force, equal in strength to the Japanese Combined Fleet, in Port Arthur was so that if war broke out, the Port Arthur Squadron could be active in the seas near Japan and make it impossible for Japan to transport troops for a landing on the continent. The Port Arthur Squadron, however, was penned up in the harbor by Tōgō; and, though a decisive battle on the seas outside the harbor was possible, the squadron chose to remain penned in, well protected by the artillery in the Port Arthur fortifications.

At any rate, the Russian Manchurian Army should not have allowed the Japanese Army to land on the Liaodong Peninsula so easily. Kuropatkin had, of course, given the matter some thought. He may not have considered an attempt at "annihilation on the shore," but he did send a large-scale field army to the area where the landing was anticipated and, using artillery fire, tried to prevent the landing.

The First Army had, however, already landed in Korea and was trying to push across the Yalu River. "The battle to be fought at the Yalu River," Viceroy Alexeyev insisted, "is the first land battle in the Russo-Japanese War. If we don't send a large force from Manchuria and annihilate the Japanese there, it will reflect on the honor of the Russian Empire."

Kuropatkin insisted on just the opposite strategy. "Your Excellency has a naval background, and army strategy is outside your area of expertise, you must forgive me for saying. The narrowness and poor condition of the roads will make it impractical to send a large force to confront the First Army. We ought rather to use all our forces to attack the Second Army, which will try to land on the Liaodong Peninsula."

Neither man would give in, and for several days the basic strategy remained undecided. In the end, a mixed strategy was adopted as a compromise. "We will divide our forces and have one section deal with the First Army, while the other will prevent the Second Army's landing." This meant that a relatively weak force would be sent against each of the Japanese armies.

* * *

As we know, the Second Army was trying to isolate Port Arthur by occupying the line between Jinzhou and Dalian, and then joining up with the First Army for a decisive battle against the Russians on the Manchurian plains.

"That's probably what they'll do," concluded Major General Roman Kondratenko, who was under the command of Stoessel in Port Arthur. "We have to fortify the Jinzhou and Nanshan areas as quickly as possible." Kondratenko offered this advice to Stoessel two days prior to the start of the war.

But Stoessel thought of Jinzhou and Nanshan as being at the northernmost outer edges of fortified Port Arthur and doubted it was necessary for him to fortify them. He was disinclined to follow Kondratenko's advice. There was a deeply rooted bureaucratic spirit among high-ranking officers of the Russia of that time, and Stoessel too always thought like a bureaucrat. He felt that Jinzhou and Nanshan were in a zone that should be mainly the concern of the field army to the north rather than being in an area he should defend.

"But if Jinzhou and Nanshan are occupied by the Japanese," Kondratenko insisted, "this small peninsula will be segmented, the railway line from Liaoyang cut off, and Port Arthur isolated!"

But Stoessel put the whole matter on ice, citing fiscal reasons.

Then the war started.

The Japanese Navy came to the entrance to the harbor of Port Arthur and applied huge pressure on the Russians. Observing the enemy fire, Stoessel came to have a sense of the reality of the situation. If by any chance Port Arthur fell, the only way of escape would be northward. If Jinzhou and Nanshan to the north were to be taken by the Japanese Army, all hope would be lost. This was the psychology of fear taking over, as was prone to happen to those inside fortifications. In war, it is not so much reason that determines strategy as psychology, to a large extent.

Stoessel summoned Major General Kondratenko and gave the order: "Those places you were just talking about—Jinzhou and Nanshan. Get to work there at once!"

More than ten days had passed since the war began. Kondratenko was the officer most respected and trusted by the troops in Port Arthur. He was not only brave but also skilled at building fortifications, since he had originally been an artilleryman.

He immediately began making plans and blueprints, and started high-speed work on the new fortifications on February 21. Since this was an emergency, the most important sections were built first, and, by April 3, the whole area had been almost completely fortified. And, because the Japanese Army had not reached there, he carried out a second stage of the plans—the construction of a very long firing trench that cut across the Jinzhou-to-Port Arthur road, extending to the seacoast. This too was completed by the time the Second Army landed.

Imperial General Headquarters in Tokyo and Oku's Second Army itself thought, "Jinzhou will fall in one day." And, indeed, during the First Sino-Japanese War, only half a day had been required to seize it. Even before the present war began, Japanese spies had entered the area, and of course they had reported that it was not well defended.

The Japanese Army's ignorance of the enemy's movements later led to appalling scenes with completely unexpected "mountains of corpses and rivers of blood."

* * *

After the battle was over, a look at the Russian Army's fortress on Nanshan Hill—or, rather, mostly their hastily built field fortifications—revealed that the artillery positions were lined up on rugged high ground. The various gun emplacements were in semi-permanent positions with some seventy cannons, large and small. On the defensive line, which connected these positions and surrounded the high ground, the Russians had built bunkers with loopholes to permit firing out. In front of these, there were minefields and barbed-wire fencing to prevent the Japanese infantry from approaching. And then, so as to cover any blank areas in the firing line, they had set up countless machine guns as well.

The Japanese Army, hitherto ignorant of what a modern defensive line should be, now learned its lesson by being showered with Russian gunfire. The Russian Empire's standing army was comprised of two million men; the Japanese Empire's was comprised of two hundred thousand. Navies are centered on mechanical force, but armies are basically different since they clearly display the essential character of a nation, showing off such things as its economic power and cultural level. In the battle at Nanshan, the army of a poor nation, still lacking in real knowledge of the outside world, based its attacks on bayonet charges, while Russia, ten times richer and stronger than Japan, held the enemy off with mechanical force.

After his army's landing, however, Oku Yasukata was amazed to learn from scouts how formidable the fortifications at Jinzhou and Nanshan were, and cabled General Headquarters in Tokyo asking them to send heavy artillery. Headquarters' immediate response was: "No need for heavy artillery. Attack at once."

The truth was that, whether there was a need for it or not, General Headquarters did not have any heavy artillery in reserve. On May 26, Oku's Second Army finished deploying and began a major attack. Akiyama Yoshifuru and his cavalry brigade, the last to arrive on the battlefield, had landed at the fishing village of Zhangjiatun three days earlier. But the cavalry had no important work to do just then. This was the artillery's moment to act.

The air in the early morning of the twenty-sixth was dense with fog. When the fog had lifted somewhat, around five-thirty in the morning, the entire artillery of the Second Army, under the sole direction of Major General Uchiyama, opened fire and rained shells continuously on the enemy positions in Nanshan. The noise of shells from both sides boomed and thundered through the Liaodong Peninsula's earth and sky. This was a tremendous spurt of artillery activity for the Japanese Army, which had from the first been hampered by limited artillery. And yet, even after one hour's, then two hours' shelling, the enemy's fire grew more and more intense—and showed no signs of letting up. The shelling ended up lasting for a full five hours.

"This is a terrible battle," said Major General Uchiyama, pale with fatigue and worry.

The Japanese artillery was almost out of shells, apart from a few held in reserve. They would have to wait for resupply from Japan. Uchiyama calculated that, in this one day's exchange, the Japanese had expended somewhat more than the total amount of shells used during the whole of the First Sino-Japanese War.

* * *

The Fourth Division (Osaka) on the right flank, the First Division (Tokyo) in the center, and the Third Division (Nagoya) on the left flank were attempting to reach the foot of Nanshan Hill. Akiyama's cavalry brigade was temporarily grouped together with the Fifth Division (Hiroshima).

There was nothing to be done but have the infantry, armed only with guns and swords, carry out the approach to the hill in the full realization that there would be massive casualties. The rapid advance of the infantry began early in the morning, together with the infantry's gunfire. As they approached the hill, their losses began to mount up at a frightening rate. They had to contend with the barbed wire strung up around the area. The infantrymen bent low to escape the smoke from the shells and were ravaged by the enemy's gunfire. When the survivors at last made it to the hill, they were fired upon from front and rear, left and right by the enemy's machine guns, which formed a tight net of fire. They were killed like so many insects. Even so, the Japanese Army, whether from valor or a sense of loyalty, entered the Russians' net of fire like creatures that knew only how to advance. Having done so, they were reduced to shreds, like human flesh put into a mixer. The fact that the enemy had machine guns was a source of amazement to the Japanese officers and soldiers alike. The Japanese infantry knew nothing about machine guns.

The Japanese Army's poor understanding of artillery was evident here. There was no excuse for the Japanese to be ignorant of machine guns. At the end of the Tokugawa period, Kawai Tsuginosuke, an elder of the Echigo Nagaoka domain, sold the objets d'art in the domain's Edo residence in order to buy machine guns in Yokohama. With the money he obtained, he bought two such guns.

Their power was demonstrated in a terrible way when his domain became, together with the Aizu domain, the last bastion of the pro-shogunate group. At the last battle in the streets of Nagaoka, Tsuginosuke himself used the machine guns by the castle gate, cutting down the imperial forces and managing to keep them at bay for a time. The commander of the imperial forces at the time was Yamagata Aritomo. Considering how badly his forces had suffered as a result of these guns, Yamagata ought to have given them a lot of thought when he became head of the army. He did not do so.

The machine guns bought by Kawai Tsuginosuke were fundamentally different in structure from the Russian ones that had spewed forth continuous fire at Nanshan. However, the Japanese Army now also had machine guns of the same sort as the Russian Army—a fact unknown to almost all the Japanese officers. Akiyama's cavalry brigade, in fact, had them. From the time of the First Sino-Japanese War, he frequently asked his superiors to supply the cavalry with machine guns. Eventually, his request was granted, and these weapons began to be imported just prior to the outbreak of the Russo-Japanese War. Immediately, a machine gun corps was formed within Akiyama's First Cavalry Brigade. In the cavalry, these machine guns were called "horse-drawn quick-firing machine guns."

The Russian Army's machine guns caused the Japanese Army much suffering throughout the Russo-Japanese War, and perhaps more than ten thousand Japanese troops died as a result of machine gun fire. The domestically produced Type 38 machine gun was introduced only two years after the war ended. An immense number of Japanese troops were killed or wounded at Jinzhou and Nanshan. It was after the attack on this area that Nogi Maresuke, passing outside the city of Jinzhou, wrote the well-known poem with the line, "For ten leagues the winds smell of fresh blood from the battlefield."

* * *

During the attack on Nanshan, a number of ships from Tōgō's fleet entered Jinshan Bay and, by increasing their guns' elevations, were able to lob shells right into the enemy camp—a great accomplishment. Tōgō had formed a detachment consisting of gunboats, from the old-fashioned *Tsukushi* (1,372 tons) on down, as well as torpedo boats, and assigned them this duty. Had he used not gunboats but larger ships of the fleet, their destructive power would have been far greater, but he could not remove the fleet's main force from the blockade of the waters outside Port Arthur, and so he employed smaller vessels. The Russian Army's artillerymen were very skillful, and they could shell this small fleet from their gun emplacements in Nanshan, shooting right over and beyond the Japanese Army's encampment. One of their shells scored a direct hit on the gunboat *Chōkai* (622 tons), killing the captain and many crew members.

The shell barrages of both sides were at their most intense until just after eleven in the morning. At this point, all of the open-air, unprotected artillery on the Russian side fell silent. These guns, which lacked a concrete overhead shelter, proved to be more vulnerable than had been expected.

The Russians, by the way, made use of their experience at Nanshan in the battle for the defense of Port Arthur, where there was also unprotected artillery. Conservative opinion at fortification headquarters had resisted the view that these guns should be provided with concrete shelters, considering this a cowardly notion. Incredible as it may seem, the spirit of medieval chivalry was still very much alive within the Russian Army. But, taking a lesson from the battle at Nanshan, the Russians quickly began building concrete shelters. If anyone failed to learn the lessons of Nanshan, it was the Japanese Third Army (Nogi's army), which later carried out the attack on Port Arthur.

Anyway, the enemy fire had greatly weakened by around noon, but those guns with concrete protective covers and the area with countless machine guns remained active. These made mincemeat of the Japanese troops that approached within several hundred meters and left a mountain of corpses in front of the enemy's barbed wire. By a little after noon on this day, Oku's staff began to feel that all was lost. At one in the afternoon, Oku assembled his staff in a Chinese civilian's house that was serving as his headquarters and began a meeting.

"We hate to say this, but we'll have to withdraw and plan how to renew our attack later," almost all of the staff said.

Oku was not satisfied with this. In his view, losing this, the first contested military landing of the Russo-Japanese War, would further weaken international confidence in Japan, which was already very weak. Still more important, Linevich's corps to the north was beginning to move to save the situation in Jinzhou and Nanshan. If Linevich's corps arrived, the Second Army would surely be annihilated.

However, one young staff officer insisted on continuing the attack. Oku took his advice, and the attack continued. In the end, two thousand dead and wounded, the equivalent of one regiment, was the only result.

*　*　*

There was a man who broke through this extraordinarily cruel and bloody situation—Lieutenant General Ogawa Mataji, the commander of the Fourth Division. Like Oku Yasukata, Ogawa had been a retainer of the Kokura domain. He became a second lieutenant in 1872, so he had been a military man even before the establishment of the Army Academy. He also resembled Oku in not having attended such an educational institution. He was quickly identified as a tactician of genius. When Meckel was a lecturer at the Army Staff College, Ogawa was already a colonel, not a student. He was an important member of the General Staff, together with Kodama Gentarō, and the two of them attended Meckel's lectures as auditors. "Kodama and Ogawa are better than our students," the Prussian lecturer remarked.

Apart from these men, the Meiji period army had formerly had that other tactical genius Tamura Iyozō, who had helped in strategic planning for the Russo-Japanese War. Temperamentally, Ogawa was a little more sharp-tongued than Tamura. So, for example, when he was auditing Meckel's lectures, he often engaged in violent controversy with this favorite disciple of the great Moltke and did not easily give in. Thus, when Meckel said that in field combat, mountain artillery was more mobile and better than field artillery, Ogawa countered that field artillery was far better. The debate grew quite heated.

"Sir, you are my respected teacher," Ogawa finally said, "but when it comes to a debate about tactics, I can't give in. If you insist on maintaining that mountain artillery is better, then please return to your country as soon as possible and bring back with you an army of German soldiers well trained in the use of mountain artillery. I will employ Japanese field artillerymen, and we will smash that army of yours to smithereens!"

Now this same Ogawa Mataji looked at the military situation and said, "Of course our army is exhausted, but the enemy must be too. I think we should attack once more, and this time concentrate all our infantry artillery's force on the enemy's weak spot. We can break them at that one spot and then widen the attack to include all the enemy lines."

Oku agreed with him.

A little after two o'clock in the afternoon, Oku's command headquarters concluded that the Russians' weak spot was their left flank and made the decision to attack again at five o'clock. "The Japanese Army reopened their attack with the aid of their fleet starting at 1700 hours," the Russian records state. The Japanese artillery lobbed all available shells at the Russians, keeping none back as reserves. At half past six, the infantry began a sudden hand-to-hand charge and took control of the Russian position. Having lost their left flank, the Russian center panicked, as Ogawa had foreseen. By half past seven, just as the evening sun was sinking into Jinzhou Bay, the whole of Nanshan fell into Japanese hands. The Russians retreated to the south, fleeing behind Port Arthur's fortifications. The Second Army had to abandon pursuit of the enemy and instead move northward to fight a decisive battle against Linevich's army corps.

* * *

"Jinzhou and Nanshan will surely not fall." Stoessel, who was in Port Arthur, had believed this right up to the moment of defeat. Typically for a Russian military man, he had great faith in fortifications. Even though Jinzhou and Nanshan had only temporary field fortifications as compared to the solid ones at Port Arthur, he firmly believed that they would still be able to hold off the Japanese Army for a month or so, resisting any weak (as he thought) Japanese attacks that might be attempted. That's how confident he was in the strong defensive positions and the superior artillery of the Russian side.

It was Viceroy Alexeyev, a former navy man, who laughed at Stoessel's too optimistic calculations: "Those fortifications aren't as strong as you think, Anatoly Mikhailovich Stoessel! They won't hold out longer than two weeks."

The viceroy was the supreme commander of the Russian Army, and he had a staff charged with forming strategy. Their plan was for the Russian forces at the Jinzhou and Nanshan fortifications to inflict maximum damage on the Second Army. After two weeks or so, Jinzhou and Nanshan would fall, and the defenders would retreat to the strong, solid fortifications of Port Arthur. The plan was to hold the two forward positions for "about two weeks." If that were done, Linevich's corps, a field army, would sweep in on the Japanese Army like a tide from the north, smashing it to pieces. But Alexeyev's plans were all for naught since the positions fell in a single day's massive attack by the Japanese.

When the Second Army landed and started heading for Jinzhou and Nanshan, the citizens of Dalian panicked. "If Jinzhou and Nanshan fall, Dalian will be completely undefended. Shouldn't Russian citizens be evacuated to Port Arthur?" suggested Vasily Sakharov, the mayor of Dalian, urging Stoessel to issue an order to that effect. Sakharov was not an elected representative of the citizens but a political officer with army connections who was also in charge of the Dalian police force.

"There's no need for that," Stoessel curtly replied. When, however, Stoessel learned that not only had these two positions fallen but also that a section of the railway to Port Arthur had been taken by the Japanese, he ordered the mayor of Dalian to begin an immediate withdrawal. But it was already too late to do things in an orderly way, and a huge stockpile of military supplies in Dalian had to be abandoned as the Russians fled.

During the withdrawal to Port Arthur, the railway was of almost no use. Aleksandr Fok, the local commander, ran to the station at Nanguanling and ordered that a special train be readied for himself and his staff. But there was only one steam locomotive remaining in the station, and it had been so badly damaged by shells from both sides that it could not be used. Fok had to make his escape by horse, which shows how bad the situation was. The roads to Port Arthur were in a chaotic state due to the flight of the defeated Russian troops.

* * *

The Russian Army at Jinzhou and Nanshan should perhaps not have retreated so readily, no matter how fierce the attack by the Second Army. If the Russian defense had continued for one more day, no one knows how many days Oku's Second Army would have needed to prepare a fresh attack. They were already out of ammunition, and the number of their dead and wounded had mounted to over ten percent of their total force. They had to depend on the Japanese homeland for resupply of shells and ammunition, and the homeland was always low on these. Thus, no one knew when the necessary shiploads would arrive.

When the Second Army sent a cable to Imperial General Headquarters in Tokyo reporting on its unexpectedly high losses, Tokyo headquarters doubted the accuracy of the figures, assuming that "they must have added a zero to the casualty figures by mistake." This was in response to the first report, which cited three thousand dead and wounded. The upper echelon of the Japanese Army could not imagine that casualties from a single battle could exceed the hundreds. Now for the first time the Japanese Army learned the horrors of modern war.

Had the Russian Army been able to hold on for even one more day, we just don't know what would have happened to the Second Army. Fok finally wrote to Stoessel requesting orders. "We must either withdraw or go on the attack during the night using everything we have—there's no other way." If Stoessel had ordered an all-out night attack, what would have happened? But the Russian Army had undergone hardly any training in making large-scale night attacks.

The Russian withdrawal to Port Arthur itself took place at night, and the Russian Army became still more confused and disordered in the dark. So, for example, when the rearguard of the retreating army (Yenisei Regiment), which was moving southward along the railway lines, came to the shunting station near Nanguanling, someone shouted, "It's the Japanese cavalry!" And, indeed, some thirty cavalrymen seemed to be in hot pursuit behind this regiment, supposedly the last part of the retreating army.

In fact, Akiyama Yoshifuru's cavalry brigade, the only one the Japanese had, was at the time engaged in defending the line—north of the Jinzhou fortifications—from Pulandian to Dashahe. It was not involved in active combat beyond that area.

Perhaps as a good tactical measure, Oku should have sent a strong cavalry force in pursuit of the fleeing Russian Army, attacking them as fiercely as possible. Oku's Second Army, however, was charged with advancing northward and could not divert attention to the retreating Port Arthur army.

One can understand, then, why the rearguard of the retreating Russian army thought that the cavalry force following them was Japanese cavalry. In tactical terms, this made sense. But this was Russian, not Japanese cavalry, a cavalry reconnaissance group from the Russian Fifteenth

Regiment. They were annihilated in a fierce hail of fire from their terrified fellow Russians.

* * *

The cavalry has two functions: attack and reconnaissance. In his present situation, Yoshifuru gave precedence to reconnaissance. Reconnaissance involves finding out about conditions beforehand in order to provide an army with information needed for making tactical decisions. To do so, the scouts have to move speedily among the enemy and then out again—this acrobatic moving in and out is of the essence in reconnaissance. Scouts are, if you like, the acrobats of the battlefield.

When the main force of the Second Army was at a loss about how to continue the attack on Nanshan, Akiyama Yoshifuru told Oku's headquarters, "I'm going north!" If the Second Army captured Nanshan, they would have to forget about Port Arthur, further to the south, and make for Liaoyang, to the north, where the main, decisive battle was supposed to take place. Akiyama's cavalry brigade was to open the way northward ahead of the advance. The cavalry was to move northward, find out about the enemy's situation, and report back to the headquarters, including, if possible, a battle plan. They borrowed two infantry companies to investigate the area around Delisi.

"Thank heavens Akiyama offered to do that" was the comment heard among the staff officers later, but his decision was only reasonable, according to the way a cavalry brigade was used in the West. The leaders of the Japanese Army brought the curtain down on Japan's military history without ever being able to appreciate the amazing capacities of the cavalry in the age we are discussing, or of tanks and planes used for reconnaissance purposes in a later period.

On the morning of May 30, Yoshifuru and his cavalry brigade set out for the enemy territory to the north. The brigade traveled for about five hours, and shortly after noon scouts led by an officer returned with their reports. "There are as many as one hundred enemy cavalry in the area of Dianjiatun, where we're headed. They know we are advancing northward and are preparing to fight us on foot."

Though the scouts saw only one hundred enemy cavalrymen, we must assume that a considerable number more waited to back them up.

"This will be our first battle," thought Yoshifuru, sending out an initial group to force these hundred Russians to retreat. He chose two companies from the Fourteenth Cavalry Regiment, adding a horse-drawn quick-firing machine gun group as well as supporting infantry troops.

The Russian side was already taking the situation at Nanshan very seriously, and Viceroy Alexeyev had ordered Kuropatkin to mobilize the First Siberian Army Corps and have them assemble at Delisi. Then they moved toward Nanshan. In the lead as this group moved south was the "hundred-man cavalry" that Akiyama's cavalry brigade had already heard about. If he did not look out, Yoshifuru would have to deal with the enemy's First Siberian Army Corps itself.

* * *

With its great intelligence-gathering ability, the Russian Army knew right away that Akiyama's cavalry brigade had begun to move northward on its own. This report was transmitted to Commander in Chief Kuropatkin, who was in the rear.

He summoned Lieutenant General Georgi Stakelberg, who was the head of the army corps, and ordered him "to take the Japanese down a peg or two." This was the first field battle of the war, and Kuropatkin wanted to deal a hard blow, crushing the morale of the Japanese Army that had just landed, and also to create good publicity abroad for the Russian Army.

Kuropatkin, however, had the bad habit of always attaching several conditions to his orders. This time, it was: "If the enemy rushes forward, and if they do not have reinforcements in the rear, then send in more men and destroy them." This was a truly artful kind of order, typical of the most brilliant general in the Russian Army. But "Destroy the advancing troops of the enemy" would have been ample as a military order. Kuropatkin's order was far too weak and did not express the resolute purpose of an army at war. Moreover, such detailed matters should have been left to the discretion of Lieutenant General Stakelberg, as head of the army corps.

Kuropatkin's instructions served only to restrict Stakelberg, who, if he had been a timid sort of fellow, could have used these attached conditions as an excuse to justify not carrying out the battle strategy. Stakelberg gave the order to advance to one cavalry brigade and two infantry battalions, with four field guns added. Both the number of troops and their firepower surpassed those of Akiyama's cavalry brigade. Yoshifuru lacked artillery, and this was his biggest disadvantage. Not only the Russians but all the European military paid far more attention to artillery support than did the Japanese Army of the time, the Europeans having experienced conquest at the hands of Napoleon, that master of artillery. Thus, whenever they put their cavalry brigades to use, they always supplied them with field guns as well.

The cavalry brigade that advanced at Yoshifuru's orders clashed with the enemy at the southern edge of Dianjiatun. Both forces fought on foot, and, after an hour of fierce fighting, the Russians all mounted their horses and began to withdraw to the north. They were not fleeing after a defeat but withdrawing, and occasionally they stopped to shell the Japanese. No doubt they were attempting to draw the Japanese forces into the area where the Russian troops were massed.

The Russian Army viewed withdrawal as an act with complex implications. For Japanese, withdrawal was simply seen as a defeat; they were interested only in advancing. So, of course, the Japanese continued to pursue and attack. As they did so, the terrain began to favor the enemy. The road was lined with mounds on both sides, and from these the Russian troops could easily fire on the Japanese. An hour and ten minutes after the battle began, six of the enemy's field pieces appeared on highlands to the south of the village of Huahung'gou, and the air was filled with the roar of their fire. Then two hundred cavalrymen arrived to fight on foot as fresh troops. Russian firepower on the battlefield rose to several times that of the Japanese.

* * *

The battle, which took place at Qujiadian, was the first large-scale battle between the cavalry of Russia and Japan. With their superiority in firepower, the Russians focused their basic strategy on establishing bases as they advanced, suppressing the enemy with firepower from those bases, and only then attempting to advance a little further. Another base would then be established and the same process continued. This strategy of continued frontal attack meant that the Russians had to have sufficient firepower.

By contrast, the basic thinking within the Japanese Army did not at all center upon such a "temporary, base-centered advance" but rather on sudden, fierce attacks—this was their usual method. Rather than establishing temporary bases and moving them gradually forward, they almost never created bases. Instead, the soldiers' bodies themselves would spearhead their advance. Naturally, this strategy depended on the bravery of both commanders and soldiers in the field. Sometimes they would dispense with strategy altogether and fight on, relying simply on the bravery of the fighters. Typifying this approach was the attack of Nogi's Third Army on Port Arthur later in the war. This became an almost chronic trait of the army and was handed down in its entirety to the military of the Shōwa period, leading ultimately to the destruction of the Japanese Army itself.

As was learned afterward, Yoshifuru was not facing head-on an enemy of such overwhelming numbers. The five or six Cossack companies led by cavalry lieutenant colonel Mikhail Svechin constituted the main force, and there were in addition two infantry companies and one cavalry artillery company. In other words, apart from the artillery, there was only a little more than one regiment. Yoshifuru fought against this relatively small force with an entire regiment of cavalry, and the battle was a harrowing one. The absence of cannon proved to be a tragic, fatal weakness for the Japanese. Yoshifuru had kept appealing to the Army Ministry right up to the start of the war, arguing the necessity of cavalry artillery, but his requests went unheeded, and then the war began.

The terrain also posed difficulties for Akiyama's cavalry brigade. They were fighting on a narrow road through hilly country, so they could not use their superior numbers to advantage. They had to press on along this single road, but the enemy had built gun emplacements at key points on both sides. Groups like the Second Company of the Thirteenth Cavalry Regiment went off in pursuit, attacking the withdrawing enemy. But they were finally lured into a valley near Longwangmiao, where they were attacked from all sides and almost completely annihilated.

The Japanese cavalry abandoned their horses and built trenches, as infantrymen would do, and from these they fired on the enemy until even their small-arms ammunition ran out. They had to turn to their machine gun bullets, which they rammed into their small arms and fired at the enemy.

* * *

The battle grew in ferocity with each passing minute. In addition, the three machine guns, the treasures of the cavalry regiment, had fallen silent—all the ammunition was gone.

"We'd better withdraw," the commanders of various units thought, and so did Captain Nakaya, an aide to Yoshifuru. We might mention here that Yoshifuru had not brought any staff officers along with him. He never gave his reasons for this, but no doubt it was because there was no one in the army with greater knowledge and ability in cavalry strategy than Yoshifuru himself.

Since there were no staff officers present, there was no one who could say, "We must withdraw." Yoshifuru himself had not the slightest intention of doing so. On the contrary, this man who was the commander of an entire army moved his command headquarters further and further forward, till he came at last to Longwangmiao, on the front line. From there, he gazed out over the flat red earth stretching before him. The enemy's artillery shells were pouring down on the Japanese machine gun emplacements, but Yoshifuru went even further forward until he came to this spot.

"There's no need for us to go right up to the machine guns," thought Nakaya.

Officers and men fell under the hail of bullets right before Yoshifuru's eyes. He knew full well how disadvantaged the Japanese were in this battle.

He knew too that, strategically speaking, withdrawal would be appropriate. The Japanese could withdraw to the narrow road to the rear, build a defensive encampment there, and hold the enemy off.

But his reason demanded another course, for to withdraw now, at this stage of the battle, would be to lose everything. He had personally taught everything to this cavalry team with him, starting from how to mount and ride a horse, and going on from there. He knew the weaknesses of these troops since he had "raised them by hand," and he knew the strengths of the enemy. But if he allowed withdrawal now, what would happen?

"This is the first battle between the Russian and the Japanese cavalry. The first battle is always vitally important. If we lose here, the Japanese cavalry's morale will be badly affected. They may get used to the idea of losing. If we withdraw here, the Russian cavalry will be much more self-confident and stronger in the battles from now on," thought Yoshifuru.

Finally, one of the front-line officers could no longer stand it. He raced up on his horse and dismounted in front of Yoshifuru. He next urged a withdrawal. "Sir," he shouted, "right now we're just barely able to push the Russians back for a while. I think we should take advantage of this chance to withdraw to the narrow road behind us."

Yoshifuru was an odd man, and to this frantic request he responded only with a grunt. He signaled to an attendant to give him a glass and his canteen, which was, as always, filled with brandy. Having poured himself a drink, he lay down on top of the low earthen wall that surrounded the Chinese house where they were at the time and turned his back on the officer. "There's nothing to be done but lie down for a bit," he seemed to be saying. Above the glass of brandy, bullets whizzed by one after the other, their noise ringing in Yoshifuru's ears.

Yoshifuru's behavior was so odd that in the very midst of this fierce battle the troops whispered, "His Excellency the regimental commander is lying down in a sulk over by the machine guns exactly at the front line!"

The top of the low wall around the Chinese house looked quite high from the standpoint of the trenches. Yet there lay the commander, drinking brandy. If the enemy had high-quality Zeiss binoculars, they would have been able to see this major general of the Japanese Army.

"Boom!" A shell landed next to Yoshifuru, and the corpse of a horse that was lying there rose up into the air, as if it had come alive again. But Yoshifuru continued to drink his brandy. "There's nothing that can be done now," he was thinking. There was no way he could take active command. In a situation like this, there was no such thing as tactics or anything like that. All he could do was to have his forces keep on firing with what remained of their small ammunition until the enemy's shells, raining down like a squall, came to an end for some reason or another.

"The battle's been going on for a good hour and a half now—they're bound to get exhausted in the end," Yoshifuru thought. At any rate, his sole strategy now was not to withdraw from where the Japanese forces were, no matter if he himself and his officers and men were blown to pieces by enemy fire. "That's all we can do," he had determined. A commander on the battlefield must not be too sharp and alert. If his responses are too keen, he's liable to make errors. It is far better to dull yourself a bit in this sort of crisis.

Again and again, Yoshifuru poured brandy from his canteen and drank it. In the First Sino-Japanese War, he had become drunk on the local liquor; by now, he could afford to drink brandy. Then a mere major, he was now a major general, and his pay had risen a good deal. Before he left Tokyo, he had spent an entire month's salary on brandy to take with him.

"The enemy too are tiring," he had thought, taking their measure, and, sure enough, around three in the afternoon, the Russians gradually began to withdraw to the north.

The Russian forces were certainly stronger than the Japanese, but their commander was not as "dull" as Yoshifuru. His nerves shattered by the violent struggle, he began to withdraw in order to set up camp for the night, offering a sound tactical excuse. "We shall resume the attack tomorrow!" He was wary of a night attack by the Japanese and therefore perhaps wanted to bivouac as far away as possible.

This battle became a test of nerves of the commanders of the two armies. The Russian commander was defeated by Yoshifuru's strength of nerve. Yoshifuru and his regiment survived the crisis. That night, they bivouacked near Longwangmiao.

"I've never been so troubled as when I was urged to withdraw today," Yoshifuru told Nakaya that same night in the Chinese civilian's house. "Tactically, of course, he was right. But, strategically, we couldn't withdraw. That's why I set myself down and pretended not to hear what he said."

* * *

At the forefront of the whole army, Yoshifuru and his cavalry regiment continued to stay in the hilly region north of Qujiadian. Unless they settled there for a time, they would be unable to grasp the state of the enemy forces far to the north near Delisi.

On the morning of June 3, Yoshifuru got two companies of artillerymen from the Fifth Division in the rear placed under his command. "Now that we have these guns, we'll be all right," he thought, greeting the arrival of the artillery companies with a ruddy, smiling face.

He had a plan. "I want you all to conceal yourselves," he ordered. The enemy would eventually attack en masse. They knew from the last few days of the battle that the Japanese cavalry regiment had no cannons, so the artillerymen should stay hidden until the last possible moment, and then, when the time came, all open fire at once. Yoshifuru knew about such matters, master of warfare that he was.

"You want us to hide our guns?" the leader of the artillery group asked in evident surprise.

"Yaah," Yoshifuru answered as if yawning. "I want you to stay quietly undercover in the hills at the critical spots and camouflage your guns with straw and shrubbery."

Around forty minutes after eleven o'clock in the morning, shortly after the artillery companies had arrived, the enemy was sighted. Then, around three in the afternoon, a scout who had infiltrated the area around Delisi, far to the north, returned with a report. "A Russian military train has entered the station at Delisi again and seems to have brought in reinforcements. Maybe that's the reason the Russian staging area in Delisi is suddenly full of activity. There are signs that they are preparing for a massive move southward."

As was so often the case, Yoshifuru's only comment was: "I see . . . "

Around five in the evening, even the naked eye could make out enemy movements.

A narrow strip of flat land created by the Hueitou River ran to the northeast around Longwangmiao, where Yoshifuru had encamped. Looking out from Longwangmiao, some foothills about 2 kilometers northwest across the river stuck out like a bird's beak, and, at five in the evening, a Russian artillery unit appeared there.

They had four cannons.

The Russian cavalry and infantry units that were already waiting in the area now began to advance, as the cannons arrived on the scene.

"Not yet," ordered Yoshifuru. He meant, don't fire yet.

Only when the front ranks of the enemy troops had come within 1.5 kilometers of Yoshifuru's command post did he give the order, "Artillery, fire!"

Then the guns that had been concealed in various elevated spots in the area all opened fire at once, immediately blasting the four enemy guns to kingdom come. At the same time, Yoshifuru ordered the infantrymen to attack and then had the cavalry advance on foot. It turned into a fierce battle, and the Russian Army was nearly crushed by this concerted attack, breaking ranks as they withdrew.

The battle here ended with a victory for the Japanese cavalry brigade. Yet as evidence that the Russians had a great fund of fighting spirit still, the corpses strewn across the battlefield were all those of Japanese cavalrymen, in their characteristic red breeches. The Russian Cossacks were skilled at scooping up the bodies of their fallen comrades while still mounted on horseback. As a result, only one abandoned enemy corpse was left on that battlefield.

9

MAKAROV

A great military leader is surely one who can vastly improve morale and thus perform a "group miracle." Vice Admiral Makarov of the Russian Navy was just such a man. After his assumption of command in Port Arthur at the beginning of March, the Port Arthur Squadron changed from what it had been under Stark.

During this period, a humorous song called "Old Man Makarov" was popular among the sailors. One of the sailors had composed the song, and, when the men got together to drink vodka, they always sang that song in chorus.

"Do just what Makarov says, and Russia will be victorious" was the confident belief that spread, not so much among the officers, as among the petty officers and ordinary seamen. Makarov was not just famous worldwide as a naval strategist, but as a commander in chief who had risen from the ranks of the sailors, he clearly felt himself a father to his men. Rather than stay cooped up in his office, he pushed himself spiritually and physically to move from ship to ship, giving appropriate directives and commands to everyone from the ship captains on down, and then seeing to it that his directives were carried out.

Makarov was more physically active than any ordinary sailor. Until he took command, the Port Arthur Squadron was criticized by the army officers and men in the fortifications. "The cowardly navy," they would say, or "They're just ducks waiting to sink themselves in the puddle of Port Arthur!"

But as soon as Makarov took over, he made his policy clear to the entire squadron. "Why can't we go out onto the open sea?" His predecessor Stark never bothered to explain the reason for this to the ordinary sailors. Makarov did.

The Port Arthur Squadron was awaiting the arrival of the Baltic Fleet. When it arrived, the two Russian fleets would combine forces and attack Tōgō's single fleet. Until then, the Port Arthur Squadron was to be circumspect, staying in the harbor. Up to this point, Makarov's policy was no different from Stark's.

"But I will not simply sit here and do nothing," Makarov declared. "We'll go out a short distance to attack as often as possible, sink as many of Tōgō's ships as possible, and that way we'll gain the advantage in the great sea battle to come."

The sailors were thrilled at this grand strategy.

"Here's what we'll do," the vice admiral continued. "We'll keep a group of ships at the harbor entrance to protect the channel, and we'll make use of the cruisers' speed to attack the Japanese. Make sure the cruisers' boilers are always fired up so we can leave harbor whenever necessary."

Normally, such policies, tactics, and stratagems are not communicated to ordinary sailors, since such matters are regarded as beyond them. That was particularly true in the Russian Navy. Makarov's method of command, however, involved letting all the sailors understand what they were doing and what they were expected to do. By making everyone aware of his strategic goals, Makarov aimed at increasing their will to fight. At this period, when the nineteenth century had just ended, Makarov's approach was truly innovative.

Makarov was somewhat old, but he hadn't a trace of an old man's excessive prudence or concern about his own dignity. "Most old men don't react to things," he was always saying, "and seem always calm and peaceful. That's just because they've lost the flexibility of mind that would enable them to react—it has nothing to do with 'the dignity of age.'" The whole world acknowledged that Makarov possessed immense intelligence, but the true miracle was that someone of his age should have muscular abilities and agility even surpassing his intellectual skills. Throughout the world's navies, the commander in chief used a battleship as his flagship, but Makarov used to say, "How can anyone command an entire fleet aboard a slow, heavy vessel like a battleship? A fast-moving cruiser should be the flagship."

This was to some extent an extreme view, as Makarov himself well understood. A battleship is so well armored with thick plating that a cruiser can't compare with it in defensive capability. Even a crushing blow is far less likely to sink a battleship than a cruiser. So the commander in chief is less likely to die in battle, and thus the chaos attendant on such a loss is avoided. Also, the commander's office is larger and can accommodate the many staff officers needed for command. For all these reasons, a battleship makes the best flagship.

Yet, at Port Arthur, Makarov chose a cruiser. Or, rather, he was willing to jump aboard any fast-moving warship, even if it was not of cruiser class, in order to go on the attack. His preference for a cruiser as a flagship was almost certainly a special case, born of conditions at Port Arthur. He wanted to lead the attacks himself. Often, he left the squadron as a whole safely inside the harbor and went off on a single ship to fight alone. His view was that "the flag of the commander in chief should always be the one flying wherever the rain of shells falls most heavily." Boldly pressing on against the enemy with his own physical self was, he felt, the only way to get rid of the sluggishness that had afflicted the Port Arthur Squadron until his arrival. This boldness and bravery of his was reflected in the song the sailors sang, "Old Man Makarov."

The battleships inside the harbor of Port Arthur were really very restricted. At low tide, their hulls scraped the bottom of the channel near the harbor mouth, making free passage difficult. In addition, the Japanese blockships had been sunk here and there in the area. As a result, it sometimes took as much as two hours to navigate the entrance to the harbor.

Here the cruisers proved their worth, and, of them all, Makarov especially loved the small protected cruiser *Novik*, at 3,080 tons. The *Novik* was not only fast—its captain, Commander von Essen was a truly brave officer and a skilled handler of his ship, and the crew was lively and efficient. Apart from the *Novik*, Makarov was fond of the armored cruiser *Bayan* (7,726 tons). He admired the daring of its commander, Captain Robert Viren, as well.

* * *

A naval port is equivalent to a fort on land. Tōgō's fleet seemed to be following a regular schedule as it passed outside the entrance to this "fort" that was the harbor of Port Arthur.

"Tōgō is as careful as the leader of some great nation!" Makarov often remarked. And, indeed, Tōgō's fleet would come to the waters just outside the entrance to Port Arthur, but, fearing the tremendous power of the fortifications' artillery, the fleet would trail its white wake just outside the range of the Russian guns. As if on parade, the Japanese warships, large and small, would file past the harbor mouth. Tōgō's principal aim was to blockade the harbor; his secondary aim was to provoke a Russian reaction.

Makarov's predecessor Stark always avoided going out on attack beyond the entrance to the harbor, staying deep within his "sea fortress." Makarov, by contrast, always went out to attack, though he did not go far into the open waters. He took care to stay within the zone protected by the Russian land artillery as he rushed madly about that limited area of the sea, lobbing shell after shell at Tōgō's fleet.

Occasionally, he would venture beyond the range of his land artillery, as if to challenge the Japanese to "come this close!" If he could provoke the Japanese into pursuing him, he would use his aft guns to fire at them as he fled and then go back within range of the Russian land artillery. If the Japanese were careless enough to continue their pursuit and come within range, shells from the land artillery, which had already taken aim, would rain down on the Japanese ships.

This splendid coordination of sea and land forces was termed "Makarov's breathing technique" by Saneyuki, who observed it all from on board the *Mikasa*. Indeed, viewed from the sea, the whole of Port Arthur seemed to be breathing in and out at Makarov's will.

"Makarov is like Uesugi Kenshin," Saneyuki sometimes thought, remembering the famed sixteenth-century military leader. Makarov moved his troops sharply and swiftly, and sometimes he would appear in person, his long sword raised in the command to attack. If Makarov was like Uesugi Kenshin, then there was something of Kenshin's rival Takeda Shingen in Tōgō's cautious and meticulous strategy.

Saneyuki hoped to use Makarov's boldness to the Russian side's detriment. "If we go there, the enemy is sure to come out to attack us," he said at a staff officers' meeting. "And they seem to follow a set pattern when they come out and go back." Just as individuals follow set patterns in their movements, so too do naval fleets. "Why don't we lay mines at the spot where the Russians always pass?"

No one considered this a particularly brilliant idea because only chance would determine whether the enemy bumped into one of these sea mines. A strategy that relied mostly on chance could not be regarded as first-rate. But on the battlefield one has to use whatever means are available to attack the enemy, regardless of whether the outcome depends on chance or is viewed as inevitable. For example, the attempt to blockade the harbor had failed so many times, but the Japanese Navy had not given up even though they didn't have any good new ideas about how to get this job done. They had asked Imperial General Headquarters in Tokyo for an additional twelve old steamers for the purpose.

So, for lack of anything better, they decided to plant the sea mines. No one dreamed that this would swing the balance of the two nations' struggle at sea in Japan's favor.

* * *

Saneyuki had Lieutenant Commander Takeuchi Jirō, the captain of the *Hayatori* in the Fourth Destroyer Division, check on the movement patterns of the enemy's attack squads. Eventually, the report came back: "The enemy always comes as far as the area around Laolucui and then goes back."

Commander Oda Kiyozō had already been put in charge of the work of laying the mines. He had studied sea mines for many years and had devised a new type of his own, named after him. He and several petty officers, who acted as his research assistants, had come to the battle area especially for this. They were aboard a special duty ship called the *Kōryū Maru*. Oda was a taciturn technical specialist, and even when he came to the *Mikasa* on official business he spoke no more than was absolutely necessary.

Saneyuki promised to provide ample protection, handing him a memo listing the names of the ships, but Oda simply nodded briefly and put the memo in his pocket. Saneyuki found himself wondering if everything would go all right. Finally, the plans for the mine laying were complete.

When Oda returned to his own ship, he assembled the petty officers assisting him as well as the ordinary seamen involved, and issued what was, for him, a rather long directive. "We're going to sneak in under the enemy's guns to do our job. I suspect that the day we go will also be the day we die, so be prepared for that."

The strategy was similar to trying to sneak into the enemy's castle carrying a load of firewood on your back. They would be carrying a great many mines with them, and, if they were hit by enemy gunfire midway, the resulting explosion would shake the sea and land of Port Arthur, and not one hair on the heads of those on board would be spared.

At last the day came. The action would take place on the night of April 12. A fine misty rain was falling on the sea outside the entrance to Port Arthur. Visibility was poor: it was perfect weather for Oda and his men to sneak near the harbor. The rain would prevent the enemy's searchlights from fulfilling their function adequately. With only a light wind and few waves, there could not be better weather for the laying of the sea mines.

As the *Kōryū Maru* moved away from the *Mikasa*, the various ships all sent a signal: "We congratulate you on your success in advance!" The escort squad consisted of the Fourth Destroyer Division under Commander Nagai Gunkichi (the *Hayatori*, *Harusame*, *Murasame*, and *Asagiri*), the Fifth Destroyer Division under Commander Mano Iwajirō (the *Kagerō*, *Muragumo*, *Yūgiri*, and *Shiranui*), plus the Fourteenth Torpedo Boat Division.

They moved forward without any lights. As time passed, the temperature fell, reaching −20 degrees Celsius, though it was April. The rain changed to snow. As they approached the target area, the enemy searchlights shone brightly as always and played over the surface of the water, but their glare could not extend far, due to the snow. They actually helped the Japanese side, since they served as aids to the Japanese in determining their own location.

The *Kōryū Maru* moved at a very slow speed, quietly circling around this dangerous area of the sea. Oda Kiyozō stood on deck, directing the laying of the mines. Snow collected on the shoulders of his cape. "Heaven is aiding us," he thought again and again. Oda insisted that his men make no noise even when they sank the mines deep into the water. When at last the operation was over, the *Kōryū Maru* slipped away, letting off only a slight amount of steam, and returned to the offing, like a burglar stealing silently away.

The escort squadron was in an area somewhat removed from the operation. It was not the same destroyer group that had brought the *Kōryū Maru* to the operation area, but the Second Destroyer Division that was on guard during the operation itself. Since neither the ship that laid the mines nor the escort squad was illuminated, it was hard to tell even whether the *Kōryū Maru* had completed its work or not.

"They must have finished by now," muttered Commander Ishida Ichirō, in charge of the Second Destroyer Division, on the bridge of the destroyer *Ikazuchi* as dawn approached. The destroyers began to move. The *Ikazuchi* led the way, with the *Oboro*, *Inazuma*, and *Akebono*, all 341-ton ships of the same type, following behind. This Second Destroyer Division had been constituted in accordance with the rules of naval strategy that had ships of the same type acting in concert. After its protective duties were finished, the division would have to engage in its regular, daily duty of patrolling just outside the entrance to Port Arthur's harbor.

As the group moved across the sea at dawn, a single enemy destroyer was sighted approaching the harbor from the east. At Makarov's orders, Russian destroyers also patrolled outside the harbor. This ship must have been on its way back from such a patrol mission.

The Japanese learned later that this particular Russian destroyer was the *Strashny*, far smaller than the *Ikazuchi* at only 240 tons. It was also slow, capable of no more than 26.5 knots per hour. The *Ikazuchi* could reach 31 knots, and this clearly shows the inferior strength of the Russian destroyer. Not a single destroyer in the Japanese Navy was as slow as the *Strashny*.

"It's going back to the port," said Ishida, deciding to engage the ship in battle. In short order, the four Japanese ships made a skillful approach and rained fire down on the Russian ship. The *Strashny* fought bravely but having received countless direct hits almost immediately, it was engulfed in flames. After a battle that lasted only ten minutes, the ship lost the ability to move in any direction and started to sink.

"Rescue them!" ordered Ishida, and the *Ikazuchi* drew nearer the unfortunate Russian vessel. The sea was already growing light in the dawn.

The *Strashny* was to sink within thirty minutes, but before that could happen, something amazing occurred.

From the Russian side, a cruiser, which a destroyer has difficulty handling, heard the firing of the guns and appeared from inside the harbor. It was the *Bayan*, an armored cruiser commanded by Captain Robert Viren, who was well known for his bravery.

* * *

In sea battles, the size of the warships almost completely determines which side wins. A big ship has correspondingly big guns, and thick armor plating. By contrast, a little ship has little guns, and, no matter how many of them come to challenge the larger ship, they will almost certainly lose.

And now, here was the *Bayan*! The four Japanese ships, each 341 tons, would be no match for its 7,726-ton power, no matter how clever their strategy might be. There was only one possible and necessary response: flight. The *Ikazuchi* hurriedly reversed course. The Russian sailors from the burning destroyer *Strashny* were leaping into the sea, one after another, but the *Ikazuchi* had no time to save them. The other three Japanese destroyers, taking their cue from the *Ikazuchi*, also began to leave the scene as quickly as possible.

"We'd never win against the *Bayan*," said Commander Ishida Ichirō, wiping the sweat from his brow as he stood on the bridge and turning to look at the ship's captain, Lieutenant Mimura Kinsaburō. For Mimura, this was no laughing matter.

The first shell from the *Bayan*, coming in hot pursuit, barely missed the *Ikazuchi*'s stern, sending up a great cloud of spray. The Japanese ship went faster, steam pouring from its funnels, and waves washing its deck.

This minor battle has the appearance of one small Russian ship being harried to its destruction by four Japanese destroyers, but in battle one event becomes a cause that gives rise to another event—so it has always been. That other event can easily be one that was quite unexpected.

Inside the harbor, the sound of the guns of the *Ikazuchi* and the others roused Vice Admiral Makarov from his slumber. He had been in bed in his commander's office on the warship *Petropavlovsk* (10,960 tons) that early morning.

"Attack!" he ordered.

On the mast of the great warship, the standard that indicated he was on board was raised. The ship already had its boilers stoked so that little time elapsed between his order and the actual attack.

Meanwhile, the situation outside the harbor had further changed. The four Japanese destroyers fled, with the armored cruiser *Bayan* in pursuit. Then in the offing the six ships of the Japanese Combined Fleet's Third Division (the armored cruisers *Tokiwa* and *Asama* had been added temporarily) commanded by Rear Admiral Dewa Shigetō were seen approaching. These were the *Chitose* (4,760 tons), the *Takasago* (4,155 tons), the *Kasagi* (4,900 tons), the *Yoshino* (4,150 tons), the *Tokiwa* (9,855 tons), and the *Asama* (9,750 tons). All had a speed of 22.5 knots, and all of them billowed forth great plumes of black smoke from their funnels.

Dewa, hoping to save the *Ikazuchi* and the other three destroyers, ordered a sudden artillery assault on the *Bayan*, which should by all rights have fled. Its captain Viren, however, showed incredible bravery in attempting to fight with his single vessel against the Japanese side's six cruisers and four destroyers. The Russian ship approached at full speed, parting the waves before it. Makarov was informed of what was happening, and he decided that now was the time for a limited battle.

One might conclude that Makarov was being too brave in this case. Like a cavalryman who hears that the enemy is in sight and then leaps onto his horse to ride off, Makarov's flagship the *Petropavlovsk* slid out of the harbor. Not many other ships joined it. The small protected cruiser *Novik* commanded by von Essen was, as always, one of the first to leave the harbor's protection. Next came the battleship *Sevastopol*, the protected cruiser *Askold*, the protected cruiser *Diana*, and the battleship *Pobeda*—a rather motley collection. There were in addition nine destroyers.

Seeing them from a distance, Commander Dewa looked at his staff officers and asked, "Isn't that Makarov?"

They had no reply, since the distance was still too great to see the standard that would indicate if he were on board or not. Yet three Russian battleships had certainly appeared, along with a group of destroyers and several cruisers. Never had such a mighty Russian force made its appearance on these seas.

"Let's lure them into the open sea," thought Dewa, but to do that he would first have to expose himself to a hail of enemy artillery shells.

When the *Petropavlovsk* opened fire, the other ships fired as well, and immediately shells fell one after the other into the sea around Dewa's flagship *Chitose*, roiling the waves.

All the Japanese ships from the *Chitose* on down opened fire, although they knew they were no match for the Russian force, and soon the surface of the water was covered in smoke from both sides' guns. The *Chitose*, scurrying about the area, almost collided with the *Yoshino*.

The Japanese side would engage the enemy and then retreat, retreat and then engage, trying to lure the Russians into the open sea by these complex maneuvers. At last, Makarov decided on pushing his attack into the open sea. He had his ships shift into single-echelon right formation. The entire flotilla increased speed and approached Dewa's force to attack.

"They're coming!" Dewa realized. He made for the spot where Tōgō's group of battleships was lying in wait and tried to draw Makarov toward it.

Relying, no doubt, on the massive size of his naval forces, and above all on his own courage, Makarov allowed himself to be led on by Dewa. He raced along and finally went outside the 15-league limit, into the open sea. Tōgō was waiting for him. He had his *Mikasa*, as well as the *Asahi*, *Fuji*, *Yashima*, *Shikishima*, and *Hatsuse*, and, in addition, the newly built cruisers *Kasuga* and *Nisshin*, which had been added to the fleet only two days before.

"There they are!" Makarov saw that he had reached a point beyond which he should not dare to venture. He immediately ordered his entire fleet to withdraw, and his flagship crashed through the waves as it reversed course, attempting to get back within the range of the land artillery. The other Russian ships followed suit. At last, they came back within their side's artillery range, but Makarov did not enter the harbor, since he was still attempting to fight.

Just then, the mists lifted from the water, and one could see the blue of the sky. In a complete reversal of weather conditions from the previous night, visibility was excellent, and each side could easily see the other's ships and their movements.

*　*　*

Makarov was too daring on this particular morning for reasons unknown. We say "too daring" because he forgot about a very important practice he customarily followed upon leaving the port: he failed to have the harbor entrance swept for mines.

Without fail, he always had sent a small ship ahead to remove any mines that might have been laid beneath the surface of the water. Only then would he leave port on his flagship. This was just normal prudent behavior for a naval commander, but on this particular day, Makarov was indignant that one of his destroyers had been beaten and destroyed by a squadron of four Japanese destroyers. He'd sent out the armored cruiser *Bayan* to save the Russian destroyer, and, when that didn't work out, his fighting spirit turned into uncontrollable indignation. He didn't bother having the harbor entrance swept for mines. He set sail at once, so he could arrive at the scene of battle without losing any time at all.

That too didn't work out when he was challenged by the main force of Tōgō's fleet. Withdrawing, he fired his guns from the stern of his ship and tried to draw Tōgō within range of the Russian land artillery. He directed the operation very deftly indeed, as was his way.

"Ah, that Makarov is something!" Saneyuki thought, as he watched the scene from on board the *Mikasa*, highly impressed.

The battleships from *Mikasa* on down fired shells at the battleship *Petropavlovsk* as far as their range permitted, but they only made one hit—the other shells landed in the water. Meanwhile, Makarov outran the pursuing Tōgō.

"Oh, he's started his usual return-to-port maneuver," thought Saneyuki, watching without the benefit of binoculars from his distant perch.

Tōgō, however, was using his binoculars. His other staff officers also continued to watch the movements of Makarov's flotilla, though their binoculars did not have the great magnification of Tōgō's. Makarov was not in charge of the handling of the flagship—that was the job of Captain Nikolai Yakovlev. The ship was, as always, moving parallel to the mountain range on the Laohuwei Peninsula, reducing speed as it moved along the coast and headed for the entrance to Port Arthur's harbor. The bell signaling the end of hostilities sounded. The sailors left the ship's guns and sat stretching their legs on the ship deck here and there.

As Makarov emerged from his battle command station, he happened to notice military artist Vasily Vereshchagin standing there and greeted him in high spirits. "How's the sketching going?"

The artist raised his eyes from his sketchbook and, seeing it was the admiral speaking to him, presented the sketchbook for inspection with both hands, rather shyly. The Japanese fleet was depicted on the horizon in the sketch.

The Japanese fleet could be seen on the actual horizon, as well. Numerous plumes of smoke colored the sky.

Just then, there was a roar so loud it seemed as if earth and sky had been blown apart. The ship's hull was lifted up, the deck sloped sharply upward, and a great pillar of fire arose. All this happened at once. Makarov was tossed into the air by the blast and then thrown down upon the deck.

When Makarov tried to make his way, he discovered that he was covered in blood. Immediately, he unbuttoned his greatcoat and took it off, and then did the same with his boots. This aged admiral, so accustomed to the sea, intended to jump into the water to save himself. Unfazed by his severe wounds, he tried to make his way to the gunwales.

The deck, however, sloped upward like the steepest part of a steep hill, and he found it hard to keep his footing. Then there was a second explosion. Knowing that escape was now unlikely, he fell to his knees and offered a final prayer. It took only one minute and thirty seconds from the time of the first explosion until the *Petropavlovsk* sank beneath the waves. Makarov went to the bottom along with his ship. More than 630 other men joined him in death.

"This is unbelievable!" shouted the Russian soldiers manning the gun emplacements near the water's edge at Golden Hill as they watched the scene.

Makarov had a fine reputation also among the soldiers, even though they belonged to a different branch of the armed forces. They had been watching the *Petropavlovsk* quietly making its way back to port after the battle had ended, together with the ten to twenty other vessels, large and small. As the flagship came alongside the reef, there was a sudden, great explosion. The seawater rose up like a wall and engulfed the ship. Then there was a second explosion, and the ship started to belch forth great clouds of greenish-yellow smoke. Almost at once, the prow of the ship sank, and the stern rose high up into the air, its screw propeller turning with tremendous force in empty space. The whole ship sank as they watched, and all that was left was smoke on the surface of the water.

That was the scene of the flagship's sinking witnessed by the solders manning the guns on Golden Hill. They all knelt down, doffed their hats, and offered prayers in the Russian manner, crossing themselves three times, with the thumb and first two fingers of the right hand brought together in a Trinitarian symbol. Thus, they mourned the death of the world-famous admiral in whom they had taken such pride.

The men of the Japanese fleet had also witnessed the sinking from a great distance—so great that they could not clearly make out what had happened. A ship that seemed to be the *Petropavlovsk* was suddenly engulfed in black smoke, and a great roar echoed across the water, audible on the Japanese ships as well. And, in the next instant, the ship could no longer be seen.

"What happened?" asked one staff officer of another. Certainly, a huge ship to the rear had vanished. But it had happened so suddenly that they thought they might have been mistaken and could not quite believe what they had seen. Saneyuki, one of these staff officers, did not have binoculars (why will be explained later) and therefore did not see what had happened at all. The staff officers were about to report to Imperial General Headquarters that "An enemy ship appears to have been sunk, though the report cannot be confirmed."

Tōgō, however, lowered his binoculars and stated as fact, "It sank, all right. And it was the flagship *Petropavlovsk*." With his high-powered binoculars, he was the only one who could confirm what had happened.

* * *

The flagship of the Port Arthur Squadron had sunk beneath the waves, together with the commander in chief. When this was confirmed by a cable from Reuters, a staff officer on the *Mikasa* proposed to Tōgō that they send a wireless message of condolence to the enemy. It was a perfectly natural suggestion. This sort of chivalrous code was still observed throughout the world at this period, and indeed the Japanese Navy had done the same kind of thing for Chinese admiral Ding Ruchang during the First Sino-Japanese War.

Everyone expected that Tōgō would nod and say, "Of course." But to their surprise, he said simply, "No." Because his refusal had been all too clear, the others fell silent, and no one said another word. Of course, everyone wanted to know the reason for Tōgō's refusal, but no one dared to raise the subject again with this famously taciturn admiral.

Ogasawara Naganari later became Tōgō's biographer, and after the war he asked the admiral the reason for his refusal. Tōgō just smiled slightly and said, "Because I didn't feel like doing it." That was the kind of man he was. He never made excuses for his behavior. It was not that he was completely lacking in such feelings as "loving one's enemies." After the naval battle of Tsushima, he went to see the wounded Russian admiral Rozhestvensky in the Sasebo Naval Hospital. When Ogasawara asked him about his reasons for that visit as well, Tōgō once again smiled slightly and replied, "Because I felt like paying him a visit."

And that was that.

Tōgō must have been in a complicated state of mind at the time of Makarov's death. The Japanese had not yet arrived at even the foothills of the precipitous pass that was this war. Makarov's death would not resolve the tremendously difficult situation that Tōgō had found himself in from the very start. The Japanese might lose the decisive battles that were to come. What happened to Makarov today might happen to Tōgō tomorrow, so it seemed pointless and disagreeable to make a show of sympathy now—so Tōgō must have felt.

At any rate, Makarov and his flagship had sunk to the bottom of the sea due to the mines that the Japanese side had laid the previous night. Right after the explosions and sinking, the entire Russian military was seized with the suspicion that a submarine had been behind this deed. The Russian ships all fired their guns wildly into the sea as they fled pell-mell into the harbor. The United States already had submarines at this date, and the Russians thought that perhaps Japan had them too, though they were in fact a "still unborn form of weapon," so far as Japan was concerned.

* * *

One month after Makarov and his flagship's encounter with the mines, the same tragedy befell Tōgō's fleet. Japan lost two battleships in a single day, and thus the mines may have done far more damage than Russia had suffered earlier.

After Makarov's death, the Port Arthur Squadron stopped coming out to attack as before. Their morale seemed to have weakened, like a flame that has been snuffed out. But this did not mean that all of the officers and men of the squadron were unfaithful to their duties. For example, Commander Fyodor Ivanov, the captain of the minelayer *Amur*, kept on showing his face at the harbor entrance, just as in Makarov's days, carefully noting the movements of the Japanese fleet on the open seas beyond. He discovered that the Japanese followed a set pattern of movements. Ivanov concluded that if he studied those movements and then laid mines accordingly, the Japanese ships would probably run into them. In short, he was trying to pay them back for what they had done, using the same ideas and operations that the Japanese had employed against Makarov. He expressed his views to Admiral Vitgeft, who was acting as commander in chief after Makarov's death.

"You want to lay mines in the open sea?" said Vitgeft, surprised at the unusual plan. Usually mines were laid near harbors and bays to prevent the entry of enemy ships, but Ivanov wanted to lay them in the open sea. He proposed using the essentially defensive weapon of a minefield in an aggressive, attack mode. "Aren't the open seas too wide an area?" Vitgeft wanted to know.

Ivanov had already made a very careful investigation of that issue. "The open seas are very wide, but Tōgō moves in a set pattern. If we determine where he customarily passes, the area won't be too wide. Then, if we lay fifty mines, he'll fall into our trap for sure!"

The plan was to lay fifty mines over a distance of 1 nautical mile at a right angle to the Japanese fleet's habitual course. The problem was that these were international waters according to international law. Territorial waters were defined as extending only 3 nautical miles from the coast, but the plan was to lay mines in the open seas more than 10 nautical miles from the coast. There was sure to be opposition from various foreign countries, but Captain Ivanov didn't say a word about this. If he so much as touched on this problem, he was sure that the timid Vitgeft would try to protect himself from criticism and crush Ivanov's plan.

But as things were, Vitgeft, who tended to be passive regarding all matters, approved the plan and implemented it with a zeal that seemed close to miraculous. Captain Ivanov was overjoyed. He crept onto the open seas under cover of darkness that night and laid the mines, finishing the job. Ivanov was an eager student of tactics, and, though at first he laid the mines in a straight line, he later revised this to a half-circle. His mines gave the Russians a military advantage beyond anything he himself had expected.

* * *

Making their greatest mistake, the Japanese failed to conceive of the simple fact that the same mine strategy they had first used against the enemy would now be used by the enemy against them. Neither Shimamura Hayao, the chief of staff, nor Akiyama Saneyuki, vice chief of staff, felt any uneasiness on that score. However, the captains of the destroyers and ships that constantly patrolled the waters just outside the entrance to the harbor of Port Arthur came to the *Mikasa* and strongly urged changes in the main fleet's routes. "If the main force of the fleet always follows the same set course in the open seas beyond Port Arthur, the enemy will do the same thing to us that we did to them—they're not fools, after all!"

"But would the Russians have the temerity to lay mines in international waters?" one of the staff officers asked. Ships other than those from the two warring sides passed through these international waters. If the Russians laid mines there, and one of the neutral nations' ships went down, international criticism would be merciless.

Still, changing the Japanese fleet's habitual patterns of movement seemed best. Saneyuki did research on possible new routes, drew lines on the map, and got Shimamura Hayao's permission to make the changes. However, when such a large fleet is engaged in repeated actions involving a number of different subgroups, it's impossible to make sudden changes, and so they decided to use the old routes until May 15. Ironically, the greatest misfortune for the Japanese in the entire war took place precisely on May 15.

Prior to that, they learned that the enemy gunships were making frequent forays into the open sea under cover of night. Their mission was unclear. Meeting in the *Mikasa*'s strategy room, the staff officers judged that they might be laying mines, and so it was decided to send the Third Squadron, commanded by Vice Admiral Kataoka Shichirō, to conduct sweeping operations. The Third Squadron began work at seven in the morning on May 12.

To carry out such an operation while under shelling from the Russian artillery emplacements was indescribably difficult. First of all, the main force of the Third Squadron would undertake the protection of the ships that were actually doing the sweeping. But the main force of the Third Squadron was made up of dilapidated ships dating from the First Sino-Japanese War: the protected cruiser *Itsukushima* was the flagship, and the *Chin'en* (this was the *Zhenyuan*, the Chinese battleship captured by the Japanese during the First Sino-Japanese War), *Hashidate*, and *Matsushima* made up the rest of the group. From the sea, they kept up protective fire against the Port Arthur fortifications, while the minesweepers did their work.

Around four o'clock that afternoon, minesweeper *No. 48* suddenly blew up during the operation and split in two. There were fourteen dead and wounded. Two days later on May 14, the dispatch vessel *Miyako* (1,772 tons) was moving about the area to be swept at 20 knots, its top speed. Charged with collecting intelligence about the enemy and firing artillery at enemy land fortifications, the ship struck a mine at half past four in the afternoon and sank twenty minutes later. There were two dead and three wounded.

The Japanese managed to destroy fifteen mines in the sweeping operations that took place from the twelfth through the fifteenth, and they felt rather relieved to have done so. But, of course, they did not realize that the Russians had laid a total of fifty mines—a very large number—in the open seas.

* * *

The destructive power of a mine laid beneath the surface of the sea is greater than the biggest artillery shell that can be fired at a warship. An artillery shell may be able to inflict particularly great damage on a battleship encased in strong steel armor but cannot sink it, unless the ammunition stores happen to be set alight and explode. A mine, on the other hand, destroys the hull of a warship—ripping out the bottom—and so can sometimes sink a huge ship in an instant.

Now Tōgō's fleet was not patrolling outside the harbor of Port Arthur every day at full force. The fleet had been divided into two parts, which alternated in going out on patrol.

There were six battleships in the fleet: the *Mikasa, Asahi, Fuji, Hatsuse, Shikishima*, and *Yashima*. Japan's destiny rested on these six ships. Out three of them went, on alternate days. When Tōgō was in charge, the *Mikasa* would be the flagship, with the *Asahi* and the *Fuji* following behind. On the fateful day of May 15, Tōgō was not on duty. Had he been, he might well have suffered the same fate as Makarov. But Yamamoto Gombei had said that he had chosen Tōgō as the commander in chief of the Combined Fleet because he was "a lucky man." And, true to his good luck, Tōgō was at a base on the northwest coast of Korea that day.

Rear Admiral Nashiha Tokioki was on board the *Hatsuse*, substituting for Tōgō. He led the *Shikishima* and the *Yashima*, as well as cruisers, destroyers, and other smaller vessels on the regular patrol. An "X-point" (close to Laotie Hill) had been set in the open sea outside the harbor entrance, and the patrol would go to that point, then turn right around, and come back. May 15 was the last day for use of this "X-point," which was to be abolished after that.

A powerful battleship of 15,240 tons and capable of going 18 knots per hour, the *Hatsuse* was the lead with the *Shikishima* and the *Yashima* following behind in that order. The group proceeded to an area near Port Arthur and reached there just as the day dawned. The thick nocturnal mist had lifted, and visibility was good.

"We moved forward calmly, without any worries," reminisced Vice Admiral Teragaki Izō, looking back on the time when he was still a captain in command of the *Shikishima*. The water was deep in that area, and since they were 11 nautical miles to the south of Port Arthur, the Japanese ships were far outside the range of the enemy's land artillery. At a little before eleven in the morning, there was a huge explosion ahead of the *Shikishima*, and, when Captain Teragaki looked in that direction, he saw a great swirl of smoke rising up near the *Hatsuse*'s stern, and then the ship began to sink, stern first.

As they learned later, the bottom of the *Hatsuse*'s stern had struck a mine, and the helm was broken. Immediately afterward, it struck another mine, and this time the ammunition stores exploded. Debris was sent flying in all directions, and the ship sank in one minute and thirty seconds. Four hundred ninety-three men died.

The *Yashima* (12,514 tons), immediately to the rear, tried to rescue the *Hatsuse*'s crew and also struck a mine. A great explosion ripped open the bottom of the hull. It was finally able to strand itself on a nearby reef but then sank before long. The entire crew, however, was saved.

* * *

Since ancient times, people have believed in the mysterious thing called fate or destiny, and the misfortunes that continued for the six days around May 15 made everyone connected with the wartime Japanese Navy think that there might indeed be such a force. All of these misfortunes involved mine incidents and accidental collisions between Japanese vessels, leading to the loss of warships.

On May 12, *No. 48* of the minesweeping squad had hit a mine and was blown up, and two days later the dispatch vessel *Miyako* struck a mine and sank. On the fifteenth, the battleships *Hatsuse* and *Yashima* were lost around the same time. In a different area of the ocean, the protected cruiser *Yoshino* (4,150 tons) and the newly built armored cruiser *Kasuga* collided with each other in the dark of night. The *Kasuga*'s ram bow, beneath the waterline, tore a hole in the hull of the *Yoshino*, which at once began to list and then sank before the crew had time to escape. Three hundred nineteen men died, from the captain on down. The *Yoshino* was by then no more than a second-rate player by the standards of the naval drama of the Russo-Japanese War, but because of its high speed, the ship had played a leading role in naval battles during the First Sino-Japanese War ten years earlier.

On the same day, the dispatch vessel *Tatsuta* (864 tons) got stranded on the southeast coast of Guanglu Island, while, on the sixteenth, the gunboat Ōshima sank after colliding with the gunboat *Akagi*. Then, on the seventeenth, the destroyer *Akatsuki* (363 tons) struck a mine in the offing near Laotie Hill while involved in a battle and sank, with the loss of twenty-three men from the captain on down.

Captain Teragaki, who had been on board the battleship *Shikishima*, later described the sinking of the battleship *Hatsuse*. "The deck sloped upward, and men fell down from there like a human waterfall." This series of tragedies befell Tōgō's fleet, which had hitherto been untouched, in the short space of six days. We can only wonder why.

The Japanese fleet had lost eight ships without receiving any hostile artillery fire. In particular, the loss of two battleships that would have been overwhelmingly effective in any forthcoming sea battles boded ill for the future of Japan's naval war. The Japanese side had up to then preserved a balance vis-à-vis the six enemy battleships in the Port Arthur Squadron, but in one day it was reduced to only four battleships, a thirty-three percent loss. Ten years would be needed to replace them with new ships, if we include the time required for the requisite political maneuverings. The ship captains there on the spot where the Japanese side incurred so much damage were stunned and found themselves wondering, "Just how are we to fight this war from now on?"

Tōgō and his *Mikasa* were at a temporary base in the Changshan Islands, 30 nautical miles to the northeast of Dalian Bay. Snippets of bad news reached the *Mikasa*'s wireless office one after the other, and, when they learned of the sinking of the *Hatsuse* and *Yashima* in particular, even the magnanimous chief of staff Shimamura Hayao could say nothing. Saneyuki's face seemed frozen, his eyes not so much as blinking for a while. The whole business of naval strategy had now become very difficult. Only Tōgō, strange man that he was, showed no signs of strain.

* * *

Tōgō had been regarded as an extremely lucky man through all the naval engagements of this war, but his steely nerves in the face of bad luck were amazing. Two battleships had been lost, and, when the captains who managed to survive returned from the entrance waters of Port Arthur and came on board the *Mikasa* to report what had happened, not one of them could look Tōgō in the face. All wept openly at the cruel fate of their ships.

But Tōgō was calm, as always. "Thank you all for your efforts," he said, and nothing more. He then pushed a dish of sweets on his table toward them, urging them to eat.

The British officers who were on board the *Asahi* as observers were amazed and impressed at Tōgō's attitude at the time, and various accounts of that scene made their way to many foreign countries.

Saneyuki, who functioned as the "brains" behind Tōgō's operations, asked himself, "In Tōgō's place, could I act the same way he has?" Tōgō seemed to be leading the fleet not so much with his brain as with his spirit. Had Saneyuki (the "brains") been in Tōgō's position, he might well have become enraged or indignant, or tried to bluff his way through.

All his life Tōgō was a strange person who never openly showed either his wisdom or his foolishness. When his appointment as commander in chief was announced, there had been discussion at the Combined Fleet's base in Sasebo about whether he was a wise naval leader. Most of the officers thought that, though he might not be incompetent, he was at best a mediocre leader.

"Tōgō was a rather vague presence, even among the officers at Sasebo." Moriyama Keizaburō, Saneyuki's close friend since Naval Academy days, offered this recollection years later at a panel discussion. "There was no agreement about his abilities. Many of us officers felt among ourselves that it was wrong of the navy to send along this half-senile commander in chief just as we were about to enter a war. They must have chosen him because he was from Satsuma. Things weren't looking good with him in charge— anyway, that's how we evaluated him at the time."

When Tōgō arrived in Sasebo by train, only three people went to meet him at the station: Lieutenant Commander Moriyama Keizaburō, Rear Admiral Nashiha Tokioki, and the captain of the *Mikasa*, Ijichi Hikojirō. "Normally, the sailors of the fleet would have been there," Moriyama recalled, "and Tōgō would have been greeted with fanfare from a naval band perhaps. But as it was, the welcoming ceremony was very subdued. It was the first time I ever saw Tōgō."

He looked like any other small, old man; there was nothing of an admiral of the fleet's impressive presence about him. "The area in front of the station was reclaimed land," Moriyama continued, "and the surface was uneven, with several puddles. Tōgō walked over this patch of land uncertainly, looking down. I felt all the more that he was a man of no importance. Yet, after he had been the commander of the Combined Fleet for a while, all of the sailors were impressed by him. I felt once more that he was a very mysterious person."

Part 4

Translated by Juliet Winters Carpenter

1

YELLOW DUST

The sun grew hotter by the day.

Although the army had landed and been deployed according to plan on its way to Manchuria, subsequent fighting was not going as well as it might have. The Second Army was advancing northward through the hills, headed for enemy headquarters at Telissu railway station. Fighting was extremely fierce, the margin of victory continually razor thin.

Imperial General Headquarters in Tokyo fretted nervously, wondering what the devil the Second Army was doing. Presumably distracted by the heavy fighting, the Second Army command was not filing up-to-the-minute reports on battle conditions but merely sending a series of wires with the identical message: "Now in the thick of battle." Of what exactly was transpiring, there was no word.

For a while, Imperial Headquarters was filled with gloom on the assumption that the Second Army must be losing badly. "They do nothing but panic," thought Kodama Gentarō disparagingly. The thing to do, in his opinion, was to establish a Manchurian army with on-site senior command over the various armies. This would mean transferring Chief of the General Staff Ōyama Iwao and Vice Chief Kodama himself from Tokyo to Manchuria.

Slipups by Kodama and others were partly to blame for the trouble. Their calculations as to the amount of ammunition required for this campaign had been fuzzy, and there was no fixed means of transport. As a result, the Second Army faced nagging problems about replenishing its supplies. Their weapons and ammunition too had turned out to be far inferior to those of the Russians. The rifles were all right, but the artillery guns were ineffective, a third less powerful than Russian guns in terms of range and speed of firing. Not only that, many of the shells failed to detonate.

The cause of the Second Army's string of victories lay rather in the Russians. Although War Minister Alexei Kuropatkin's simple, grand strategy aimed at gathering a large army in the vicinity of Liaoyang and using it to destroy the Japanese Army as it advanced northward, Viceroy Alexeyev took seriously the defeats at Jinzhou and Nanshan, and ordered Kuropatkin to rescue Port Arthur. As a result, the army's purpose was divided, and Kuropatkin sent half his soldiers south.

Lieutenant General Stakelberg, commander of the southbound corps, was known for his intrepidness. South he went, clashing on the way with the northbound Second Army at Telissu. He fought with great courage and put intense pressure on the Japanese forces wherever he encountered them. However, he was laboring under a serious misapprehension: he overestimated the strength of the Second Army several times over.

In the end, Stakelberg pulled back. Had his military intelligence been accurate and had he swept southward with sufficient force to penetrate the Second Army's zone of control, the Japanese forces, unable to resist, would undoubtedly have suffered a crushing defeat.

* * *

The great battle of Liaoyang was fast approaching. This was to be a major engagement of the sort where two sides come together at a preset location, concentrating all the manpower and firepower they each have at their disposal, and clash at a predictable hour until the fated outcome is reached. The looming battle of Liaoyang would be a pitched battle on a scale rarely seen in world history.

With Japan clearly in need of senior officers in command on the scene, it was a given that the man who would actually command the Manchurian Army would be General Kodama Gentarō. Everyone knew that only he had the brains to be head of military strategy for the Russo-Japanese War. The question was: who should be his commander in chief?

Field Marshal Yamagata Aritomo volunteered enthusiastically for the job, once again causing a slight difficulty for Kodama. All his life long, Yamagata was dogged by the childish grand ambition—or the poetic delusion—of proving his manhood by leading a great army in a decisive battle on which hung the fate of the nation. His battle experience was limited to his days in the Chōshū irregular militia, and he had been involved almost exclusively in military administration ever since. This born statesman was highly accomplished in that area, and from the earliest nation-building days of Meiji had been the respected head of Japan's military. But there was no getting away from his particularly disagreeable personality and narrowness of spirit that would not allow talented underlings to exercise their full abilities.

"I can't do the job under old man Yamagata," Kodama let on, appealing to Prime Minister Katsura Tarō and Army Minister Terauchi Masatake. Both Yamagata and Kodama were men of Chōshū, as were Katsura and Terauchi. Though he and Yamagata were bosom friends, Kodama knew that he couldn't fight a war under the leadership of the strongly idiosyncratic Yamagata, who was bound to second-guess every strategic decision until Kodama would be more worn out from dealing with him than with the enemy.

Kodama had had someone else in mind from the first: Ōyama Iwao. A former Satsuma general, Ōyama was a man of immense generosity and a born leader. Kodama campaigned on his behalf, but Terauchi and Katsura deferred to Yamagata as a genrō of the military. Finally, Kodama appealed to Emperor Meiji, hoping he would issue a direct command. The emperor was not particularly enamored of Yamagata, preferring Ōyama's expansive style, so he willingly intervened. Ōyama got the job.

* * *

Soon after Ōyama was made commander in chief of the Manchurian Army, he went to the Naval Ministry and presented himself at the minister's office, reporting formally to Yamamoto Gombei, who had already been informed of the appointment and so showed no surprise. He did express regret, however, telling Ōyama outright that it was a shame, that Ōyama belonged in Tokyo and the promotion should have gone instead to Nozu Michitsura, commander of the Fourth Army.

"Yes, I know," answered Ōyama, equally forthrightly. "He's a better man for the job." A fellow native of Satsuma, Ōyama knew all too well Nozu's brilliance in war. "But all the army commanders are heroes," he said. The First Army was led by Kuroki Tamemoto, the Second by Oku Yasukata, the Third by Nogi Maresuke, the Fourth by Nozu Michitsura. All four men had played active roles during the upheaval at the end of the Tokugawa period and had come through the fires of war in the Meiji period. Moreover, they were equals. Singling out Nozu as commander in chief would be likely to raise the hackles of the rest, creating a difficult situation. "That's why I have to go."

That same day, Ōyama had an audience with Emperor Meiji at the palace. The emperor shared with him the thinking behind his decision. "Yamagata is a good man but too prickly. He criticizes every little thing, which seems to upset the other leaders, but you're not so demanding. That's why I picked you."

Ōyama laughed. "So you're saying I'll make a good commander in chief because I'm fog-brained, is that it?"

The emperor laughed back. "Well, something like that."

Later, Ōyama relayed this conversation to Yamamoto Gombei with a chuckle. Then he added, "Since I was chosen for my fogginess, I'll leave the details of fighting to Kodama. But if it turns into a losing battle, I'll take the reins."

Then he made a request. "I want you to decide when it's over." He meant, decide when to make a peace feeler. The two men had previously spent much time discussing this very thing and had begun the war with the understanding that in the end they would appeal to a third country for peace negotiations. With Ōyama off on the battlefield, it would be up to Yamamoto Gombei to carry out this mission single-handed.

"I accept," said Yamamoto. He personally filled a clay teapot with tea and served his friend. Ōyama picked up his cup and emptied it in one gulp as if it were medicine, then paused before drawling a thank you in Kagoshima dialect. He had some odd ways.

* * *

On July 6, 1904, at ten o'clock in the morning, Ōyama Iwao and Kodama Gentarō set off from Tokyo's Shimbashi Station with their staffs in tow. They arrived two days later at Hiroshima, where the *Aki Maru* was waiting in Ujina Harbor to carry them to the scene of battle. They set sail on July 10.

On board ship, Kodama spent little time in his cabin, preferring to roam around and strike up random conversations or look out at the scenery. He was like a windup doll, constantly in motion. This small man had always been that way. Traditionally, brilliant strategists seem always to be calm individuals whose every spare moment is devoted to reading. If such a pattern exists, Kodama Gentarō was an exception. With no formal schooling in the ways of the modern military, this self-taught man read little once he was furnished with the necessary knowledge. Only in moments of extreme boredom would he sprawl on the floor with a popular historical narrative, reading at random. The bookworms in the military used to marvel that stratagems so ingenious could emerge from a mind like Kodama's. The only explanation was that he was a man of genius.

At this time, Jacob Meckel was in the Ministry of War in Berlin. Germany itself was allied with Russia, and so supported Russia in the Russo-Japanese War, but Meckel personally rooted for the Japanese. He also assured the newspaper reporters assigned to the ministry that Japan would win, an outcome of which he had no doubt. Once he told a journalist, "Japan has

Kodama. As long as he's there, the Japanese Army is bound to come out on top." Even to Meckel, the most brilliant tactician in the German Army, Kodama's strange faculties came across as genius.

To digress a bit, here's what Meckel said about the Japanese military around the same time. "German and French military officers show great zeal for study, but there's no comparing them with Japanese officers. The Japanese make amazing efforts to increase their own knowledge of military matters. The other distinguishing characteristic of the Japanese military man is his fearlessness of death, which will doubtless play into the coming victory."

The *Aki Maru* was heading for Dalian Harbor with Ōyama and Kodama aboard, but stopped along the way to call on the Combined Fleet, anchored at the base in the Changshan Islands. This was to allow the two leaders to meet with Tōgō Heihachirō on board the *Mikasa* and discuss the joint operation.

Saneyuki sat in on these talks as a member of Tōgō's staff. Kodama kept a cigar in his mouth throughout. Every so often, he would drop it in a burst of hearty laughter, then scramble to pick it up off the floor.

* * *

Saneyuki firmly believed that the army's sensibilities were dulled where Port Arthur was concerned, and he freely shared this view with Shimamura Hayao, chief of staff of the First Squadron of the Combined Fleet. Inside the enemy harbor at Port Arthur lurked one of the world's largest fleets, a fact recognized though unappreciated by the army. If this fleet should ever get out and have its way on the open sea, Japan's seaborne supplies would be cut off. Left to its own devices, the army in Manchuria would wither away before the enemy could ever get to it.

For the Combined Fleet, consumed with its blockade of the enemy fleet inside the harbor, laying siege was a painful chore. Sailors had no time off and grew ever more fatigued, but the warships suffered even more. Barnacles grew on their hulls and scale accumulated in their boilers, draining their power and speed, but they couldn't go into dry dock. If the blockade went on without letup, by the time the main Russian fleet arrived from Europe and it was time to do battle, the Japanese would not be able to summon their trademark speed and thus would be vulnerable to defeat.

"If the enemy comes out of the harbor, that's a different matter. Then we fight them at sea and destroy them, and that's that. But they know that, and so they won't come out." Saneyuki explained this at the joint navy and army summit meeting aboard the *Mikasa*. "The enemy is smart. They're hiding in the harbor, waiting for the Baltic Fleet to arrive. If they keep on waiting, when the time comes, they'll be at double strength. Then they'll attack our fleet and sink it, establishing right of passage over the Sea of Japan and isolating the Japanese Army in Manchuria."

"That would be a disaster," said Kodama in a loud voice. If that happened, Japan would lose the war.

"Launching an attack from the sea on a fleet inside a fortified military harbor is next to impossible. We have to lure them out, and the only way to do that is to attack from land. If the army attacks the fortress and captures it, the fleet will have no choice but to leave the harbor."

In Tokyo, the Navy General Staff had already submitted a formal request for combat troops to the Army General Staff.

Attack Port Arthur? The Army General Staff had hesitated at first, but finally gave in to the navy's insistent demand and belatedly created the Third Army to do the job. This army, under the command of General Nogi Maresuke, had only recently been dispatched to the Liaodong Peninsula. The operation was yet to begin. The meeting aboard the *Mikasa* revolved around this point. The navy wanted the fortress taken as soon as possible so it could wrap things up at Port Arthur and move the fleet back to Sasebo. Unless the warships were overhauled soon, they would turn into unseaworthy tubs.

* * *

Ōyama and Kodama replied that they would do their best to comply with the navy's request and soon thereafter boarded the *Aki Maru*, headed for Dalian.

"To be honest," confessed Kodama in Ōyama's cabin, "Port Arthur was our oversight."

Successive vice chiefs of the General Staff had drawn up various plans for campaigns against Russia. The late Kawakami Sōroku had laid his plan, and Tamura Iyozō had come up with a very detailed one. Soon after becoming vice chief, Kodama had dusted off the Tamura plan and used it in designing his own strategy. None of the three men's campaign plans had called for an attack on Port Arthur.

Of course, in Kawakami's day Port Arthur had not really been fortified, and even in Tamura's day there'd been little indication that Russia was in the process of rebuilding the Port Arthur defenses as authentic, European-style forts. Nor was that all. The Japanese Army did not even fully understand what modern fortifications consisted of. And, even if they had understood, Kodama's plan for a decisive battle in Manchuria treated Port Arthur "as an extra," as he himself admitted. He thought it could be safely ignored.

Since the Port Arthur fortifications were on the extreme tip of Jinzhou Peninsula, jutting off the end of Liaodong Peninsula, we know that Kodama's plan had the army leaving that extreme tip untouched, while occupying the Nanshan area north of Port Arthur (this had already been accomplished) and building a powerful line of defense there with which to contain Port Arthur. After that, the main force could proceed northward to the Manchurian plains. This time, imagine the Jinzhou Peninsula as a pinky finger—they would tie a string around it at the top knuckle and cut off the blood supply, making Port Arthur rot.

His plan's focus was the Manchurian plains. Specifically, the army would subdue first Liaoyang and then Mukden, apportioning its scant (compared to the Russian Army) strength to get the job done.

But then the navy requested this attack on Port Arthur, which they had to carry out. Even though the request came from the navy, in a broad sense it was aimed at the support of Japanese soldiers in Manchuria. They had no choice but to comply.

For that purpose, the Third Army was formed, bringing together the First, Ninth, and Eleventh divisions. If it weren't for Port Arthur, thought Kodama regretfully, he could have used those three divisions in the battle of Liaoyang. Still, the business at Port Arthur wouldn't take long, he comforted himself. Not even he had any inkling of what lay ahead. He intended to send the Third Army on to the decisive battle on the Manchurian plains as soon as the Port Arthur fortifications fell. During the First Sino-Japanese War, it had taken a single day to capture the Chinese defenses at Port Arthur, which had been designed by a German; this time, it might take as long as five days, no longer than ten, by his reckoning.

On July 15, the *Aki Maru* entered Dalian Harbor, which had already fallen into the possession of the Japanese military. The men disembarked.

* * *

For its staff headquarters, Ōyama Iwao's Manchurian Army took over the just-vacated official residence of the Russian mayor of Dalian, an imposing brick building.

"Hard at it, I see!" Kodama went around the staff officers' table, talking to the men. Each one was busy preparing for the battle of Liaoyang. Not one had time to spare for the attack on Port Arthur. One major even predicted optimistically that the city would fall in a single day. Since the Japanese had already laid claim to cities north of Port Arthur, including Jinzhou, Nanshan, and even this city of Dalian, the expectation that Port Arthur would fall like a ripe persimmon was understandable.

"Any word from Nogi?" Kodama asked Colonel Matsukawa Toshitane. Matsukawa was from Miyagi Prefecture and had a methodical mind.

"Nothing, sir."

"Hasn't made any move yet, I'll bet."

"No, sir, he hasn't," replied Matsukawa, and at this, for some reason, Kodama laughed out loud. Not only were he and Nogi both men of Chōshū, they were also comrades in arms from the siege of Kumamoto Castle back in the Satsuma Rebellion. In Kodama's mind, his old friend Nogi was eccentric in a lovable way. Though earnest, Nogi was not a capable commander.

"Tomorrow we'll go to Nogi together and hold discussions to get him to hurry up." Leaving detailed instructions with Matsukawa, Kodama headed for the stairs.

Nogi had arrived on the scene a month ahead of Kodama and the others, but he hadn't been killing time. He had carried out preparatory operations needed as a springboard for the eventual attack on Port Arthur. In particular, shortly after arriving, he had attacked a hill west of Dalian, which the Japanese called Tsurugizan—"Sword Hill"—and taken out its stronghold.

The attack on Sword Hill was carried out by the Forty-third Infantry Unit from the island of Shikoku. They attacked on June 26 under heavy artillery cover and took the fort after five hours of fierce fighting. The mountain was defended by a Captain Lopatin, who held on ably with only half the troop strength of the Japanese, making the rounds from position to position to cheer his men and fighting on until he had lost three-quarters of them. This Captain Lopatin was one of the most valiant battle commanders in the entire Russian Army, but after he withdrew to Port Arthur, Stoessel, commander of the fortress there, held him responsible for the retreat and had him court-martialed. Incensed at this treatment, Lopatin committed suicide in prison.

Nogi was impressed by the fighting of the Russian soldiers, but Sword Hill's quick surrender made him all the more optimistic about the Port Arthur fortifications. What he did not know was that the mountain stronghold was not a permanent fort like the one at Port Arthur. It was more like an entrenchment, something built by Lopatin and his infantrymen for field maneuvers.

* * *

General Nogi and his staff, meanwhile, were in a village called Beipaoziya, just before Dalian on the railway line laid by the Russians. There was a railway maintenance center in the village with a two-story brick building that Nogi made his headquarters, using the second floor for his living quarters.

Generals Ōyama and Kodama rode up on horseback to this building, accompanied by nine staff officers. The sun was already high in the sky and scorching the red dirt. The building was surrounded by a grove of poplars, and there was a little flower garden by the front door. The trees and the flowers had been planted by the Russians.

"There are even apple trees!" After Kodama dismounted, he looked around, taking note. Nogi came out to meet them, accompanied by his staff, and as soon as Kodama spotted the general he rushed over and gripped him by the hand. "Please accept my condolences on the loss of your son."

Nogi's older son Katsusuke, a second lieutenant, had participated in the attack on Jinzhou as a platoon leader in the infantry's First Regiment, but at dawn on May 26, two months before this encounter, he had been shot by a Russian defending the eastern city gate with a machine gun. The bullet lodged in the flesh, and he died in the hospital the following day. Ten days later, his father had landed at Yandaao, and the next day passed through the fresh battlefield at Jinzhou. That was when he composed the celebrated elegiac poem, "Outside Jinzhou City Walls."

> Hills, rivers, grasses, trees turned desolate.
> For ten leagues the winds smell of fresh blood from the battlefield.
> Horses are still, and men are silent.
> Outside Jinzhou city walls I stand in the sinking sun.

Kodama expressed his sincere sympathy. Nogi nodded wordlessly, then invited the party indoors.

Kodama seated himself and announced in a loud voice, "It's hot as the devil!"

Nogi's staff sat down quietly. Chief of Staff Ijichi Kōsuke, a specialist in artillery from Satsuma, and Toyoshima Yōzō, artillery commander of the Third Army—both of them major generals—were among those present. Somber as Nogi was, his staff officers were equally so. Kodama wondered momentarily if these people were all right.

* * *

Few high-ranking officers of the day had taken as much leave as Nogi in their career. His military philosophy was already out of date, so the General Staff couldn't use him to plan operations, and since he lacked administrative ability they had not been able to give him an administrative post either. He went on leave in May 1901, and when the fighting began he was called up to command the Imperial Guard Division held in reserve.

Eventually, when Imperial General Headquarters formed the Third Army, Nogi was appointed as commander, partly on the recommendation of Yamagata Aritomo, boss of the Chōshū clique. Commanders of almost all the armies from First to Fourth, as well as the Army of the Yalu, were from Satsuma. The sole exception was Oku of the Second Army, who was from Fukuoka. There were no Chōshū natives in command. By the standards of the day, therefore, Nogi inserted a needed balance into the personnel arrangements.

Nogi knew little about campaign planning in modern warfare. However, his personality was eminently suited to commanding a field army. The officer in command should be the object of his troops' admiration, and in that respect Nogi was ideal. For the rest, he could be assigned someone well versed in the tactics of modern warfare to assist him, and so Major General Ijichi Kōsuke of Satsuma was made his chief of staff. Ijichi had spent years overseas at the German General Staff Office and was a specialist in artillery. Only a chief of staff who was a specialist in artillery was qualified to lead an attack on the enemy stronghold.

In the end, however, Ijichi's dreadful incompetence and stubbornness made Nogi miserable. Worse, they caused the Third Army to shed needless gallons of blood. The fort at Port Arthur became a vast pump that sucked up Japanese blood.

Here is an example of Ijichi's blundering.

The plan suggested by the navy was an attack on 203-Meter Hill, a bare elevation that was the sole place left defenseless after Russia set in place an array of concrete defense works in the peninsula hills. Its defenseless state was evident to Tōgō's fleet on the sea. The first to discover the peak's vulnerability was Akiyama Saneyuki. But the justification for taking that particular peak was less the sheer ease of the operation than the more important fact that its summit was perfectly situated to look down on the harbor at Port Arthur. If the army captured 203-Meter Hill, hauled a big gun to the top, and fired at the Russian fleet in the harbor, they could make direct hits as easily as dropping stones on the road from a second-story window. Since the point of the land campaign was to get the fleet to leave the harbor, going after 203-Meter Hill was a vital and sufficient tactic.

But Ijichi laughed off the idea. "The army does things its own way," he said and settled on the direct approach—a frontal attack on the great fort. As the focus of the assault, he chose a point midway between Panlong, the northern fortification, and East Cockscomb Hill, the northeastern fortification, planning to penetrate the fort after slipping through there. Even though the route was between fortifications, there were countless strongholds on each side, providing enfilading fire. You could send millions of troops to storm that corridor, but still all would be instantly killed.

To summarize the rest of the story, when Ijichi's attack plan failed, at the last moment Kodama Gentarō set aside his work at General Headquarters of the Manchurian Army and came to Port Arthur to take charge of matters himself. He adopted the navy's proposed strategy and led a full-scale offensive against 203-Meter Hill. By then, the Russians had also realized the hill's strategic importance and had set up a defense network, so the assault involved enormous bloodshed. The hill's capture abruptly changed the course of the attack on Port Arthur. In the beginning, it was estimated that Port Arthur would fall in a single day, but counting from the preliminary struggle over Sword Hill, it took 191 days in all. Japanese casualties numbered sixty thousand, a bloody toll without precedent in world military history.

* * *

But we are getting ahead of ourselves, so let us return to where we left off.

Ōyama, Kodama, and Nogi climbed Sword Hill soon after its capture, guided by Ijichi. Once on top, Kodama marveled aloud at the view; indeed, the mountain's defensive position was high. On one side, they could look down on Dalian Harbor and, on the other, beyond waves of green hills to the south, they could see the cluster of defense positions around the fort at Port Arthur.

Ijichi explained his plan of attack, and Ōyama and Kodama listened in silence. Ōyama offered a single comment: "So the navy will bring its guns ashore?"

"Well, that's the agreement." Ijichi's reply lacked energy.

After it was decided to attack Port Arthur in line with the navy's request, deliberations had constantly taken place at Imperial General Headquarters between the army and the navy. Captain Yamashita Gentarō of the navy had declared his willingness to "put as much of the navy's heavy artillery at your disposal as I possibly can." Ijichi Kōsuke and Matsukawa Toshitane, both of whom were present, thanked him cordially for the offer before turning it down.

"The army is using all the manpower it can spare on the Port Arthur campaign," Matsukawa said, again proving that Japanese Army leaders had no idea of what they were up against. "On the siege line there are as many as three soldiers per meter, a huge number. Seeing that this is such a grand-scale operation on our part, I don't think we'll be needing any assistance from the navy."

Matsukawa was from the infantry arm of the military. His understanding was that the army could grab the big fort by using rifle-carrying infantrymen in sufficient numbers. Even Ijichi Kōsuke from the artillery arm thought the same way. In the beginning, Ijichi attached the Second Infantry Brigade to the Third Army to supply the main firepower. He believed this would be sufficient, and that led him, one of the designers of the plan, to leave Imperial General Headquarters and become chief of staff of the Third Army.

The assumption that the fort could be destroyed using only the shells from field artillery shows a pathetic lack of understanding. The Russians used over two hundred thousand barrels of cement to fortify Port Arthur. They made enormous underground chambers for batteries and barracks. The underground defense works were interconnected by tunnels. Field artillery shells would only blow up dirt and sand off the batteries without causing the least bit of damage to the actual fortifications.

The navy, meanwhile, having been engaged in an artillery duel with the fort ever since the opening of hostilities, was keenly aware of how resistant it was. Full-scale siege artillery was needed, and if the army could not supply it then the navy would have to remove the guns on its warships and carry them ashore to be used as a substitute. In the end, around the time of the Third Army's assault on Sword Hill, Ijichi reluctantly accepted the navy's offer. The heavy artillery squad headed by naval commander Kuroi Teijirō was then placed at the Third Army's disposal.

* * *

The army's fighting was not going according to plan. Had they been on schedule, by the time Ōyama and the others climbed Sword Hill and took in the view, the battle of Liaoyang, a major objective, should have been well underway. But needed supplies were not forthcoming, and that battle appeared likely to run beyond August.

Japanese military planners evidently lacked a strong sense of logistics. At this point, actual daily rations were short, never mind supplies for coming battles. The situation was so desperate that for a week in June the whole Second Army, including the First Cavalry Brigade headed by Akiyama Yoshifuru, went on half rations. For units on active combat duty, this was an especially painful show of ineptitude.

Yoshifuru's cavalrymen grew markedly weaker. Yoshifuru himself declared, "I've got my wine, so I don't need food." He declined rations and drank the brandy he always carried with him. When that ran out, he drank Chinese wine.

Supplies were the business of the logistics unit, but nobody had worked out a plan for hauling supplies to the front once they were unloaded in Dalian

Harbor. There was a railway at hand but no steam engine—nothing but some three hundred freight cars abandoned by the Russians. These were loaded with supplies, then surrounded by troops on all sides and pushed manually along the tracks. Chinese workhorses were also used. The head of the veterinary section, who was named Kishimoto, went around the Zhuanghe area buying up Chinese horses until he had around six hundred. He fitted them with Chinese-style pack saddles, and used them to transport bales of rice and the like. This emergency transport squad was dubbed the "workhorse queue," but the horses weren't strong, and most of them developed saddle sores, so in the end they weren't of much use. As a result, the men at the front edged closer to starvation.

In the meantime, Major Makino, a military administrator on Great Orphan Hill, fastened his eyes on Chinese horse-wagons. He bought up a big supply of them, calling them the "wheeled queue." This method proved fairly effective.

In the midst of these privations, on June 21, the Second Army captured Xiongyuecheng, and remained there a fortnight waiting for rations before occupying Gaiping on July 9. The First Army, based in Fenghuangcheng, captured Aiyangbianmen, and Beifenshuiling on the Liaoyang Road, preparing for the battle of Liaoyang.

This was the situation around the time Ōyama and Kodama landed in Dalian.

Around then, Yoshifuru was busily sending out spies to reconnoiter in the city of Dashiqiao and the Yingkou region, which were still in enemy hands. Now and then, a great burst of shellfire would descend on brigade headquarters. When he heard the scream of shells, Yoshifuru would reach for his ever-present liquor bottle. "I can't stand it without a drink," he said honestly, valiant a soldier as he was. He occasionally took a swig straight from a whiskey bottle. Apparently, he had no particular need for food to accompany his drinking. Sometimes when visiting the front, he would pull out a stick of pickled radish from his pocket and gnaw on it absently as he watched.

Out on the water, the Japanese Combined Fleet continued carrying out fixed exercises while continuing its blockade, keeping the Port Arthur Squadron penned in the harbor.

"Why doesn't the Port Arthur Squadron go out and fight on the open sea?" Voices of criticism rumbled within the Russian military. Even Stoessel uttered the same curses over and over again.

British Admiral Sir Cyprian Bridge, a naval tactician who later wrote about the Russian fleet under these conditions, expressed doubt about the sentiments of the Port Arthur Squadron. "Tōgō and Vitgeft"—Port Arthur

Squadron commander in chief—"were almost evenly matched in fighting strength. If Vitgeft had made up his mind to fight a decisive sea battle and engaged in fierce, close combat, then, even if he lost the greater part of his naval vessels as a result, he would undoubtedly have inflicted huge losses on Tōgō's fleet. Russia still had its main fleet in reserve, but Japan had only Tōgō's fleet. When Russia's main fleet arrived, Russia would have held sway over the Far Eastern seas."

This was probably true. This daring plan is what Russia should have followed. Vitgeft's fleet would have had to be steeled for destruction as it clashed with Tōgō's fleet in a fight sending both to the bottom of the sea. By sacrificing themselves, Vitgeft and his men could have saved their country. Admiral Bridge's plan would have succeeded by sacrificing Vitgeft. But Russian people at this time were deficient in such raw vitality, partly because Russian society itself was lacking in spirit, its systems superannuated.

Russia's Imperial Headquarters gave Vitgeft no such orders in the first place. If the tsar had ordered a fight to the death, the Russians might well have complied out of habitual loyalty. The only order that came down insistently was this: "Escape from Port Arthur and flee to Vladivostok." Not "Destroy Tōgō at sea and then report to Vladivostok."

But the end result was the same. The only way to get to Vladivostok was to leave Port Arthur. When they set out, Tōgō would be waiting.

Vitgeft had already gone out of the harbor entrance with his fleet on June 23, intending to obey the order, but Tōgō had immediately appeared with his main force, and Vitgeft beat a hasty retreat. Then Japan's Third Army began to step up its assault on Port Arthur, causing Vitgeft further panic. Moreover, he had information that the Japanese battleships *Hatsuse* and *Yashima* had hit mines and sunk. This news was reported in a highly sensationalized manner. Port Arthur was abuzz with rumors that Japan had lost almost all of its capital ships.

What with one thing and another, among Vitgeft and his staff the desire to make a run for it began gaining rapid ground.

* * *

In the streets of Port Arthur, drunken Russian soldiers who caught sight of a Russian sailor yelled for the squadron to leave. Such incidents happened frequently. Sometimes they led to a brawl, and the law would have to intervene. Stoessel fumed at his staff. "What the soldiers say is only right. What the hell is the navy doing? Their sailors do nothing but chase skirts in Port Arthur bars and cower in fear of Tōgō. Our men are only stating the obvious. Why shouldn't they!"

One time when the naval and army leaders met to debate whether the fleet should leave the harbor or stay, Stoessel got worked up. "I speak on behalf of the entire army. The Port Arthur Squadron should sortie in order to exterminate Tōgō, and, if it does not, the entire squadron should be punished for treason toward tsar and country."

Vitgeft, the normally placid commander in chief of the fleet, became so furious that he lost his equilibrium. "I beg your pardon. My ships are not under the command of you, an army lieutenant general. On the honor of the navy, I cannot allow such reckless talk."

"The honor of the navy?" scoffed Stoessel. "What honor is that? The honor of napping at Port Arthur like a duck in a puddle?" The quarrel stopped just short of a scuffle.

The Russian Army was far from sanguine about having the navy sit tight. Tōgō was blockading the harbor to cut off the Port Arthur Squadron, and Nogi was threatening to attack from the rear. If the squadron weren't there, the Japanese military wouldn't be so hell-bent on attacking Port Arthur. Such grousing spread throughout the troops.

While we're on the subject, it must be said that General Stoessel was committing a colossal error. Russia had turned the harbor at Port Arthur into a naval base. To protect a military harbor, the army must build fortifications in the surrounding area. The army at a military harbor is secondary to the navy, and it was incumbent on Stoessel to be more adaptable regarding the navy's plan of operations. He had no sympathy for the navy, but clung obstinately to the army's interests. The fault lay not in any character flaw on his part, but rather in the superannuated Russian bureaucracy and the bureaucratic mentality. All Russian government officials and military men of the era were like Stoessel, to a greater or lesser degree.

After the failed effort to venture out on June 23, Vitgeft held a council of generals, and they decided to revert to their former policy: the squadron would be maintained in the harbor as before and would not go to Vladivostok.

August came. Though the attack of Japan's Third Army had yet to yield results, the navy's heavy artillery began to make its presence felt, raining shells on the far-off streets of Port Arthur, churning up the occasional pillar of water in the harbor, and sometimes, though rarely, causing damage to warships. Vitgeft had no alternative but to leave.

* * *

The naval engagement that would be known as the "battle of the Yellow Sea" and that would exact a grisly toll on both sides began with Vitgeft's decision to exit the harbor. He had received a telegram from Viceroy Alexeyev informing him that this was the tsar's desire. His orders were to leave at once and go to Vladivostok. Vitgeft made up his mind to do so and devoted August 9 to preparations. For security reasons, no one but his private staff was informed.

To begin with, they had to lay in rations and coal, the latter a particularly grueling job for seamen of this era. After sundown, every warship began firing up its boiler. From these developments, the crews divined that the time had finally come to leave. "Watch out for Japanese spies" was a watchword aboard the ships, but Port Arthur counterintelligence was strict, infiltration by Japanese agents impossible. Out at sea, Tōgō remained unaware of these stirrings in the Port Arthur Squadron on the eve of battle.

The date changed to August 10. Shortly before dawn, Vitgeft ordered the ships out of the harbor.

The flagship *Tsesarevich* went first. As protection from torpedo attack, it was flanked by eight destroyers, headed by the cruiser *Novik*. The ships glided silently over the dark, predawn waters.

The convoy consisted of eighteen ships, with the hospital ship *Mongolia* bringing up the rear. Six were battleships. They outnumbered Tōgō's fleet, which had lost the *Hatsuse* and *Yashima*. The six left the harbor in this order: *Tsesarevich*, 12,912 tons; *Retvizan*, 12,902 tons; *Pobeda*, 12,674 tons; *Peresvet*, 12,674 tons; *Sevastopol*, 10,960 tons; *Poltava*, 10,960 tons. After that came the cruisers, in this order: *Askold*, 5,905 tons; *Pallada*, 6,731 tons; *Diana*, 6,731 tons. In addition, two gunboats and a number of destroyers prepared the way for the squadron's departure, busily carrying out minesweeping operations.

When the *Tsesarevich* passed by Golden Hill outside of the harbor, on its mast were flags bearing the message: "The tsar has ordered our fleet on to Vladivostok." By this means, each captain was officially apprised of the purpose behind the sortie.

First to spot the mass exodus was the destroyer *Shirakumo*, which had been keeping a watchful eye. The Third Division was quickly informed, and Division Commander Dewa Shigetō wired an alert to the *Mikasa*: "Enemy fleet leaving harbor." Fortunately, Tōgō's *Mikasa* and its squad were not anchored at the base by the Changshan Islands but were cruising north of Round Island.

Akiyama Saneyuki was in his cabin on lower deck.

Before going further, we'd like to relate an anecdote about Saneyuki from just before this. In the middle of the night, a torpedo boat patrolling outside the harbor at Port Arthur wired this alert to the *Mikasa*, which was anchored in the Changshan Islands: "High smoke in the harbor tonight. Signs of enemy movement." The officer on duty grabbed the telegram, went below deck to Saneyuki's cabin, and opened the door. Saneyuki was leaning back in his chair with his jacket off. On closer inspection, the officer realized he was asleep. He went over and shouted in Saneyuki's ear the news that a wire had come in. Saneyuki didn't stir but opened his eyes. The officer proceeded to read the telegram aloud. As soon as he had finished, Saneyuki said, "The whole navy is to prepare at once to move out. Signal the *Taihoku Maru* to open the midship boom and fasten torches at either end. Convey this order to the commander in chief and chief of staff on the double." Then, to the officer's surprise, he closed his eyes and was again sound asleep.

Before delivering Saneyuki's order to Tōgō and Shimamura, the officer glanced at the notes he had made, wondering briefly if the message was all right. However, both commanders trusted Saneyuki so implicitly that they didn't doubt his plan for a moment and nodded their approval.

Despite this previous incident, when the alarm came on August 10, Saneyuki was not asleep. He was on the bridge. He held out a map before Tōgō and indicated the route to take, obtaining the admiral's approval. The swift cruiser squadron, having received orders to find the enemy fleet, was already on its way. The rest of the fleet set off, cutting through foaming waves.

"Can we win?" wondered Saneyuki. He had never been less sure of anything in his life.

Saneyuki had prepared for this day by cudgeling his brains to come up with several plans, none of which could clinch victory. In his later years, he would often look back on this moment and recall, "Victory seemed impossible, no matter what."

* * *

Tōgō had brought along four battleships. Added to this were the *Kasuga* and *Nisshin*, armored cruisers brought in as emergency replacements for the sunken *Hatsuse* and *Yashima*. In an artillery battle, however, the Japanese main squadron would be at a disadvantage.

What decided the fate of the enemy's capital ships in an artillery battle were the battleships' main guns. The six battleships of the Russian squadron had a total of twenty-four 12- and 10-inch guns, the six Japanese ships, seventeen. Herein lay the biggest reason for Saneyuki's pessimism. Battle outcomes were determined by the number of artillery shells that could be rained on the enemy in a given unit of time. With this big a difference in firepower, gaining the advantage by a meticulously executed strategy was next to impossible.

Tōgō's mission was the destruction of the entire enemy squadron. Even one escaped ship could haunt the area, putting the transport of Japanese troops gravely at risk. The enormous task of sinking every ship put the military leaders in this battle under a great psychological strain.

Skies were clear. There was a slight breeze from the south, and virtually no waves. A light mist lay over the water, but visibility was good. It was a fine day for a sea battle.

Tōgō's fleet was lined up in this order: *Mikasa, Asahi, Fuji, Shikishima, Kasuga, Nisshin.* They steamed forward in a line-ahead formation.

At half past twelve in the afternoon, from a point 10 nautical miles westnorthwest of the reef that the navy called "Encounter Rock," the enemy squadron was sighted making its way southeast.

"Let's lure them out into the open sea," Saneyuki suggested, and this later turned out to be a mistake.

Chief of Staff Shimamura Hayao nodded in agreement and so did Tōgō. That was because, on June 23, when the Russian squadron previously sortied, Tōgō's fleet had made its move immediately on receiving the notification, intercepting the enemy on its way south. But, before any engagement could take place, the enemy had suddenly reversed course and slipped back inside the harbor.

This previous mischance was constantly on the minds of Tōgō and his staff. They were determined this time to lure the enemy out so far that retreat to Port Arthur would be impossible, and then, after a good fight, destroy them. There would be no rest for Tōgō's fleet until the enemy was utterly destroyed. To repeat, if even one Russian ship made it back to Port Arthur, Tōgō would have no choice but to put off the longed-for trip to Sasebo and continue the blockade. The only route to victory was to prepare for the arrival of the Baltic Fleet from Europe by getting the warships home for muchneeded overhauls in dock. Anxiety over this point robbed Saneyuki and the others of flexibility in their thinking.

At one o'clock in the afternoon, Tōgō ordered his entire fleet to change course 8 points to port—turn left 90 degrees—putting the ships in line abreast. Then there commenced the flip-flop maneuvers that British naval historian Allan Westcott would denounce as "four hours of incomprehensible fleet exercises."

* * *

It was partly exhaustion from the long blockade that caused Tōgō and his aides to misread the enemy's very simple intent. Saneyuki, convinced that the enemy would fly straight at them, slowly paced the bridge deck as the *Mikasa* altered course, his eyes intent on the smoke pouring from enemy funnels in the offing. Not for a second did he doubt the enemy's will to fight. The Russian squadron was at full strength, with seven more heavy guns than the Japanese. If the squadron charged straight ahead, it had a very good chance of sending Tōgō and his fleet to the bottom of the sea. To a military man's way of thinking, it only made sense that the enemy's purpose in leaving the harbor must be attack.

But the Russian commander Vitgeft was also less warrior than bureaucrat. One characteristic of tsarist Russia in its waning years was that its bureaucrats were at their most bureaucratic, a poisonous influence that seeped into the disposition of even military men who should have been active. Vitgeft was less interested in crushing the enemy than he was in preserving the Russian tsar's precious fleet, a feat for which he hoped to win a medal. The imperial order he had received was a simple "Go to Vladivostok." The tsar may well have expected Vitgeft to encounter and destroy the Japanese fleet along the way, but to a man of Vitgeft's bureaucratic mindset, taking the order at face value was safer.

"One way or another, to Vladivostok it is." This being Vitgeft's unshakable plan, when he saw the Japanese fleet looming on the horizon, his one thought was flight.

As Tōgō bore down upon him from the north in line abreast formation, Vitgeft's proper response would naturally have been to enter battle formation and face up to the enemy. Saneyuki was puzzled to see that, instead, the Russian ships maintained their southeasterly course at full steam. In an attempt to cut off their progress, Tōgō ordered another turn 8 points to port, changing to reverse line-ahead formation, with the rear ship *Nisshin* in the lead.

Watching from the bridge deck of the *Tsesarevich*, Vitgeft was filled with admiration. Japanese fleet maneuvers might even be superior to those of the British Navy, he thought. The irony was that Tōgō's fleet was doing an acrobatic dance far ahead of the enemy, all alone.

Forty minutes after Tōgō discovered him, Vitgeft was heading southeast, Tōgō east-northeast. The distance between the two fleets was too great for an artillery duel, but each side began to fire its big guns sporadically to test the range. Vitgeft, bent on flight, was moving at top speed. Tōgō and his aides, still unaware that the enemy fleet was going to Vladivostok, thought only of preventing a return to Port Arthur as had happened on June 23. The flip-flop maneuvers that ensued were conceived with this sole purpose in mind.

*   *   *

Determined to head off Vitgeft's squadron, Tōgō veered northeast and sent his battleships charging ahead full steam, water foaming at their bows. The succession of changes in direction was dizzying. Saneyuki's trademark nimbleness was put to the worst possible use.

Vitgeft, no less determined not to be headed off, swerved abruptly to starboard and began steaming south, putting Tōgō's fleet in the van. It was as if Vitgeft had pivoted behind Tōgō's back and was fleeing headlong south. Or, to put it another way, it was as if Tōgō the attacker had stood with his sword held high, rushed forward holding it aloft and, after crossing swords with his opponent a single time, passed by on the run, momentum carrying him off to the north, while his opponent kept on going south, leaving the match far behind.

"Vitgeft's dodge," Saneyuki would call it, the memory of this moment bitter to him for the rest of his life, as well it might be. Once the Russian squadron was gone, it would be no easy feat to catch up with it again.

Having steamed too far, Tōgō had to shift helm yet again. He ordered the fleet to change course 16 points to starboard—that is, turn right 180 degrees. This had become Tōgō's one-sided acrobatic show. The *Mikasa* was back in the lead, the formation single line ahead. The fleet picked up speed and raced southwest, spray rising high like mist around the ships' bows. This time, they would cut across the enemy line, roughly crossing the T. The maneuver posed grave risk to the attacker, but as a way to sink the enemy's lead ship it was highly effective. Saneyuki had devised the tactic after being inspired by an account in the book of ancient Japanese naval strategy that he had borrowed from his friend Ogasawara Naganari.

The distance from the enemy was 6,000–8,000 meters. Tōgō's main battle squadron began to concentrate fire on the enemy's lead ship, the *Tsesarevich*. The Japanese tactic was to sink the enemy's flagship and so plunge the enemy command into disarray. To accomplish this, the fleet had to "cross the T" in what was to become a signature battle tactic of the Japanese Navy.

Shell after shell landed on the *Tsesarevich*—but battleships of the day, fitted with waterline belts of armor, did not sink easily from shelling alone. The enemy naturally responded by setting its sights on the *Mikasa*, inflicting huge damage. Enemy shells ripped through the ship without a moment's cease, the great 12-inch guns in particular scoring a direct hit on the rear of the shelter deck, killing many men and severely damaging the mainmast. Two-thirds of the area around the mast was blown away, leaving it like a great tree attacked by a woodsman's axe, on the verge of toppling.

"If we go too fast, it may collapse" came the report. As a result, at this critical juncture, the *Mikasa* was unable to travel at high speed and so delayed its chance to engage the enemy in a second round.

* * *

The vicious pounding inflicted by Tōgō's tactic of crossing the T began to take a toll on Admiral Vitgeft, who returned to his former policy of flight rather than fight. This faintheartedness on his part would eventually lead to his own doom. Yet, had he taken action at this time, resolved to fight Tōgō to the bitter end, a different fate would surely have awaited him. Never at any point in the war was Tōgō as hard pressed as at this moment.

To escape from Tōgō, who was hard on his heels, Vitgeft swung his flagship hard aport. For the Russian crew, unskilled in fleet maneuvers, nothing induced such chaos aboard each ship as these mid-battle changes in formation. The line promptly began to undulate, ships coming together like tango dancers locked in embrace, and the fleet's speed plummeted.

Tōgō adroitly changed course, turning north. He had no intention of letting this opportunity pass. From the relative positions of the two fleets, the armored cruisers at the Russian rear were in sight of all Tōgō's gunners. The Russian cruisers panicked, picked up speed, and caught up with their own battle squadron, sticking to its shadow. As a result, the squadron moved in an irregular double-line formation.

In that awkward formation, the Russians simply blasted away while fleeing, racing southeast for all they were worth. During this brief interval, the two sides exchanged heavy fire, Russian gunners showing deadly accuracy as they pounded away at the *Asahi* and *Nisshin*, inflicting heavy damage.

The *Mikasa* was the hardest hit, one shell striking the central waterline and opening a great cavity. Another pierced the deck and exploded, and still another hit the rear stack, causing massive casualties. The deck was covered in blood, body parts flying in all directions. As Saneyuki looked on from the bridge, he saw an arm come flying straight at him, strike something, and fall.

But Tōgō's fleet had not yet fought effectively. Constantly caught off balance by Vitgeft, it had been unable to engage sufficiently in the artillery duel, wasting the greater part of the battle in movements to tangle with and disentangle itself from the enemy. Time was going by fast. Tōgō had yet to sink a single enemy ship.

The enemy was fast receding, without giving Tōgō an opportunity to engage it. He gave chase. In line with Yamamoto Gombei's policy, the Japanese fleet was put together for speed. But in this chase, the Japanese warships were slow, their hulls and parts worn out from the long blockade.

The Russian squadron was considered slow, and yet here they were making a quick escape. That was because while confined in the harbor Vitgeft had kept his ships in top condition, sending divers to scrape the hulls clean of barnacles before making his exit.

At twenty minutes past three in the afternoon, going on three hours since the discovery that the Russian squadron was on the move, Vitgeft had sailed far out of range of Tōgō's fire. Tōgō issued a ceasefire and went after the enemy with every ounce of speed he could muster.

"We've got to catch them before dark." The thought was on everyone's mind. Once night fell, warships of the day were helpless, unable to trade fire or even to determine the enemy's location.

* * *

In the end, Tōgō let Vitgeft get away. The direct reason was the time it took his fleet to turn around in a circle and a half. While Togo was pirouetting, Vitgeft raced off full tilt, and, by the time Tōgō swung into full pursuit, already 30,000 meters separated the two forces. The effective range of Tōgō's main artillery was around 7,000 meters, so at that point there was little hope.

Tōgō was hot in pursuit. All his staff was consumed with one familiar, anxious thought: if Vitgeft got away, the Russo-Japanese War itself would be thrown into chaos. The enemy squadron would enter Vladivostok. From that base, it could cruise Japanese waters at will, playing havoc with military transport routes. The navy would have no choice but to devote all its energies to the task of troop transport—pushing men and ships alike to their limits—and then, when the Baltic Fleet arrived, fight an enemy doubled in strength. There was no doubt that victory in the war hung on the outcome of this chase across the Yellow Sea.

"The fleet was delayed three minutes by tactical maneuvers," wrote Akiyama Saneyuki after the war. "For that reason, it took us three hours to catch up with the enemy."

This was Saneyuki's take: an initial three-minute delay ended up causing the waste of three precious hours chasing the enemy. The hours were precious because the fleet was racing against the onset of darkness.

As for why they were three minutes late, opinions differed even among battle participants. Vice Admiral Yamaji Kazuyoshi said later that for a moment, when he saw the movements of Tōgō's main squadron (the First Division), "I thought the First Division was going to go around the enemy's rear and prevent them from returning to Port Arthur. I was sure that was it."

That assumption was foremost in everybody's mind, and that's how they interpreted what happened: the enemy was bound to head back to Port Arthur as it had on June 23, and so the Japanese fleet took swift action to prevent that from occurring, attempting to cut off their retreat.

But that's not what Saneyuki said. "At 1400 hours, when the shelling was at its fiercest, the First Division slipped around to the enemy's west (that is, the Port Arthur side) without realizing it. The enemy quickly lost no time in changing course for the Shandong promontory. Admiral Tōgō turned the head of his fleet, but unfortunately that caused a three-minute delay, and so the First Division was put in the disadvantageous position of following the enemy."

Whether this happened without their realizing it or by order is impossible now to say, since it took place at the height of the battle. In any case, as British historian Westcott noted, "incomprehensible maneuvers" were the decisive characteristic of this battle.

The experience was a bitter one for Tōgō and his aides, who, vowing not to repeat the same mistake at the subsequent battle of Tsushima, would work out and implement a special plan of attack with that in mind. Later, in different venues, Tōgō and Saneyuki would separately say the exact same thing: "Without the lessons of the battle of the Yellow Sea, the battle of Tsushima would not have gone as well as it did."

* * *

Tōgō gave chase.

Vitgeft was fleeing in desperation, but Tōgō's pursuit was pathetic. He chased the enemy not as victor but as one who risked becoming an ignominious loser. Never was there a wartime chase so comical. The stronger side fled, and the weaker side took off in hot pursuit, like a dog nipping at the heels of a bear. Moreover, if the bear made it to its lair in Vladivostok, another bear would come, doubling its strength. Flight was the winning tactic. History had never seen such a battle.

"Is the mainmast all right?" Captain Ijichi of the *Mikasa* asked over and over again. If the mainmast toppled, the ship's speed would be drastically cut, spoiling the formation and preventing them from ever catching up.

"It was only by the grace of God that the mast held," Saneyuki would later say. During this chase, under conditions beyond human control, he performed a spiritual feat without precedent in his life: he prayed. In later years, what fixed his spirit in unconventional realms was this early spiritual experience in the Russo-Japanese War, when he prayed for divine deliverance.

The prayers were strictly internal, of course; nothing showed on the outside.

At one point, a late meal was served. Usually the staff gathered for meals in the admiral's galley, surrounding Tōgō at the table, but this time the admiral was delayed, his seat empty. Following protocol, no one else lifted a fork, but Saneyuki nonchalantly began to eat. He was always like that. He spent so much time immersed in thoughts of battle strategy that he had no energy to spare on other matters. The others habitually stayed around to chew the fat, but after eating Saneyuki would go straight back to his cabin, sprawl on the bunk with his shoes on, and stare up at the ceiling.

Tōgō and Shimamura both treated him as a special case, and the others followed suit.

The ship sliced through the waves at top speed.

While the chase was on, Saneyuki came down from the upper deck and sprawled on the sofa in the staff quarters. In the event that they ever caught up with the enemy he would be ready, having come up with a variety of different battle plans based on every conceivable scenario, but for the moment there was nothing to do but stay the course. He would doze off and snore for a quarter of an hour, then suddenly spring up, grab his compass and square, and work out an idea that had come to him, shaping it according to logical principles. He looked like a madman.

Because of the maintenance work carried out in the harbor at Port Arthur, the enemy's speed was 14 knots, faster than the Japanese had expected. Saneyuki later had praise for this accomplishment. "At Port Arthur, there were no docks for ship repair. For the Russians to repair and restore their damaged battleships to the point that each one could achieve its maximum speed meant surmounting a host of difficulties. I must say I admire what they did."

But during its headlong flight the Russian squadron suffered its first misfortune. Just before leaving harbor, the *Retvizan* had sustained a gash along the waterline. Quick emergency repairs had been done, but the tear had since reopened, and if the ship went too fast it would take on water badly. The shell that caused the damage was not from a Japanese warship but was fired by the navy's heavy artillery squad on loan to General Nogi's Third Army. Headed by Commander Kuroi Teijirō, the squad had taken up position behind Mt. Huoshi just three days prior to the battle of the Yellow Sea, bombarding the streets of Port Arthur and the Russian fleet. One shell had landed broadside on the *Retvizan* as it lay at anchor in the harbor, rupturing it amidships below the waterline and causing a commotion as the ship immediately began to take on water. Repairs were stopgap and insufficient. In the midst of Vitgeft's desperate strategic getaway, this signal went up the *Retvizan* mast: "Damage at our waterline, speed cut by 4 knots."

Seeing this, Rear Admiral Nikolai Matusevich, Vitgeft's chief of staff, gave a howl of dismay and raised a fist. "Commander, what shall we do?" He awaited Vitgeft's decision—whether to leave the *Retvizan* behind or take it along. If the latter, the entire squadron would have to lower its speed as well, at great risk.

The issue of the injured battleship had come up before, as they were preparing to leave the harbor. A majority had been in favor of leaving it behind, but Vitgeft had cast the deciding vote to take it along.

Before Vitgeft could reply, another signal went up: the *Retvizan* had been repaired and could safely maintain a speed of 12.5 knots. With an overall speed of 12 knots, 2 knots slower than before, the squadron would be overtaken that much sooner. Tōgō, racing at 15.5 knots, was hot on their tail.

Tōgō kept up the chase for three hours, and before sundown at half past five, at a point 45 nautical miles north of Shandong promontory, his *Mikasa* saw the smoke from Russian smokestacks on the horizon. "We're saved," Saneyuki thought. Unaware that damage to one battleship had slowed the enemy, he rejoiced at overtaking them sooner than expected. "It's providential," he thought. Any accident that befalls the enemy is always an act of providence.

* * *

Aboard the *Mikasa*, the atmosphere was lively and brisk, the preparations for battle soon done. It was summer, and the day was long. Since they had caught up sooner than expected, at half past five, there remained another two hours of daylight in which to fight. For Tōgō's fleet, which needed to wipe out the enemy in this limited amount of time, two hours was all too short. There might not be enough time to finish the job, but at least they had caught up before sundown. That much was lucky.

The rearmost ship of the enemy fleet was the battleship *Poltava* (10,960 tons). When its 12-inch main artillery turned toward the *Mikasa* and started to spit fire, round two of the battle of the Yellow Sea began. A cloud of dark cannon smoke enveloped the *Poltava*, and the heavy-caliber shell grazed the *Mikasa*'s port hull and fell into the water, raising a great column of spray.

Tōgō's fleet did not lower its speed but kept firing as it steamed ahead, parallel with the enemy. The intention was to cut off the enemy's lead ship. Eventually, the vans of the two columns closed to a distance of 7,000 meters. Firing on both sides was intense, the air filled with spray from shells landing in the water. Clouds of dust and smoke covered the sea. Shells landed on every ship, friend and foe alike. Fires broke out and were extinguished. On the Japanese side, for these two hours, they had to keep firing and firing even if the gun barrels burned out.

The accuracy of these enemy gunners was far and away superior to that of the Baltic Fleet, which came later. While penned in the harbor, the Port Arthur Squadron had not wasted time but had carried out plenty of target practice.

Damage to the *Mikasa* was severe. From this engagement alone, the ship suffered ninety-five hits. Fifteen minutes into the battle, a shell struck the rear 12-inch guns, the ship's main armament, destroying one cannon. One seaman was killed outright, his body split vertically in two. Another eighteen men and officers were felled in the same instant. Among the wounded was Prince Fushimi Hiroyasu, a lieutenant commander.

The thunder of gunfire and the screech of flying shells covered the ship incessantly, rending the air. Explosive blasts carried men away, and shrapnel rained everywhere, sticking jaggedly where it fell.

When a shell struck the crowded bridge at half past six, an hour after hostilities had begun, the ensuing havoc made hell seem tame. A great column of fire erupted, and an instant later body parts flew through the air, entrails spilled, and everything was painted red with blood. Tōgō, Shimamura, and Saneyuki were all on the bridge at the time. The ship's captain Ijichi, who had been standing beside Tōgō, was injured; next to Saneyuki, five officers including the staff officer Ueda Kenkichi were injured, along with ten petty officers and crewmen.

Tōgō kept his eyes trained on the enemy's position on the horizon, not a flicker of change in his expression. Concerned for the admiral's safety, his chief of staff Shimamura implored him to take shelter in the conning tower. The bridge was out in the open where flying shrapnel filled the air, but the conning tower was protected by steel. Nevertheless, Tōgō customarily remained on the bridge during battles, never setting foot in the conning tower. All he said to Shimamura was: "It's hard to see out from there." This small man from Satsuma showed greater pluck than any enemy officer.

* * *

To a greater or lesser extent, most of the enemy ships were on fire, but none of them sank. Although the Japanese purpose in this battle would not be achieved unless they all went down, Japanese gunners were not as adept this time as in the later battle of Tsushima. Even so, hits on the *Tsesarevich* included fifteen 12-inch shells. But ships fortified with belts of armor were not easy to sink. Bits of the superstructure, large and small, were blown off like scrap, and the gruesome state of the wounded trapped between those destroyed structures was incomparably worse than anything aboard the *Mikasa*.

Twelve-inch shells are visible as they come at you. The Japanese shells were different from the Russian ones, with such a distinctive, long shape that Russian seamen nicknamed them "suitcases." Their destructive capability was vastly superior to that of Russian artillery shells. They contained Shimose powder, the invention of a little-known naval engineer named Shimose Masachika, which was then the most powerful explosive in the world. Its blast power was said to be two and a half times greater than that of most explosives, but the actual force was even greater, as much as three and a half times stronger than the standard. Shells containing this explosive would explode even when coming in contact with water. The sight was extraordinary: towering pillars of water breaking out of the sea accompanied by clouds of dark-brown smoke and shooting flames.

Based on the experience of the First Sino-Japanese War, Japanese shells were aimed not so much at sinking enemy ships as at crippling their fighting ability, a strategy that the world's collective naval wisdom found strange. It was considered common sense to use armor-piercing shells, as the Russians did. One of those would rip a hole in the side of the ship, go through, and detonate inside, whereas Japanese shells, unable to pierce the waterline belt of armor, would explode on board instead. Powerful Shimose powder not only blasted all shipboard structures to bits but was certain to start a fire as well. With the ship in flames, its guns could no longer function. This way of crippling enemy ships rather than sinking them had been adopted by the Japanese ever since they battled the *Zhenyuan* and *Dingyuan* in the First Sino-Japanese War. Shimose powder, cruel as it was to enemy soldiers, was the one physical advantage that the outnumbered Japanese forces could rely on.

During the hours of this battle, the six Russian battleships were hard pressed by this Japanese explosive. Seeing that the tide of battle was going against his squadron, Admiral Vitgeft decided to free his speedy cruisers from this hell and sent up the signal, "Cruisers flee south." This would be his final command.

* * *

For Tōgō, time was running out. With sundown fast approaching, he had yet to deliver a fatal blow. Since he had pulled closer, the two fleets were steaming ahead on a parallel course 5,000 meters apart. The accuracy of each side's firing was steadily climbing.

In the conning tower of the *Tsesarevich*, Vitgeft and his staff tensely gazed out to starboard. The *Mikasa* was about to pass them by.

"Sir, why don't we spread out?" said one of the aides. Both fleets had sustained roughly equal damage, he reasoned, and so rather than firing their guns while making a run for it they should engage Tōgō directly, line abreast, and seek to overpower him. That is indeed just what the Russians should have done. Had Vitgeft taken his aide's advice, the fate that came upon him in the next moment would have been averted. The damage to the Japanese fleet would have been incalculable.

But, remember, Vitgeft was a bureaucrat. All he did was stubbornly repeat his orders: "The tsar ordered us to go to Vladivostok."

The *Mikasa* overtook them.

The *Mikasa*, keeping the enemy flagship *Tsesarevich* beside it toward the rear, fired off large and small artillery with a constant roar in a steady barrage. It was then exactly thirty-seven minutes past six. Just which gunner fired the *Mikasa*'s 12-inch main gun will never be known, but at that very moment the "fateful shell," as it would be celebrated in Japanese naval history, flew toward the *Tsesarevich*. Akiyama Saneyuki called it the "uncanny shell." Throughout this naval battle, which was, he had confessed, unwinnable, he had stood on the upper deck praying for a stroke of good fortune. The word "uncanny" seems to express his acknowledgment of some unknowable power.

The 12-inch shell landed with a huge explosion around the conning tower of the *Tsesarevich*, blowing Vitgeft and his staff to bits. There was little blood; it was rather as if the men had vanished into thin air. Only Vitgeft's leg could be seen rolling around the vicinity of the mast. His chief of staff Matusevich was severely wounded.

The senior officer remaining was the flagship's captain, Captain N. M. Ivanov. He had one brief moment in which to think of signaling Rear Admiral Pavel Ukhtomsky aboard the *Peresvet* to take over the flag of the squadron before a second 12-inch shell made a direct and fatal hit, blowing up him, his navigator, and his helmsman. Yet this alone was not what made the shell so fateful.

What was fateful was the felling of the helmsman. At this point, the conning tower contained only corpses; the *Tsesarevich* was under a dead man's command. No one aboard knew this, however, much less anyone else in the squadron. The flagship went on clipping through the waves. During battle, in the absence of any signal to the contrary, the vessel astern was to carefully watch the movements of the flagship and follow along.

Of the annihilated senior officers, the one who died last (by a matter of seconds) was the helmsman, who took a piece of shrapnel in the back much as if he'd been stabbed with a carving knife. To support himself, he fell against the helm and in his agony writhed to the left. As the ship's prow moved, he perished where he had fallen. Guided by this dead man's hand, the huge bulk of the *Tsesarevich* began turning to port.

Eduard Schensnovich was captain of the crippled *Retvizan*, which was following behind the *Tsesarevich*, and he instructed his navigator to look at the flagship. The navigator decided that Vitgeft was deliberately altering course. The captain agreed with this assessment and immediately turned the *Retvizan* to port. Captain Vasily Zatsaryonny of the third vessel in line, the *Pobeda*, naturally followed suit.

But the movements of the *Tsesarevich* were bizarre. It kept turning to port until it plunged straight through its own line as if gone wild. The

Peresvet, fourth in line, narrowly missed being struck broadside. To avoid impact, its captain, Captain Vasily Boisman, quickly swung to starboard—bringing the ship that much closer to the Japanese fleet. He promptly swung to port again. Rear Admiral Ukhtomsky, who was on board this ship, decided that something was amiss with the flagship. Eventually, a signal appeared on the mast of the death ship (put up by a Lieutenant Kamigan, it was later found out): "Commander Vitgeft has relinquished command."

Seeing this, Ukhtomsky realized that it was up to him to assume command of the squadron. But he made up his mind that under the circumstances he would not follow the same policy as his late superior. Instead of going to Vladivostok, he would return to the haven of Port Arthur.

Ukhtomsky summoned his signalman and tried to put up the signal "Follow me," but both masts where the signal flags could have flown were gone. In the end, he put the flags out on rails next to the conning tower and changed course to the west, assuming that the other ships would get the message and follow him. This action deepened the general confusion.

* * *

The greatest misfortune for the Russian side was that, in this decisive battle, none of the ships knew where to go. The degree of chaos beggars description. The *Tsesarevich*, its conning tower full of dead men, continued going around in crazy circles. The second ship, *Retvizan*, turned first to port, then to starboard. The third ship, *Pobeda*, naturally followed suit. To escape the *Tsesarevich* as it ran amok, the fourth-place *Peresvet*, which took over as flagship, veered to starboard and then to port before finally setting a new course for the west. But the other ships had difficulty in realizing that this was the new flagship. Only the fifth-place *Sevastopol*, following behind, understood and went along. The sixth battleship, the *Poltava*, was too far away to see what was happening.

"What's going on?" the ship's captain, Ivan Uspensky, hurriedly asked his navigator.

"I can't really say," answered the navigator with a quaver, peering straight ahead. "All I know for certain is that the flagship *Tsesarevich* has fallen out of line."

Naturally, he knew that. The *Poltava* was just then passing by the *Tsesarevich*, which had stopped running in circles. Though listing to starboard, the former flagship was in no danger of sinking. Lieutenant Kamigan had attempted to take command of the ship again but hesitated, unsure where to go. Because the fleets had continued steaming on while they fought, the battle site was now far off.

Kamigan decided to go to Jiaozhou Bay. This was in the opposite direction from Vladivostok, but it wasn't far, and it would be safe. Jiaozhou was leased to Germany, a Russian ally.

The former flagship steamed south, aiming for Jiaozhou and luckily managed to make good its escape, arriving the following night at nine o'clock, without having encountered any Japanese warships along the way. Damage to the ship was so severe that it could not withstand any more voyaging, let alone fighting. As allies of the Russians, the German authorities ought to have broken international law if necessary to minister to this hobbled ship. However, in what was perhaps a national trait, Germans venerated victors but were indifferent to losers. Governor Oskar von Truppel, citing international law, summarily requested the ship to leave. Only recently, Germany had cooperated with the Russian Navy and Army in Port Arthur, relaying military wires between Port Arthur and the Russian mainland there at Jiaozhou.

When the Russians demurred, saying the ship was incapable of leaving, Germany did what any neutral country should have done in such a situation. They removed the ship's guns and armor, and interned it until the end of the war. Three Russian destroyers also fled to this same harbor and met with the same fate.

* * *

Out on the battlefield at sea, night was coming on, forcing Tōgō regrettably to order a ceasefire. The time was twenty-five minutes past eight. Though great damage had been inflicted on each enemy ship, not one had been sunk.

"This is bad," murmured Saneyuki in the gathering darkness, stunned. "How could anything this bad be happening?"

Tōgō showed no sign of frustration as he ordered a company of destroyers and torpedo boats to clean up. Their crews, accustomed to night attacks, would close in and finish off the enemy with torpedoes at point-blank range. It was far more effective to sink ships from below with torpedoes than from above with a hail of gunfire. The operation was essentially picking off fallen warriors on the run.

Leaving the rest to the smaller ships and boats, Tōgō gathered up the warships in his command and prepared to make a leisurely return to his base in the Changshan Islands.

Saneyuki took a late supper. As he worked his knife and fork, his mind filled with visions of the vast seas of the Far East: the Yellow Sea, the Sea of Japan, the Sea of Okhotsk. Where would the enemy go? Most likely, the ships would not move together, but would each make good their escape individually. In any case, five battleships and a great many cruisers of the enemy fleet were now scattered around the perimeter of the isles of Japan. If they were only bunched up in Port Arthur as before, they'd be far easier to deal with. With the enemy so spread out, from tomorrow Japanese ships would no longer be safe on the Yellow Sea or the Sea of Japan.

"Well, what do you think?" broke in the voice of Chief of Staff Shimamura Hayao.

Absorbed in his own thoughts, Saneyuki had failed to notice when Shimamura, across from him, addressed him. He looked up as if to say, "Huh?"

"You think they can sink three at least?" He meant, could the destroyers and torpedo boats send at least three enemy battleships to the bottom.

"I doubt it."

"You do? Why?"

"The squadron commanders and captains are worn out from the long siege operation. The boats aren't moving energetically, judging from what we saw this afternoon."

During the battle between the main forces, a barrage of countless shells, large and small, had fallen into the sea, making it impossible for smaller boats to play any role. It was true that Japanese destroyers and torpedo boats did nothing but roam around the battle area without contributing anything. But even if conditions weren't right, weren't you supposed to leap in, even in the face of certain death? Wasn't that the nature of war? That's what Saneyuki thought. Even though the mother ship *Mikasa* was being heavily bombarded, the smaller boats had only wandered around aimlessly.

Given that attitude in the daytime, how could they engage in desperate nighttime combat at close quarters?

* * *

At the very beginning, when they first struck Port Arthur, Saneyuki had anticipated that the destroyer flotillas would sink at least five enemy warships. Of course they would. The Russian fleet at Port Arthur had been anchored and defenseless, like so many "sitting ducks," as someone had said. There were no booms to speak of. And they were in the outer harbor at Port Arthur.

The ships had attacked at night, groping their way forward, and fired off some twenty torpedoes, managing only to damage three enemy vessels in all. As soon as they had fired their torpedoes they had turned back, all of them returning without a scratch. For attackers to return unharmed could only mean that they had not, after all, been at close quarters with the enemy. In other words, the high-value Japanese flotilla commanders placed on their destroyers meant that they were unwilling to sacrifice them when necessary.

"There are only nineteen destroyers in all of Japan," mused Saneyuki. "Are the captains too concerned that the loss of a ship would adversely affect the fleet?"

Or was it something else? He couldn't forget the Americans in the Spanish–American War. They'd been amateurish in the extreme, yet far more adventurous in spirit than any Japanese. Among naval officers, the torpedo-craft captains had been a much more interesting lot than the ship captains, he thought. Maybe it was because the adventurous nature of light craft suited them better. In any case, those Americans were a rowdy bunch. They were drifters from Europe or their descendants, so maybe it was in them to like daredevil stunts.

In contrast, look at the Japanese. For the three hundred years of the Tokugawa period, they'd been farmers, each tending to his little plot of land—a way of life deeply ingrained in Japanese bones. Since the shogunate had outlawed adventure in every sense of the word, the adventurous frame of mind was generally lacking. On the other hand, Japanese were loyal and good at sticking to a set plan, which made them well suited to serving on big warships. A Japanese sailor might see his officer fly through the air in front of him or his mate be torn to shreds, but he would never leave his post. Therein lay the strength of the navy's main force.

The world of destroyers, demanding individual courage and an individual spirit of adventure, seemed suited to Japanese but ultimately was not. Saneyuki, who had made a study of ancient Japanese naval history, thought privately, "We've forgotten the long-ago days when we roamed the coasts as pirates." Destroyer crews were pirates, pure and simple, but modern descendants of those pirates of old were shockingly inept, to his mind.

* * *

When the Japanese destroyers went into action, the sky was still light. The enemy couldn't have gotten far. "Our lead destroyer," wrote Lieutenant Yoshida Takeshi, captain of the *Shinonome* (274 tons) in the Third Destroyer Division, "was the *Usugumo*"—279 tons—"with Commander Tsuchiya Mitsukane on board."

> We kept going so as not to lose sight of the *Usugumo*. But then in the pitch dark all the destroyers and torpedo boats started swarming at once toward the enemy ships and nearly ran each other down. It was extremely dangerous. The *Usugumo* would stagger one way and then the other to keep from running into friendly boats. The rest of us were following behind, and every time the ship did something like that we would come to a dead halt or turn or do something. In the meantime, we lost sight of the enemy completely.

It was a considerable traffic jam.

The battle tactics were crude. Following the First Sino-Japanese War, the Japanese Navy suddenly put together a world-class fleet, miraculously mastering the strategy and seamanship required for a great navy within ten short years—and yet there were oversights. Too much emphasis was laid on the strategy, operation, and offense and defense techniques of heavy ships, at the expense of learning the same about destroyers and torpedo boats. It is simply ridiculous that friendly boats got tangled in a tango on the broad sea and let the enemy give them the slip.

Some of the boats did fire off torpedoes, but all of them were afraid to get in too close to the enemy and fired from a distance, so none of the torpedoes hit. The enemy ships had been damaged in the earlier round of battle, but they were great warships. If they trained their countless guns large and small on one point in the sea and fired, even if they didn't hit anything, the waves and mist that erupted would be enough to capsize a torpedo boat. That's what the Japanese feared. None of the boats had the audacity to charge full tilt at the enemy and damn the consequences.

Then there was a night search. They never did relocate the enemy until dawn, when they saw three ships traveling slowly and unsteadily, the very picture of a vanquished foe. The *Usugumo*, *Shinonome*, and *Sazanami* of the Third Destroyer Division attacked, but then, unable to close in and finish off their prey, they fired torpedoes, did a U-turn, and returned to their fleet. Not a single torpedo found its mark.

And so the squadron commanders and captains returned to the base in the Changshan Islands with a dismal record of zero accomplishments to report to Admiral Tōgō.

After this incident, Tōgō replaced all these commanders and captains, though this was not his idea. Tōgō was a man of uncommon generosity, and, even when the officers came to report their utter lack of achievement, he thanked them as usual for their efforts and at the end only nodded without further comment. They deserved a tongue-lashing. Rozhestvensky, commander of the Baltic Fleet, would probably have sneered, "Worried about saving our skin, are we?" And he would have been well justified.

"We lost sight of the enemy in the dark of night," they claimed.

Even letting this statement pass, once at dusk and once again at dawn they had sighted the enemy and attacked. But torpedoes couldn't hit their target if fired from a distance by officers with cold feet, thought Saneyuki. As far as he could tell, the destroyers and torpedo boats had been in ceaseless motion ever since the fighting began. The commandants and captains were surely exhausted, their reflexes dulled.

And, even if the attack on Port Arthur had fallen short of his expectations, on paper it amounted to a sterling deed of arms for which these officers were guaranteed medals. That alone wouldn't be enough to make a man hold life dear, and yet probably they did feel something like that. The depth of fatigue of those on smaller ships must be twice that of the men on the larger ships. A man's will to fight declines as his fatigue increases. Wasn't it asking too much to expect these men to rise and fight the coming Baltic Fleet, let alone to win?

"Replace the lot," Saneyuki recommended to Shimamura Hayao, who nodded and passed on the recommendation to Tōgō,

"Changing horses midstream?" Tōgō was disinclined to act on this suggestion. "You think that's wise?" The commander in chief's primary job was keeping up morale. Making reckless personnel decisions was the last thing Tōgō wanted to do just then.

"It's the principle of rewarding good work and punishing bad. It will charge up the men," Shimamura insisted.

Tōgō gave his approval.

"And," Shimamura went on, "to change public sentiment I must be transferred, too. It's got to be done."

Tōgō was taken aback, but Shimamura was adamant. From his point of view, since he had recommended the punishment of the destroyer commandants and captains, it would be wrong for him alone to keep his job. Transferring him would clearly settle the question of headquarters' responsibility and prevent any sapping of morale.

"Let me command one of the cruiser task forces," he suggested. "For the rest of it, I think Katō Tomosaburō would do a fine job. Anyway, as long as Akiyama's here, everything will be all right no matter who becomes chief of staff."

In the end, this was exactly what happened.

* * *

The battle of the Yellow Sea was a failure. If the measure of a battle's success lies in the extent to which its strategic purpose is achieved, then for the Japanese Navy this battle was, if not an outright defeat, at best a failure. The reason is that it scattered the Port Arthur Squadron far and wide across the ocean. It was as if a creel full of fish, large and small, had inadvertently been overturned, spilling its contents into the river.

Of course, the battle was a failure for the Russian side as well. The Russians' strategic purpose was to leave Port Arthur and make it to Vladivostok—but not one vessel did. Only the *Novik* managed to get almost all the way there. Small at 3,080 tons, the small protected cruiser *Novik* had been continually in the van of the battle. Even when the main force was under siege in the harbor, it was the *Novik* that had bravely ventured out. Its behavior was so different from that of the other Russian ships that it might have been from some other country. Its captain, Commander von Essen, was that sort of man. If someone like him had been commander in chief, the Japanese fleet would never have made it safely through the war.

The *Novik* fled the scene of battle and made straight for the German protectorate of Jiaozhou, as did the protected cruiser *Askold* (5,905 tons). Grammatchikov, captain of this ship, was a valiant man with a strong desire for fame. However, the Germans turned both ships away. After leaving Jiaozhou Harbor, the *Askold* went to Shanghai, where it was interned and disarmed. The *Novik* alone broke through the enemy forces and started on the perilous route to Vladivostok.

With no word on the *Novik*'s whereabouts, the Japanese were on edge. In Jiaozhou, the *Novik* had taken on so much coal that it was piled high on the deck. The light cruiser went past the Kagoshima Osumi Peninsula and entered the Pacific Ocean, pushing north past Kunashiri Strait.

The Japanese cruisers *Chitose* and *Tsushima* went looking for the *Novik*. They proceeded north over the Sea of Japan, entered Hakodate, and snooped around but found no trace of a Russian warship in Tsugaru Strait. Early in the morning on August 19, having pulled anchor and left Hakodate, they were searching along the Hokkaido coast when they received hot news that the enemy had been sighted just after seven o'clock, proceeding northwest by the Atoeya lighthouse in the Kuril Islands. The Japanese cruisers immediately headed for La Pérouse Strait at full speed. Just before dawn the next day, they arrived in the sea off Rebun Island on the northwestern tip of Hokkaido. The two cruisers then split up to hunt their prey.

The *Tsushima* came upon the *Novik* outside the town of Korsakov in Sakhalin and drew in. The *Novik* emerged from the harbor, but after an hour of heavy fighting suffered heavy damage and retreated to safety. The *Chitose* came running, and both Japanese cruisers went into the harbor only to find the *Novik* scuttled in shallow water by its own crew. Von Essen and the other survivors had all gone ashore, and so managed to avoid being taken prisoner.

* * *

One reason the Russians basically self-destructed without fighting sufficiently was that so many officers in their high command were nobles. Some of the ships, however, did show surprising mettle. The destroyer *Reshitelny* (240 tons) fled to Yantai, where its captain, A. A. Kornilov, told his men, "The real fighting starts now," and took on a huge amount of coal.

The *Asashio* and *Kasumi* of the First Destroyer Division went in pursuit of *Reshitelny*. As they were doing night reconnaissance of the harbor, they discovered the presence of the Russian ship. Intending to advise surrender, the Japanese sent out a boat containing Sublieutenant Terashima Usami from the *Asashio*, ten petty officers, and an interpreter.

Terashima boarded the *Reshitelny* and negotiated on deck with Lieutenant Kornilov. Realizing that escape was impossible, Kornilov covertly ordered his men to prepare to blow up the ship and went on conversing with Terashima. He stalled for time, giving the same vague responses over and over until an hour had passed. Finally, Terashima had had enough and decided to capture the ship. He looked back over his shoulder at Machinist Warrant Officer Sakamoto Tsunetsugu. Kornilov understood what Terashima was about and sprang at him, striking him in the face. Terashima grabbed Kornilov's arm and tried to fling him off, but the other man was so outsized that the technique didn't work. Terashima saw that grappling on the deck with a giant like that would leave him at a severe disadvantage, and so on the spur of the moment he grabbed Kornilov and toppled overboard with him in his arms. Once in the water, the two men came apart, and Terashima tried to climb back aboard.

On the deck, a brawl had broken out between the Japanese and Russians. The Russian sailors pounced on Sakamoto and tossed him overboard. At first, the men fought unarmed, but gradually they resorted to firearms. Though outnumbered, the Japanese fought hard. One was killed, and the remaining eleven all were wounded. On the Russian side, of a crew of fifty-one there were over thirty casualties. Just as Terashima was scrambling back on board, the ship trembled, and an explosion went off in the fore part. The Russian sailors leaped into the water in fear and swam for shore. There were no further blasts, and so Terashima took *Reshitelny* in tow as prize.

"The Russian fighting man was not at all weak," Tōgō later commented. "In fact, the Russians were powerful fighters. The main reason they lost lay in the difference in their basic concept of war. Russians didn't think of war as something fought by individuals. The army thought it was fought by units of troops, the navy by ships—so, when a warship was seized, the men felt their duty was done and, with extremely rare exceptions, stopped putting up a fight. Japanese soldiers and sailors, on the other hand, were set to fight as long as they had breath, even if their unit was defeated or their ship destroyed. This difference in concept was the determining factor in victory and defeat."

It was true. Although no Russian battleship was sunk on the Yellow Sea, the Russians went ahead and adopted a posture of defeat. This greatly benefited the Japanese.

* * *

After the battle of the Yellow Sea, the Russians did indeed see themselves as losers. The *Tsesarevich* fled to the neutral territory of Jiaozhou and was disarmed. The cruiser *Askold* also took refuge in Jiaozhou for a brief time but was chased away by the Germans and went instead to Shanghai, where it was disarmed. The cruiser *Diana*, after stopping in Jiaozhou, went all the way to Saigon, where the French authorities disarmed it. The destroyers *Grozovoy*, *Bezshumny*, *Besposhchadny*, and *Besstrashny* all chose similar fates. The bulk of the squadron, including the five remaining battleships, returned to Port Arthur.

On shore, word that the ships were back caused a commotion. The fleet that had left harbor on August 10 in such high spirits with the Russian Navy's St. Andrew flags flying high limped back with their superstructures torn to pieces, leaking and listing, little more than floating scrap. Seeing the sorry state of the ships, the soldiers at Port Arthur who had yelled, "Navy, get out!" regretted their former taunts.

A joint summit council of naval and army leaders was quickly held. General Stoessel, who disliked the navy, expressed heartfelt condolences and respect for the navy's "gallant fighting." Rear Admiral Ukhtomsky and a dozen other navy officers were present. Every one of them was wounded.

"Japanese shells are powerful," said someone, and everybody chimed in, agreeing. They still did not know about Shimose powder, but they knew plenty about the devastation it caused. They talked about the unthinkable impact of exploded shells. "Even if one doesn't hit home but falls in the water beside the ship, the damage is still terrific. It releases a gas with heat so intense that it melts the joints on the steel plates in the side armor belt, so the ship takes on water." The shells released a great deal of gas at very high temperature. Since even the protected areas of the ship were so vulnerable, the damage to unprotected areas was even worse.

"The explosive power of that gas goes way beyond our shells. It doesn't just destroy the metal on the side of the ship and the decks, it knocks down smokestacks, smashes ventilators, topples steel masts, and destroys steering gear. The temperature is unbelievably high—it must be a good 3,000 degrees Celsius. The proof is it's hot enough to melt the coat of paint on steel surfaces. The paint evaporates and burns like alcohol."

"That's not a shell, it's a flying torpedo," said someone.

"There must be six times as much powder in a Japanese shell as there is guncotton in one of our shells," said a navy medic. "When a Russian shell explodes, the casing just breaks into large pieces, but a Japanese shell disintegrates into numberless tiny fragments. If one of those hits you, it penetrates to the bone."

* * *

Shimose powder was invented in 1888 and, after extensive testing, adopted by the navy in 1893. The powder was not used in the First Sino-Japanese War, however, which began the following year. Sawa Kannojō, superintendent general of naval ordnance, was quoted in the September 4, 1911 edition of *Hōchi Shimbun* as saying, "Shimose powder was already available by the time of the First Sino-Japanese War, but we couldn't use it yet because the machinery wasn't perfected." To implement the powerful explosive, various ordnance and other mechanical conditions had to be met. Until the First Sino-Japanese War, the all-important percussion fuse used in Japanese artillery shells was mainly of Dutch make, but this was ill-suited to Shimose powder. The later invention of the Ijūin fuse finally made Shimose powder a practical alternative, and, by the time of the Russo-Japanese War, all shells, torpedoes, and mines of the Japanese Navy were packed with this explosive.

The explosive's inventor, Shimose Masachika, was the son of a musketeer in Hiroshima domain. His grandfather pored through Dutch books to learn about explosives. Shimose was born in 1859, the same year as Akiyama Yoshifuru, and so both men experienced the upheaval of the Meiji Restoration at around the age of ten. They were also affected in much the same way by the decline of the samurai class, which left their families in straitened circumstances.

After graduating from Hiroshima Middle School, Shimose entered the Imperial College of Engineering in 1878. There was a two-year preparatory course followed by a five-year specialized course. Shimose majored in chemistry and after getting his degree entered the Naval Ministry, where he worked in the arsenal.

Around this time, the head of the arsenal was a Satsuma man named Harada Sōsuke, who went to study in Britain with Tōgō Heihachirō, among others, in 1871. Harada studied weapon manufacturing at William Armstrong's company in Newcastle. He was fond of saying, "Without superior arms, no nation can be free." This may well have been the slogan of the arsenal, where invention was prized above imitation.

When Shimose came to work there, Harada told him, "Japan is a weak country. There's just one way for a weak country to survive in this age of imperialism, and that's by inventing weapons. Concentrate on the powder used in munitions. Rather than improving on what's already there, come up with something revolutionary."

Shimose was convinced and spent three years developing a kind of powder completely unlike the guncotton then in use in Western countries. His invention used picric acid, taking advantage of the shock-sensitive picryl chloride that forms when the acid comes into contact with steel. The terrific explosions that occurred when the acid was driven into steel plates revolutionized the world's concept of explosives.

In quantitative terms, Japan had little chance of winning the war. The country's one slim advantage lay in Shimose powder, which produced temperatures so high that people actually said, "If a shell detonates anywhere on a warship, the deck will be too hot to set foot on." In the beginning, the Russians complained to the world that Japanese artillery shells released toxic fumes. They justified the claim by citing examples such as the time when, after a Japanese torpedo struck the coal bunker on the cruiser *Pallada*, six sailors approached the scene to put out the blaze and collapsed on the spot as if poisoned by gas. It wasn't toxic gas that did them in, of course. The temperature of the gas released when the blasting charge went off was extraordinarily high—as high as 3,000 degrees Celsius—and this was the cause of the six sailors' unhappy end.

Unable to believe that, only thirty-odd years after modernizing, Japan could have created its own new artillery, the Russian naval officers at Port Arthur announced that Japan was using British-made Lyddite shells.

Meanwhile, a Japanese naval research lab did an analysis of Russian shells and found they had extremely low explosive power. Because Russia had formerly been on close terms with France, the Japanese thought at first that they might be using mélinite, an explosive invented by the French, but apparently France never shared the invention with Russia. Russian fuses, moreover, were rather crude, and many shells failed to explode.

Russia first took a serious look at the power of Shimose powder when, in the naval battle off Ulsan after the battle of the Yellow Sea, the cruisers *Gromoboy* and *Rossiya* finally staggered into port at Vladivostok. They were both afloat, but neither one was good for anything but scrap. "Damage to both ships was so severe that people shivered at the sight," declared one newspaper. The ships' boats lay in shambles, the gun barrels were destroyed, and there were gaping holes in the ships' sides large enough for a man to walk through. Of the Russians' twenty cannons, barely three remained usable.

Foreign newspapers also reported on the Japanese explosive. On July 31, the *New York Times* speculated: "Since Japan is treating this explosive as a top national secret, it is impossible to say for certain, but it appears to be quite revolutionary. Russians were put in the unlucky position of having to learn the powder's potency through physical experience."

Based on Shimose powder, which was for naval guns, the Japanese Army developed its own new "yellow powder" (picric acid), successfully producing it on an industrial scale in 1897. This powder never achieved the potency demonstrated by Shimose powder against steel enemy ships.

* * *

After deliberation, the Russian Army decided the warships that had fled back to Port Arthur were "too damaged to be of any use as warships" and so would be left to sit unused in the harbor. Most of the crew members were assigned shore duty, and the ships floated empty on the water. Most of their guns were removed and taken ashore for use as heavy artillery in the fortress.

Due to a failure of intelligence, the removal from active duty of what was left of the fleet at Port Arthur remained unknown to Admiral Tōgō, out at sea. Although Japanese intelligence was extremely good in Europe and on the battlefields of Manchuria during the Russo-Japanese War, Port Arthur was an exception. There the Russian military kept city streets under such heavy surveillance that Japanese intelligence was paralyzed. Accordingly, Tōgō did not learn of the fleet's state until the fall of Port Arthur, and until then maintained the difficult blockade with its heavy price in exhaustion of men and machinery. Naturally, he was impatient to leave and fit out his ships, but until General Nogi's Third Army prevailed at Port Arthur, he was stuck. The situation was no different from the beginning of the war.

One big worry was gone, however, as a result of the naval battle off Ulsan on August 14.

The Russian naval force based at Vladivostok was an independent cruiser squadron that in the end worked the hardest of any unit in the Russian Navy and did the most damage, not to the Japanese Navy, but to the army. The squadron consisted of three armored cruisers, one protected cruiser, and one armed merchantman, for a total of five. These five ships scoured the Sea of Japan and the Korea Strait, harassing and sinking Japanese transport ships heading to and from Manchuria.

On April 26, the cargo ship *Kinshū Maru* went down. On June 15, the *Hitachi Maru* was attacked and sunk with an Imperial Guard regiment on board, and the *Sado Maru*, transporting a railway engineer corps, was severely pounded and suffered enormous damage. The squadron freely sank everything from large ships like the *Izumi Maru* (3,229 tons) to, over on the Pacific side, tiny ships like the 100-ton *Kihō Maru*, *Hokusei Maru No. 2*, and *Fukujū Maru*. Finally, they grew emboldened enough to venture over to Tokyo Bay on the Pacific side, graze Izu Peninsula, and wreak havoc on Japan's naval transport system.

The Japanese assigned Kamimura Hikonojō's Second Squadron to pursue the Vladivostok Squadron, but the waters were vast, the enemy elusive. For a time this situation cast a pall of gloom over Imperial General Headquarters.

The Vladivostok Squadron was highly mobile. Its sole purpose was to evade the Kamimura fleet and, operating out of Kamimura's line of sight, disrupt Japanese lines of transportation. The two forces played a constant game of hide-and-seek in the waters around the isles of Japan.

Satō Tetsutarō, staff officer of the Second Squadron, would later write, "Kamimura's squadron did not enjoy good fortune in war." Satō was at this time classified together with Saneyuki as a naval strategist.

Kamimura's mobile attack unit went as far as Askold Island off Vladivostok in an attempt to lure the enemy out to open sea but was unable to get in close as the sea was frozen over. Finally, by breaking through areas of thin ice, the fleet approached the harbor and attacked by long-range firing, but the enemy did not emerge. Subsequently, on hearing that the Vladivostok Squadron had attacked the port of Wŏnsan in Korea, they rushed over but arrived too late. When the Vladivostok Squadron showed up in the Tsushima Strait and fired on the *Sado Maru* and *Hitachi Maru*, Kamimura was nowhere nearby. The nation was coldly unsympathetic to Kamimura's ill-fortune, labeling him incompetent or worse; some called him a traitor. His house was constantly pelted with stones.

Kamimura assiduously continued to hunt for his prey. On the evening of July 1, while cruising southwest of Tsushima, he spotted thin smoke 22,000 meters offshore and tore off in desperate pursuit, but the enemy again fled, managing to disappear as the sun set.

Most painful of all for Kamimura were the events of July 24. At one o'clock that afternoon, he received a wire from Imperial General Headquarters to the effect that three ships of the Vladivostok Squadron were cruising off Izu Peninsula, posing a threat to merchant ships. His orders were to proceed swiftly to Tokyo Bay. He promptly headed the fleet south along the west coast of Kyushu, but as they were speeding on their way, around eight o'clock in the evening orders came in from the Combined Fleet to proceed immediately to Hokkaido instead. The fleet thus was given simultaneous conflicting orders. The orders from the Combined Fleet were to "give up guarding the Tokyo Bay area, go straight to Hokkaido, and wait in Tsugaru Strait to intercept the Vladivostok Squadron on its return." This clearly contravened the earlier orders.

The reasoning behind the Imperial Headquarters order was that the Vladivostok Squadron intended to proceed down Japan's Pacific coast, threatening the Tokyo Bay area, before merging with the Port Arthur Squadron. The basis of the Combined Fleet's order was the contrary supposition that the enemy would pull back and return to Vladivostok via Tsugaru Strait.

After hesitating, Kamimura decided to obey the order from Imperial General Headquarters, the navy's supreme command. However, the order from the Combined Fleet was the correct one. Akiyama Saneyuki had had a vision accurately foretelling the movements of the Vladivostok Squadron.

* * *

Saneyuki's vision was to a great extent mystical.

During this time, Saneyuki spent all day every day trying to visualize which route the Vladivostok Squadron would take. One night he was unable to sleep. That's when it happened.

To digress for a moment, an officer once commented, "When I go into Akiyama's cabin, his eyes will be looking straight at me, but when I speak to him he makes no response." When Saneyuki was deep in thought, there was something abnormal about him. Idle chatter didn't bother him. Once, as he lay on the sofa with his shoes on, reading a book, some junior officers began bragging among themselves, half joking, about what they would do if they were in charge of the next operation. Saneyuki suddenly threw aside his book, jumped up, and said, "Say that again. What would you do?" He got out his compass and square and, after listening in all seriousness to the others' braggadocio, worked out a logical battle plan on the spot.

This time was different. As he lay on the bed with his shoes on, absorbed in thinking, he dozed off from fatigue. Before his eyes spread a scene of pale sky and sea, just after dawn. In the background were rolling hills. It was clearly a scene on Japan's eastern coast, near Tsugaru Strait. He could see three dark war vessels—the *Rossiya*, *Rurik*, and *Gromoboy* of the Vladivostok Squadron—heading north to Tsugaru Strait.

Saneyuki was disposed to trust this vision that had mysteriously come upon him. The vessels must be on their way back to Vladivostok via Tsugaru Strait. Strategy was something to be worked out with every ounce of brainpower at your disposal, but in the end, as he was well aware, once the plan was pared down to its essentials, you had to fall back on native instinct. He believed the voice of instinct to be the expression of a transcendental state, one that he sometimes attained and one that was worthy of his trust. His involvement with spirituality in later life stemmed from these experiences.

But at the time he said nothing to anyone of this mysterious vision, knowing that if he did, Tōgō and the other superior officers would lose faith in what he said.

He went directly to the stateroom of the chief of staff and gave a reasoned explanation of the Tsugaru Strait theory. The Combined Fleet promptly overrode the orders from Imperial General Headquarters and wired Kamimura to proceed to Tsugaru Strait. Kamimura, however, had already taken action based on the earlier orders. Had he acted on Saneyuki's hunch instead, the defeat of the Vladivostok Squadron would have come about sooner than it did.

* * *

When his fleet was unable to intercept the Vladivostok Squadron, Kamimura Hikonojō was subjected to a barrage of bitter criticism in letters, newspapers, and speeches. After it was reported that the fleet had lost sight of the enemy in dense fog, one member of the House of Representatives made a speech in which he railed, "Turn 'dense fog'"—*nōmu*—"upside down and you have an incompetent"—*munō*!

All of this shows the spirit of the times. This was an age when the Japanese people were hard taskmasters. In essence, they had formed the fleet with their taxes and put Kamimura in charge. He was their representative, and so they found his incompetence to be offensive. Later on, in the militarized state of the late 1930s and early 1940s, the military clique would rule Japan on the borrowed authority of the emperor, acting for all the world as if they had taken over the land where Japanese people resided. The people were their servants and, toward the last, their slaves. The nation at the time of the Russo-Japanese War was qualitatively different from the nation of the 1930s and 1940s.

Later, Kamimura's staff officer Satō Tetsutarō would recall, "The attacks from the populace were vicious. They even called us the 'Russian spy fleet.'" Letters like the following poured in: "The Kamimura fleet would make lousy bird catchers. If a bird appeared in Ueno and you gave chase from Shimbashi, do you think you'd catch it?"

Kamimura Hikonojō was a typically pugnacious man of Satsuma. Quick to quarrel as a youth, he hated losing and was a valiant general. The "owner" of the navy during this war, Yamamoto Gombei, chose Tōgō to lead the Combined Fleet and Kamimura to command the Second Squadron, which Yamamoto Gombei needed to carry out brave hit-and-run tactics. Kamimura was chosen because his character suited the job. This must have made the lashing criticism he received all the more intolerable.

"While the fleet was anchored in Tsushima," Satō wrote in his memoirs, "the commander would often go fishing in a small boat." Whether Kamimura did this to raise morale by showing his men that, despite the barrage of public criticism, he could relax and go fishing, or whether he did it to calm himself down after a fit of rage, no one knew. In any case, while in Tsushima, Kamimura often had his men engage in sumo wrestling or go mountain climbing to refresh their spirits.

Even when speeding back to Tokyo Bay on orders from Imperial Headquarters, the fleet would frequently be troubled by unverified reports of enemy sightings. On July 25, this wire came in: "Russian fleet is just off Katsuura, Bōsō Peninsula." The following day came this wire, naming a completely different area: "Off Cape Shionomisaki, Kishū Peninsula." The second wire was in error.

Eventually, Kamimura's fleet searched painstakingly around the Izu islands, but by then the enemy had gone, and they returned to Tsushima empty-handed.

Such was the ill fortune that had dogged the Second Squadron. Luck finally came their way when, on August 12, the Vladivostok Squadron left the harbor at Vladivostok and headed south of its own accord. This was essentially an addendum to the battle of the Yellow Sea. When the Port Arthur Squadron set out, it contacted the Vladivostok Squadron with a request to be met halfway. Once the two forces had met and converged, they would then return to Vladivostok together. But, before this could happen, the Port Arthur Squadron was routed and scattered to the winds. Unaware, the Vladivostok Squadron steamed across the Sea of Japan on its way to the rendezvous.

Once the Port Arthur Squadron made its move, the Vladivostok Squadron was bound to respond. From past experience, this was easy to predict. Saneyuki came to this conclusion and, with Tōgō's permission, issued orders to Kamimura to be on the alert for the appearance of the Vladivostok Squadron.

Even without such an order, Kamimura and his staff officer Satō were well aware of the situation. Resolved to wait north or northeast of Tsushima for the enemy to appear, they assigned ships of the Fourth Division to patrol strategic points, stationing the *Niitaka* south of Tsushima. On August 11 at forty minutes past ten in the morning, the main force left Ozaki Bay and sped toward its destination. At Tōgō's order, they stopped west of the island of Heuksando along the way, arriving east of Tsushima at dawn on the thirteenth.

At half past one in the morning on August 14, they arrived off Ulsan to the east and changed course, heading south-southwest. In the early morning, they discovered the Vladivostok Squadron heading south. The discovery came at twenty-five minutes past four, when a dim glow was detected far off on the port bow. There was no moon that night.

What could this be? Excitement stirred aboard the flagship *Izumo*. As they continued along, the sun came up. Twenty minutes after the light was first sighted, they discovered the three ships of the Vladivostok Squadron moving through the morning mist.

That morning, there was a southerly breeze. The weather was fine, the sea calm. Both sides were in single line-ahead formation. The enemy consisted of the flagship *Rossiya* (12,195 tons) in the lead, followed by the *Gromoboy* (12,359 tons) and the *Rurik* (10,936 tons), all great armored cruisers. The Japanese side consisted of four armored cruisers, with the *Izumo* (9,906 tons) in the lead, followed by the *Azuma* (9,450 tons), the *Tokiwa*

(9,855 tons), and the *Iwate* (9,906 tons). The *Asama* and *Yakumo* were also part of this fleet, but both were then in the Port Arthur area.

Around five o'clock, when the two sides were approximately 6 nautical miles apart, Admiral Kamimura sent off the wireless message: "Enemy sighted," and went into battle position. The encounter took place just off Ulsan in Korea. Partly because the sun was not yet fully risen, the Russians were slow to spot Kamimura.

From the psychological pressure that had been brought to bear on him, Kamimura was out for blood. His desperation in this battle can be told from the speed with which his *Izumo* raced across the sea, far outstripping the *Azuma* and the rest. He was prepared to leap into the enemy's midst with the *Izumo* alone and open fire. The rearmost ship at this time, the *Iwate*, was left far behind. One of the officers on board the *Iwate* saw smoke far off on the horizon, assumed it was from the Vladivostok Squadron, and took a photograph. Afterward, everyone looked at the photograph and had a good laugh, realizing it was their own *Izumo*. That shows how close the *Izumo* drew to the enemy in its headlong dash.

Kamimura stood on the bridge. A staff officer beside him, observing the enemy through binoculars, remarked aloud on the unexpected size of the enemy fleet: "They're huge, sir."

"Then they will be that much easier to hit," Kamimura spat out. Full of fighting spirit, he was jumpy and irritable before his first engagement.

Finally, the enemy caught wind of them. In confusion, they suddenly changed course to port, apparently intending to flee east. Kamimura was enraged. If they escaped his clutches this time, he would have no choice but to atone with his life. To keep the enemy from stealing away, he changed course to east-southeast and saw them on the starboard bow. He kept his eyes on them, seeking to shorten the intervening distance.

There was not quite enough light yet to begin a gun battle, and the distance was a little far. But to prevent the enemy from escaping, Kamimura had no choice but to open fire. It was twenty-three minutes past five, when from a range of 8,400 meters he opened fire on the enemy's rearmost ship, the *Rurik*. The enemy returned fire.

Every 8-inch shell from the main gun on the *Izumo* must have been imbued with Kamimura's resentment. Few if any shots missed; they hit the *Rurik* as if drawn by a magnet, exploding and setting the ship instantly on fire.

During the entire battle off Ulsan, it was later said, the gunners on the *Izumo* had to keep shooting without replacements before there was adequate light, straining their eyes. The *Rossiya* and *Gromoboy* began to open fire. Soon every ship in the Japanese fleet was keeping up a thunderous fire. Every shell increased the tension over the water; clouds of smoke and soot filled the air, and gigantic pillars of water rose and fell.

* * *

The Japanese tendency toward hypersensitivity made Japanese soldiers poor marksmen with small arms. In the First Sino-Japanese War, they seldom did as well as the Chinese soldiers, and, in the Russo-Japanese War, Russian officers and foreign observers were united in their opinion that the Japanese infantry were poor shots. The Japanese Army actually had a phrase *shageki baka*, "firing idiot." The idea was that those who were a bit dull-witted were better suited to firing rifles, which requires a calm frame of mind. The general inferiority of Japanese small-arms marksmanship is probably attributable to soldiers' hypersensitivity to their environment, causing them to become overly excited.

Yet the accuracy of the cannons, even in the army, was slightly better than that of the Russian artillery. In the navy, the difference was greater. You could almost say they were poles apart. It was part of Tōgō's basic policy to emphasize marksmanship, and in between battles he drilled his men constantly. Not only that, he gathered superior gunners from the entire fleet and put the best on his battleship fleet, the second best on Kamimura's heavy cruiser fleet. Tōgō's simple, clear enforcement of his belief that the outcome of a battle depended on big guns on great ships lay behind his fleet's success.

The accuracy of Kamimura's fleet was miraculously high. Within thirty minutes of the outbreak of hostilities, all three enemy ships were on fire. What worked in Kamimura's favor was that the rising sun was continually at his back. He strove mightily to maintain this advantage. With the sun behind them, his men had a clear view of the enemy, and their aim was spot on.

The Vladivostok Squadron's blunder lay in shooting in the direction of the sun. With the light against them, they could see Kamimura's fleet only in silhouette, and their gun crews' eyes quickly tired from squinting.

At fifty-two minutes past five, twenty-nine minutes after the fighting began, the *Rossiya* and *Gromoboy* turned to starboard and fled south, leaving the still-burning *Rurik* alone on the scene of battle. But the Russians of the Vladivostok Squadron were so valiant that they might have been a different race of men from those of the Baltic Fleet. Their devotion to their consort ships was exceptionally strong. The *Rossiya* and *Gromoboy* escaped, only to come back and draw near the *Rurik*. Kamimura's fleet quickly went forward to block their path, changing course to west-northwest. They saw the enemy off the port side, steered a parallel course, and opened fire.

There was something deeply moving in the efforts of the *Rurik* to make a comeback. Finally back with its consorts, it got back in formation and savagely returned fire, but at half past six, its steering gear was disabled, and it began to drift.

Kamimura went after the *Rossiya* and *Gromoboy*. At 6,000 meters, he subjected them to enfilading fire. With high accuracy, a vast quantity of concentrated shells landed squarely on the ships; but these were great warships and did not sink. Amazingly, after this much hard fighting, at around seven o'clock, the two ships again returned to the *Rurik* in the midst of the battle. But this time, the *Rurik* was beyond help.

With its rudder destroyed and a large fire raging on deck, the *Rurik* could not be saved. The *Rossiya* and the *Gromoboy* approached but soon fled north again. They put out their own shipboard fires only to come under heavy raking fire from Kamimura's fleet, hot in their pursuit, and have flames break out all over again.

But the consort ships were surprisingly unwilling to leave their fallen comrade behind, returning still yet again. Kamimura intervened, firing incessantly until the air was dark with clouds of smoke. Finally, the consort ships had no choice but to give up and change course for the north.

"They mean to go back to Vladivostok!" yelled Kamimura from the bridge. He meant he would see to it they did not.

The *Izumo* and the three ships behind picked up speed. But, after the long battle, their hulls were in need of cleaning, and none of them could reach their allotted speed. The enemy ships were surprisingly swift. They kept on breaking out in fires, and every man on board enlisted in the fight to extinguish them. The Russians' guns had largely fallen silent, probably put out of commission by all the shelling, yet their engines were intact and their waterline armor unharmed, it seemed, for they flew along with no diminution of speed.

Herein lay the weakness of the Japanese naval artillery shells known as "flying torpedoes." As we mentioned before, deliberate emphasis was laid on destroying everything on board enemy ships and taking away their fighting capacity, rather than rupturing their armor and sinking them, or piercing their bottoms and blowing them up.

Though the *Rossiya* and *Gromoboy* had managed not to go under, the damage done to them was so extensive that they were little more than junk. On the *Rossiya* the upper deck was completely smashed, almost all the casements on the main deck destroyed, the mast fallen. Even both smokestacks had collapsed. On the *Gromoboy* also the defenses on all three decks were utterly ruined. The two ships had only three usable guns between them. Half of the officers had been killed, and few crew members survived unscathed. Those able to work were forced to spend their time extinguishing fires rather than fighting the enemy.

Even so, they maintained a good speed of 19 knots. The *Izumo* and the rest pursued them at the same clip, which made capture impossible. The Japanese could only continue firing as they gave chase.

Kamimura tried hard to sink the two Russian ships, causing five conflagrations aboard the *Rossiya* and three aboard the *Gromoboy*. Throughout the pursuit, he remained on the bridge glaring at the enemy without moving, but after ninety minutes his chief of staff wrote something in chalk on the blackboard and showed it to him. The roar of winds and waves made normal conversation impossible. On the blackboard were these words: "Out of ammunition."

Kamimura grabbed the blackboard and threw it to the deck. He must have been bitter indeed. But there was nothing for it but to turn around.

After that, the two Russian armored cruisers made it back to Vladivostok, ready for the scrap heap. The *Rurik* sank. The Vladivostok Squadron was no more.

2

LIAOYANG

Next to Mukden, Liaoyang is the largest city in southern Manchuria, with some thirty thousand households. The city's history is surprisingly ancient. From the time of the Han dynasty, Liaoyang was a local hub, and in the later Liao dynasty it became one of the five capital cities of the Khitan nation. It was laid out in a square with a neat grid of streets and enormous protective walls, each one as much as 1.5 kilometers long. Those walls, with eight outer gates in all, were extensively rebuilt in the early Ming dynasty.

Five years before the outbreak of the Russo-Japanese War, imperialist Russia took over Liaoyang and forcibly made it a semi-protectorate. The Russians saw the city as having greater strategic value than Mukden to the north. To borrow from Sunzi's discussion of terrain in *The Art of War*, Liaoyang was a crossroads: roads from all directions led there.

The streets of Liaoyang showed how much effort the Russians had put into administering affairs in Manchuria. In only five years, a fine Russian settlement had gone up. Just west of the city was the Liaoyang railway station, with various modern facilities clustered around it. The locomotive yard had a great fan-shaped switchyard of a type not yet seen in Japan. The Russian enclave by the terminal was lined with Western-style brick buildings— everything from official residences and trading houses to churches and clubs. The view from any street corner called to mind a European city. Only the seasonal blanket of yellow dust—airborne sand swept up from the roads—marked this as Manchuria.

General Kuropatkin's headquarters and official residence were located near Liaoyang Station. Europe's great military strategist arrived in town three months ahead of the battle. His main task, which he was resolved to accomplish, was to assemble a great army that would wipe out the Japanese

Army at one blow. Defeated at Nanshan and Telissu, he had driven his troops further and further north, finally making camp in Liaoyang. He needed to prepare for a major battle that he had to win convincingly to avoid losing favor in the St. Petersburg palace. His reputation had suffered, and he needed to take steps to restore it.

Far East Viceroy Alexeyev, in the role of nagging mother-in-law, kept sticking his nose in matters of strategy and had to be handled with tact. Kuropatkin reminded himself repeatedly, "This is turning out just the way Witte warned it would." Sergei Witte's warning had been blunt: "Capture Alexeyev and send him back to Moscow or you won't be able to fight the war." Military genius though he was, not even the great Kuropatkin had that much nerve.

* * *

Kuropatkin's plan for the coming battle may be described as grand. Although the battle of Liaoyang would be a field battle, the Russian general introduced elements of siege warfare as well. Besides turning the town into a fortress, he also constructed semi-permanent fortifications and field works nearby where Russian soldiers could lie in wait for Japanese troops. In this way, he artfully combined elements of offense and defense, an approach in keeping with traditional Russian strategy. Vast amounts of materials went into the making of these fortifications.

Northwest of town flowed the Taizi River. Kuropatkin positioned the far right wing of his inner defenses along the river's lower reaches and extended the line to the south and west to enfold Liaoyang. Along the way, he constructed fifteen heavily guarded strong points. With these as base, he added rows of concealed fortifications and batteries large and small bound together organically by fields of interlocking fire. The Russians excelled at building such fortifications. The one responsible for this design was General Konstantin Velichko, a renowned authority in the field of military engineering.

Kuropatkin requested that the fortifications be made as strong as possible. There was little time to build them since they had to be ready in three months. Major General Nikolai Aleksandrov assured him that, no matter how manfully the Japanese fought, the fortifications would last one hundred days. According to Kuropatkin's calculations, that would be more than enough time, as he was expecting reinforcements. All he needed to do was hold out till those arrived.

Kuropatkin had two hundred thirty thousand troops at his command, while the Japanese Army numbered only one hundred forty thousand. With those superior numbers, there's no telling what might have become of the Japanese

Army had he gone on the attack. But Russian strategy laid primary emphasis on defense. Kuropatkin practiced "safe attack" by inflicting damage on the enemy (the Japanese Army truly suffered heavy damage), while defending his territory and waiting for the enemy to weaken. The Japanese preferred to leap boldly into the fire like Edo firefighters, but that approach was alien to Kuropatkin. Despite commanding a large field army of two hundred thirty thousand men, he was eager for reinforcements from European Russia, expecting to increase his troop strength by as much as two corps.

Kuropatkin's battle plan had depth. However, the great strategist did do one peculiar thing: he opened great holes in the city walls as potential escape routes. While constructing elaborate defenses, he prepared simultaneously for the possibility of defeat and flight. This mindset would be a main contributing factor to his defeat in the battle of Liaoyang.

* * *

The truth is that the Japanese Army should have reacted swiftly to the deployment of Russian troops in Liaoyang but could not, due to a shortage of ammunition. The Japanese Navy had entered the war with ammunition to spare, but not so the army. As war preparations got underway, army leaders blithely underestimated the amount of ammunition they would need. They were simply unable to conceive of the rate of consumption of material resources in modern warfare. This failure of imagination was a constitutional flaw in the Japanese Army and not just in this era, either—it persisted all the way up to the army's demise at the end of the Second World War.

A longstanding myth in the Japanese Army was that battles are won by officers' strategy and daring. Before the war, staff officers devoted themselves wholeheartedly to mapping out strategy, becoming immersed in strategic problems with all the ardor of chess enthusiasts. Liaoyang strategy was one "chess problem" that the General Staff had been working on since around 1902. Army officers made the unfortunate assumption that actual warfare was like chess—an equation that they clung to till the very end. In their simplistic way of thinking, all that it took to convert a "chess problem" into real-life combat was do-or-die fighting on the field. When a strategy that looked good on paper didn't pan out as expected on the battlefield, they berated the troops on the assumption that men at the front had shown cowardice.

This thinking was shared by all tacticians in the Japanese Army, whether in Tokyo or at the rear. As they prepared to put their Liaoyang strategy into action, instead of ammunition, the army prepared ten thousand boxes to store the bones of the soldiers who would die in battle (according to a Russian source). They failed to grasp that what was needed to flesh out a chess problem and make it into a workable battle plan was not soldiers' blood, but material resources.

During the buildup to war, the General Staff Office considered how much ammunition to procure. If the amount needed were, say, ten times as much as in the First Sino-Japanese War, they would have to place an order overseas or else expand production in the Osaka Arsenal. But army leaders reached the jaw-dropping conclusion that they could get by with fifty rounds per gun, per month—when, in fact, that much would be used up in a single day.

This plan, totally devoid of any understanding of the exigencies of modern warfare, was the brainchild of the Army Ministry's artillery section chief. The pervasive evil of kowtowing to experts—or the rigidity of the bureaucracy—led his superiors to approve his proposal. The vice minister approved it and so did the army minister, thus giving it the ministry's official endorsement. Imperial General Headquarters swallowed the plan whole. The resulting cost in bloodshed would be enormous, yet, due to the smokescreen of bureaucracy, no one was called to account after the war.

* * *

And so it was due to lack of ammunition that Japanese troops were not able to promptly start the battle of Liaoyang, their first major land engagement with the Russian Army. Meanwhile, Nogi's Third Army, struggling to besiege Port Arthur, was exhausting its ammunition supply to no good effect. Imperial General Headquarters was flooded with frantic wires warning that Nogi's army was scraping bottom. The sheer idiocy of trying to fight a war with insufficient bullets and shells boggles the mind.

This is how an artillery section chief's catastrophic decision to order fifty rounds of ammunition per weapon before the outbreak of war played a crucial role in the nation's history. Early on, after a baptism by Russian fire in Nanshan and Jinzhou, the allotment was expanded to "at least one hundred rounds per gun," but it was already too late. Japan's arsenal could not expand production overnight, and ordering from abroad (though this was done) could not fill the gap in time. In the meantime, the war proceeded on course. The Russian Army was not about to wait for the enemy to lay in ammunition.

During these battle preparations, the Japanese Army carefully set aside ammunition from the domestic supply. The First Army managed to stockpile 205 rounds per weapon, the Second Army 180 rounds, the Fourth Army 140. Still, it was all too clear that, once fighting began, those paltry amounts would quickly be used up. Requests rained on Tokyo for more. From Nogi at Port Arthur came this appeal: "Stop making ammunition for field guns and mountain guns. Make ammunition for siege guns instead. Six hundred rounds per gun needed immediately." But Tokyo was unable to grant even this request.

Meanwhile, with the onset of fighting only days off, the following incident took place in Manchuria. On August 23, Kodama Gentarō, chief of staff of the Manchurian Army, received a secret wire from Imperial General Headquarters. It was sent by Major General Nagaoka Gaishi, vice chief of the General Staff. The wire began "For your eyes only" as showing it around carelessly was sure to deplete morale. The gist of the message was this: "The Third Army hasn't got enough rifle bullets, let alone larger ammunition. We need to give it all the ammunition piled up around Dalian, large and small. There are no more bullets to be had. No matter how much we press the Army Ministry, all we can produce is a mere sixty thousand rounds each month." The wire ended with an admonition to "resolve to attack Liaoyang with what arms you have on hand." This admission of the state of affairs was less pathetic than absurd.

* * *

The world's attention was focused on the looming battle. From Japan's perspective, victory in this first major encounter of the Russo-Japanese War was essential to facilitate diplomatic peace maneuvers and float foreign loans. In the event of defeat, Japan's international standing would be drastically diminished, and no country would be likely to offer aid.

On August 3, shortly before the opening of hostilities, Imperial General Headquarters sent a wire to Commander in Chief Ōyama Iwao: "In the coming battle, lead us to victory in the Russo-Japanese War." But not only were ammunition supplies pitifully low, rations at the front were insufficient as well, with some units actually on half rations. The cause was inefficient supply lines. The simple yet urgent business of maintaining supplies, an activity that requires careful planning, was perhaps unsuited to the Japanese temperament. Yet the navy carried out the task punctiliously, managing to get through the entire war without slipup. If army negligence regarding supplies was rooted in some Japanese character flaw, then it was perhaps unavoidable, since a nation's essential roots are largely evident in its army.

Any deficiency in supplies could be made up for by valor in fighting. This supremely Japanese way of thinking, pervasive in Imperial General Headquarters, was peculiar to the national character and persisted in the Japanese Army to the last.

On August 14, Ōyama ordered the armies under his command, all except Nogi's Third Army, to march toward Liaoyang. Both in Tokyo and on the continent, there was concern that any further delay would only allow a greater buildup of enemy troops. But the day the command went out marked the beginning of the rainy season. Flooding was rampant, transportation cut off. As a result, two days later, the command was withdrawn.

"The rains that began on the thirteenth still have not let up," wrote Kodama on a postcard to a friend in Tokyo. To while away the time during the torrential rains, he sat in headquarters and wrote postcards to people all over or composed Chinese verses. On August 22, he received permission from Ōyama and issued orders for the attack on Liaoyang to begin August 26 (for some units, August 28).

Naturally, they couldn't charge Liaoyang immediately. Their first task was to attack the enemy line from the camps at the front along the Taizi River to Anshanzhan, and then occupy that entire area. Kuroki's First Army would be the detached force. The frontal assault on Liaoyang would be carried out by Oku's Second Army, to which Akiyama Yoshifuru belonged, and Nozu's Fourth Army.

The army marched through seas of mud. When gun carriages and ammunition wagons stuck in the muddy ruts, soldiers gathered round and pushed them slowly forward by brute strength.

* * *

On August 3, Yoshifuru's cavalry had received orders to proceed far to the north toward Anshanzhan to check on the enemy's situation. They spent the next twenty days doing so by sending small parties to reconnoiter or by having cavalry officers made up like Chinese infiltrate enemy territory. Those who undertook this latter perilous assignment were First Lieutenant Gotō Hideshirō and Second Lieutenant Kobayashi Tamaki.

There is a story connected with this assignment. After the war, when Yoshifuru was sitting in the officers' lounge of the Imperial Guard Division headquarters, he scrutinized his aide-de-camp and said, "Gotō, you've got the face of a Chinese."

Unsure what had prompted this sudden remark, Gotō felt rather annoyed, yet he had to mumble some sort of reply. "I do?"

"Yes." That was the end of it. But as he spoke, Yoshifuru's eyes misted over momentarily.

This Gotō was the very man who, on the eve of battle, had disguised himself as a Chinese and penetrated enemy territory. Though challenged a number of times by Russian soldiers, he had miraculously returned alive.

Remembering this, Yoshifuru wanted to express thanks but said only, "Gotō, you look like a Chinese," without further comment. Perhaps he assumed that those cryptic words would convey his reminiscence and emotion.

Gotō did not immediately catch on. The next day, it dawned on him what Yoshifuru must have been referring to. When he brought it up, only then did Yoshifuru say, "That was a brave thing you did." That's the sort of man he was.

For the rest of his life Yoshifuru would be seen as the last of the old-time samurai. Fearless in battle, he alone of Army Academy graduates did not become a staff officer (and thereby involved in planning and strategy) but served as a unit commander to the last. He cared little for war, however. In a letter home on the eve of the battle of Liaoyang, he wrote this poem.

> My grandmother's spirit:
> I want to stop warfare
> and live in peace.
> Make war for the sake of peace.

On rare occasions, he would compose poems in Chinese or Japanese, but his efforts were bumbling. This one can't be called a poem, but it shows something of his state of mind.

* * *

In the battle of Liaoyang, the role of Yoshifuru's cavalry was to position itself on the left of the Japanese Army's central force and move forward in tandem with it, protecting the left flank. The army's biggest concern was the possibility that Mishchenko, the head of the Cossack cavalry, might appear. If the Japanese troops were sideswiped on their way to Liaoyang in that stretched-out formation, they would suffer a rout. Yoshifuru was to prevent this from happening.

"They don't know how to use cavalry," Yoshifuru thought again. The purpose of cavalry wasn't just to protect against enemy cavalry. The thing to do was to take advantage of the cavalry's mobility—send it deep into enemy territory to scout strategically high ground from which to gauge the optimal time to strike, and use that information to launch a surprise attack. That was what a cavalry was all about. But it took a genius like Napoleon to exploit the cavalry to the full. Expecting Oku's aides to be capable of such a thing was asking too much, as Yoshifuru well knew.

He requested that another unit be formed for the purpose of defense. The cavalry brigade on its own would not be enough, and so he suggested adding on another unit with independent fighting potential. Oku's headquarters accepted this idea. This is how Yoshifuru came to command not only his First Cavalry Brigade but infantry, artillery, and engineers as well. Together these formed a highly respectable force with fighting power greater than that of Mishchenko's brigade.

As an aside, Mishchenko had fully ten companies of Cossack horsemen but only ten field guns. Even if Yoshifuru came across the powerful Russian brigade somewhere along the way, he could easily crush it. "The only way to go up against Mishchenko's long-coated Cossacks and win is with firepower." That's what Yoshifuru thought.

The Japanese cavalry were attired differently from the infantry. Their jackets were decorated with epaulets, and their trousers were red. When seated on a rather small horse, a Japanese cavalryman looked quaint rather than intimidating. Russian Cossacks wore big fur hats and long coats that fell below the knee. The Japanese carried sabers, the Russians lances. All in all, the Japanese cavalry was at a disadvantage, with smaller men and horses.

To overcome these inherent shortcomings, Yoshifuru came up with his idea of mobile units combining infantry, artillery, and engineering, centered around the main force of the cavalry. His innovation eventually disappeared in Japan but was picked up in the Soviet Army, in the use of combined infantry, artillery, and engineering corps centered around tanks—a development that would lead to the defeat of the Japanese Army at Khalkhin Gol in 1939.

* * *

On the night of August 25, Oku's Second Army swung out.

The Nagoya Division (Third Division) took Liaoyang Road. This division, known for its strength and bravery, consisted of men from Gifu, Nagoya, Toyohashi, Hamamatsu, and Shizuoka. The Osaka Division (Fourth Division) took Niuzhuang Road. Ever since the Satsuma Rebellion, the Osaka Division had acquired a reputation for weakness, but it proved the bravest by far in the thick of the fighting at Nanshan, grappling hand-to-hand with the enemy and occupying the territory in no time. But at the battle of Liaoyang, the shortage of rations hit this division harder than the rest. They became rather listless and received this encouragement from military headquarters: "Remember your valor at Nanshan, where you played such a leading role, and make renewed strenuous efforts."

Between the Nagoya and Osaka divisions was the Kumamoto Division (Sixth Division), said to be the strongest of all. As the plan of operations unfolded, an order went out officially changing the appellation of Yoshifuru's command: "Effective immediately, it will be known for the time being as Akiyama's detachment." An army directive aimed at Yoshifuru read, "The enemy's right flank and rear should be threatened with the powerful cavalry detachment." Yoshifuru and his detachment were assigned to actively menace the enemy's right flank and rear, and passively protect the left flank of Oku's army from attack by Mishchenko.

The night of August 27 brought heavy rain. Under cover of this rain, Oku's army launched an attack on Anshanzhan, which his staff was convinced was the enemy stronghold. After reconnaissance there, Yoshifuru had reported, "It doesn't amount to much. The main camp is further back at Shoushanpu." However, Oku's headquarters dismissed his report. General Headquarters, where Ōyama and Kodama were, agreed with Yoshifuru. Yet, even though they were the headquarters superior to Oku, they could not step in and order Oku to follow his advice.

Oku's chief of staff was Major General Ochiai Toyosaburō of Shimane Prefecture, who started out as a military engineer. He graduated from the Army Academy in the same class as Yoshifuru and from the Army Staff College in the second graduating class, one behind Yoshifuru. Later on, he would write a book called *Explaining Sunzi by Examples* in which he dispassionately analyzed the underlying failures of Japanese military strategy in the attack on Port Arthur. Partly because of his background in engineering, Ochiai had profound knowledge of modern fortifications and firm views on how they should be attacked. He was not sent to Port Arthur, however, but was transferred to Oku's field army instead. Whether he was the right man to be a field army's chief of staff is not entirely clear.

At dawn on August 27, Oku's army launched an attack on Anshanzhan only to find that the Russian main force had already retired to Shoushanpu. They were able to occupy the area with ease. Ochiai's assumption thus proved wrong.

* * *

General Oku's masterful performance at Nanshan was, then and later, a mainstay of his high reputation. When the army's top echelon was choosing commanders for the Russo-Japanese War, the general opinion was "We can't leave Oku out," even though he was not from Satsuma or Chōshū but from Kokura, one of the "renegade" domains. Of the four armies that made up the Japanese Manchurian Army, three had commanders from Satsuma or Chōshū: Kuroki of the First Army was from Satsuma, Nogi of the Third Army was from Chōshū, and Nozu of the Fourth Army was from Satsuma. That only Oku differed indicates the army's high estimation of his abilities.

Here is an interesting sidelight on personnel affairs in the Russo-Japanese War. The General Staff Office paired each army commander—survivors of the Meiji Restoration all—with an Army Staff College alumnus of the rank of major general. In general, the commanders led by force of character, while chiefs of staff were responsible for tactical planning. Commanders assigned a brilliant chief of staff, someone like Kuroki's Fujii Shigeta, were fortunate. Those saddled with someone of lesser ability (like Nogi's Ijichi Kōsuke) were not.

Oku Yasukata was an exceedingly broad-minded man who stayed aloof from the minutiae of tactical planning and decisions. From the beginning, it was his policy to leave such things in the hands of his chief of staff. He would step in only when they were cornered, he always said, or the fighting was out of control. In staff meetings, he took a central seat but scarcely spoke. There was a good reason for his taciturnity: he couldn't hear. He wasn't stone deaf, but anyone who wanted to address him had to write out what he wanted to say. All his aides did so, from the chief of staff on down. This physical handicap served to increase the role played by Oku's chief of staff Ochiai Toyosaburō in determining troop movements. Ochiai was not calm and flexible in his approach, and tended to reject any military intelligence that conflicted with his preconceptions and judgments.

Oku's army advanced by driving back the enemy in light fighting, but at Shoushanpu the situation changed. There they were dealt a blow great enough to reverse the course of the battle. At first, Ochiai lacked the mental flexibility to register this altered state of affairs. "That can't be!" He clung stubbornly to his preconceived opinion, insisting loudly that Shoushanpu was no big deal and lambasting the soldiers at the front.

* * *

"Shoushanpu" refers broadly to the second line of defense of the Russian Army. The defense line, with the 97-meter hill at Shoushan on its western edge, extended east all the way to high ground in the northeast, where there was a fish-breeding reservoir. Kuropatkin sought to inflict damage on the Japanese Army along this east–west line.

The Japanese forces headed there were Oku and Nozu's armies. The attack began before dawn on August 30.

"I never fought in a battle so bitter in all my life," Oku would often remark later. European military history had seldom seen combat on such a scale. Japanese soldiers, moreover, had never before participated in so large an encounter.

The eight hundred guns of both sides went off simultaneously and continued firing all day long. The ground shook. Smoke from exploding shells became a thick cloud that covered the sun, and smoke from belching cannons crawled along the ground. Not only shells flew. Rifles—three or four hundred thousand on both sides—spat fire at the same time.

Akiyama Yoshifuru's detachment advanced much farther north than Oku's army, boldly going behind enemy lines and inflicting painful damage on the right flank. The Russians could not dismiss this threat. Their supreme commander was Lieutenant General Stakelberg of the First Siberian Army Corps. His work began at four in the morning when he received an urgent message that Japanese infantry had appeared in front of the camp of his right wing. He tapped the edge of the table where a map was spread out. "The right flank is in danger."

Blessed with the natural ability to remain calm under any conditions, Stakelberg swiftly ordered the Thirty-fifth Rifle Regiment to face the Japanese Army. The Ninth Division, the one across from the Japanese, was commanded by Major General Kiprian Kondratovich. He gave his forty-eight artillery pieces the order to fire. Up to this point, the Russians had always had numerical superiority in artillery, but not any more. Japanese guns were concentrated here, all 150 of them. They went off simultaneously, aimed at the forty-eight Russian pieces, and inflicted huge damage.

"Freedom to concentrate lies with the attacking side." Stakelberg addressed the remark to his staff as if delivering a lecture on military strategy. He had always been opposed to Kuropatkin's defensive strategy. A strong defense required three times the strength of the enemy, in order to be safe whichever way they came. The Russians did not have three times the strength of the Japanese, and so they had to spread their troops thin. The attackers, however, were free to choose the point of their attack and concentrate their fire.

* * *

That morning, the appearance of Japanese troops south of Shoushanpu set off alarm bells in Stakelberg's mind. "What, here already?" It was unbelievable. This was far past the front where heavy fighting was taking place. Later, he found out that it was Japanese cavalry leader Akiyama Yoshifuru, Major General Mishchenko's counterpart, who had ridden a great distance to attack with guns blazing.

Yoshifuru covertly sent his artillery battery all the way to Wangerdun and had it set up camp there secretly. This hush-hush operation was something he could well be proud of, but he never once boasted of it after the war.

Russian records indicate the intensity of the assault by the "rifle cavalry." Rifle shells and shrapnel rained on the camp of the East Siberian Rifle Artillery Brigade. In two hours, the Third Company of that brigade lost all its officers and nineteen noncommissioned officers and men, as well as having two cannons blow up. In the end, all its guns were forced into silence.

Determined to silence the enemy in turn, General Stakelberg pulled an artillery corps from the reserves. This was the Second Company of the Zabaikal Cossacks Horse Artillery, which rushed to the scene. As they tried to hurry, unsure which direction Akiyama was shooting from, their field artillery got stuck in the mud. The officers gazed off in the likeliest direction, listening for the sounds of gunfire and searching for the sight of smoke, but Yoshifuru's battery was like a phantom, its whereabouts a mystery.

All the while, Akiyama's rifle cavalry kept firing. Not only did this single battery silence the Russian company by ten in the morning, but by noon it had struck down all officers but one of the First and Second Companies of the Rifle Artillery Brigade—an unbelievable outcome.

"Japanese cavalry on the right flank." This wire reached Stakelberg's headquarters at six in the morning. It was followed by an urgent message that the Japanese cavalry main force had taken Wangerdun, and a separate band had occupied Wulonghe and Shuiquan. This was Akiyama Yoshifuru.

Stakelberg gave immediate orders to pursue the Japanese cavalry. The recipient of the order was the cavalry leader Colonel Vasily Gurko, who set off with two and a half regiments of Cossack horsemen. The names of his outfits were the Mounted Hunting Corps, the Coastal Dragoon Regiment, and the Border Defense Cossack Cavalry Regiment.

"When Akiyama came to Siberia as an observer of the grand maneuvers," Gurko commented to his aide-de-camp as he set off, "we went drinking together."

* * *

The attack on Shoushanpu was the most bitterly fought engagement in the battle of Liaoyang. Lieutenant Colonel Tachibana Shūta died in this battle and later became famous in the epic song "Commander Tachibana," which portrayed him as a war god—*gunshin*—who died bravely, a smile on his lips, "scattering like cherry petals . . . for the emperor's land."

The main Japanese forces of Nozu and Oku's armies had their work cut out for them. Time and again, they were driven back, even facing the danger of collapse. At Manchurian Army headquarters, Kodama Gentarō grew apoplectic over the inactivity of Oku's army and fired off wire after wire asking essentially one thing: "What are you doing?" He had intended to hold the Osaka (Fourth) Division in reserve but quickly dispatched it to Oku's left flank. The reinforcements too failed to perform well, adding to Kodama's woes.

On the night of the thirty-first, after two days of heavy fighting, alarming news came in. In the enemy's rear, an enemy force of unknown numbers had appeared at Beitai (4 kilometers west of Liaoyang) and was pushing south. If the report was true, the Osaka Division on Oku's left flank was about to be penetrated. The Osaka Division was the weakest element in Oku's army, and, if it disintegrated, the result could be ugly. In the end, though, the enemy went off in another direction.

From the Russian perspective, Oku was fighting the First Siberian Army Corps, while Nozu engaged in mortal combat with the Third Siberian Army Corps. Commander in Chief Kuropatkin inspected the front line and, seeing the fierceness of Nozu's army, came to the mistaken conclusion that this must be the Japanese main force. (Oku and Nozu commanded armies of comparable size.)

Stakelberg requested reinforcements many times, only to be turned down by Kuropatkin every time. Kuropatkin's reasoning was as follows: "You aren't facing the enemy's main force. The Third Army Corps needs replenishing more."

Kodama erred even more than Kuropatkin in assessing the enemy's strength. His error proved fatal. Though inwardly surprised by the enemy's stubborn persistence at Shoushanpu, he saw that as an outpost, and believed that, if pushed, the enemy would pack up, withdraw to Liaoyang, and establish a base for a great battle there.

Kuropatkin was different. He began deploying reserve corps in Liaoyang to fight the Japanese at Shoushanpu. Even Kodama, berating Oku's army from behind, did not take the situation seriously enough.

During this time, only Akiyama Yoshifuru's cavalry brigade, off to the north on the enemy's right flank, defeated the enemy at every turn and filed continual reports with Oku's army. The accuracy of those reports was verified after the war, but at the time they went virtually ignored, due to Chief of Staff Ochiai Toyosaburō's poor judgment.

* * *

If the war had continued in this vein, both Nozu and Oku would have been forced to withdraw. They had suffered heavy casualties and their ammunition was nearly gone. Two main factors turned things around for the Japanese Army, saving it from the brink of disaster and leading on to eventual victory.

One was that Kodama borrowed two long-range cannons from Nogi's army at Port Arthur and gave them to Oku, although Oku had little use for them. Yoshifuru learned about the cannons when he advanced into a small village west of Shoushanpu, where his men engaged in repeated fierce shooting contests with the enemy. While there, Yoshifuru set up headquarters in front of a small roadside shrine. Whenever possible, he chose not to locate his battle headquarters in private houses, preferring to be out in the open air. He spread husks from the *kaoliang* grain on the road and sat down, folding his long legs into a cross-legged position. He then proceeded to read maps, plan strategy, listen to reports, and dispatch orders. Shells fell in the village frequently, but his expression never flickered.

At this time, fresh gunfire broke out in the northwest corner of the village, as the enemy launched a counteroffensive. They were three hundred strong. Apparently, these were cavalry daring to attack on foot—their uniforms identified them as Cossacks. Without getting up, Yoshifuru sent for an orderly to dispatch the order for a company of infantry to repulse them. When he had done this, he summoned his aide-de-camp.

"Nakaya, tell me something." As he spoke, bullets hit the roof of the shrine over his head, shattering tiles, but he kept right on talking. The gunfire coming from Oku's main force to the rear struck him as sounding different from usual. "Isn't that siege artillery?"

Nakaya thought so too. The target was apparently the enemy camp at Shoushanpu. But even though the ground in that area had been heavily fortified, there could be little advantage in using big guns to pound what was not a proper fort but a mere cluster of small field works.

"Go tell them that if they want to use siege guns, they ought to fire them at Liaoyang Station in the distance." Yoshifuru knew from reconnaissance that Kuropatkin's headquarters was nearby. He knew also that ammunition and other military supplies were stored at the station. Firing the big guns there would be sure to shake enemy morale and give the enemy's senior command a sense of defeat.

Nakaya tore off to the rear on horseback. Oku's headquarters accepted the recommendation, for once, and shortly thereafter began bombarding the station. The psychological toll on Kuropatkin was devastating.

* * *

The greatest contribution to victory in the battle of Liaoyang came from Kuroki's First Army. The armies of Oku and Nozu, the main force of the Japanese Army, made a strong frontal assault on the enemy's main defense line, but Kuroki's army wasn't there. It was playing the role of flying column off to the right. Far off in the mountainous region to the east, Kuroki was on the move. His mission was to make a great detour, cross the Taizi, and encircle Liaoyang from behind or else attack from the side.

Kuroki's chief of staff, Fujii Shigeta, had long been an outspoken proponent of this plan, which he declared was their only hope of taking Liaoyang. Like Yoshifuru, Fujii was a member of the first graduating class of the Army Staff College, where, again like Yoshifuru, he had received no awards for excellence. But before the outbreak of war, he had carefully prepared for the impending battles in his role on the General Staff and had grown convinced that the walled city of Liaoyang could be taken no other way.

When Fujii first proposed making a detour and crossing the river in a surprise attack, Kuroki had responded with lightning quick understanding. "Right. Like Yoshitsune at Hiyodorigoe Cliff."

Only a military genius could have devised the strategy so brilliantly executed by medieval warrior Minamoto no Yoshitsune. The enemy forces of the Heike were then encamped in what is now the city of Kobe, where sawtooth mountains press up against the sea leaving a narrow strip of land extending east and west. The Heike main force was securely wedged in this stronghold with its head to the east and its rear to the west. The leader of the main force on the other side, the Genji, was Yoshitsune's older brother Noriyori. He attacked straight from the east, making a frontal assault where the Heike had erected a stockade. As the two armies clashed before that stockade, all at once the rear of the Heike camp was attacked by a separate division. Out of the blue, soldiers on horseback came thundering over the ridge of mountains that extended like a folding screen beside the camp. This was the celebrated attack at Ichinotani.

Before the battle, Yoshitsune had been in the capital, and then suddenly he had taken off. On the way to Kobe, he had made a quick detour north over Tamba Road, racing along lightly equipped. Some sources say he had with him seventy men, others put it at roughly double that number. In any case, it was a small force, no more than two hundred strong. They had charged to the top of Hiyodorigoe Cliff and then poured down into the valley of Ichinotani, raiding the enemy camp with a rush of men and horses. This incident led to the Heike's ultimate defeat.

Kuroki's army would play the role of Yoshitsune, who had accomplished his daring feat with a handful of soldiers. Common sense seemed to dictate that to be successful, the detour strategy must rely on a few lightly equipped men. Kodama, however, decided to devote an entire army to the mission.

Kuroki's army was large. The divisions under his command included the Imperial Guard as well as the Sendai Division (Second Division), the Kokura Division (Twelfth Division), and the Imperial Guard Mixed Brigade. This great army went on the march days before the armies of Oku and Nogi, who would make the main frontal assault. (For convenience, let us call the front where Kuroki's army fought the "eastern front.")

Kuroki would circle to the east and attack Liaoyang from that direction. Along the way, his men would have to attack and destroy numerous enemy fortifications. Their path was far from easy. Some in the main army headquarters worried that the men would be so hard pressed, going from battle to battle without adequate rest, that their strength might give out. The prelude to the battle of Liaoyang would be so long for Kuroki's army that it was feared his men and officers might collapse from exhaustion.

The limits to human endurance mean that no battle, however momentous, can continue indefinitely. The epic battle of Sekigahara in Japanese history lasted roughly five years, surely close to a record. In early modern times, the 1809 battle between France and Austria at Wagram went on for fourteen hours, and, in 1812, the battle of Borodino lasted twelve and a half. But for Kuroki's army, the battle of Liaoyang began on the evening of August 25 and did not stop for a full eleven days. For Oku and Nozu's armies, it lasted eight days.

Foreign observers were astounded. How could Japanese soldiers withstand such draining battles when they were so small of physique, with a diet that was significantly poorer than Europeans? In any case, on August 24, Kuroki went on the march. His men began by attacking the enemy's first line of defense, stretching from Hongshaling Peak to Sunjiasai and to Gaofengsi Temple. After two full days of hard action, they conquered the entire area in a display of almost unbelievable daring and persistence.

After that, they carried out a series of follow-up attacks. The Sendai Division carried out a bold night attack, climbing Mt. Gongzhang and wiping out the enemy camp there. Doing this with a full division of twenty thousand men was unheard of and inspired much admiration as a feat unique in the annals of warfare. Night raids were a specialty of the Sendai Division, one which they practiced with special vigor before the battle of Liaoyang.

But what accounts for the unparalleled strength of Kuroki's army overall? For one thing, Kodama had used a combination of particularly strong divisions in constructing it. At the time, Japan's best soldiers were thought to come from Tōhoku in the north and Kyushu in the south. The Sendai Division was from Tōhoku and the Kokura Division was from Kyushu.

* * *

Kuroki's army would cross the Taizi River. It never occurred to Kuropatkin that this was the Japanese Army's plan. The Taizi, muddy and swollen from days of driving rain, was in no condition to be crossed by a large army. The Russian general considered the river a natural defense.

Kuroki's pattern of actions to that point had led Kuropatkin to expect a standard method of attack. In desperate fighting on the eastern front outside Liaoyang, Kuroki's army was making a standard frontal assault and had already breached the Russian first line of defense.

When news of Kuroki's occupation and breakthrough was rushed to Kuropatkin in his lodgings near Liaoyang Station, he was nonplussed. "That can't be!" Kuroki, he knew, commanded the strongest force in the entire Japanese Army, while he himself commanded the strongest units in the Russian Army: the European Russian Tenth Corps and Seventeenth Corps as well as the Siberian Third Corps.

"The tsar himself would applaud the bravery of our men," said his staff. True enough.

When the Kokura Division attacked Hongshaling Peak, it was defended by the Thirty-first Division of the Russian line infantry. After a fierce exchange of gunfire, the Kokura soldiers climbed the slope under raking fire from every Russian stronghold. For a time, the slope was covered with the bodies of Japanese soldiers, so many that there was no place to set foot. Even so, the attackers kept up the attack. Such a phenomenon was unthinkable according to the European logic of warfare.

When Japanese soldiers had advanced far enough to see the mountaintop just overhead, the Russian soldiers not only fired their muskets but threw rocks as well. Then followed a hand-to-hand battle with bayonets. The defensive battle lasted a full twenty-four hours. Only then did Russia's Thirty-first Division retreat. They held on that long to allow their allied armies, the Siberian Third Corps and Thirty-fifth Corps, time to retreat.

"They say Kuroki's army is made up of three divisions, but that's a damned lie. He's got another three on top of that." This became Kuropatkin's view. From the perspective of European military experts, the conclusion made perfect sense. The fearless aggression shown by Kuroki's army could only mean that he had plenty of troops in reserve. In fact, Kuroki had only the three divisions, exactly as advertised. If the Russo-Japanese War dragged on, Japan would inevitably suffer from a shortage of manpower. Japanese strategy depended on winning the war quickly, and so, in a manner of speaking, Kuroki's three divisions had to serve as both work clothes and Sunday best. No fresh change of clothes was available.

Once his first line of defense had been penetrated, Kuropatkin had to stop Kuroki at the second line of defense. He was a good general who feared the attrition of troop strength. Surviving troops from the first line were taken in at the second line in large numbers. The trouble was, the second line of defense was in danger as well.

* * *

The Russians' first line of defense that Kuroki's army took over after a full day of intense fighting consisted of the following fortifications: The Kokura Division took the high ground from Shuangmiaopu Fort to Yingshoupu Fort. The Sendai Division took the high ground east of Caojiayu Valley. The following day (August 29), the Imperial Guard and the Sendai Division overcame their exhaustion to push ahead further, advancing to the area from Dashimenling Peak to the high ground south of Mengjiafang.

These high hills afforded a good view of the Russian Army's second line of defense. The land extended skyward in a series of waves, and at each knoll representing the crest of a wave there were numberless pillboxes and earthworks. Each of these positions was connected by trenches in the zigzag shape of lightning bolts, and all around the trenches was barbed wire. It was a death factory without an inch of unprotected ground.

Word came to the railway station that Kuroki had come far enough to look down on the second line of defense, again catching Kuropatkin by surprise. He even wondered if perhaps Kuroki was possessed by an evil spirit. From the first, the name "Kuroki" had been for Kuropatkin a kind of unlucky omen. Kuroki had fought the first land battle of the Russo-Japanese War, landing on the Korean Peninsula and handily defeating the Russian Army defending the Yalu River.

From that time forward, Kuropatkin and his staff took it for granted that Kuroki would always hide out somewhere and come swooping down from the side. To use a term from ancient Japanese military tactics, this was the technique of "hidden chessman." It seemed to the Russians that Kuroki's entire army was employed as the "hidden chessman" of the Japanese Army and had been from the very beginning. When the war started, the Japanese main field army abruptly went ashore near Dalian on the Liaodong Peninsula and just as abruptly squared off against the Russian main field army. Only Kuroki's army entered Manchuria by crossing Korea overland, across the Yalu. His army's strength was so overpowering that compared to the rest of the Japanese Army, his soldiers seemed to belong to another race of men.

And this has been stated before, but let us reemphasize: putting the strongest divisions together in Kuroki's army was the doing of Kodama Gentarō. The strategy of organizing an army with one force of especially strong soldiers goes back in Japanese history to the time of Tokugawa Ieyasu, who did this from his middle period on. After the downfall of the Takeda, Ieyasu, with Nobunaga's permission, took into his service all the Takeda officers and men, and assigned them to his general Ii Naomasa. Ieyasu gave them all matching red armor to wear and made them the vanguard. The army vanguard is like a spearhead with which to penetrate enemy strongholds. The stronger, the better.

The difference between Ieyasu and Kodama is that, while Ieyasu used his spearhead for standard frontal assaults, Kodama used his for an attack by a flying unit, that is, as a "hidden chessman." This strategy of using a powerful army was unique to Kodama. In all the history of European warfare, there is nothing like it.

* * *

Kuroki showed his deftness on the eastern front in the way he kept bearing down on the enemy's second line of defense while his real intention lay elsewhere, in crossing the Taizi River. Kuropatkin naturally had no inkling of this, and he can hardly be blamed for that. Kuroki had taken the Russians' first line of defense on the eastern front after a fierce and persistent onslaught. He did not rest on his laurels afterward but pushed further until the second line of defense was before him.

"Kuroki has his eye on our second line of defense, and he means to take it too." How could Kuropatkin think otherwise? He was convinced of it. At this time on the western front (as we shall call it), the Japanese main force, consisting of Oku and Nozu's armies, had begun their own bitter assault in Kuroki's wake. The roar of cannon fire split the skies. Kuropatkin had to deal with simultaneous attacks to the east and west. Developments on the west were a distraction, as this was where the main defensive strength of the Russian Army was concentrated.

Kuroki's entire army faced west (properly speaking, northwest), poised to charge the second line of defense. But the plan was for the army to vanish into thin air like smoke, falling back all the way to Liandaowan, a crossing point on the Taizi, and then rush across in one swoop.

To accomplish this, Kuroki had to deceive the Russian Army. To that end, he left behind a small number of soldiers. Approximately two thousand men under the command of Major General Matsunaga Masatoshi would stay put, spread out in a long, thin formation. They might be compared to a silken thread—a long, narrow thread to use as bait to lure the massive enemy force. With the enemy hoodwinked, the main force would creep stealthily down the mountain under cover of night, fall back, and pick its way northward between the mountains until it came to the river. This was no sneak attack by a mere handful of men. A full army of thirty thousand men was setting out, field artillery in tow.

Max von Hoffmann, a young officer sent from the German General Staff Office as military attaché, wondered privately if such a stunt was even possible. A small-sized youth who had just been made captain, he was a particularly outstanding member of the illustrious German General Staff Office. For the rest of his life, he would speak about this daring strategy of Kuroki's—not only speak but write about it too. He found it utterly new. Success would mean that the Japanese, who had learned the art of modern warfare from Meckel, had surpassed their teacher with a brilliant creative tactic. Hoffmann estimated the chances of success as below twenty percent.

* * *

Kodama was fussy to a fault. His fussiness caused headaches for the headquarters of the various armies. Occasionally, an officer would yell back over the phone in exasperation, "I'm not a child!" However, the great benefit of his fussiness was that, even under intense battle conditions, the intentions of the General Staff Office were duly communicated to each army.

On the twenty-ninth, Kodama wired Kuroki. "When will you cross the Taizi River?" The content of this question is tactically masterful. Rather than simply urging action, he conveyed his grand plan for the battle and sought to obtain Kuroki's full understanding. "The reason I ask," he went on, "is that I intend to use your army's crossing as the basis for an all-out attack." If Kuroki was successful in crossing the river on the eastern front, he would order Oku and Nozu to conduct a simultaneous all-out attack on the western front. "The key to Japan's victory is in your hands," he was saying in essence, lecturing his colleague Kuroki as if he were a child.

Kuroki fully grasped the immensity of his task. For that reason he pounded the table in a rage and spat out, "Does he take me for a fool?" Kuroki was known as a rough-and-tumble general on the order of Sassa Narimasa in the era of Warring States. He knew that Kodama had persistent doubts about his mental abilities, which enraged him all the more.

Kodama added, "Inform me of the time of the crossing and your troop strength."

Kuroki wired back a reply through Fujii Shigeta. Assigning Fujii to Kuroki as chief of staff was Kodama's inspired personnel decision. Of all the chiefs of staff of Japan's four field armies, Fujii was the ablest. He was not only brilliant but also constantly cheerful, never pessimistic no matter how dire battle conditions became—a trait that would enable him to get along well with Kuroki. His one flaw was a slight tendency to be unfocused.

At this point on August 29, it was not possible to write a reply that Kodama would find satisfying. Fujii sent off a wire to the effect that neither the time nor the troop strength had as yet been decided, but he added detailed information about the prospects for the crossing. Kuroki had already had his engineers investigate where the best place to cross the river might be. Not until after the wire went off did he learn that the river was shallow at the great bend called Liandaowan.

* * *

Preparations were ready, and it remained only for Kuroki to decide the timing of the crossing. A small incident helped him make up his mind.

At noon on August 29, Kuroki spotted fires raging west of Liaoyang, northwest of his position. He consulted his chief of staff.

"Fujii, what do you make of that?" Located on the army's extreme right flank as they were, they had no way of knowing what the fires might signify.

"Beats me," said Fujii, stumped.

The flames were caused by long-range firing from Akiyama's cavalry brigade on the army's extreme left, which reduced the Liaoyang railway terminal to rubble and made the surrounding structures go up in flames. But neither Kuroki nor Fujii knew this.

The Russian report reads, "The Liaoyang railway terminal was destroyed by enemy howitzer shells, so a new terminal was built north of there."

But Fujii got the strange idea that the Russians might be on the retreat, burning piles of stores as they went. It was in his nature always to take an optimistic view. In fact, the Russians were doing anything but beating a retreat. They were clashing fiercely with Oku on the left flank and Nozu in the center, landing painful body blows. Both Japanese armies faced certain defeat, but, from where he was, Fujii could not tell any of this.

Fujii wasn't the only one in the dark. Kuroki's response did not show any sign of worry. "Okay, if the Russian Army is retreating, then now's our chance. Tomorrow night, the thirtieth, we'll cross the Taizi and surround them, come what may." This was how he decided on the date and time of the operation.

But the mission was successful.

Nearly the entire army of thirty thousand men sneaked across the river on the night of the thirtieth and thirty-first. That an army so large should have managed to cross undetected by the enemy was a signal achievement. The basis for victory in land battles of the Russo-Japanese War came, it is fair to say, from just such hairbreadth successes.

Kuropatkin, learning about it after the fact, was furious with his own army. He had squared off against Kuroki with an exceptionally large army, readying three divisions totaling seventy-eight thousand men, and a total of two hundred eighty-four field guns and mountain guns.

Kuroki surreptitiously moved his large army under cover of night, slipping away and crossing the river at a point the Russians had left largely undefended. In so doing, he breached the outer moat of the enemy castle.

* * *

Kuropatkin filed a report about the fighting on all fronts during this time. "The fierce attack by the Japanese Army began on the twenty-fourth. We went on the offensive on the afternoon of the twenty-seventh." He used heated rhetoric to describe the fighting style of the Japanese Army, calling it "frenzied to the highest degree." While, for Russia, the war was being conducted in what was a stolen colony, for Japan, the nation's very survival depended on the success of the main force in this first encounter. The Japanese Army could not help being "frenzied."

In his report, Kuropatkin attempts to convey the fierceness of the fighting by pointing out that of the fifteen hundred casualties suffered by the Russians in the vicinity of Anshanzhan, most were by bayonet and sword. "Everywhere on the front there were close encounters. The attack was do-or-die." Of his clashes with Oku and Nozu's armies, he writes with pride, "At 2000 hours on August 31, a heated battle began that finished in the middle of the night. The battle ended in a complete victory for our side."

This was true. Kuropatkin did achieve a complete victory. As an example of the fierceness of the fighting that led to that victory, he cites the valiant action by the troops under the command of his subordinate, Major General Kondratovich.

> The Japanese Army fired off countless shells but our men hung on and defended their positions stubbornly to the point of death. Our front batteries fell partially into the hands of the enemy for a time, but with repeated bayonet attacks, our army recovered them. After each round of hand-to-hand combat, the Japanese Army would retreat, leaving numerous dead behind. To dispose of the bodies we dug many huge holes in the fields of kaoliang, but dig as we would, there were too many enemy bodies to bury them all.
>
> The damage suffered by the Japanese Army must be very great indeed. The damage to our own army is also great, to be sure, but at this time I cannot make even a rough estimate. Major General Rozovsky was wounded, as was Lieutenant General Stakelberg. But the lieutenant general is still in the line of battle.

* * *

This report was evidently written amid the confusion of battle. Until August 31, Kuropatkin remained hugely confident of victory. Kuroki's crossing of the Taizi River dealt him a powerful blow.

"It became clear on August 31 that Kuroki's entire army had crossed to the right bank of the Taizi," he wrote. "On this point, I had suspected something of the sort. That is because, on August 30 and 31, Kuroki's attack on the Russian left flank weakened conspicuously. I wondered then if he might be planning a detour around our left flank with his main force." Despite this glimmer of suspicion, clearly Kuropatkin never expected that such a large army would be able to cross the river successfully.

In any case, Kuropatkin lashed out in fury at the incompetence of his generals on the eastern front (from the Russian perspective, this was the army's left flank, from the Japanese perspective, the right). "How can I describe this incompetence? How could you not realize that tens of thousands of Kuroki's men had vanished before your very eyes? This goes beyond any question of competence or incompetence. What I want to know is, have you got eyes in your heads?" He scolded his own adjutant and chief of staff as if they themselves were the incompetent generals.

Kuropatkin was known as the finest tactician in Europe. His strategies and troop deployments were textbook examples of the art of war, a fact universally acknowledged by all foreign observers. The generals under his command were undoubtedly incompetent. Had their senses been alert and their reflexes nimble, they might have gone off in pursuit of Kuroki as he withdrew, stopped him cold on the banks of the Taizi, and destroyed his army, turning the waters red with Japanese blood.

For Kuroki, the danger had been real. Captain Hoffmann conveyed his doubts to Fujii. "As far as I can tell, your chance of success is minuscule, your risk of failure immense. What if the Russian Army catches on and comes after them? What then?" All hell will break loose, he meant, but he did not say so.

Yet Fujii's decision was well grounded in the facts. As usual, he took a positive, indeed an optimistic, view of the facts, rather than a negative one. "It's a gamble, but I'm betting the enemy won't give chase. Look at the way General Bilderling does things. It's obvious he won't come after us."

Hoffmann, still unconvinced, expressed his misgivings to Kuroki. "If I were you, I wouldn't do it this way. I'd go after the enemy—Bilderling—in front of me with all my might, push him way back. Once I'd gained a little breathing room, then I'd cross the river."

Kuroki, a veteran of the Boshin War, scoffed at young Hoffmann's idea. "You're talking nonsense." Hoffmann was technically right, he admitted. In war as in wrestling, once you were grappling with the enemy, you couldn't magically disentangle yourself and run around behind him. Logic was on Hoffmann's side—but wars didn't unfold according to the rules of logic. Granted, the risk was huge, but if you spent all your time calculating risk, you couldn't fight a war.

* * *

Kuroki's army went across.

You might say that Kuropatkin's attitude and response to the crossing had a powerful influence on the fate of the Russian Army in this war. He had set the table for the Japanese left flank (Oku) and center (Nozu), but, when he swung completely around, he faced Kuroki instead. It was foolish of him. As he himself wrote in his report, "I resolved to pull out divisions from the forward outposts and bring them back to base camp, concentrating full troop strength on Kuroki's army." This move marked a drastic change whereby the eastern front became the major battlefield.

Russian officers and men fighting actively on the western front were left to scratch their heads and wonder what had happened. They were winning against Oku and Nozu. Although victory was in their grasp, the order from the rear was "Retreat!" "Abandon the positions you are now fighting to defend, you're being transferred out of here" was the message. It is fair to say that every Russian subordinate officer handed this incomprehensible order in the thick of fighting went into a rage. They were distrustful of senior headquarters to begin with. This was the chronic disease of the Russian military (including the navy). This order fanned the flames of their distrust.

"What the hell are they thinking?" yelled one artillery officer from his fort.

The one small bright spot in the Russian Army was the personal popularity of Commander in Chief Kuropatkin, whose astuteness every army leader trusted without question. All of them, from generals commanding corps and divisions to field officers leading regiments and battalions, silently obeyed this new command.

The changeover went smoothly. It was on the morning of September 1 when Oku and Nozu's armies learned the astonishing fact that the enemy had begun to retreat. Army staff officers congratulated themselves on having put up a ferocious fight, a laughable conclusion under the circumstances. The Russian Army was withdrawing of its own accord, not because it was losing to the Japanese.

"The enemy shows signs of retreat." When Ōyama and Kodama of the Japanese Manchurian Army received this urgent message, they were puzzled. That the strong stimulus of Kuroki's maneuver might produce such an unexpected result had never occurred to either of them, which was only natural. This turn of events grew largely out of issues in Kuropatkin's psychology rather than his strategy.

* * *

We know that from the first, in the battle at the Yalu River, Kuropatkin had been impressed with Kuroki's might—an impression reinforced by a string of defeats. He viewed Kuroki's might with a mixture of fear and hatred. That psychological state must have overpowered his reason; there seems no other explanation. How else could a military strategist of his stature have made such an elementary mistake? Standard military strategy dictates that a general does not abandon a battle he is winning. Kuropatkin ought to have kept up the pressure on Oku and Nozu on the western front until he wiped them out. Kuroki's flank attack (though, in point of fact, he had just crossed the river and had yet to launch an assault) required only minimal attention. Kuropatkin had plenty of troops to spare for that. Instead, he turned the entire table around to face in Kuroki's direction.

Neither Kuroki nor Fujii had any notion of the deep psychological impact on Kuropatkin of their crossing of the Taizi. On either side of the river, fields of rippling kaoliang spread as far as the eye could see, with knolls rising above the plain here and there. Russian field fortifications had covered certain of those knolls with well-entrenched positions. Kuroki, however, thought the area scantily guarded and did not see it as much of a Russian stronghold.

"Those two are good hills," Kuroki said to Fujii, who also understood the hills' value as an axis from which to take Liaoyang. They were called Mantou Hill—"Steamed Bun Hill"—and Wuding Hill—"Five-Headed Hill." As the names suggest, they looked eminently assailable. Neither Kuroki nor Fujii could have foreseen that these would become the scene of bloody battles that would rip and scar the land. They didn't know about Kuropatkin's altered state of mind (rather than altered strategy). Kuropatkin was busy withdrawing infantry, shifting artillery, even sending in reserves. He was determined to concentrate his strength against Kuroki's army, exterminate it, and bring glory to the Russian military by winning this first major land campaign of the Russo-Japanese War.

* * *

Kuroki sent the Sendai Division to take Mantou Hill, the Kokura Division to take Wuding Hill. But once the divisions got down to business, they realized that the positions were extremely well defended after all. Kuropatkin had given specific orders to yield no hills to the Japanese. Both of those in question afforded a good view of the plain and were therefore strategically important to Kuropatkin as well. One regiment was already in place, and he had ordered General Bilderling to send in reinforcements.

The Japanese began their attack just as the Russians were increasing their troop strength. The fierceness of the Russian artillery set a new record for the battle of Liaoyang, but the Japanese artillery, limited by restrictions on the consumption of ammunition and by the lack of appropriate battle positions, gave its most lackluster performance to date.

There were frequent instances of hand-to-hand combat. The Harada Regiment in the Sendai Division carried out one of the night raids for which the division was famous, closing in on the enemy to a distance of 50 meters before charging them with fixed bayonets. The Russian gunners at first stayed put and mowed them down, but soon they too came pouring out of the trenches to grapple man to man. Countless blades of friend and foe glinted under the stars, blood spurted, flesh was slashed in a spectacle of gruesome carnage—and then the Russians withdrew. This was midnight on September 1.

The Kokura Division took Wuding Hill, but the struggle to defend it was greater than the struggle to possess it. Russia made every effort to reclaim the hill. The most violent fighting unfolded at Heiyingtai on September 2 and 3. During that time, Kuropatkin had easily three or four times Kuroki's troop strength. In artillery and cavalry, his advantage was overwhelming. Kuroki, floundering in the surging sea of the Russian Army, never realized that he was fighting the central Russian force—and herein lies the strangeness of war. Sheer foolhardiness sometimes enables men to maintain their courage.

Mantou Hill fell—but this victory too was brief. At dawn on September 2, for the sake of this hill alone Russian artillerymen raked the enemy with concentrated fire from 140 field and mountain guns and then, with an army at newly doubled strength, charged the hilltop, which the Japanese were holding with a single brigade. The bitter contest kept up all day. Atop the hill, the defenders gallantly hung on.

Kuroki Tamemoto was quite a character. At some point during these grisly exchanges, he stretched out on the ground and took a nap. At first he sat and puffed on a pipe, but soon lay back and drifted off to sleep. "What leadership could I offer at a time like that?" he commented later. "All I could do was sleep." But while he was napping, the tide turned against Japan.

* * *

Mantou Hill became the scene of a decisive, all-out stand like that at Tennōzan, where warlord Toyotomi Hideyoshi won a historic victory. On the afternoon of September 2, the Japanese Army yielded the hill, but that evening they went back on the attack and charged to the top. Every last man of them knew that if the Russians retained control of the hill, the army would fall like dominoes and be pushed back into the Taizi.

Kuroki began an evening offensive, leading a valiant charge with hand-to-hand fighting. By eight o'clock that night, they had dislodged the Russians at the point of the bayonet, and the hill was at last secure.

But Kuropatkin was no less determined. He too at once launched another offensive to take the hill back, and, after using up a great amount of artillery, carried out a series of night raids, sending men out in successive waves. Close-range musket firing and hand-to-hand fighting went on for a full four hours, an amazing record in the annals of warfare. Such drawn-out, desperate fighting could take place only in an era when—setting aside questions of moral value—the existence of the fatherland weighed heavily. To soldiers on both sides, the commands of the fatherland were absolute, and the existence of the fatherland ruled every aspect of life. Dying for country was beyond all doubt (for Japanese of this era, at any rate) a noble death. Without these underlying assumptions, the phenomenon would have been impossible.

In the end, the Japanese won by behaving like sumo wrestlers relentlessly moving forward, no matter what. Russian divisions began to struggle separately down the hill, then retreat.

Kuropatkin's report contains this comment: "The Russian Army frequently occupied the high ground. But, in the end, temporary retreat became an unavoidable necessity." Kuropatkin here uses the phrase "temporary retreat" for literary effect, but it was clearly a retreat. From then on, he erased from his mind all thought of how determined he had been to take the hill. This is another example of the working of human psychology, not of a tactical approach to combat. Kuropatkin still had an abundance of manpower and ammunition. Had he persisted once or twice more, Kuroki's army might well have collapsed. In the end, the psychological makeup of those two men, Kuroki and Kuropatkin, determined the outcome of the battle.

Kuropatkin subsequently began doing something that the Japanese found hard to believe: he began to withdraw his entire army. The Russians abandoned Liaoyang itself. When Kuroki heard the news, he scratched his head and muttered to himself, "That's funny, they're not even losing." Only Mantou Hill had been lost, so why on earth withdraw from the entire front line?

* * *

Kuropatkin the strategist may have been an absolutist, as brilliant people tend to be. His battle plan at Liaoyang fully deserves a passing mark. The only problem was his change of heart midway.

In the beginning, he overwhelmed Oku and Nozu's armies on the western front, pushing them to the brink of defeat. In the east, no sooner did Kuroki begin his detour than Kuropatkin changed strategy and swung around to confront him. In this battle, the two sides came out roughly even.

But Kuropatkin grew obsessed with recapturing Mantou Hill, and Kuroki too saw it as his Tennōzan. He wanted to use it as the axis for an operation that would let him encircle Kuropatkin (although, in point of fact, he lacked the numbers to carry this off). Kuropatkin had a similar plan in mind. They fought as if they had a compass and kept stealing it back and forth, the needle pointing continuously at the contested hill. But, after stealing the compass from each other time and again, Kuroki narrowly won the hill in the end. This apparently left Kuropatkin so demoralized that he gave up on the more important task of defending Liaoyang itself.

"There's still Mukden." This was Kuropatkin's plan for a second major engagement. "Things didn't go as planned at Liaoyang, so I'll back off, deploy the troops on the front at Mukden, and carry out my strategy there." Something like this must have gone through his mind. He was a remarkable genius, a man of extraordinary intellect and sensitivity, but not the man to command a great field army.

Kuroki didn't have half the military knowledge of his Russian counterpart, nor a tenth of his Western-style education. He was a simple samurai from Satsuma. But he was leagues ahead of Kuropatkin when it came to having both the right stuff to lead an army of tens of thousands and the indomitable will to do battle.

After the war, Kuropatkin was judged to have carried out a nearly perfect, textbook example of a tactical retreat. Without allowing the Japanese Army to come after him, he left behind squads in strategic locations along the way, while removing his large army in stages and dispatching it to Mukden. "The Japanese Army goofed and let the prize get away." This was the general assessment. Despite having emerged victorious, the Japanese Army had surprisingly little to show for it. This is one reason for the malicious reports circulated in the foreign press that Japan did not win at Liaoyang.

* * *

The Japanese killed and wounded numbered twenty thousand. Russian casualties were about the same or slightly higher. These numbers in themselves eloquently reveal how desperately both sides fought.

On September 7, Japanese General Headquarters pulled out of Shaho at eight in the morning and entered a still-smoking Liaoyang at one in the afternoon. There by the railway terminal was the building that until a few days earlier Kuropatkin had used as General Headquarters for the Russian Army. Ōyama, Kodama, and their aides went in and decided to take it over for their own purposes.

"Went into Kuropatkin's former HQ," noted Ōyama in his diary, writing the Russian general's name with Chinese characters for "black" (*kuro*), "pigeon" (*hato*), and "gold" (*kin*). The headquarters contained a fine bed that Kuropatkin had left behind when he retreated, and the officers from an impoverished Far Eastern land gawked at its splendor. Since it was too good to throw away, someone suggested deferentially to Ōyama that he use it, if he could possibly bring himself to do so. Ōyama delightedly consented, commenting that he had a fondness for afternoon naps. The acquisition must have given him inordinate pleasure, for he commemorated it in his diary with a haiku.

> Entering the nest
> of the black pigeon, I take
> my afternoon nap

There was one problem with the Japanese General Headquarters, however. They were poor at handling the various foreign war correspondents tagging along after them and offered little in the way of hospitality. Worse, even young staff officers behaved superciliously (as the foreigners thought) and were excessively secretive.

Japanese of the Meiji period had poor understanding of journalists and public opinion. Even Japanese journalists were treated like military porters; many of them even dressed like military porters. Others showed up at the field of battle in striped kimono with the hem tucked up and breeches showing, using an umbrella as cane. Staff officers looked on reporters as a nuisance and drove them off like flies. This treatment roused the indignation of foreign journalists, many of whom packed up and went home. Thus, articles written by reporters with the Russian Army were the ones that got sent around the world.

Kuropatkin was clever here. Amid the confusion soon after the battle of Liaoyang, he held a press conference to spell out what was happening. "We are simply carrying out a planned withdrawal. As proof, you see that we left behind only two cannons."

Japanese headquarters also held a press conference, but theirs consisted simply of reading aloud a few lines of text. The news that raced around the world was that Japan had failed to clinch a victory. As a result, subscriptions to Japanese war bonds plummeted in London, dealing a severe blow to Japanese wartime financing.

Exactly who treated foreign correspondents lightly isn't clear. Imperial General Headquarters in Tokyo was lacking in the sensitivity and ability to handle international opinion from the first. As soon as war broke out, correspondents from newspapers and news agencies of Britain, the United States, and France flocked to Tokyo, but Imperial General Headquarters took no steps to deal with them. Naturally enough, each correspondent intended to do his reporting from the front, attached to a particular army. "Hurry up and let us do our job!"

Flooded with requests to follow the troops, the reporters' respective embassies notified the Foreign Ministry. A ministry section chief conveyed the request to a counterpart in Imperial Headquarters whose response was airily dismissive. "That's the last thing we need to worry about now. They'll just leak military secrets to the enemy anyway, won't they?" Imperial Headquarters officials never dreamed that this attitude would have major repercussions on Japan's ability to float war bonds.

The correspondents languished unhappily in Tokyo. From the first, therefore, they had reason to nurse resentment against the Japanese. The one who showed greatest understanding was Kodama Gentarō. He believed that foreign war correspondents should be taken to the battlefields and took steps to see that they were. Thanks to his intervention, correspondents were assigned to each Japanese army.

But the armies differed in their treatment of war correspondents. Fujii Shigeta was confident enough to allow reporters free access to his tent. He answered their questions without evasion, even explaining what the army was about to do, all of which earned him enormous goodwill. Oku's staff, however, was secretive. His aides forbade visits to the front and gave no solid answers to questions about the war situation. The same treatment was meted out to foreign military observers, one of whom blustered, "We're being treated like swine!"

Oku had faced a mighty foe and had, in the latter stage of the Liaoyang attack, shown unmistakable signs of defeat. In the absence of any explanation to the contrary, what conclusion could reporters reach except that the Japanese Army was losing? They extrapolated from this one instance to apply their observations to the entire front line. As soon as the battle ended, they scattered from the field of operations, racing to the ports of Yingkou and Yantai to file stories in their home countries.

"The Japanese Army did not win at Liaoyang. They just got carried along by Russian strategy. The Russian Army withdrew with aplomb." This was the gist of the reports that spread around the world from telegraphers' keys.

Racial prejudice played heavily into this development. The phenomenon of members of the yellow race demonstrating any superiority over the white race in an armed conflict was difficult for Western reporters to accept. At the battle of Liaoyang, Japan began to project its image on the world's screen for the first time.

* * *

In the world's eyes, the Russian bear had stepped back a little, preparatory to delivering the final, fatal blow. Wounded head to toe, little Japan had barely managed to reach Liaoyang, but that constituted no victory. Japan had merely fallen forward because the Russian bear stepped back.

When Imperial General Headquarters realized that this was the tenor of the world's reporting, a slight case of panic set in. This may have been the first time that Japan was startled by the image of itself reflected on the screen of the international community. When that unflattering image led to a steep decline in London subscriptions to Japanese public loans, the genrō were scared witless.

Japan had no money. On the eve of war, the total (gold) specie in the Bank of Japan was only one hundred seventeen million yen—not enough to fight a war. Some seven or eight times this amount would have to be raised through public loans. Takahashi Korekiyo, vice governor of the Bank of Japan, was working hard in London to float this government debt. Then came word of the "defeat" in Liaoyang. Anticipating a Japanese defeat, people at once sold their bonds or gave up buying them.

In order to devise a countermeasure, genrō Itō Hirobumi, Inoue Kaoru, and Matsukata Masayoshi met with government representatives including Prime Minister Katsura Tarō, Foreign Minister Komura Jutarō, and Army Minister Terauchi Masatake. Yamagata Aritomo, chief of the General Staff, also attended the meeting, where it was decided to issue a directive to the military fighting overseas: "Demonstrate to foreign military observers the empire's sincerity with your cordiality and openness, and without revealing military secrets." In other words, don't miss a chance to propagandize the war. This directive was issued to Ōyama Iwao in the name of Yamagata Aritomo.

When Kodama Gentarō, chief of staff of the Manchuriann Army under Ōyama, read the directive, he let loose with a characteristic blast of temper. Aware of Imperial General Headquarters obtuseness on this matter, he had taken special foreign correspondents with him to Manchuria, mingling with them in his natural convivial style. His reputation among them was accordingly high. Imperial General Headquarters itself was to be faulted for its complete lack of savvy where propaganda was concerned. To fault the army on this matter was an egregious miscarriage of justice.

Kodama promptly wrote out his resignation and sent it to Tokyo. "I deeply regret that my assistance has been insufficient, thus doing injury to the moral influence of Commander in Chief Ōyama. Painfully aware of my responsibility, I hereby beg to be relieved of my command."

Yamagata was taken aback but managed to talk Kodama out of resigning. That incident, at any rate, was smoothly resolved.

* * *

Eventually, Japan published a detailed report concerning the battle of Liaoyang, and so the world recognized Japan's victory. As a result, the flotation of Japanese loans not only recovered but prospered.

For Japan, the Russo-Japanese War was a tightrope walk in terms of financing and troop strength. As an example, there was no money to pay for the warships *Nisshin* and *Kasuga*, which set out from Italy just prior to the outbreak of war and went into action just afterward. The Japanese government looked to the flotation of foreign securities in London in order to make the payments. Success in floating bonds hinged on military success at Liaoyang.

The Japanese government and Imperial General Headquarters fretted continually over the issue of procuring war funds, which kept them needlessly on edge. The Army Ministry and Imperial Headquarters both had the dominant impression that Kuroki was at fault at the battle of Liaoyang. "Why didn't he go after the Russian Army when it was on the run? He made no effort to go after them and achieve greater success. If he had, there could have been no possible doubt about Japan's victory, and conditions would have been more favorable for the flotation of loans. But instead of pursuing his advantage, he halted in the occupied zone." That's how they saw it. Their constant sense of looming crisis over war finances gave rise to heartless carping.

Thanks to the First Army's crossing of the Taizi River under the leadership of Kuroki and Fujii, and the subsequent heart-stopping, furious fighting, the Japanese Army managed to eke out a victory in the battle of Liaoyang. But neither the Army Ministry nor Imperial General Headquarters could bring itself to accept what had happened on those terms. Their censure of Kuroki for failing to pursue the retreating enemy was beyond cruel; it was idiotic. After crossing the Taizi, Kuroki's army fought against a Russian Army four times its size in the struggle for Mantou Hill. Not only that, Kuroki was up against tremendous offensive firepower—fully seventy percent of the artillery in the Russian Army. He finally managed to dislodge the enemy only by throwing in all his reserves.

When the Russians decamped, he had no energy left to go after them. Not only that, the departing Russian soldiers were deliberately deployed so as to prevent pursuit. To expect Kuroki to chase after them anyway under those circumstances was unrealistic.

Even so, Imperial General Headquarters was unrelenting. As a result, Kuroki ended his days a general, even though the other army commanders in the war—all except Nogi, who committed suicide—were made field marshals. Fujii never rose above lieutenant general. This unbelievably mean-spirited way of thinking was dominant in the Japanese military, perhaps because of the nation's extreme financial difficulties during the war.

The Osaka Arsenal was supposed to manufacture all the ammunition needed to send to the front, but consumption of shells far outran their production capacity, and the country was reduced to making hasty purchases from overseas. After the battle of Liaoyang, there was no ammunition left over for the next campaign. On September 15, the Army Ministry sent out orders for munitions to weapons manufacturers around the world, including names like Armstrong, Kynoch, Kings Norton, and Nobel.

These companies naturally had to be paid. Takahashi Korekiyo, vice governor of the Bank of Japan, was then touring Europe with his secretary

Fukai Eigo in tow, trying to dredge up the needed funds. Looking at the situation objectively, one would have to say that surely no country ever fought a war with such a ridiculous amount of scurrying around.

Takahashi had set sail from Yokohama on his mission back on February 24 of that same year, 1904. Barely two weeks had passed since Japan's declaration of war against Russia. A send-off party was held for him at Yokohama Specie Bank, where a rather strange scene was enacted. Genrō Inoue Kaoru, who had been in charge of government finances ever since the Meiji Restoration, stood up and tried to deliver a speech. "If the flotation of foreign loans does not go well, and war funds cannot be raised, what will become of Japan? Unless Takahashi succeeds, Japan will be finished." He got that far and then choked up with tears. Unable to say more, he hung his head in silence while an awkward hush fell over the room.

Takahashi went first to New York. There he contacted several bankers, none of whom held out any hope. Just then the United States was eagerly introducing foreign capital from Britain, France, and elsewhere to develop domestic industry. As a result, there was no money available for lending elsewhere. Takahashi gave up on the United States and crossed over to Europe.

France was then a country of great financial resources, but, out of consideration for the Franco-Russian pact, it was lending money to Russia. Takahashi went to Britain. Though there was an Anglo-Japanese Alliance, this arrangement did not require Britain to help Japan defray war costs. Takahashi went around to all the major banks and capitalists in London. The results were hopeless. All were sympathetic to Japan's situation, but none could see their way clear to extending financial assistance.

* * *

In Europe, Takahashi observed that the outbreak of the Russo-Japanese War had caused no decline in Russia's credit. Rather, the market value of Russian bonds in Paris and London actually showed a slight increase. Japanese bonds did not fare as well. The value of Japanese bonds fell from eighty pounds sterling to sixty as soon as the war began.

"Since we are so unpopular, will the British people respond even if we issue new war bonds?" The gloomy thought weighed on Takahashi's mind. Banks were willing to lend money to Russia as a matter of course. Russia had vast lands and mines at its disposal, and with that as collateral, a lender had no fear of suffering any loss, come what may. But Japan had neither land nor mines to offer as collateral. Despite these unfavorable circumstances, Takahashi succeeded in having war bonds issued by offering tax income as security. Unfortunately, the interest rate on the bonds was an extraordinarily high six percent, at so-called "colonial terms," referring to the harsher terms imposed by Western powers on Asia.

As he was running around making deals under these difficult circumstances, Takahashi met with an unlikely piece of luck. Jewish financier Jacob Schiff, a United States citizen who happened to be visiting London just then, approached Takahashi of his own accord with an offer: "I've heard of the struggles you are going through. Let me be of such service as lies in my power." Jacob Schiff was of German extraction, born in Frankfurt, but he had traveled to the United States at a young age and worked his way up by selling used clothing. At that point, he was owner of the American firm Kuhn, Loeb & Company and head of the American Jewish Committee. Concerning the ten-million-pound war loan at six percent that Takahashi had scraped together, Jacob Schiff volunteered without hesitation, "I'll underwrite half."

From that time on, Schiff stayed in close contact with Takahashi and played a key role in his success in selling bonds. At first, Takahashi had trouble understanding why this American Jew would be so willing to come to Japan's aid. Schiff explained that Russia persecuted Jews. Six million Jews lived in Russia, and, according to Schiff, the history of imperial Russia was a history of anti-Semitic atrocities. It was still going on, he added. "We Jews pray earnestly for the fall of the Russian tsar. It so happens that your country Japan in the Far East started a war with Russia. If you win, there is bound to be a revolution in Russia. Revolution would mean the end of the Russian monarchy. That is what I want to see happen, and that is why I am offering you this perhaps unreasonable assistance."

* * *

When Jacob Schiff explained his reasons for backing Japan, Takahashi's secretary Fukai Eigo was mystified. "Are racial issues that serious?" he asked Takahashi later. To the Japanese mind, Jews were money worshippers. Why would a Jew take his precious money and give it to Japan, when Japan's victory was by no means assured? Schiff had said that Russian anti-Semitism was the reason. In Japan, where the population was far more homogenous, such tensions were hardly likely to become a problem.

Fukai Eigo used all his connections in London's financial world to check up on Jacob Schiff. He also explored the issue of Russian persecution of Jews. The more he learned, the more he realized that the problem was horrifying in its scope. The history of Russian persecution went back to the sixteenth century, when Ivan IV attempted to convert the Jews to Christianity, and the Jews resisted. An imperial order then went out, stating that all who refused to convert should be thrown into the river, and thrown they were.

Persecution intensified in the late nineteenth century, reaching cruel extremes. As head of the American Jewish Committee, Jacob Schiff did all in his power to remedy the situation. He appealed to the governments of Britain and other nations, but no country was willing to interfere in what was clearly a domestic problem in Russia.

Schiff lent money to the Russian government as a private citizen, asking in return an immediate halt to the slaughter of Jews for the crime of being Jews. This ploy was effective in the short term, but, after a year, the situation reverted to what it had been before. Schiff lent money repeatedly but ultimately lost faith in the integrity of tsarist Russia. Revolution, he began to think, was the only answer. One thing that tsarist Russia had in greater supply than any other country was rebels. There were easily over one hundred different parties interested in overthrowing the government, including freedom parties in Poland and Finland, both of which Russia had subjugated.

Schiff doubtless provided financial assistance to these various groups as well. In the meantime, along came the Japanese military, with strength far greater than that of any revolutionary or freedom party. The Japanese military was bold, well organized, and mighty. To Schiff, it seemed obvious that Japan would be Russia's downfall. He didn't even care if Japan lost the war. The important thing to him was that the Russian state would be seriously weakened. That was why he came to Japan's assistance.

The world was certainly a complicated place, mused Fukai, who had worked as a reporter for *Kokumin Shimbun*, a pro-government newspaper, before going into government work. Later, he became governor of the Bank of Japan. He would live on to witness Japan's defeat in the Pacific War, before dying on October 21, 1945.

* * *

Racial issues taught Fukai Eigo the world's complexity, but Takahashi Korekiyo shared the sentiment with even more intensity. "Indeed, the world is truly complex," he told Fukai. When Schiff had offered to support Japan in order to save the Jews in Russia, Takahashi quickly understood that the reason was eminently realistic. He himself, as a young man living in the United States, had once been sold as a slave.

Takahashi Korekiyo was curiously optimistic by nature, with a background strikingly out of the ordinary. The adopted son of Takahashi Kakuji, a low-ranking ashigaru samurai from the Sendai domain, he never knew his true parents until after he grew up. His birth father was Kawamura Shōemon, a master painter in residence at Edo Castle, his mother a maid in the Kawamura residence and the daughter of a fishmonger in Shiba Shirogane. He was handed over to the Takahashi family soon after birth.

One day, when Korekiyo was a small child, as he was playing at a small shrine next to one of the domain's Edo mansions, who should come along to worship but the daimyo's wife. Unafraid, he toddled up to her as she knelt on the wooden floor of the hall and climbed up into her lap. In the feudal society of those days, this was a bizarre and wholly unexpected event. The tot was all smiles, however, and attendants didn't have the heart to scold him. He soon captivated the daimyo's wife, who ended up inviting him to visit her in the castle the following day.

The story created a sensation in the ashigaru tenements, where people talked of nothing but how lucky the Takahashi kid was. This conclusion reached the boy's ears, and he came to believe himself luckier and better off than anyone else. This became a lifelong article of faith, he recorded in his autobiography. "No matter what blunders I made or what difficult straits I fell into, I always made great efforts, believing luck would turn my way in the end." No one but a fellow with this sunny outlook could have succeeded in touring Europe to scrape up money for the Russo-Japanese War. Others went over fearing the worst and, sure enough, came back empty-handed.

In 1867, just before the fall of the shogunate, Takahashi had gone off to study in the United States. Using his connection to a Yokohama shopkeeper named Eugene van Reed, he sailed to San Francisco, where van Reed's parents lived, and moved in with the elderly couple. Not long afterward, he received an introduction to a family named Brown and moved in with them instead—completely unaware that he had been sold as a slave. When the truth came out, he raised an uproar, but curiously, Takahashi never, for the rest of his life, considered this a tragedy or indulged in any self-pity over the incident.

When Fukai Eigo brought up the topic of the seriousness of racial problems in the world, Takahashi merely smiled broadly and said, "I know."

* * *

In any case, a Jew supported Japan. "If possible," Takahashi wrote in his memoirs, "Schiff wanted Japan to win."

> But even if final victory was beyond Japan's grasp, the longer the war continued, the more internal strife there would be in Russia, leading to a change of government. Schiff felt the war should go on at least that long. Besides, since Japanese soldiers were well disciplined and strong, as long as Japan's military expenses were met, he was sure to get what he wanted

in the end. The Russian government would change, and Jewish families would be spared persecution. This was the real reason why Jacob Schiff underwrote Japanese war debts.

Not only in the case of Takahashi, but in other cases as well, racial friction worked in Japan's favor. Nothing is so fierce as the rebellion that arises when a people or a nation is subjected to oppression.

Nineteenth-century Russia had invaded and conquered a vast area, and among its conquests was Poland. What was once the kingdom of Poland became a state in the Russian Empire, and Polish young men were drafted to fight the Japanese Army on the Manchurian plains. Ever since Russia annexed Poland in 1815, patriots there had pushed steadily for independence, only to be put down each time by the Russian police or army.

Finland, which Russia seized in 1809 in a deal with Napoleon, was the same. For a time, the Finns were granted autonomy, but the father of Tsar Nicholas II began a policy of Russification that his son continued with a vengeance, sending in troops and ending Finnish autonomy, halting the legislature, and making Russian the official language. In 1903, the year before the Russo-Japanese War began, he suspended the constitution and placed the country under the autocratic rule of a governor general. This wave of Russification provoked many forms of resistance, culminating in the assassination of Governor General Nikolai Bobrikov in 1904—the very year the Russo-Japanese War broke out. That same year, there was also a nationwide general strike.

The tsarist regime was saddled with issues like these. In Russian satellite areas, dissident parties and independence parties continued active underground campaigns, while, in Russia proper, the contradictions and tyranny of the regime bred more and more revolutionaries each year.

When contemplating war with Russia, Japanese Imperial Headquarters decided to conduct a large-scale intelligence operation aimed at inciting resistance among discontented elements in the Russian Empire in order to topple the tsarist regime. The coordinator of this operation was Colonel Akashi Motojirō, who had served as military attaché in France and Russia, and was accordingly well informed about European affairs. Akashi hailed from the Fukuoka domain and had graduated from the Army Academy in the sixth class, somewhat after Yoshifuru. He was a hero in the rough Asian mode, careless of his appearance, but what he managed to accomplish is nothing short of astonishing. He spent capital liberally. At a time when Japan's annual revenue was two hundred fifty million yen, the General Staff allotted Akashi the colossal sum of one million yen to carry out his mission. This fact alone gives some idea of the scale of his activities.

Colonel Akashi was a man of great imagination, and this trait made him well suited for espionage. He was also capable of passionate involvement, which perhaps made him a fitting choice to coordinate a large-scale intelligence operation in the West. His great untidiness is well known. Fortunately, he joined the Japanese military in its formative period, since the military bureaucracy would certainly have rejected anyone like him later on.

Uehara Yūsaku, general and chief of staff of Nozu's army, once took Akashi to see Field Marshal Yamagata Aritomo, a genrō whose power within the Japanese Army was so great that he had dictatorial powers in personnel matters. According to Uehara, Akashi became engrossed in a certain topic and began to talk enthusiastically without stopping, forcing Yamagata to listen closely. It was a chilly time of year and Yamagata, having caught cold, was sitting next to a heater with his legs wrapped in silk floss. Akashi, talking to him from the other side of the heater, became so caught up in what he was saying that he wet his pants—and kept right on talking without even noticing. His pee rolled down his trousers and onto the floor, wetting Yamagata's silk floss and chilling the great man's feet. Even so, the intensity of Akashi's passion was such that Yamagata could not even shift the position of his feet but had to keep on listening.

Akashi established contact with virtually every major revolutionary, dissident, and freedom fighter in and out of the Russian Empire, gaining their trust in every instance. His characteristic intensity may well have made him more attractive in their eyes. He met Lenin too and spoke about him after the war. "He was absolutely devoted to the cause with no regard for anything but the nation and no thought of his own life, let alone greed or self-interest. The person who will bring about the coming revolution will probably be Lenin."

Once, when he was in Europe, Akashi was smoking a cigar at a certain meeting when Lenin said to him laconically, "Nice taste in cigars." Akashi instantly stubbed his cigar out, having grasped the meaning behind Lenin's words. Lenin was surely trying to warn him that anyone planning to be a leader of workers must be careful even about his choice of cigar.

Lenin also had a firm policy that those instigating demonstrations or riots were not to pass out arms. As long as the people were unarmed, he told Akashi, the police and army could not brandish weapons either.

* * *

The great success of Akashi's work as agent provocateur owed less to his talents than to his capital of one million yen. Nagaoka Gaishi wondered privately if it was wise to hand over such a huge sum of money. In Nagaoka's eyes, Akashi was annoyingly argumentative as well as untidy and unprepossessing in appearance. Worse yet, he was no linguist. Nagaoka later admitted that he only realized how capable Akashi was after his spectacular success in sowing disorder in Russia.

In the end, not even a man of Akashi's gifts could probably have accomplished so much without extraordinary financial support. His power was the power of money. Russian revolutionaries gathered around him not because of his personal magnetism, but because of his boundless (so they thought) generosity. Though he seemed slapdash, he was skillful at handling money and kept scrupulous accounts. Unable to use up the entire million, he returned to Japan with over two hundred thousand yen in cash, and receipts and notations accounting for every penny of his expenses.

In the end, the vast sum of money that he spent was fully justified by the scale of the disturbances that took place within the Russian Empire. Key government officials were preoccupied not by foreign campaigns but rather by the threat of internal collapse. When they thought about the problems that required their attention, foreign campaigns were last on the list. Every loss in Manchuria and every domestic riot filled them with fresh conviction that the war must be ended at the earliest opportunity.

In its conduct of the Russo-Japanese War, the Japanese government adopted a policy of quick, decisive battles. Every leading figure in the government, the army, and the navy was well aware that Japan would lose the war unless it achieved a rapid series of victories in an extremely short time and then negotiated for peace. The conditions had to be ripe for Russia to agree to a peace feeler, which meant bringing Russia's domestic crisis to a head—in other words, fomenting revolution. To accomplish that goal, Japan was willing to spend any amount of money. Pulling off a revolution would more than balance the books. Akashi was entrusted with this job.

He consorted with too many revolutionaries to list them all here, but the full list would surely amount to a who's who of the Russian Revolution. There was Lenin for starters and also Father Georgi Gapon, a priest who headed his own political party; thinker Pyotr Kropotkin; Konni Zilliacus, activist for a Finland free of Russian influence; Georgi Plekhanov, founder of the Social-Democratic movement; writer Maxim Gorky; Pyotr Struve of the left-leaning Party of Popular Freedom; and countless more. They all had one thing in common: they wanted to see Japan win the war with Russia. In this respect, they were no different from Jacob Schiff.

In any case, this war with its complicated political and strategic background had passed the Liaoyang stage.

3

PORT ARTHUR

The harbor at Port Arthur with its great fortifications was, and went on being, a thorn in the side of the Japanese military. Tōgō's plight was pathetic to the point of absurdity. The army's failure to capture the fortifications meant that his fleet was stuck at the harbor entrance, posting guard to ensure that what remained of the Russian fleet didn't sneak out and overrun the seas—a terrible waste of manpower. Japan's chances of victory had never seemed so unpromising.

Reports on when the Baltic Fleet might be expected to arrive from Europe were inconsistent, the timing of that fateful encounter impossible to predict. One disturbing rumor had the fleet reaching the Sea of Japan as early as October. Port Arthur was still an impregnable fortress, the season already late summer. Even if Port Arthur fell immediately (a dream), repairing the Japanese fleet would take at least two months. And, unless each warship was repaired and restored to full fighting power, what hope was there of defeating the Baltic Fleet? Taking Port Arthur immediately would leave barely enough time (assuming the October rumor was true). The navy was frantic.

Imperial Headquarters in Tokyo was beyond frantic. A consensus had already formed that General Nogi was unequal to the task at hand, and evaluation of his chief of staff Ijichi Kōsuke was even harsher. It was the top leaders in Tokyo who had put the two men in their posts, however, so nothing could be done. There were calls for a shake-up, but changing the army commander and his chief of staff in the middle of fighting would devastate troop morale. Within Imperial Headquarters some fumed. "Their strategy is to use up huge numbers of men at Port Arthur—enough to fill in the harbor—with no discernible effect. What on earth are they thinking?"

Even more surprising than this failure of leadership is the docility with which nameless soldiers of Meiji Japan went obediently to their deaths. "People must be made dependent on the authority of the government." This thinking had prevailed during three centuries of Tokugawa rule, and well into the Meiji period Japanese soldiers still retained the old feudal virtues of fear and obedience. An order was absolute. The same order to attack the same target was given monotonously over and over again, and successive waves of soldiers silently obeyed. Before the gigantic killing machine of the Russian Army, whole companies were mowed down en masse.

But Nogi's staff stayed too far in the rear. The young staff officers seldom visited the front and were slow to grasp the wretched situation. When Kodama Gentarō finally came on the scene at the end of the siege, this was what drove him wild. Toward Nogi, who was expected merely to oversee the army, he was tolerant, but he lambasted Chief of Staff Ijichi and the others whose job it was to carry out actual operations. To reprimand an officer for gross failure to monitor battlefield conditions, he tore off his shoulder sash in front of a large assembly.

But Kodama did not come along until the very last. In the meantime, following the chain of command, the situation was left to the discretion of Nogi's staff.

General Nogi was not solely to blame for the failed attack on Port Arthur fortifications: the entire Japanese Army had been remiss. "It was our moment in the new twentieth century. What in blazes were we doing with antiquated bronze cannons?" wrote Captain Satō Kiyokatsu with hot indignation in his book *The Russo-Japanese War As I Saw It*. He was referring to 15- and 9-centimeter bronze mortars. The army used weapons like these to attack the world's newest, most modern fortifications—a miscalculation of appalling proportions. (Later, they would borrow artillery from the navy or remove them from domestic coastal defenses.)

It was more than a simple miscalculation. There was an inherent tendency in the army to look down on technology, even to take pride in countering enemy technology with Japanese courage and human bullets. This way of thinking owed much to the character and proclivities of the architect of the Japanese Army. Japan's military system was first modernized by an expert in military technology named Ōmura Masujirō, but he died in 1869, the second year of the Meiji period, and was replaced by Yamagata Aritomo from the Chōshū militia. It is fair to say that Yamagata's conservative temperament weakened the tradition of emphasizing technological expertise. From that time on, the army would seek to offset second-rate technology with the blood of its soldiers.

In a sense, the Japanese Army did possess weaponry of greater sophistication than the Russian Army. Their rifles in particular were superb. But no matter how many of Japan's vaunted Type 30 rifles the infantry had, the concrete armor of the Port Arthur fortifications held firm.

Nogi's army made the greatest inroads by destroying clusters of smaller defenses in front of the harbor. Those were easy to take. After that, Nogi prepared to attack the main defenses. On August 16, he advised General Stoessel to surrender. Stoessel naturally refused. "News of the invitation to surrender spread quickly through the ranks," wrote General Mikhail Kostenko, one of the Russian officers stationed at Port Arthur. "The effect was to lift the morale of the entire army, just the opposite of what Nogi intended. Our officers and men figured he sent the invitation because he lacked the power to take the fortress."

Nogi launched his first full-scale attack on August 19, slightly before the battle of Liaoyang began. Ignoring the maxim that attacks should be aimed at the enemy's weakest point, he selected the well-nigh impregnable Panlong and East Cockscomb forts, intending to drive a wedge between them and split the area in half—a perfect example of a "desktop plan." Implementation of this plan resulted in devastating losses. After six days of fierce fighting, Japan had 15,800 casualties. Damage inflicted on the enemy, meanwhile, was minimal, and not a single fortification fell.

* * *

General Nogi Maresuke's greatest misfortune was the selection of Ijichi Kōsuke as his chief of staff. He had no say in the matter. The choice was made by the army's top echelon. Final authority in all such personnel assignments rested with Yamagata Aritomo, who also picked Nogi to head the Third Army.

Yamagata was the supreme arbiter of personnel decisions based on domain loyalty. As the grand old man of the Chōshū military faction, he naturally had a deep affection for Nogi, a fellow native son. Ironically, Nogi himself was completely lacking in domain loyalty where personnel matters were concerned and, if truth be told, secretly disapproved of such cliquishness. But Yamagata was inordinately fond of him.

"Chōshū on land, Satsuma on sea." This division of the Japanese military was an unequivocal fact. Men of Satsuma controlled the navy, but ahead of the First Sino-Japanese War, Yamamoto Gombei himself went through the roster of Satsuma veterans to eliminate the deadwood, and by restructuring the navy and enhancing its functionality he succeeded in defeating the Qing. The Chōshū-dominated army never underwent any such radical reform. Yamagata retained his grip on personnel matters, creating a peculiar system where any washout could rise high so long as he hailed from Chōshū.

Yamagata's choice of Nogi grew out of this climate. At the time, Yamagata himself was chief of the General Staff, and the army minister was Terauchi Masatake, who had served in the Seibutai militia in Chōshū. Terauchi had little flair for the military and virtually no battle experience. Despite his high position in military government, he made no attempt to keep an eye on the future and improve the army's capability. He was a conscientious administrator, skilled at insider appointments (based on domain cliques) and fond of paperwork.

The key figure in command of operations in the Russo-Japanese War was Vice Chief of the General Staff Nagaoka Gaishi, a man of sufficient ability that he could probably have attained the position on his own merits, even without the advantage of being a Chōshū native. A visionary in the best sense of the word, he combined a hard-nosed ability to grasp reality with a sweeping imagination. Though lacking the genius of Kodama Gentarō, yet another man of Chōshū, he was an able strategist. It was he who gave Akashi Motojirō, a mere colonel, the million yen to foment revolution in Russia.

Nagaoka was among the first to matriculate at Japan's Army Academy and a member of the second graduating class there. In other words, he was one of the first Japanese to receive a formal military education under the modernized system. Everyone in that first group became a major general in the Russo-Japanese War.

* * *

Let us continue the discussion of factionalism.

The highest army echelon in charge of waging the Russo-Japanese War was overwhelmingly dominated by men from Chōshū, among them Terauchi Masatake, army minister; Yamagata Aritomo, chief of the General Staff; Nagaoka Gaishi, Yamagata's deputy; and Kodama Gentarō, chief of staff for the Manchurian Army. Indeed, virtually every important administrative and tactical post went to an officer from Chōshū.

Interestingly, however, Chōshū did not produce many officers fitted for field command. Among military men independent of any domain clique, there was a widespread sense that Chōshū lacked generals of sufficient toughness to lead a siege or field operation. Satsuma generals were better suited for such roles. Ōyama Iwao, a Satsuma native, was made commander in chief of the Japanese Manchurian Army, while the First Army, of which daring deeds were expected, was put under the command of Kuroki Tamemoto of Satsuma. Oku Yasukata, commander of the Second Army, was not from either Chōshū or Satsuma, but Nozu Michitsura of the Fourth Army was another Satsuma man.

This preponderance of Satsuma generals grated on Yamagata. "Surely we can have at least one from Chōshū," he protested, and that's how Nogi Maresuke was put in charge of the Third Army. In the beginning, army brass were inclined to believe that Port Arthur posed little challenge, and accordingly Nogi was chosen less for his fitness for the job than for his birth credentials. Since he had withdrawn from active service, being awarded this post was no doubt an honor. But as he faced up to the reality of Port Arthur, it may not have seemed unmitigated good fortune after all.

Even more unfortunate was the fact that clique rivalry figured equally in the assignment of Nogi's chief of staff. "Since the commander is from Chōshū, in fairness we ought to make his chief of staff a Satsuma man." Following this line of thought, Yamagata and Terauchi chose Ijichi Kōsuke for the job. Though Ijichi was tapped in part because of his artillery experience, his Satsuma roots carried far greater weight. He did not have a reputation as a great strategist. Indeed, his friends and former subordinates were well aware that he lacked the flexibility to adapt to shifting circumstances.

Nogi too lacked the tactical ability necessary to carry out modern warfare, but he was known to be a man who lived by spiritual values. After the war, his spiritual side would become widely bruited in Japan and abroad, but, at this point, it was known only to a limited number of individuals. Yamagata counted heavily on the general's leadership and ability to inspire his men.

The siege of Port Arthur put Japan at continuous risk of overall defeat, and Army Minister Terauchi and Chief of the General Staff Yamagata must bear responsibility for this.

* * *

When Nogi left Tokyo, he was of the opinion that ten thousand casualties would suffice to take Port Arthur. That low estimate was his basis for approving the plan of attack—a plan devised by Ijichi Kōsuke, needless to say—but the first all-out assault alone produced Japanese casualties of sixteen thousand, a devastating defeat. Not only was Port Arthur not taken, but the great fortress came through unscathed. It was a total victory for the defending side. The second assault followed the same basic plan, with no better results. Though there were four thousand nine hundred casualties, the fortifications held firm as a rock.

"You would think," Nagaoka wrote savagely in his diary, "that after bringing death or injury to more than twenty thousand men below that impregnable fortress, they would have changed their mode of attack."

The General Staff Office tolerated the loss of so many dead and wounded in the first assault—the equivalent of an entire division—only because it took that great a sacrifice for them to realize just how formidable the fortifications at Port Arthur really were. Such miscalculations and misapprehensions are an inevitable part of any war. What made Nagaoka and the others question the intelligence of Ijichi was his failure to acknowledge the error, extract a lesson, and alter course.

The lesson involved was elementary. To gain knowledge about fortifications that any encyclopedia would have yielded, Ijichi paid dearly, sacrificing many thousands of soldiers' lives. The knowledge was not even gained directly at the battlefield but pieced together behind the scenes from various reports. That's because the Third Army headquarters was so far back that they were completely out of range of enemy fire. Concerned, Nogi would later suggest to Ijichi that they move forward, but Ijichi declined on grounds that, in that case, he would be unable to make cool, rational decisions. He kept his distance from the fighting to the end.

Nogi was no coward. To raise the men's morale, he frequently rode his horse to the front amid a hail of bursting shells. But even when he saw with his own eyes the horrors of the front, working out a new strategy was beyond him. (Of the four army commanders, the only one capable of waging war without the aid of his chief of staff was General Oku.) In the alien world of strategy development, Nogi had no choice but to trust Ijichi and go along with what he said.

"Too benevolent to be severe." This was the assessment of Major Ōzawa, a battalion commander in the Eleventh Division who admired Nogi's warmth and humanity, yet regretted that these very virtues made the general excessively generous to everyone on his staff from Ijichi down. Ijichi's news from the front line was largely secondhand, relayed by young officers, yet Nogi did not object. He had lost his elder son at Jinzhou, would lose the younger one on this battlefield, and was himself resolved from the beginning to die at the front. His supreme misfortune, however, was his failure to gain a topnotch chief of staff.

* * *

The second attack on the fortifications was not a simple headlong assault like the first. This time, it was preceded by an artillery barrage. It still ended up a pointless exercise in hurling flesh and blood at concrete.

Concerning attacks on fortresses, Sebastien le Prestre de Vauban had already laid down the great operating principle involved: the attacking side must erect its own fortification for use in offense. This approach was known in Japan as early as the era of Warring States, when an army attacking a castle would build an opposing castle as a base of operations. Toyotomi Hideyoshi, the brilliant conqueror, used this technique with great effectiveness from early in his career.

According to the Vauban principle, an attacking army not only built additional fortifications but also dug parallel trenches to protect the lives of infantry. Then they dug tunnels to blow up the enemy walls from below and, once they had taken the outer walls, they blew up the breastworks. Only then would they make their assault. This procedure was the basic principle of offensive battle and had by the time of the Russo-Japanese War become standard practice in the world's armies. "There is no other way to do it," Vauban declared unequivocally, an opinion backed by countless examples from European warfare.

Nogi's army did not completely ignore this orthodoxy. The soldiers did apply the Vauban approach in their second attack, however incompletely. They dug trenches and a network of tunnels leading to the enemy stronghold from a variety of directions. But Russia was second to none in the sophistication of its defense. The Russian Army dealt swiftly with the crude tunnels, cutting them off so that they were of little use.

From the first, Ijichi was of the optimistic view that gunfire would be enough to demolish the fortress. Offensive power rated higher than defensive power in his book, a view that was, in the light of modern siege warfare, utter nonsense. Some members of Nogi's staff were aware of the Vauban principles of defense but dismissed them as the arguments of "foreigners without souls." Japanese soldiers had *Yamatodamashii*, the indomitable spirit of the Japanese people. Faith that this spirit could melt steel was necessary for troops in the thick of battle, but the high command had no business relying on it. The respect accorded the high command was based on the faith of the state and the nation that they would attain victory on the battlefield with the fewest possible casualties.

If the Japanese soldier was docile, Japanese privates in particular were surely the most docile of any in the world, yet even among their ranks there was muttering. "We can't fight the war under a chief of staff like that." Replacements would cheer if assigned to the army fighting its way north, but among those who joined Nogi's army, there was a noticeable drop in morale.

* * *

Had he not been a man of Satsuma who attained his majority around the time of the Meiji Restoration, Ijichi Kōsuke would doubtless have spent his life in obscurity. Due to those circumstances, however, he was blessed with opportunity from the first. In 1871, he went to Tokyo along with some other

Satsuma youths and joined what was then called the Imperial Bodyguards. When the army preparatory school opened the following year, he enrolled based on someone's recommendation from home. Then, in 1875, when the Army Academy was founded, he naturally entered that too and was a member of the second graduating class. On becoming a second lieutenant, he was ordered overseas to study in France. Others said jealously that Ijichi was like "Satsuma's cherished son."

During his three years in France, Ijichi studied artillery, but soon after his return it happened that Ōyama Iwao, then the army minister, was about to tour Europe and needed an interpreter, so Ijichi went along. When his services were no longer needed, he remained in Europe, going to Germany to study. In the meantime, the Army Staff College was established in Japan, but since Ijichi happened to be abroad at the time, he never studied there. "That's all right," people said. "Ijichi got his training from the horse's mouth." They said this in reference to his studies in Germany.

Ijichi's bond with Nogi Maresuke came about during his German sojourn. Nogi, at the time a major general, was on a study tour of Europe, and Ijichi went along as his interpreter.

After the First Sino-Japanese War, Ijichi became a colonel and served as military attaché to the British embassy. He spent a long time overseas, in other words, with almost no experience as division or other unit leader in Japan. He was promoted to major general and, in 1900, became chief of the First Section of the General Staff, a great honor and a piece of luck for an army bureaucrat. "After all, Ijichi was trained in Britain, Germany, and France," the higher-ups enthused, their hopes for him high.

The main fruit of Ijichi's extended time abroad was undoubtedly linguistic prowess. His next most important acquisition was not strategic studies or practical experience but a certain concept of military affairs—a concept drawn from modern army and military science. Nobody had any idea how he might perform in an actual war. The fact that four years before the fighting began he was made the First Section chief of the General Staff, the nerve center of Japanese tactical planning, is a strong indication of the temper of the times. It was an era when certain words carried great prestige: *hakuraihin*, "imported goods"; *kichōsha*, "someone returned from abroad"; *yōkōgaeri*, "back from a Western tour." Having spent nearly the whole of his military career abroad, Ijichi was to the Japanese a quasi-foreigner, a man of whom much was expected. "Ijichi can handle anything." And so he attained his post. If not for the Russo-Japanese War, he would undoubtedly have lived out his days happily as a nameless military bureaucrat.

His luck held. Even though he perpetrated that preposterous disaster at Port Arthur, he was made a baron after the war, thanks to his Satsuma connections. He never made general, though, rising only as high as lieutenant general.

*　*　*

As Nogi's senior command fell out of touch with sensibilities at the front because of Ijichi, one frustrated brigade commander wrote directly to Nagaoka Gaishi in Tokyo. "Ijichi doesn't know the first thing about strategy. He continually issues commands that don't match conditions at the front or the enemy situation, sacrificing more and more men to no purpose." In the letter, he refers to Ijichi as a "superannuated anomaly."

Tokyo was alarmed. This was why Imperial Headquarters sent people (Lieutenant Colonel Tsukushi Kumashichi, among others) to learn on the sly what was going on. The inside information they gained was sobering: division leaders under Nogi's command had no confidence in Nogi's staff.

Ijichi's report to the Manchurian Army after the first all-out assault was amateurish in content, so simplistic that Kodama and the rest were taken aback. "To sum up, enemy fortifications and gun batteries are unexpectedly strong. The fortifications are securely concealed and equipped with loopholes from which the area outside can be swept with gunfire."

Amid the carnage of the assault, the senior command lacked adequate knowledge of the fortifications there. And, although grasping the enemy situation is admittedly never easy in the thick of war, they failed to exert themselves to learn what they could. For example, in one preliminary operation before the assault, Nogi's army captured Great Orphan Hill. Although the summit afforded a clear view of the eastern fortifications and gun batteries, Nogi's staff climbed to the top only on the day of occupation. After that, none of them visited there.

Each Russian battery was equipped with a large number of machine guns. For Japanese troops at the front line ordered to attack with bayonets, nothing was so fearful as this new weapon. Unlike an encounter with a standing army, in storming a fortress, Japanese attackers were forced to follow a set course. All the defenders had to do was mow them down as they came. It was as if Japanese troops kept coming for the sole purpose of being mowed down.

Nogi's senior command at the rear was aware that the Russians possessed something called a machine gun, but they failed to go to the front in person and see with their own eyes just what it was the troops were up against. When a new weapon appears among the enemy, military strategists must go to the front to experience directly how formidable it is. Otherwise, any strategy they work out risks ending up a mere desktop plan, detached from reality.

*　*　*

In the staffroom of Tōgō's fleet anchored off the harbor at Port Arthur, hope lingered that Nogi might yet use the main force of his army to attack 203-Meter Hill. "Why doesn't he do it?" they wondered, but no one spoke up to criticize the competence of Nogi's headquarters.

"The army has its reputation to maintain," someone said. Nogi's headquarters wanted to attack the Port Arthur fortifications straight on, fair and square. Although 203-Meter Hill was virtually undefended (later, the Russians hastened to fortify it), their answer was unvarying. "Capturing a hill off at one side like 203-Meter Hill won't help us occupy the Port Arthur fortifications. Our mission is the occupation of all fortifications."

To the navy, gaining 203-Meter Hill meant being able to look down on the harbor. If observers were positioned at the peak, and the Russian warships in the harbor were attacked with a barrage from heavy navy guns, that would be the end of what remained of Russia's Port Arthur Squadron. Tōgō's fleet would finally be free to return to Sasebo to dock and prepare for the arrival of the Baltic Fleet. But Nogi's headquarters would not go along with this plan.

At the time of the first assault, Imperial Headquarters sent navy commander Kamiizumi Tokuya to Nogi's headquarters to check on the situation. After the assault failed, Kamiizumi prepared to return to Tokyo, first visiting Nogi's quarters to pay his respects. Nogi's eyes were red from days without sleep. On his return voyage, Kamiizumi planned to call on the Combined Fleet and visit Tōgō as well, so he inquired if Nogi had any message for the admiral.

Nogi pondered awhile before replying. "As you see, our attempt to storm the fortress failed. There is no use continuing with this line of attack, so I have decided to employ a standard direct attack next. For the rest, while I wonder about the appropriateness of an army officer offering any opinion regarding naval matters, it seems to me desirable that ships should slip off to Sasebo one or two at a time for repairs to ready themselves for the coming of the Baltic Fleet."

Kamiizumi asked Nogi how much longer he thought the fall of Port Arthur would take. Nogi answered honestly that the fortress showed no sign of yielding in the next few weeks. Beyond that, he could not predict.

Kamiizumi returned from Port Arthur to Dalian and from there borrowed a torpedo boat to call at the *Mikasa*. He met first with Chief of Staff Shimamura Hayao and reported what Nogi had said. Shimamura's only comment was: "Well, that's war. Can't be helped."

Kamiizumi then called on Tōgō and relayed the same message. To his surprise, Tōgō responded with the exact same words: "Well, that's war. Can't be helped."

That was the navy's only reaction. Kamiizumi then reported Nogi's suggestion about repairing the fleet and sought Tōgō's response. The reply was curt: "No change." Tōgō was a man of swift decisions.

To Imperial Headquarters, the incoherent strategy of Nogi's Third Army, along with the stubborn refusal to change it, had become like a cancer. The matter ought to have been simple enough. "All they need to do is turn the main force of the offensive to 203-Meter Hill. That's all there is to it. Why can't they just do that?" Once 203-Meter Hill was in hand, even if all the fortifications had not yet fallen, the fleet in the harbor could be sunk, thus fulfilling the mission of the attack on Port Arthur. Troop losses would be held to a minimum.

"Advance on 203-Meter Hill." In a variety of ways, Imperial Headquarters put this request through to Nogi's headquarters. But the chain of command dictated that the request be relayed locally, through the Manchurian Army's General Headquarters. It was standard policy to leave matters of strategy to the army in the field. Tokyo could only suggest, not order, what needed to be done.

"Just do this one thing—capture 203-Meter Hill!" This plea was made by the navy at every liaison conference of the Imperial Headquarters. The army was also of the same opinion, but Nogi's headquarters turned a deaf ear. Imperial Headquarters had the authority to dismiss Nogi and Ijichi, but in the middle of fighting that was something to avoid at any cost.

* * *

At one point, the navy sent Commander Iwamura Danjirō from Tosa (the present Kōchi Prefecture) as liaison officer. Iwamura stood before Nogi and Ijichi, and vociferously argued the urgency of capturing 203-Meter Hill.

Ijichi coldly dismissed his remarks from a different perspective. "We will not tolerate navy interference in army operations."

Iwamura, a hotheaded man of Tosa, flared up. "Sir, do you mean to say that you do not care if the empire is destroyed?" He gave Ijichi a shove and, in his excitement, also laid a hand on Nogi.

Later on, Nogi testified, "I was merely sprayed with spittle from Commander Iwamura. There was nothing to make a fuss about," and so Iwamura narrowly avoided being expunged from the navy rolls.

Another time when a fellow staff officer of the Manchurian Army confronted Ijichi, pointing out his obstinacy and urging a major shift in tactics, both men got worked up and traded blows.

At the time of the second major assault, the question of 203-Meter Hill took another turn. The chief of staff of the First Division recognized the importance of the elevation and, during a council of war at the headquarters of the Third Army, enthusiastically proposed attacking it.

Ijichi gave his approval. "Very well, if the First Division has reserve strength." It was to be a secondary attack, nothing more.

As a result, a portion of the First Division attacked the hill, which was defended only by a rifle pit, but the attackers were so few in number that they were easily driven off. Their sole accomplishment was to demonstrate to Stoessel the tactical importance of 203-Meter Hill. The Russians then hastened to fortify the hill to the maximum.

* * *

Here again we must return to the fact that the Japanese Army did not have a superior "owner" comparable to the navy's Yamamoto Gombei. From the first, Yamamoto had a clear vision of what the Imperial Japanese Navy ought to be. The theme of how to beat the Russians gave his vision substance and wrought fundamental changes in the navy, affecting everything from its character to its weapons. But there was no one like him in the army.

Yamagata Aritomo was Yamamoto Gombei's counterpart in status and authority, but he was so enamored of authority, so enthusiastic about fiddling with personnel, and such a conservative to the core that coming up with a new vision for the army was the farthest thing from his mind. His background as a *shishi*, one of the young men of action who took on the establishment at the end of the Tokugawa period, seems incongruous—but, in fact, Yamagata was not a true shishi at all. When the Chōshū domain he served as a lower-ranking samurai rebelled against the shogunate, he participated in the rebellion as a matter of course. Not even the most careful examination of his record from that era will turn up any evidence qualifying him as a shishi, someone filled with a revolutionary new vision for the nation of Japan. He was not a man who rose because of his powers of imagination.

As a young man, Yamagata sought to shake off his low status. That was the driving force behind his actions in the years leading up to the Meiji Restoration. He was born into a family of ashigaru samurai. "Deep down in Yamagata there was always something mean. After all, the man rose from ashigaru parentage." This remark is attributed to Hara Takashi, who was born into a samurai family of high status. His father was a chief counselor to the daimyo in the former Nambu domain (the present Iwate Prefecture), which joined the pro-shogunate forces at the end of the Tokugawa period.

And yet surely the mere fact of being from an ashigaru family is not enough to invest a man's every thought and action with meanness. Yamagata's overweening determination to succeed in life, to make it to the top, and also to protect his own authority, cast a shadow on the figure he cut and made him seem mean-spirited. While Yamagata had eagerly devoted himself to mastering the Hōzōin school of spear-fighting in his youth, this was not from any love of that martial art, but because, once he became a master, he could leave the ashigaru class and become a full-fledged samurai.

Just when Yamagata was thus consumed with the desire to make something of himself, the imperial loyalist Yoshida Shōin of the same domain was driven to act, impelled by a frantic sense of crisis over Japan's place in the world. Later on, Yamagata would join what amounted to a local political party founded after Shōin's death by his disciples. These were the young men of the Shōka Sonjuku, the private school that Shōin established in his house. Evidence that Yamagata was actually a disciple is rather tenuous. However, he styled himself one all his life. Certainly after Shōin's death, he joined that party and so became a commander in the Chōshū irregular militia, a record that won him a position of importance in the later Meiji government. Besides such things, there were his gifts as a highly accomplished composer of tanka and a skilled garden designer. He did not have the sort of talent to strike out in any new direction, however, but was conservative in all things. This was the man known as "the army's pontiff."

Yamagata's character explains why, unlike the navy, the army was not superior to Russia in structure, equipment, or armaments.

* * *

When, on the eve of war, Kodama Gentarō had decided that he alone was fit to become chief of staff of the Manchurian Army, he had to find someone to replace him as vice chief of the General Staff, the post he would be giving up for this new assignment. Kodama wired the forty-seven-year-old major general Nagaoka Gaishi to "Come immediately." Nagaoka, chief of the Ninth Infantry Brigade (Hiroshima), was waiting for mobilization orders when he received this peremptory summons. "Bring your family and horse with you," the wire added. Nagaoka hurried to Tokyo and went to the General Staff Office, where he met with Vice Chief Kodama.

"I'm going to Manchuria," Kodama informed Nagaoka. "You take over here."

Nagaoka was thunderstruck.

Kodama would have much preferred the next head of overall strategy for the Japanese Army to be a longtime specialist of Russia, but, given the crunch the army was in, he could not insist. Why then did he choose Nagaoka Gaishi?

The army's personnel policy for both Imperial Headquarters and field headquarters was to place graduates of the Army Staff College, trained by Meckel, as chiefs of staff. Operations were to be conducted uniformly in the style of Meckel. This is why people said that "the Russo-Japanese War was fought with Meckel's strategies." The entire first crop of Meckel's students to graduate from the Army Staff College were all major generals already. That bunch included Akiyama Yoshifuru, who was sent to the field to take on the Cossack cavalry. His grades were not particularly outstanding. Top honors in war strategy went to Tōjō Hidenori of the former Nambu domain, who rose from petty officer to major general. But Kodama did not appoint Tōjō as chief of staff and instead sent him off as head of an infantry brigade.

Of the ten members of that first graduating class, only Nagaoka was from Chōshū. Kodama was not overly concerned about factions, but with Chōshū stalwart Yamagata Aritomo as commander in chief, he chose Nagaoka for one reason only. "Whoever is vice chief of staff will have to get along well with old man Yamagata." As Kodama saw it, Yamagata was likely to interfere, and, when he did, it was vital to have someone in place who could calm him down and persuade him to withdraw his suggestions. That was why he picked Nagaoka, a Chōshū man. A deputy from anywhere else would either be unable to stand up to Yamagata or would get into fights with him, neither of which would work. Nagaoka Gaishi was not awarded this important post for his ability.

* * *

There was a society of sons of Chōshū called Ippinkai—"Top Quality Society"—so named because the characters for the word *ippin*, "top quality," resemble the crest of the Chōshū daimyo. Every military man from Yamaguchi Prefecture—that is, the former Chōshū domain—of the rank of major general and above was a member. This was a private association and, among all the organs of the army, the one most feared by soldiers since almost all personnel decisions—who was promoted, who was shifted where—were made in its secret deliberations. Nogi and Nagaoka's fates were almost certainly settled here.

Yamaguchi soldiers with the rank of colonel and below had their own association, called Dōshōkai— "Same-Costume Society." This was a junior version of the Top Quality Society and answerable to it. To men from other prefectures, the existence of these organizations was a bane. Later on, to counter the Chōshū faction, other factions were formed with other geographical ties, and those developed in the early years of the Shōwa period into overtly ideological factions like the Imperial Way faction and the Control faction. But that is not a main consideration here.

To repeat, the reason that Nagaoka Gaishi took on the weighty role of vice chief of the General Staff, with the future of Japan in his hands, was not because of his sterling abilities.

"Nagaoka will do." It was Kodama Gentarō who gave this assurance to Yamagata. Kodama believed that no one but himself was qualified to conduct the Russo-Japanese War, and objectively speaking he was right. The virtue of Chōshū men lay in their high intelligence, a trait that Kodama possessed in abundance. Also, like so many Chōshū fighters, he was ready at any time to put his life on the line. In short, he embodied all the finest aspects of Chōshū tradition. "Nagaoka will do," he said, because he believed that the Army General Staff of Imperial Headquarters ultimately did not matter. As long as he was heading to the field with Ōyama Iwao, he was resolved to take every single moment of the war's management with him. For that reason, he undoubtedly thought of the vice chief of the General Staff as a caretaker, the General Staff as little more than a glorified supply center for soldiers, weapons, and ammunition. That is what he meant by "Nagaoka will do." And, indeed, the ablest members of the General Staff followed Kodama overseas.

Nagaoka was a peculiar fellow with an enormous mustache that he proudly called the "world's longest." That mustache made him seem like nothing so much as a humbug. "Show-off," some called him behind his back. While there may have been some truth to the charge, basically he simply took a child's delight in flaunting his wit and heroism. His imagination occasionally was visionary. In time, he would introduce skiing to the army, and later, when the airplane came on the scene, he not only was the first to see its potential usefulness to the military but also enlightened the army staff about his views. These accomplishments are proof of the strength of his imagination.

Nagaoka's mustache was 19.7 inches long, fashioned in the shape of the airplane propellers he eventually became so engrossed in. Had the two sides of the mustache only rotated, it seems entirely possible that he would have taken flight. He was rash by nature. At the time, there was a man in the United States with a 22-inch mustache, the world's longest. The second-longest mustache in the world belonged to Nagaoka Gaishi of Japan. "It's an expression of my patriotism," he would explain in all seriousness. Diffidence was clearly foreign to him.

Was Nagaoka an able man or a third-rate soldier who bluffed his way up the ladder? This question lingered on in the army for years. Even after he died, the matter was never resolved. But the fact that he tended daily to the second-longest mustache in the world and wore it boldly in public without the least embarrassment is perhaps one key to unlocking his character. Nagaoka was a creature of impulse.

There were many mysteries about the great fortress at Port Arthur. One was that, even though Japan's army and navy together had the harbor and town so tightly encircled and blockaded that not even an ant could crawl out, comments from General Stoessel appeared off and on in the world's newspapers. Apparently, it was possible to communicate with the outside world from the safety of the fortress, by some means or other.

"How in the world do they do it?" The General Staff Office spurred its spy network to investigate and found that the enemy was using carrier pigeons.

The report came from Colonel Aoki, who was stationed in Beijing. There was a dovecote for carrier pigeons in Weihaiwei, he said. It belonged to the United States, but the Russians were the ones actually using it. Weihaiwei was a neutral part of Qing territory, and, moreover, the Japanese had no wish to stir up a diplomatic skirmish with the United States.

Nagaoka struggled to come up with a ploy, and at last he did, finding a solution entirely in keeping with his character. "Send hawks to attack the pigeons." He promptly took up the matter with the Imperial Household Ministry, which had an office with the old-fashioned name "Hunting Division." Count Toda Ujitaka was the division head, with many hawk-keepers under his supervision. Nagaoka quickly summoned the keepers to Imperial Headquarters and handed out formal notices of appointment, making them members of the strategic planning team.

However, it soon became clear that Imperial Household Ministry hawks were not accustomed to attacking pigeons. "Peregrine falcons might work," the keepers suggested, and Nagaoka jumped on this idea, asking them to follow through. They had to start by finding wild peregrines, which were most plentiful in the prefectures of Kōchi, Kagawa, Shimane, and Wakayama. Men were dispatched to those areas, and so Imperial Headquarters was able to get its hands on the necessary birds—but training them took time. Port Arthur fell before Nagaoka's peregrines ever had a chance to wing their way across the harbor there.

* * *

Nagaoka Gaishi did not have a gift for careful, precise reasoning, but in his ability to dream up new ideas one after another he was second to none. For one thing, since Kodama Gentarō had authority over strategy in the field, the General Staff of Imperial Headquarters was relatively idle. It was Nagaoka who came up with the idea of floating a balloon over Port Arthur. This was an ingenious scheme. They would put observers in a balloon high in the air and have them look down inside the fortifications to spot hits. Nagaoka's later focus on airplanes and his attempt to send hawks after carrier pigeons suggest a strong interest in flight.

Balloons had long since been put to practical use by European armies, but since the Japanese Army put little faith in technology, their lone balloon had been tested just once, in December 1901. Nagaoka ordered the old balloon hauled out of storage and re-tested. There was no rope, so a rope-manufacturing company in Fukagawa was told to produce some. The quality of the resulting rope was poor. In April of that year, 1904, the balloon was successfully launched in the Hama Rikyū Garden, but at 300 meters the rope broke, and the balloon floated off, eventually falling into the sea off the port of Ōarai, about 160 kilometers north of Tokyo.

A new balloon had to be hurriedly constructed. The gas bag was ordered from Shibaura Engineering Works, the precursor of Toshiba. The finished balloon, known as *Mooring Balloon No. 3*, joined Nogi's army at Port Arthur in August and flew high in the sky over Zhoujiatun and Fenghuang cheng. It turned out to be of little use, affording a view of the harbor and part of the enemy forts but not the all-important gunners. Its military effectiveness was virtually nil. This was not Nagaoka's fault but rather that of the Japanese Army itself for failing to make the balloon operational all along.

Nagaoka agonized over Port Arthur. "If Port Arthur doesn't fall, the country will be destroyed." He muttered these words nearly every day.

While Ōyama Iwao and Kodama Gentarō of the Manchurian Army had the right to issue direct orders to Nogi's Third Army, Kodama was in the process of moving troops farther north after the pitched battle of Liaoyang, oblivious to all else. With no time to spare for Nogi's army in Port Arthur, he followed protocol and left matters entirely in the hands of Nogi and Ijichi.

As a result, Nagaoka ended up stepping outside the chain of command to supervise Nogi's army in various ways. He had no choice. The tactics of Third Army headquarters were all too plainly bumbling and ill-considered as well as deeply entrenched. At this rate, losses would continue to pile up while enemy positions remained unscathed. Some new approach was required, something unconventional. Nagaoka may be called a showman with some justification, but his ability to come up with unconventional solutions may have made him exactly the right man for the job. Yet, because his ideas were too eccentric for the dignity of his position as vice chief of the General Staff, he failed in everything he attempted.

* * *

What saved this crisis in Port Arthur, where the fate of the nation hung in the balance, was not the strategic competence of Nogi's headquarters. It was rather the human blood that headquarters spilled by driving successive waves of soldiers at the Russian fortress in blatant disregard of Nogi's personal feelings and sentiments. This blood was not the agent of change. But the fact that blood was spilled was important. To explain further, those deaths represented the spiritual condition–the grand spiritual condition, let it be said—of tens of thousands of Meiji period Japanese soldiers striding willingly (or helplessly) into the jaws of death. Nogi's military headquarters relied on Japanese men's loyalty to the state and, using that as base, issued death orders again and again on a scale never before seen in world history. The many deaths finally motivated Imperial Headquarters to take drastic steps.

Earlier, we touched on Nagaoka Gaishi's showmanship and affectation. But his show-off personality played a significant role in saving the Japanese at Port Arthur. It predisposed him to enjoy discussions of quick-wittedness or resourcefulness and to listen avidly to new ideas. He was as different in personality as he could possibly have been from Nogi's chief of staff Ijichi, who was stuffed full of preconceived notions.

One time, when Nagaoka went to the Army Ministry to call on Colonel Yamaguchi Masaru, head of the artillery section, he happened to run into someone else. It was technician Arisaka Nariakira, famed as the inventor of the "Arisaka rifle." A major general, Arisaka was from Iwakuni domain in Suō (ruled by a branch family of the Mōri family of Chōshū)—the next best thing to being from Chōshū itself. The Type 31 quick-firing field gun that he invented, a vastly improved version of a quick-firing rifle, would prove its worth many times over in field battles of the Russo-Japanese War. Arisaka was eventually promoted to lieutenant general, then made a baron before he died in 1915.

"About Port Arthur," ventured Arisaka, at this point head of the Army Technology Investigation Department. "The way things are, it will never fall."

Nagaoka looked at him with annoyance. He knew very well that Port Arthur wasn't about to fall. That was precisely what he was agonizing over, why he kept intimating to Nogi's headquarters that a change of strategy was in order.

"Do you have a good strategy in mind?"

"No, sir," said Arisaka. "I don't know anything about that. What I know about is guns. And the ones you sent over there can't get the job done."

"The hell you say," thought Nagaoka. Senior command had taken the trouble to place Ijichi and Toyoshima, both artillery experts, on Nogi's staff.

"What I say may sound odd, but I would like to send over some 28-centimeter howitzers."

Nagaoka gasped. The 28-centimeter howitzers were great guns mounted in Japan's coastal defense zone.

* * *

"Send soldiers." This message, a request for troop replenishments, came without cease from Nogi's Third Army in Port Arthur. Any troops sent there were bound to become fodder for the trenches in front of the fortifications (not even making it as far as the fortifications). In Imperial Headquarters, loud mutterings were heard. "The only tactic Nogi's staff knows is killing people." Nogi's brain trust was so obstinate that they never seemed to realize that their failures should serve as a springboard for new approaches.

"The Japanese Army keeps coming at us in the same way." This comment appears in Russian sources.

Among the men and officers under fire on the front line at Port Arthur, there was increased criticism of military headquarters at the rear. Major General Ichinohe Hyōe was a born soldier and a talented field officer who served under Nogi as brigade commander. He led the Sixth Brigade from Kanazawa in the assault and succeeded in capturing a rise that was renamed "Fort Ichinohe" in his honor. Even he—we say "even" because Ichinohe shared with Nogi the character of an old-time samurai—criticized Nogi in private. While fighting at the front during the siege of Port Arthur, he wondered, "Why does the army chief"—Nogi—"keep issuing orders that are so nonsensical, so completely unconnected to the situation?"

Under such appalling leadership, the rank and file went obediently to their deaths, but one or two generals faked illness and actually were transported to the rear. To Meiji period Japanese, the state and the emperor were absolutes, and yet there was undoubtedly some wavering among high-ranking officers. Even common soldiers began to sense that the commander was too far back, too unaware of what was happening at the front. And, at Imperial Headquarters, the phrase "needless killing" came into daily use.

In later years, Major General Shigi Moriharu gave a special lecture at the Army Staff College on the battlefield psychology of Japanese officers and men during the siege of Port Arthur. He was a colonel at the time of the siege. "General Nogi was not at the time anything like the General Nogi so highly revered today," read the stenographic notes of the lecture.

> Before the third all-out assault, a rumor reached the front that if Port Arthur didn't fall this time, the chief was prepared to die. But the rumor did not encourage or inspire the troops in the slightest. They sloughed it off. "If he wants to, let him" was the attitude. Knowing that the general lost two sons in the war supposedly stirred up the troops' morale to a great degree, but this is a complete fabrication. The First Division knew nothing about it, and the Eleventh Division thought it was only a matter of course.

* * *

Big guns: the appellation perfectly fits the 28-centimeter howitzers, then known as "coastal guns." They were positioned strategically at Japanese straits, at the entrance to Tokyo Bay, and on promontories and islands along the Kitan Strait leading into Osaka Bay. In the event of an attack by enemy warships, they would be used to sink the ships.

The prototype of the 28-centimeter howitzer was of Italian make and had a fairly long history in Japan. As far back as 1883, the army had ordered the Osaka Army Arsenal to build a replica. Lacking the technology to make good-quality cast iron of its own, the arsenal used imported Gregorini cast iron from Italy, completing the replica in 1884. When the finished gun was test-fired at Shinodayama in Osaka Prefecture, it let out an earth-shattering roar and was declared a success. The army promptly built a battery on Kannonzaki Point in Tokyo Bay and mounted the gun there.

This howitzer could not yet be described as being entirely manufactured in Japan. Comparable guns of purely Japanese make did not come about until 1893, when Gregorini cast iron was abandoned in favor of Kamaishi pig iron. After that, several dozen more were made and placed in strategic coastal spots around the country. The gun barrel was cast iron. The exterior was covered in steel.

Previous army cannons, field guns for example, would rattle backward when fired, due to recoil. After each blast, they had to be muscled back to their original location before they could be fired again. The new cannons were equipped with buffers so that recoil affected only the barrel, which was returned to its position by hydraulic pressure. The pump contained a spring and glycerin.

As coastal defense, the howitzer did not need to be moved about, and it was so big that the chassis was fastened down. Concrete was used for the groundwork, with impressive results. The gun was mounted on a rack able to turn 360 degrees, allowing it to be fired in any direction.

"Those would be powerful enough to destroy the concrete in the Port Arthur fortifications," said Arisaka. "The psychological impact alone would be enormous."

Nagaoka, fond of new ideas as he was, began to be excited about the suggestion, but then his expression darkened slightly. "If they are removed, won't the country's defenses suffer?"

"Port Arthur has the country teetering on the edge of destruction anyway" came the pointed reply. "With the country destroyed, what need will there be of coastal defense?"

For Nagaoka, this was a plan of great magnitude. Unable to make the call on his own, he consulted Commander in Chief Yamagata and was told, "If Arisaka says so, you can count on it. Go talk to the army minister." He then sprang into action, immediately going to see Army Minister Terauchi Masatake, laying out the plan and the reasoning behind it. Terauchi balked, however, and refrained from committing himself. He had always thought Nagaoka rash, and generally took a dim view of his speech and behavior. But Nagaoka was relentless, calling on Terauchi repeatedly until finally he obtained the minister's consent.

Nagaoka later said that he felt "great joy" at that moment, but when he conveyed the news to Nogi's headquarters in Port Arthur, he was told, "No need to send them."

* * *

"Nagaoka is out of his mind," Ijichi told Nogi.

The sound of gunfire never ceased, although none of the shelling reached as far back as headquarters. It was significant that none of Nogi's aides had acquired the habit of creeping to the front on hands and knees. So their uniforms were clean, their gold braid decorations brightly shining.

Nogi's expression never varied. In years to come, he would be known as a man of great virtue, and indeed there was always a gentleness in his eyes as he looked on others. He never once lost his temper with his aides, nor hurled abusive language at them. His mouth, the shape of which suggested an introverted temperament, would sometimes curl in a light smile, but he had what people call a "tear-stained face," so that even when he smiled, he appeared to be crying.

"Did you talk to Major General Toyoshima?" Nogi asked Ijichi. Toyoshima Yōzō was the one in charge of all the siege artillery in Nogi's army.

Neither Ijichi nor Toyoshima had ever studied under Meckel, nor were they graduates of the Army Staff College. On that point, the two were of one mind, agreeing that "just because you've gone to the Staff College doesn't mean you know anything about war."

This, by the way, is perfectly true. Strategists and commanders possess innate ability. Like artists and sculptors, they are not produced by a fixed course of training. Akiyama Saneyuki acquired his knowledge of naval strategy completely on his own. While he did take up a teaching position at the Naval Staff College, he was never a student there. Geniuses of the likes of Minamoto no Yoshitsune, Toyotomi Hideyoshi, and Napoleon never received formal training either.

But let this be clear: in the case of the Japanese Navy, nearly all the tacticians of the various fleets and squadrons that made up the Combined Fleet had studied under Saneyuki in the Naval Staff College. This shared background was of enormous benefit, providing unity of approach and aiding in the communication of strategic goals.

In the army, Kodama Gentarō was previously not a student of Meckel's but a college administrator. We've told of how he attended lectures alongside the students and absorbed the German advisor's tactics. Nagaoka Gaishi of Imperial Headquarters was a follower of Meckel, as were most of the chiefs of staff and other staff members of the various armies. Their thoughts regarding strategy were therefore easily conveyed to one another. Only Nogi's headquarters was a nonconductor of this electricity.

"Those idiots in Imperial Headquarters know absolutely nothing," Ijichi informed Nogi when discussing the howitzers. "Toyoshima had a good laugh about it too." He and Toyoshima were accepted experts on artillery. Not knowing anything about modern warfare himself, Nogi had no choice but to go along with what his "expert" aides told him.

* * *

The surprising news that these enormous guns would be shipped to Port Arthur came by wire. "Preparations are underway to send four 28-centimeter howitzers" went the text of the wire that Nagaoka sent to Ijichi, "two with disappearing carriages and two with ordinary gun carriages. Will arrange for them to arrive at Dalian Harbor around September 15. If you have any opinions on this matter, please advise." Nagaoka's enthusiasm shows between the lines. The last line, with its deferential approach, demonstrates Tokyo tactfulness toward the Manchurian Army.

That reply from Nogi's headquarters deserves to go down in history: "No need to send them." In the history of the world, has any military leadership ever been so impossibly foolish and deluded?

"Nagaoka was in the infantry. He has no idea what a hassle it is to move 28-centimeter howitzers." This is what Ijichi and Toyoshima, the two artillery experts, said to Nogi.

"You have to start by building an emplacement," Toyoshima explained. "It would take a good month or two for the concrete to dry. After that, there's no telling how long it might take to put the thing together. The people in Tokyo don't even know that much."

Ijichi echoed this opinion. He was not fool enough to suppose that it would take "a good month or two for the concrete to dry," as Toyoshima said. Still, it might well take a good three weeks, he thought, which would not be in time for the next assault. And so he wired back, "No need to send them."

In fact, neither Toyoshima nor Ijichi had much real technical knowledge. Tricky as it was to disassemble and transport the big guns, ten days would suffice to set them up again. This was common knowledge in artillery circles. The two men's knowledge and understanding were piecemeal. They merely put on the airs of being experts as opposed to the "amateurs" in Tokyo.

But Tokyo had Arisaka Nariakira, a world authority on guns, as well as an expert on these 28-centimeter howitzers. A team was set up to construct emplacements, headed by Captain Yokota Minoru, who assured Nagaoka that he had no cause for worry.

A special ship was prepared for the purpose of transporting the howitzers. It entered Dalian Harbor and arrived at Dazifangshen. Barely nine days later, the emplacements were set up and all was finished, the howitzers ready to fire. Yokota's struggles were monumental, but he got the job done.

The number of guns increased from the four in the original plan to six. Later, the number would go all the way up to eighteen.

* * *

In discussing the Japanese approach to the assault on the Port Arthur fortifications, we've covered the same ground several times from different angles; sometimes we've inverted the order of events in our relentless pursuit of the matter. We find the degree of repetition embarrassing. And yet "Port Arthur" is not an ordinary place name or phrase, but one that has acquired a fateful sound and meaning associated with the very survival or extinction of Meiji Japan. Everyone at the time felt a dark foreboding that Port Arthur might spell the end. After the unprecedented agonies of the late Tokugawa period through the Meiji Restoration, Japan had built a modern (that is, nineteenth-century) state—a state which, barely thirty-seven years on, lay in mortal peril.

From the first, Nagaoka Gaishi believed that the thing to do was to make an all-out effort to capture 203-Meter Hill. Nagaoka had done all he could to win Nogi and Ijichi over to this idea, even dispatching Lieutenant Colonel Igata Tokuzō to the front to try to talk some sense into them.

When Igata had reached Manchuria, instead of going straight to Nogi, he called at the headquarters of the Manchurian Army. "As I am only a lieutenant colonel," he told Kodama, "I doubt if my words will carry weight with the commanders in Port Arthur, Nogi and Ijichi. If possible, I would like to go there in the company of Major General Iguchi." He was referring to Iguchi Shōgo of Shizuoka, known along with Colonel Matsukawa Toshitane of Miyagi as one of Kodama's two top thinkers.

One hot day early in August, Iguchi and Igata had set off for Nogi's headquarters in Shuangtaigou. The first words out of Ijichi's mouth were: "What does either of you know about the conditions here, or the suffering? The Third Army doesn't need half-witted advice from you, Igata. It needs soldiers and bullets." In other words, send us more blood and iron.

Iguchi and Igata had done their best to convey the dire straits the navy was in, hinting at the need for a fundamental review of tactics, but Ijichi had flatly dismissed their concerns. "We are in constant communication with the Combined Fleet," he maintained. "They're in no particular hurry." A heated argument arose, during the course of which Ijichi called Iguchi names. Iguchi became so incensed that he was sorely tempted to cut down Ijichi on the spot, commit seppuku and so save Japan from its moment of crisis.

* * *

For the Japanese nation, so keen to modernize in the wake of the Meiji Restoration, the attack on Port Arthur was its first intimate encounter with the fearsomeness of modernity, as symbolized in those impregnable fortifications. The lesson cost Japan dearly in the blood of its soldiers.

"Leave Port Arthur alone." This was the essential line of thinking developed over a period of years by the General Staff as it geared up for war with Russia. "The enemy is holed up in its castle fortress," reasoned army leaders. "Why draw it out?" That approach was essentially correct. Had the Japanese Army landed at Dalian Harbor, proceeded northward without bothering about the fortifications at Port Arthur, and then won a string of victories in the field, the fortifications would have eventually fallen of themselves. Better to have left them to their fate.

"Yes, but what if the foe emerges and threatens the Japanese Army from the rear as it moves north? Then what?" This consideration was of course valid. "Then we leave behind sufficient troops to handle that possibility." That was what everyone thought—correctly, it must be said.

In laying out an early blueprint of the war, even Kodama Gentarō spoke about the possibility of enemy soldiers coming out of Port Arthur. "Just put up a bamboo palisade." A bamboo palisade was a temporary impediment used in medieval Japan to stop an enemy attack. In the Tokugawa period, bamboo palisades were set up to mark areas that were off limits. Kodama did not mean that his suggestion should be taken literally. It was his way of saying that a minimal contingent of soldiers could do the job.

But then, on the eve of fighting, the navy put in a request that Port Arthur be attacked by land. The request was not unreasonable in itself. Had the Japanese Navy succeeded in sinking every last ship in the Port Arthur Squadron (a virtual pipe dream), an overland attack would have been unnecessary. They gamely did what they could to sink the entire enemy fleet unaided, but because the squadron refused to leave the harbor, their only recourse was to continue the blockade.

At one point, the squadron did emerge. Tōgō then took off in hot pursuit and fought the battle of the Yellow Sea, but too many enemy ships slipped away unharmed and retreated to the safety of the harbor, leaving the navy no choice but to resume the blockade. From the navy's perspective, the fleet in the harbor needed to be sunk. For that to happen, the army needed to capture a hill where spotters could be placed (203-Meter Hill, as it turned out) and then sink enemy ships with heavy artillery fire. That was all. That would have been enough to wrap up Port Arthur in the Russo-Japanese War. Instead, Nogi's misguided attempt to obliterate the fortifications caused an unprecedented and unmitigated disaster (one not to be dignified with the name of war).

4

SHAHO

The battle of Liaoyang had ended in a Japanese victory. However costly a victory it may have been, the fact that the adversary retreated (having suffered minimal damage) put the battle undeniably in Japan's win column.

General Kuropatkin insisted on calling the pullout a "tactical withdrawal," but since the bed he left behind when he fled Liaoyang became Ōyama Iwao's favorite place to take a nap, the only logical conclusion was that Russia had indeed suffered a defeat. The world saw it that way too. The Russian court was beside itself, dubbing Kuropatkin "General Retreat."

"What does a young punk like Kuropatkin know anyway?" growled the old general Linevich, stationed in Manchuria under a separate command. Because Linevich had taken a personal hand in the Russian Army's looting of the Beijing palace during the Boxer Rebellion, Witte saw him as lacking in common sense, someone who ought not to be entrusted with any position above regimental commander. Others murmured that Linevich spoke ill of Kuropatkin to the tsar just because he wanted his job. Kuropatkin's retreat was no libel, though, but incontrovertible fact.

Witte, having opposed the war from the first, had been shoved aside and forced into semiretirement. He was an enlightened patriot who, on receiving news of Russia's defeat at Liaoyang, said, "Russia's in for it now."

Witte's Western education colored his view of the Russian Empire. "What makes the world fear Russia?" he asked rhetorically. "Is it Russian culture? Russian wealth? Unfortunately, no. At first Russia was just a small semi-Asiatic kingdom. One thing alone made our country the greatest power in Europe—military might. Russian power comes from its soldiers and bayonets, and that's what other nations fear. But now," he maintained, "the weakness of the Russian military has been exposed for all the world to see.

The world knows now that the Russian Empire is a sand castle. The overestimation of our strength by other nations will make them even more inclined to look down on us now."

Russia would indeed be taken more lightly from this point on. Witte predicted that "Russia's enemies within and without" would lower their opinion of Russian strength. By "enemies within," he meant the dissidents seeking to foment revolution. "This succession of defeats," he wrote, "has dealt an unprecedented blow to every level of Russian society, a blow that has expressed itself in a certain uniform reaction. By that, I mean dissatisfaction with the political status quo." He referred, of course, to the tsarist regime.

Russia was well and truly "in for it." Outside the country, the Russian military threat had been exposed as a sand castle, and, at home, dissatisfaction and animosity were eating away at the empire's foundations.

"Tactical withdrawal" is how Kuropatkin characterized the pullout, but, generally speaking, troop morale and order are maintained by attack and undermined by retreat. Two Russian brigade commanders, both major generals, came to blows near the station at Mukden over the question of where to assign blame for the retreat. Such incidents were typical. And, no matter how Kuropatkin defended the move, its political ramifications for him personally were severe. Along with Russia's international reputation, the general's own status at court went into precipitous decline. Some thought he should be relieved of command, but the court as a whole understood the folly of firing the top general in the middle of a war. Most saw the problem as structural.

The Russian Army was modeled differently from the Japanese Army. The Japanese Manchurian Army was divided into the four lesser armies. Each army was commanded by a general who presided over several divisions, each one headed by a lieutenant general, with Ōyama Iwao the commander in chief. But Russia's massive Manchurian Army was in Kuropatkin's sole control. Leaders below him in rank were delegated only as much power as Japanese division commanders, not generals. In overseeing an army of such size, Kuropatkin had to display enormous versatility.

The burden was too great for one man's shoulders, Tsar Nicholas II decided, and so he split the army in two, creating the First and Second Manchurian armies. Kuropatkin was given command of the First Army, but since he had been supreme commander until then, this was effectively a demotion. Command of the Second Army (the Sixth and Eighth Siberian Army corps and a cavalry division) went to General Oskar Grippenberg, who was dispatched to Manchuria for that purpose.

When news of the change reached Kuropatkin, he was beside himself with rage and frustration. He resolved that the outcome of the war must be shaped while he was still in charge. His original plan was bold: he would withdraw as far as Harbin and then, after amassing a million troops, go on the attack. Had he been allowed to carry out that plan, the Japanese Army would have stood not one chance in a hundred of winning the war. Pursuing the Russians as far as Harbin would have overextended the Japanese supply line. As it was, ammunition was perennially scarce, and with transportation bottlenecks the situation would have been dire. Not only that, the Japanese field army numbered at most around two hundred thousand men. Against a Russian army of a million, they stood no chance of winning, however brilliant a strategy they might employ.

But Kuropatkin had to abandon his plan, for reasons that were not military but political in nature. Any further retreat would have caused his standing at court to drop still further. Besides that, his superior Viceroy Alexeyev (whose raison d'être was unclear to Kuropatkin) was convinced of the need to hold the line at Mukden, and this was an opinion he could not ignore.

* * *

Kuropatkin's army emerged from the battle of Liaoyang virtually intact. From among his two hundred twenty-five thousand troops, casualties numbered a mere twenty thousand. While the general's original plan was to retreat all the way to Harbin, instead he stopped and held the line at Mukden. Having done so, he was surprised at the failure of the Japanese Army to give chase. What could it mean? Genuinely puzzled, he sent an intelligence officer to find out what was going on. The report came back that the Japanese were suffering from a shortage of ammunition. Still, Kuropatkin went on overestimating his adversary.

The term "shortage of ammunition" no longer sufficed to describe the Japanese Army's plight, which was so severe that joining in a large-scale engagement would be impossible for months to come. Giving chase to a retreating army was out of the question. Though the Japanese Army had suffered approximately the same number of casualties as the "defeated" Russian Army, its situation was vastly different. Where the Russian Army was being steadily beefed up with fresh troops from the homeland, reinforcing the beleaguered Japanese Army was proving extremely difficult.

Despite Kuropatkin's tendency to inflate the size of his adversary, his estimations grew more accurate after repeated clashes with the Japanese Army. When he left Liaoyang, he estimated the army's size as "around two hundred seventy thousand." Even this number was inflated, but at last the brilliant Russian general realized that he held the advantage.

The Russian Army had great prospects. Amassing a million men on the plains of northern Manchuria was the brainchild of Transport Minister Mikhail Khilkov, who managed the Trans-Siberian Railway and oversaw troop transport and replenishment. A man of outstanding ability, he came up with a variety of ways to increase the transport capacity of the one-track Siberian railway, including adding on passing tracks and building a subsidiary line to Lake Baikal. The *Times* expressed admiration for his abilities, allowing that "A more fearful general to the Japanese than Kuropatkin is the civil servant Prince Khilkov." His strenuous efforts created an odd phenomenon: despite the Russians' defeat at Liaoyang, their numbers increased until they were at full strength.

"The enemy gets stronger with every battle," commented Kuroki Tamemoto, commander of the First Army. The reverse was equally true: short on supplies, the Japanese Army grew progressively weaker. The moment of gravest crisis for the Japanese nation came with the "victory" over Russia at Liaoyang that coincided with the ongoing battle of attrition at Port Arthur.

* * *

The Japanese victory at Liaoyang could be described as "merely territorial" in nature. "What our army has so far purchased with much bloodshed is only land," wrote Iguchi Shōgo, staff officer of the Manchuria Army, in an opinion paper at the time. "Far too great a price has been paid for the capture of enemy positions." The enemy had been let off relatively lightly, simply vacating one area and moving to another. "This sort of thing can't go on," declared Iguchi. "The main purpose of a battle must be to destroy the enemy's main force and overwhelm the enemy so that it is incapable of rising again." He was only stating the obvious.

But, compared to the defensive Russian Army, the attacking Japanese Army was always slightly inferior in manpower and firepower. Having paid dearly in blood just to break up the Russian encampment, now for the army to enlarge on its success by going after the Russians and wiping them out was impossible. To succeed, Iguchi's plan would have required twice the men and ammunition of the defending Russians.

When Kodama Gentarō read Iguchi's opinion paper, his only comment was "Quite true." If Japan did not end the war quickly, it was in danger of exhausting its resources. Already, at Liaoyang the army was scraping the bottom of the barrel. Unless the enemy's main force was roundly defeated and peace restored quickly, the country was doomed.

"Wartime finance will be the end of Japan"—this was the consensus among nations and the fear that gnawed at Japan's leaders. Kodama Gentarō was not only a brilliant strategist but also a savvy politician. His mindset was not that of an ordinary military man, but represented the state itself. He knew exactly what the country's financial resources were and how much artillery its arsenal could afford to manufacture, figures that he kept constantly in mind as he planned and implemented strategy. Kodama's illness and death shortly after the war's end speaks volumes about the toll the war took on him.

Once Liaoyang was captured, Ōyama and Kodama were ready to collapse with exhaustion and halted the army. The main reason was the need to stockpile ammunition. There was nothing to do but steadily pile up supplies as they came trickling in from the mainland—rather like trying to fill a barrel with water dribbling from a broken tap. Having to focus patiently on the task despite mounting anxiety and frustration was an ordeal.

Prince Khilkov's success in using the Trans-Siberian Railway to supply the Russian Army was a laudable achievement on a grand scale befitting a country of Russia's enormous size, an achievement without precedent in the annals of war. The extraordinary patience exhibited by Ōyama and Kodama as they slowly built up enough ammunition to go on shows all too clearly the wretched plight of a tiny nation. That display of patience, itself an arduous feat for military men of action, also deserves high marks.

* * *

Japan was at an impasse. If the Japanese Army had only had sufficient field ammunition at this stage, the war would have soon been over. When the troops first burst into Liaoyang, morale soared.

"Troop morale is high," Kodama wired Yamagata Aritomo at Imperial Headquarters. "If we could deliver a blow to the enemy now, there is no telling how great our advantage would be, but for lack of shells we cannot. It is truly a shame." He was merely letting off steam. He knew perfectly well how difficult it was for Japan to get hold of the needed shells.

After the First Sino-Japanese War, Japan's army and navy had foreseen the likelihood of imminent war with Russia, and each had made preparations. For the army, the equivalent of a navy battleship is a division, the largest unit of a standing army. A division commander holds the rank of lieutenant general. The size of a division isn't fixed, but averages around ten thousand men, closer to twenty thousand in time of war. Below a division comes a brigade, then a regiment, then a battalion. Maintaining a division is an extremely expensive undertaking.

Japan began the war with thirteen active divisions (plus seven in reserve), numbering over two hundred thousand men. Since the structure of the Russian Army differed, comparison is difficult, but overall the Russian side had two million soldiers and a budget ample enough to maintain so vast an army, including all the ammunition that might be needed. Maintaining divisions involved stockpiling ammunition for them in time of peace, just as for every battleship it was necessary to lay in a supply of shells ready to be used when the time came. Japan pushed its luck by doubling the number of army divisions in eight short years before the Russo-Japanese War. Even then, there were a mere thirteen. Still, maintaining so many divisions stretched the country's resources so thin that there was not enough money to cover the cost of ammunition.

Russia, however, was finding the Trans-Siberian Railway a highly satisfactory way of transporting supplies and troops. By the end of 1904, the equivalent of thirty-five Japanese divisions was expected to be in place on the Manchurian plains. United States president Theodore Roosevelt privately expressed the opinion that a long war would mean defeat for Japan—no doubt because he was privy to data on the situation regarding Japanese supplies.

Japan's Manchurian Army was on edge. But there was nothing to do but wait for the mainland to increase production so they could acquire a decent supply of artillery. Until that happened, they were in no shape to fight a large-scale engagement.

* * *

At the same time, the siege of Port Arthur continually siphoned ammunition. The trouble was that Japan's main fighting force in Liaoyang was painfully short of ammunition just as that unprecedented war of attrition was going on in Port Arthur. Ijichi wired Kodama desperately, "Send more shells." He seemed to be howling in rage. "How do you expect us to win the battle like this!" He was absolutely right.

"Just tell me what we're supposed to do?" Ijichi wired Kodama on October 16. "All we have is 101 rounds per field gun and 103 per mountain gun. Mounting an attack under these conditions is preposterous." He concluded by requesting "at least three hundred rounds per weapon."

But, at that point, Kodama himself, facing a decisive battle in the field, had fewer than a hundred rounds per field gun. General Headquarters was irritated that Nogi's staff thought only of itself. Kodama wired back, "I am well aware that you lack sufficient shells. But the deficiency and the urgency of the need here is far greater. It is accordingly impossible to resupply only your army with field ammunition."

Kodama advised the Third Army to make full use of 28-centimeter howitzers from Imperial Headquarters instead of field guns and mountain guns. Ijichi, however, had never studied their proper use. Used like ordinary siege guns, they were of little practical value, apart from the psychological effect of intimidation. Instead of using them to attack Russian warships in the harbor as he should have done, Ijichi turned them on the Port Arthur fortress. Gigantic though they were, all they did was raise enormous clouds of earth and sand in the sky over the unharmed fortress.

* * *

When the once-feisty Japanese Army fell silent after the battle of Liaoyang, Kuropatkin finally took its true measure. The severity of the enemy's struggle to replenish its troops and ammunition became clear.

This was the moment for Kuropatkin to go on the offensive. From the first, the Japanese Army had seized the initiative, pushing him into a passive role. Here he could regain the initiative, attack the Japanese and overwhelm them, driving them straight into the Yellow Sea. He had plenty of troop strength. His troops having suffered little damage at Liaoyang, they far outnumbered the other side. Moreover, nine trains carrying reinforcements arrived daily. By throwing all this manpower at the enemy, he was poised to deliver the anemic Japanese Army a crushing blow.

Rapidly falling out of favor, Kuropatkin was about to be demoted from commander in chief to army commander, and General Grippenberg was shortly to be dispatched to Manchuria as his counterpart. But, for the time being, the entire Manchurian Army was at his command. Now was his chance to restore his honor; the impulse to do so set his pulse racing.

As Kuropatkin prepared to launch a major offensive, he delivered a moving proclamation to the Russian forces on October 2. According to him, despite the various minor setbacks they had suffered, morale was higher than ever. "The troops of the Manchurian Army," he said defensively, "have not been numerically strong enough to defeat the Japanese."

This was not the case. At all times, in every battle, the Russian Army had consistently held the advantage in manpower and firepower alike. But what Kuropatkin sought was not just a numerical edge. He wanted triple the strength of the Japanese Army. The war strategy of a great power is always based on size—even Napoleon always worked from the assumption of an overwhelming advantage in men and arms. Kuropatkin's demand was by no means excessive. He was merely following conventional wisdom.

"You retired to new positions at Mukden as planned," he told his forces. "You carried out the retreat while set upon by General Kuroki's army, under the most difficult conditions imaginable. Our successful retreat to Mukden, overcoming various obstacles, is worthy of admiration. But now," he assured them, "the tsar has assigned for the conflict with Japan forces sufficient to secure Russia the victory." He announced that the time had come to go on the offensive and, with words of praise for the bravery of the Russian forces valiantly defending Port Arthur, urged the army to rouse itself for a great push forward.

"God is with us," he concluded. "Victory is assured."

* * *

In contrast to Kuropatkin's army, the Japanese Army was in a deplorable state. On the mainland, there were only two active divisions (the Seventh and Eighth), and all that could be deployed were standby reservists hastily called up. The soldiers were older veterans, and the officers and non-commissioned officers had declined in quality. There was no hope of mustering an army equal in strength to the Japanese Army that had fought at Liaoyang.

There weren't even any rifles for the reinforcements. For lack of an alternative, they were given Murata rifles used during the First Sino-Japanese War and confiscated Russian rifles, but Japanese rifle shells didn't fit the confiscated arms. The Japanese Army's fighting power was spent. Everyone, down to the last private, felt this in his bones.

Prime Minister Katsura feared that the nation's poverty was affecting morale on the front lines. On hearing reports that a rich vein of sixty percent gold-bearing ore had been discovered in Kesennuma, a town north of Sendai, he ordered that General Headquarters in Manchuria be so informed—even though he must have known the story was bogus. He sought to raise morale by assuring troops at the front that the empire's military expenses were covered. Only a truly poverty-stricken nation would resort to such a ruse. The imaginary mine was supposed to have yielded four billion yen's worth of gold—more than enough, if it were true, to pay all the expenses of the Russo-Japanese War. Heartened by this glad news, the troops could fight with spirit and die without misgivings.

When the news was conveyed to General Headquarters near the station at Liaoyang, the rejoicing was general. Kodama lost no time in informing Ōyama, who chuckled with amusement. "Sounds like something Katsura dreamed up." He dismissed the report with an indulgent smile. "Even if they did find a gold mine, digging up all that gold would cost billions of yen. Do you really think the nation could afford to spend money that way in the middle of a war?" He laughed. "Just take it as a comic story Katsura spun for our enjoyment, and let it go."

Kodama laughed too. At the same time, he was filled with admiration at the commander in chief's acumen.

What made the army's state even more pitiable was an outbreak of what was then Japan's national disease, beriberi. It began spreading through the ranks. Certain divisions had a thousand sufferers already, and severely stricken soldiers were incapacitated, unable to pick up a rifle and fight. This was on top of the extreme shortage of ammunition.

At that point, on October 4, a Chinese spy that Kuroki had dispatched to Mukden returned with a dire warning: "The Russian Army that had stopped at Mukden is now on the move, heading south." Fujii Shigeta hastily relayed the news to General Headquarters.

* * *

On learning that the Russian Army was southbound, the Japanese command hesitated over how to react. The word "react" is not usually found in the lexicon of warfare, but it aptly conveys the level of consternation—which is not too strong a word—among army leaders at this juncture.

Frankly, given the Russian Army's conduct of the war thus far, no one had expected any action so bold. Certainly, the Japanese Army leaders had prayed that nothing like this would happen. Now that it had, what were they going to do about it? They dithered.

The strategic approach of the Japanese Army until this point had been to get the jump on the enemy and launch a preemptive strike. Superiority over the enemy had been maintained by consistently getting in the lead punch, one that packed a wallop. But at this point they lacked the necessary troop strength and ammunition. Should they go on the defensive? That was the question.

Already, at Liaoyang, they had taken a defensive stance. Each division had dug trenches and surrounded them with wire entanglements. This was the first time the Japanese Army had taken up a defensive position.

Earlier, Colonel Fujimoto Tarō of the Thirty-third Infantry Regiment (Nagoya) had presented himself at General Headquarters and met with Matsukawa Toshitane. "I wish to respectfully offer my opinion," he had said, and proceeded to do so, standing at attention.

The gist of Fujimoto's remarks was this. The nation's military strength had lasted only as far as Liaoyang. If the army spurred itself to fight at Mukden, the resulting attrition was bound to be still greater, the army's ability to recover from its wounds seriously impaired. The best course was to set up a strong defensive position at Liaoyang from which to engage the enemy when it attacked. This plan was backed by strategic theory. The Russo-Japanese War had been undertaken in the first place in order to repulse the Russian threat on the Korean Peninsula. Send four divisions there for protection, Fujimoto advised, and leave the rest to diplomatic peace negotiations.

"I know for certain that you have a lot on your mind." Matsukawa Toshitane, Kodama's most trusted staff officer, was sardonic. "You are a regimental commander. All you need to do is obey orders and fight hard, pressing forward. Never mind debate."

Fujimoto responded that he had no intention of neglecting his duty as a regimental commander. Whenever orders came, he was prepared to lead his men through fire or water. He had come only to offer his private opinion. With that, he turned and walked away.

A cool appraisal of the realities of Japan and its armed forces would indicate that Fujimoto was correct. But there was no need to focus solely on Japan's reality. The enemy, too, was enmeshed in its own complicated reality. The Russian Army and the Japanese Army were intertwined in the abnormal circumstance of war. If Japan veered away from its reality and took matters into its own hands, there was no telling how the situation might change. Matsukawa Toshitane, for one, favored action.

* * *

What was most inconvenient at this critical time was the absence from Liaoyang of Kodama Gentarō. Having decided that one reason why the siege of Port Arthur was dragging on so long was a dearth of strategic ability on Nogi's staff, he vacated his post for twenty days beginning in mid-September to go to Port Arthur. In this way, he considerably shortened the time it took for the fortress to fall, but only at the cost of neglecting the army's main battlefield.

While Kodama was away, the alarming warning that the Russian Army was marching south sent a chill through Ōyama's headquarters. Without Kodama there to take charge, opinion split down the middle, and confusion reigned. Matsukawa declared that the only viable alternative was to take the initiative and strike. Even if signs pointed to an imminent move south by the Russian Army, intelligence reports indicated that preparations were still underway. The best thing to do was attack swiftly before the enemy was ready.

But Major General Iguchi Shōgo thought otherwise. "Too risky," he insisted. His plan was rather for the army to maintain its stronghold, draw the enemy there, and launch an attack only after bombarding them first.

Deep down, Ōyama was troubled. When he left for the front, he had announced his intention to leave day-to-day matters in Kodama's capable hands and take charge only if Japan began losing badly. Until now, he had stuck to that policy, but with Kodama gone he had no choice but to step in and decide this crucial issue himself. Although inclined to agree with Matsukawa, he wanted to check whether the colonel had a firm enough basis for his opinion and so summoned him to his quarters for questioning. At the same time, he ordered Kodama back immediately.

Kodama returned to headquarters in Liaoyang at six o'clock in the morning on October 6. He quickly absorbed the full complexity of the situation, but his twenty days' absence had broken the rhythm of his thought processes. For once, his famously clearheaded thought processes were nowhere in evidence.

The next day, October 7, marked the fourth day since the warning that the Russian Army was on the move. A general staff meeting was held with Kodama presiding. Iguchi and Matsukawa clashed, and, with neither man willing to give an inch, the meeting went on interminably. For the famously brisk Japanese leadership to allow a war council to drag on so inconclusively was unprecedented.

Back in the sixteenth century, leaders of a clan centered in Odawara met to discuss what to do about warrior Toyotomi Hideyoshi, who was headed their way with his troops. The debate dragged on for weeks, until finally Hideyoshi besieged the castle and the hapless leaders were forced to surrender. The phrase "Odawara council" thus came to refer to any long and empty negotiation. As history shows, such futile debates have no place in war. All the same, Kodama could not make up his mind.

* * *

Perhaps Kodama should never have gone to Port Arthur to check on Nogi's army in the first place. With a decisive battle in the offing, he should have stayed on the job to lead Japan's main force. "Kodama lost his edge at Port Arthur," his aides murmured. Though normally this man of quick insight could make snap decisions about what needed to be done, with the enemy heading south from Mukden he was distracted.

Whether brooding over war strategies or carrying out simple daily tasks, people follow a certain rhythm. The workings of the mind fall into that rhythm which, if neglected for days on end, cannot be picked up again right away but need time to recalibrate. That is the position in which Kodama found himself. At this critical juncture and for the first time since the war began, his brain was foggy. That was all there was to it, really.

But if anything else did hold his powers of thought captive, it was the fact that the siege at Port Arthur was unfolding in a far more tragic way than he had ever imagined possible.

In hindsight, it has to be said that the organization of the Japanese Army was flawed. Nogi's army, which was responsible for attacking Port Arthur, should have been under the direct command of Imperial Headquarters in Tokyo, not in the Ōyama–Kodama line of command. Ōyama and Kodama had their hands full commanding the main force of the Manchurian Army in a showdown with Kuropatkin. Port Arthur was a completely different situation. Only supermen could have managed them both at the same time.

That's how Port Arthur ended up being left entirely to Nogi's discretion. Other staff officers of the Japanese Manchurian Army made backbiting remarks: "What in God's name is Nogi up to?" "Ijichi's a damned fool and no mistake." But their concern went no farther than sarcasm. No one had the time or energy to come to Nogi's aid. The Manchurian Army was mired in its own problems, without the men or the ammunition to do what needed to be done.

"If only Nogi would hurry and take Port Arthur so he could come to our aid!" This unspoken wish was so intense they could have screamed it. To have a military force so large bogged down in Port Arthur, just when Japan was suffering from a severe shortage of manpower, was no way to win a war.

* * *

On May 2, Tsar Nicholas II had decided on the commander of the large fleet he intended to send to the Far East. He had appointed a man he trusted absolutely, his aide-de-camp Rozhestvensky, a rear admiral. As soon as his appointment was official, Rozhestvensky set about preparing for the expedition of the century.

The Japanese Navy panicked. A series of urgent messages were fired off, urging the army to capture Port Arthur and be done with it. Enough was enough. That is why Kodama had traveled to Port Arthur in person, meeting with Nogi and his staff and touring the battle site. His visit coincided with the second all-out assault, which succeeded only in wasting precious blood and iron without hurting the enemy significantly. The assault was a total failure.

On the train back to Liaoyang, Kodama had not been able to shake the horrors and failure of the Port Arthur attack from his mind. Nor was that the only ongoing crisis. The fortunes of the Japanese Manchurian Army seemed to change hourly.

On September 26, the Trans-Siberian Railway opened a subsidiary line that detoured to Lake Baikal, greatly increasing the ability of the Russian Army to resupply itself. The Russians were strong adherents of the European idea that supply lines were of paramount importance in warfare. Kuropatkin, greatly heartened by the swelling ranks in Manchuria, announced in his October 2 proclamation that there were now sufficient forces to move forward.

* * *

At this point, we would like to insert a slight digression.

The Russian Army had a tradition of not assuming the offensive unless it had two or two and a half times the men and arms of the enemy. The reason was not cowardice. In all times and ages, victorious generals are those who make a point of assembling greater armies than the enemy so they can overwhelm and destroy their foe. Oda Nobunaga's youthful victory in the surprise attack at Okehazama was an exception; after that, he always followed the above policy. Therein lay his greatness. Even though he began his career with a surprise attack against a vastly superior fighting force, he never attempted to imitate that early success. Nobunaga knew better than anyone that his chances of success at Okehazama had been one in a hundred—that's what made him a great warlord.

At the time of the Russo-Japanese War, the Japanese military was fighting desperately with its back to the wall, rising up against a superior opponent in circumstances similar to those at Okehazama. Hence, Kodama's pain and effort. Greatly outnumbered, he was constantly racking his brains for a way to rout his superior foe.

Japan's subsequent military leaders were incompetent precisely because they took as precedent the victory in the Russo-Japanese War, a victory won in the unlikely style of Nobunaga's Okehazama. The Japanese military establishment clung to that method of attack all the way to the demise of their army in 1945.

What's surprising about the Russo-Japanese War, to pursue this line of thought a little more, is that Okehazama-style fighting should have been so successful. It is also surprising that the sweetness of that success determined the course of the Japanese military thereafter—a ridiculous state of affairs that cries out for explanation.

Though plagued with shortages, including a chronic scarcity of ammunition and of the new weapons known as "machine guns," the Japanese Army was otherwise one of the best-equipped armies in the world. But, following the Russo-Japanese War, its equipment would remain second rate all the way until 1945. "Look how we won the war with Russia." That thought occupied the minds of elite military leaders, who ought to have known better. Of course, Oda Nobunaga never tried to repeat the success of his raid at Okehazama but was careful to surround himself ever after with troops double the size of the enemy's, troops that he kept well supplied. The difference is so stark that one has to wonder if Japan's subsequent military leaders deserve to be called professionals.

The bungling of Japan's military leaders is demonstrated in the limited war fought between the Japanese and Russian armies in 1939. Although Japan's Kwantung Army staff officers had greater military knowledge than those who served during the Russo-Japanese War, their operational planning abilities were far inferior. That's because the military organization was rigidly bureaucratic and behind the times.

At the time, the Soviet Union wanted to stir up conflict along the Manchuria–Mongolia border and so provoked the skirmish intentionally. The Kwantung Army got wind of what was happening, but continued to underrate Soviet strength and supply capacity even after trouble broke out. The battlefield was over 200 kilometers away from the railway, which led the Kwantung Army to believe that the Soviet Army would assemble only a small force. Unbelievably, army leaders were so dense that it never occurred to them that the Soviets might use trucks to transport soldiers and goods. Back then, the Japanese military relied on horses and men for non-rail transport. Military use of motor vehicles was not yet widespread, and Japanese leaders extrapolated from their own experience to predict Soviet logistics and troop strength. But the Soviets made liberal use of motor vehicles for troop transport and supply.

The Kwantung Army flung twice as many troops as the enemy into the war. But where Japanese infantry equipment had improved but little since the days of the Russo-Japanese War, the Soviet military had undergone a radical revision. At a time when the infantry was still widely considered the mainstay of the military, the Soviets had built a military force centered around tanks, with the infantry merely offering support. Their artillery strength too was vastly improved, and they had switched to a style of fighting that relied on massive firepower. Japan's best military leaders, in contrast, were interested in politics and believed that armies were formed by praising men's spiritual strength. Thus, the Japanese military was merely an extension of its previous self during the Russo-Japanese War, and the results showed this clearly. The Japanese withdrew after suffering a catastrophic defeat with a casualty rate of seventy-three percent.

* * *

The digression has gone on too long. We must turn our sights back on Kodama Gentarō after his return to Liaoyang from Port Arthur.

Though there was regional factionalism in military circles at the time of the Russo-Japanese War, there was as yet no sense of bureaucratic order in the decision-making process. Kodama was able to carry out his own ideas on his own authority. The nation's future rested squarely on his shoulders in a real, not a rhetorical, sense. That made him so far removed from the military leaders of the subsequent Shōwa period that he might have been from a different country and race of men. The crushing responsibility was sometimes too much for the nerves of that diminutive, 5-foot-tall man to endure. He was able to bear up under the daily pressure not only because of his natural cheerfulness, but also because his partner Ōyama Iwao continually supported him and soothed his nerves.

For some time after his return, Kodama was at a complete loss. Though the Russian Army had strengthened considerably, the Japanese Army had declined in the quantity and quality of its troops and ammunition supply. On the vast Manchurian plains, there was no way to rely on natural defense. No general in history would have known what to do under the circumstances.

The opinions of Kodama's staff split down the middle. Kodama would have to choose between Major General Iguchi's plan urging defense and Colonel Matsukawa's plan urging a counteroffensive. He and Ōyama both inclined toward the latter. Given their few troops and paltry supply of ammunition, a counteroffensive seemed like the right idea. It had always worked before.

Unable to make up his mind, Kodama did the equivalent of drawing lots. He wanted to hear from someone besides his own staff, and so decided to send for Major General Fujii Shigeta, chief of staff of Kuroki's army, and Major General Uehara Yūsaku, chief of staff of Nozu's army.

Fujii Shigeta could always provide a clear-cut answer to any question. "Liaoyang," he pointed out, "is extremely difficult to defend against an enemy coming from the north. The only way out is to go after the enemy yourself."

Uehara lacked Fujii's acuity, but he came to the same conclusion for this reason: "The soldiers' morale is extremely high."

After listening to the opinions of these two men, Kodama made his judgment.

* * *

It wasn't until one o'clock in the afternoon on October 7 that an order went out from Ōyama and Kodama's headquarters in connection with the enemy's changed situation. The order can be summed up very simply: "The army will assume standby positions." The funny thing about that order was that it failed to make clear whether the army was supposed to attack or defend. "Man your positions" was all it said. Kodama's vacillation was plain to see. He had resolved to go on the offensive but, as this command shows, he was also giving himself leeway. Needless to say, unclear orders are taboo in military leadership—as Kodama well knew.

Kodama was famous for his nimble decision-making. But a person doesn't always act according to a single set of traits. At this point, Kodama gave the impression of being not a brilliant strategist but an ordinary, worn-out old man. The loss of his customary perspicuity was owing not just to the lingering effects of his time in Port Arthur but also in large part to the extreme shortage of ammunition. Kodama's psychological state at this point is a textbook example of how the fatal flaw of a shortage in supplies can dull a person's mental agility.

Back on the mainland, Japan's arsenals were unable to produce even half the amount of ammunition needed. With the Port Arthur siege eating up ammunition at a rate far beyond anything the army leaders had imagined, the need was only going to become more acute. Shells for heavy guns were needed above all. Imperial Headquarters took the drastic step of ordering a temporary halt to the manufacture of shells for field guns and mountain guns. Given the arsenals' meager output capacity, desperate measures were called for. "As a result," Imperial Headquarters in Tokyo wired Manchuria General Headquarters, "no field ammunition can be manufactured until October 15." After the battle of Liaoyang, fighting in Manchuria would become even more difficult.

"It's true what they say—poverty dulls the wit." Chagrined at his own slow-wittedness, Kodama murmured this privately to Matsukawa Toshitane.

The ambiguous "standby" order was issued on October 7. But, to everyone's surprise, by the following day, the enemy had still barely made contact with the Japanese front-line troops and was acting generally sluggish. Kodama began to wonder if the news of Russia's move southward had been a lie after all.

* * *

Word that the Russian Army had halted also came from the head of Akiyama's brigade, which remained on the left flank of Oku's army, providing protection and carrying out reconnaissance activities. General Headquarters picked up the following intelligence: the enemy's first line had advanced as far as Kangdaren Hill, Mangjiagu, and Banqiao Fort, and then stopped. Now they were entrenching.

"What's going on?" Kodama was stumped. If the enemy troops had kept on coming like a tsunami, they might well have broken through the Japanese line of defense, since the Japanese Army was wavering between defense and attack. In any case, the battle was shaping up to be a devastating loss for the Japanese. Now might well be the time for Ōyama to make good on his famous pledge to "leave everything to Kodama and take charge only when Japan is fighting a losing battle."

Letting Kodama fight all the winning battles shows Ōyama's greatness as a general. When fighting turns brutal and lines collapse in defeat, it's axiomatic that only the top leadership can stave off disaster. The one who saves the day has to be a war hero the whole army looks up to and trusts, someone as immovable as a mountain. He must fill officers and men with hope as he spurs them on, demonstrating leadership with calm boldness. Ōyama knew he was better suited to this role than Kodama. That is the sort of partnership he and Kodama had. Ōyama was fully persuaded that as long as the army was winning, he wasn't needed.

Ōyama took as his model his cousin Saigō Takamori, that leader in the overthrow of the Tokugawa shogunate, who was later forced out of semiretirement to become the reluctant leader of a ragtag rebel army. Ōyama grew up near the great man in Satsuma and was greatly influenced by him. At the end of the Tokugawa period, he stayed by Saigō's side and served him devotedly. For him, Saigō was the supreme model of a leader.

But what to make of the enemy's movements?

"They're entrenching?" For Kodama, the news brought surprise and joy. The Russian Army would not be coming their way any time soon.

"Why didn't they keep going south?" wondered Eberhard von Tettau, a German observer embedded with the Russian Army, in later writings about this strange development. "I had no idea what was going through Kuropatkin's mind." And yet Kuropatkin had his reasons.

Kuropatkin's army had two flanks, one on the east and one on the west. The eastern corps was to make a detour in order to surround the Japanese Army, and so its arrival at the appointed battle site was delayed. The western corps advanced alone. Kuropatkin ordered the western corps to entrench and await further orders in order to keep the two corps in synch. He was a perfectionist. The proper thing for him to do would have been to make the western corps attack the Japanese Army and breach its defenses, then to bring the eastern corps into play from behind in a pincer operation. But, to someone like Kuropatkin, that strategy would have seemed like reckless adventuring.

* * *

Kodama's vacillation and indecisiveness were more than his aides could bear. This was not the Kodama they knew. He seemed like another man, they said later.

Kodama gathered all the staff officers of the various armies at Kuroki's headquarters in Luodatai. Fukuda Masatarō, Kuroki's staff officer, agreed with the plan to launch an offensive strike and approached Kodama, who was still unable to make up his mind.

"Sir, what is there to think about? If you decide to adopt the plan to draw the enemy to our camp"—Iguchi's defensive plan—"the First Army will have no choice but to abandon our position on Lake Benxi."

This was because the positions occupied by Kuroki's army formed a zigzag pattern, not a straight line. Drawing the army into formation would necessitate handing over to the enemy the protruding part, the Lake Benxi camp, and pulling back from there. As a member of Kuroki's staff, Fukuda cared less about the situation of the Manchurian Army as a whole than about Kuroki's army. He didn't want to give up the stronghold they had established, not only for strategic reasons but also for the negative effect that doing so would have on morale.

With a venomous look, he lashed out at Kodama. "Sir, the situation is what it is. If we are to go on the offensive, we should do so now. If you are still torn between the two proposals at this point, how can you go on as chief of staff of the Manchurian Army, with the nation's fate resting on your shoulders?"

Always hot under the collar, Kodama saw red. "Damn you, are you looking for a fight?" Though his opponent was a mere lieutenant colonel, the general lost his temper and his dignity, jumping to his feet and overturning his chair. If only he had had enough manpower and shells for an attack, Kodama would not have agonized so much.

At that point, he finally made his decision. "Starting tomorrow, the army goes on the offensive," he announced. "I will present the plan to Commander in Chief Ōyama straight away."

Fukuda let out a howl of protest. As long as they were going on the offensive, why do so "starting tomorrow"? Shouldn't the order to attack go out right away?

"Give the order now!" Fukuda's expression was so fierce as he hounded the general that Kodama's aide Fukushima Ansei, an intelligence officer known for his daring, reached out impulsively, caught his sleeve, and pulled him back.

"He looked so bloodthirsty I was afraid he was on the point of drawing his sword," Fukushima later commented.

Fukuda's fierceness had helped Kodama come to a decision, but the order had yet to go out.

* * *

Kodama made his final decision after returning to headquarters, but deep down he continued to harbor doubts. The proof is that he didn't go directly to Ōyama's room. Usually, he would head straight there and briskly propose a strategy. Kodama respected Ōyama, and he knew better than anyone what it meant to be commander in chief. He didn't want Ōyama to detect his wavering. As top commander, Ōyama needed to issue the order with a mind as unclouded as a mirror.

Whatever hesitation Kodama might feel, he had no desire to implant any similar hesitation in Ōyama's mind. He stayed away from Ōyama's quarters because he feared that Ōyama would read his mind and be influenced accordingly. Even under ordinary conditions, it frequently happens that an aide's state of mind affects that of his commanding officer—but this was no ordinary time. The fate of the nation hung on the order that was about to go out in Ōyama's name. If he issued the command resolutely, without the least sign of wavering, then, by the peculiar psychology of the battlefield, morale would lift, as surely as electricity travels through air.

That was why Kodama didn't go in person but instead summoned Colonel Matsukawa, author of the counteroffensive plan, and had him go in his place. He chose Matsukawa rather than his superior, Iguchi, in hopes that the man's enthusiasm would prove infectious.

When Matsukawa appeared, Kodama was sitting at his desk. He laid down a piece of paper and said, "I am going to read out a draft of an order. I need you to write it up properly and take it to the commander in chief so that he can decide if he agrees." He proceeded to dictate, first touching on the enemy's movements and then outlining the commander in chief's decision. "The enemy is now amassing forces on the left bank of the Hun River. I want it attacked before it finishes doing so." That was the nub of the matter. Kodama told Matsukawa to add an estimate of the situation and other details, and submit the document to Ōyama for his approval.

Matsukawa went straight back to his room, where he spent the next hour and a half drafting the order. He took the finished document to Ōyama's room and knocked on his door. From inside came a leisurely response. Matsukawa entered, went up to Ōyama's desk, and handed him the draft.

Ōyama read it through once, then read it a second time before looking up. "Does Kodama know about this?" When Matsukawa said yes, Ōyama nodded. "All right, let's do it." He handed the paper back to Matsukawa. The order was in effect.

* * *

With the issuing of this order, the Japanese Army swung into action. The front line was over 70 kilometers long. The army was to go on the offensive, but it was outnumbered, and so the line could not be ragged. The slightest irregularity anywhere would render the whole line vulnerable. The enemy could seize upon any protrusion, surround it, cut it off, and destroy it. The enemy's major force could then push through the resulting breach and divide the Japanese Army in two, encircling each half and wiping both out.

"Press forward in a smooth line abreast." This was the Matsukawa plan that Kodama had approved. But the battlefield was hilly, the terrain unusually difficult for Manchuria. Keeping a large army together and advancing in step was well-nigh impossible—yet, if they did not, the operation would fail.

This concern was what had prompted Iguchi to advocate the defensive plan. "How the hell can the army pull off a stunt like that?" he had shouted at Matsukawa at one point.

Kodama too was worried. At dawn, he turned toward the east as the sun was coming over the horizon, his palms together in an attitude of prayer. Though not a man of faith by any means, he was convinced that at this point there was no alternative but to seek divine aid.

But Matsukawa was unfazed. "This is why we've trained the army so well and hard ever since the Restoration—just so it can pull off this stunt!" Expert opinion concurred that the Japanese Army of this era was indeed the world's best-trained military force, top to bottom. The ability of high-ranking officers alone could not account for such distinction. The level of ability of combat leaders and noncommissioned officers had to be extremely high.

The upshot was that the advance of the great, 70-kilometer-long Japanese line went off without a hitch. Dressing the line was fiendishly difficult under the circumstances. The operation took place at night. Portions of the line jutting forward had to fall back, and those lagging behind had to catch up.

One section in particular was a source of great concern—a spur which, if attacked, was likely to cause the whole army pain. This was the brigade of Major General Umezawa Michiharu (from Miyagi Prefecture), a particularly isolated section of Kuroki's army, which of the three was closest to the enemy camp. Umezawa led a mixed standby reserve brigade with a large percentage of older draftees bearing obsolete weapons. They had taken up their position only recently and had not yet built any fortifications. This brigade had to be pulled back—but if the Russian Army caught on to its retreat and came in pursuit, the fighting was bound to be grisly.

* * *

The Umezawa brigade, which was to receive the brunt of the Russian Army's immense thrust, was held in mild contempt by the supreme command and friendly troops as "standby reservists." Umezawa himself was already an old man. On top of all this, it was an Imperial Guard brigade—at the time, the Imperial Guard were commonly believed to be weak fighters.

Though the Russians were continually sending up fresh soldiers on active duty from home, Japanese soldiers went on getting older and older—a source of worry to Manchurian Army headquarters. The Umezawa brigade was a prime example of the graying of the Japanese Army. Umezawa was not a graduate of the Army Academy but a samurai from Sendai who had participated in the Boshin War. In rebellion against imperial forces, he had entered the fortress Goryōkaku in Hakodate, fighting under naval commander Enomoto Takeaki in his final show of resistance to the new government. He prided himself on being a veteran of that war. Had he been from Satsuma or Chōshū, he would certainly have risen above major general to rub shoulders with Kuroki and Nogi in the high command.

Other veterans of the Boshin War who fought in the Russo-Japanese War include Ōyama Iwao, Kodama Gentarō, Kuroki Tamemoto, and Nozu Michitsura, all of whom had fought in the imperial force, as well as Oku Yasukata and Tatsumi Naobumi, who had fought in the pro-Tokugawa force. All of them had gone on to become generals. Umezawa, a major general, was the only other veteran of that war involved in the current campaign.

Of Umezawa, it was said, "He knows the scent of battle." As someone who had learned the art of war in actual battle, not in the classroom, he had developed instincts that made him keenly sensitive to the constantly shifting enemy situation and psychology. He also had something of a genius for command. He did all he could to instill confidence and pride in the men in his brigade, which the other units derided. He even composed a *sanosabushi*, a popular type of ballad ending with the refrain *sanosa* that his men liked to sing.

> Did you see them?
> The glorious Umezawa brigade
> Taking Jilin and Harbin easily
> on empty stomachs *sanosa*.

Indeed, the members of the Umezawa brigade were formidable fighters, not a whit inferior to the active forces.

To backtrack, on September 17, Umezawa went out to the front to do his own inspection. A master of warfare, he didn't bother taking along an aide or a mounted orderly but went out blithely by himself. He stood at the sentry line on the right flank, looked out at the enemy through his binoculars, and saw what appeared to be movement. They were on the march, heading straight toward him. The mounted corps were deployed in front, with the infantry corps following behind.

Umezawa immediately instructed a nearby sentry to go tell the news to the troops behind. But the sentry, thoroughly imbued with a sense of duty, refused to leave his post. This answer delighted Umezawa, who took over the post while the sentry dashed back. Thanks to Umezawa's swift action, the brigade was able to get a jump on the enemy.

Kuropatkin had already focused on the Umezawa brigade as the Japanese Army's weakest link. He had decided his first step would be to cut off the rear communication line between Pingtaizi, where the brigade was positioned, and Lake Benxi, encircle it, and so wipe out the enemy's extreme right flank.

Kodama and the other strategists had seen this coming and ordered Umezawa to retreat—all well and good, except that withdrawing in the face of the enemy was a fiendishly difficult stunt to pull off. Stakelberg's great army was right in front of them.

Umezawa's pet phrase came into play at this time: "There is a scent to war."

When Kuroki's chief of staff approached Umezawa to discuss the timing of his retreat, his answer was prompt: "Let's withdraw immediately."

The young officer demurred; surely it would be more prudent to observe the enemy a day or so before deciding on a method of retreat.

"But there is a scent to war," insisted Umezawa. "No matter how we try to hide our plans, the enemy will find them out. The wind carries the news. If we wait a day and give the enemy a chance to sniff us out, they'll gladly come after us. That's the last thing we want to have happen."

It is practically a physical law of war that being overtaken by the enemy while retreating leads to a rout. Umezawa's point was that, since the enemy was bound to ferret out their movements anyway, once the order to retreat had been given, the best thing to do was slip away immediately, giving the enemy less time to react and so keeping damage to a minimum. This was the wisdom of a hard-bitten veteran of many a campaign.

On October 7, Umezawa waited for night to fall and then began his retreat. His brigade left and moved to its new camp on Lake Benxi as noiselessly as the wind. To be precise, Lake Benxi was on the right flank, and from there the new camp extended through the hills south of Mt. Zhaoxian.

The Russian Army found out afterward that Umezawa had disappeared, but they weren't disappointed. Because Umezawa's camp on Lake Benxi had incomplete fortifications and was thinly manned, that, Kuropatkin decided, was the place to commit a large force and break through.

Twenty days earlier, in order to check up on the state of Umezawa's detachment at Pingtaizi on the Japanese Army's right flank, Kuropatkin had ordered two generals—Pavel Rennenkampf and Aleksandr Samsonov—to organize a large unit to conduct reconnaissance in force and then attack. The purpose of the exercise was to test the waters.

This was what Umezawa had seen on September 17 when he had gone out alone to the sentry line at the front to reconnoiter enemy movements. He was there from dawn until after eleven in the morning. At eleven-thirty, he had spotted the advance unit of the reconnaissance in force through his binoculars. There were some two battalions of infantry and several companies of cavalry. The troops behind them, according to his report, stretched "on and on, seemingly without end." He had taken prompt steps to deal with this change in situation.

* * *

The grizzled veteran Umezawa felt less alarm on discovering the presence of the enemy than he would if a stray dog had wandered into his front yard. He adopted the tactic of having his troops lie low and wait for the enemy to approach. The brigade was in a hilly area where it was easy to conceal themselves. He deployed the old soldiers under his command stealthily and shrewdly. The Fourth Standby Reserve Infantry Regiment was on the right and the first battalion of the Second Imperial Guard Standby Reserve Infantry Regiment on the left, like two spread-out wings, while in the center he placed the First Imperial Guard Standby Reserve Infantry Regiment. His brigade also had an artillery company attached. This Umezawa divided into three, assigning one platoon (with two guns) to each flank and the center.

The Russians were unaware that the enemy had discovered their forward movement. They probably figured that, as is bound to happen in war, a scout might have observed them. They certainly did not count on the brigade commander doing his own scouting and assigning troops to their battle stations on the spot.

"Don't fire until the enemy is well within range," Umezawa ordered. His men obeyed.

It was around noon when the Russian Army came within range of the Japanese artillery. The gunners waited till the last possible moment and then, under Umezawa's capable direction, all three branches opened fire simultaneously.

The infantry saw with their own eyes how astonished the Russians were—and then they carried out their own sudden strike. Fighting lasted for more than three hours. Finally, at a quarter to four in the afternoon, the Russians took flight, having sustained enormous damage. Umezawa ordered his men to give chase, and the fighting went on until sundown, when they returned to their base. Umezawa had suffered the loss of a single noncommissioned officer, but Russian casualties were heavy.

Still, the defeat didn't affect the Russians' overall strategy. The original purpose of the sortie had been a reconnaissance in force. Despite having lost this small, localized battle, the Russians had successfully ascertained that Umezawa's position was "thinly manned with scarcely any fortifications," a harvest of intelligence that amply rewarded their efforts. Twenty days later, Umezawa's advance posts came under heavy attack from Russian forces.

When day dawned on October 8, soldiers in the garrison at Lake Benxi on the extreme right of Umezawa's camp discovered that the hills ahead of them were black with a swarm of enemy troops—the left column of Stakelberg's corps and Rennenkampf's division. Enemy units had assembled in front of Lake Benxi shortly after noon, opposite a single Japanese battalion. Faced with a task as hopeless as trying to hold back a raging flood with a wooden board, the Japanese soldiers began to retreat. Umezawa, who was behind them, did not leave the men unaided but hastily sent in reinforcements. Heavy fighting ensued, but Umezawa's men were isolated and outnumbered, and their outlook appeared bleak in the extreme.

* * *

On learning that the Umezawa brigade was on the verge of annihilation, Kuroki took bold steps to rescue it. He was well aware that its loss would put the entire army at risk. If the Japanese Army's defense line could be likened to a long dike, the Umezawa brigade marked its weakest point. Once that point gave way, the Russian Army could flood through the resulting hole in the dike and sweep away the rest of the Japanese Army.

Kuroki ordered the Twelfth Division (Kokura Division), led by Lieutenant General Inoue Hikaru of Yamaguchi Prefecture, to use every means at its disposal to rescue Umezawa. The Twelfth Division sprang into action, but the Russians had blockaded the roads and clearing them took time. By the time they reached Umezawa's position, it was half past eight at night.

Kuroki further ordered his Second Cavalry Brigade to the rescue. However, that cavalry brigade was surrounded by an enormous force at Gujiazi, engaged in a desperate struggle and pinned down, unable to move.

Kuroki went still further, ordering the line of communication garrison to Lake Benxi—an order that broke the bounds of military common sense. Deprived of its garrison, the line of communication consisted of noncombatants only. Men who normally never laid a hand on weapons were forced to take up rifles and stand guard.

In any case, by October 9, Kuroki's army, the right flank of the Japanese Army, was in grave danger, especially Umezawa's brigade. At headquarters, Kodama decided that Kuroki's army would have to pay a sacrifice. He had come up with a grand strategy. With the enemy's main force bearing down hard against Kuroki's army on the right, now was his chance to have Nozu's army in the center and Oku's army on the left wheel around the major Russian assault forces and encircle them. This was an operation beyond Kuropatkin's imagining. Indeed, it was a strategy like few others in history. Japanese troops were far outnumbered. The idea of a smaller force surrounding a much larger one was, tactically speaking, preposterous.

The embattled First Army under Kuroki would function as a pivot around which the other armies could wheel to the right, driving the enemy forces into the hills where the Japanese forces, in their element, could wipe them out.

Nozu and Oku's armies were to take the initiative in this offensive, but they too were embroiled in fighting. Unless they cleared away the enemy troops before them, they couldn't begin the wheeling action. General Nozu, having consented to the plan, sought the permission of Ōyama and Kodama to attack the enemy at night on Sankuaishi Hill. There was no precedent in history for a night raid by an army consisting of several divisions. Ōyama and Kodama gave permission. On the night of October 12, Nozu's army carried out this daring nocturnal assault, putting the enemy on Sankuaishi Hill to flight. That same day, Oku's army routed the enemy forces at Qianlangzijie and thereafter saw light action.

* * *

Akiyama Yoshifuru and his cavalry brigade were positioned on the left flank of the Japanese Army, carrying on their campaign. Back when Yoshifuru was garrison commander in China, he had won the trust of the powerful Qing leader Yuan Shikai, who now sent him a gift of alcoholic beverages as a gesture of friendship. There were as many as four dozen bottles, a mixture of wine, champagne, whiskey, and brandy. For Yoshifuru, who had had nothing but cheap Chinese wine to drink, this was an especially welcome gift—but, at the time, no leader on the battlefield could be so heartless as to monopolize such a gift and not share it with his men. He took only a tiny amount for himself and gave away the rest to the men in his command.

The main force of Yoshifuru's detachment advanced to Heigoutai, keeping a search party constantly to the north. From around October 11, the fighting was fierce. The detachment was continually pressed by a superior foe, and from time to time the enemy cavalry would descend like a storm and attempt to destroy them. Yoshifuru's survival tactic was to have his forces bear up under this storm as best they could and, when it had finally swept on, crawl like inchworms to establish the next position.

To endure the storm, he had to make his cavalry cease being cavalry. They moved the horses to the rear, established a position, and opened fire. The attached infantry, artillery, and engineer units came to their aid, helping to press forward steadily.

"If it weren't for them, we could never win out against the enemy's superior cavalry." This was what Yoshifuru thought. Cossack men and horses were so large in size that, in a one-on-one battle, the Japanese cavalry would have stood no chance. The fighting tactic that Yoshifuru adopted was similar to the one used by Oda Nobunaga in 1575 against Takeda Katsuyori's cavalry in the battle of Nagashino, where Oda's innovative use of wooden stockades and rotating volleys of fire led to a decisive victory. Even if it was born of necessity, the technique of pushing forward as they established positions followed European precedents.

In general, the Japanese style of fighting in the Russo-Japanese War can be likened to that of the powerful medieval warrior whose name has come up several times—Uesugi Kenshin, who was revered as the "god of war" by his followers. The Russians, having never before experienced such intense forward charges, were astonished, and repeatedly ceded ground. Yoshifuru's detachment alone was different. The Russian Cossack cavalry was extremely aggressive, as cavalry always should be, and Yoshifuru resisted their whirlwind attacks by tenaciously hanging on to his positions.

"Of all the officers at every level, none had as hard a time as Akiyama." This was the oft-repeated assessment of Lieutenant Colonel Naganuma Hidefumi, leader of the famous Naganuma cavalry raiders, who would later ride out long distances and wreak havoc behind Russian lines. Yoshifuru, at the head of Japan's inferior cavalry, endured a harrowing ordeal.

*　*　*

"If attacked, endure." This policy of Yoshifuru's was also evident in his personal conduct on the battlefield. He had learned in Europe that the brigade commander himself flourishes his saber, leading charges and overtaking the enemy with his mobility, and then tramples the enemy underfoot. But because Japanese cavalrymen and horses were so inferior to their Cossack counterparts, any such attempt to take the foe by storm would have spelled their doom.

Although they were cavalrymen, the Japanese cavalry was constantly digging holes in the ground and shooting at enemy horses. They were not supposed to be farmers but hunters, and yet like farmers they were always digging in the ground.

"This is the only way." Yoshifuru spent all his time studying maps in brigade headquarters and planning his next move. Whenever there was an enemy raid, he would take out his pistol and lay it on the table. He kept the weapon fastened to a cord around his neck. Since his fighting strategy was to endure the enemy's intermittent whirlwind attacks and then creep forward when they were over, he was never able to step away from his post even for a moment. The pistol was to be used for suicide should the enemy cavalry come storming into his headquarters.

He was always drinking and thinking. Once, when Naganuma came to report to him after sunset he was surprised to find Yoshifuru's room at headquarters dark and thought perhaps he wasn't there. Looking closely, he saw Yoshifuru leaning back in his chair, deep in thought. From time to time, he would pick up a blue and red pencil and make some sort of notation, then cast the pencil aside and be lost in thought again. Naganuma was amazed that Yoshifuru could see the map in front of him in the twilight gloom. It angered him that Yoshifuru's aide-de-camp, who should have been seeing to his needs, hadn't bothered to light a lamp for him. He summoned the aide, Nakaya, and admonished him for leaving Yoshifuru to sit in the dark.

Nakaya apologized for his remissness, but people typically found it hard to be of service to Yoshifuru. He kept a canteen filled with liquor at his side and would from time to time pour some into a teacup and sip it. He asked nothing else but a few pickles and a map. That was all he needed. Having graduated from the Army Staff College, he had no need of aides. The Japanese cavalry was his own personal creation so he knew all its characteristics, both strengths and weaknesses, as well as the abilities and temperaments of all the officers and noncommissioned officers in his command. His years in Europe had taught him exactly how fast Western soldiers could ride Western horses. Before the Russo-Japanese War ever began, he had observed Russian military exercises in the Far East and grown acquainted with General Linevich and many other Russian officers and cavalrymen. There was nobody whom he had any particular need to consult about anything. The man's very self-sufficiency led to his adjutant's inadvertent neglect.

* * *

The battle of Shaho—that is, the battle by the Sha River—was a classic pitched battle.

The Russian Army was driving south. Unprepared to defend itself from the coming onslaught, the Japanese Army instead went on the offensive and began moving its entire line north. Both sides knew the clash was inevitable. When it came, the fierceness beggared description.

In one small bit of good fortune for the Japanese side, this was purely a pitched battle. Until this point, the Japanese had attacked and captured Russian positions without concern for the immense bloodshed involved. Strictly speaking, the battles at Jinzhou, Nanshan, and Liaoyang were not so much field battles as attacks on enemy positions. But now the Russian Army had abandoned its position at Mukden to head south. To be striking an army in motion was a boon for the ammunition-strapped Japanese Army.

But the enemy was too numerous. At every turn, the Japanese Army was in danger of being surrounded. That must not happen—and therein lay the difficulty. If one part of the army were surrounded, the whole army would succumb. To keep from being surrounded, they had to spread out and push forward, and, if the enemy jutted out, the right and left flanks needed to work together to encircle and drive them back.

The Japanese Army tried to seize the advantage by carrying out night assaults, its specialty. The Russian Army was ready for this, however, not only repelling the Japanese but also carrying out night assaults of its own.

The Japanese cavalry had two active brigades. One was Yoshifuru's brigade, protecting the left flank, and the other was on the right. The cavalry took up these positions on either extremity because the Russians' vaunted Cossack cavalry was in constant motion, taking constant sideswipes at the outermost flanks.

The brigade on the right was called the "Miyasama brigade," or "His Highness's brigade." It was led by Prince Kan'in Kotohito, a close relative of the imperial family. After graduating from the military preparatory school in 1881, he went to France to study military tactics and receive cavalry training. He graduated from the Military Academy at Saint-Cyr and the Academy of Saumur, then from the Army Staff College in 1894, specializing in cavalry. Later, he became a field marshal. During most of his career, he was merely decorative and showed no particular ability, but at the battle of Shaho he made a major contribution.

The Second Cavalry Brigade that the prince led was mobilized considerably later than Yoshifuru's First Brigade, not arriving in Manchuria until after the battle of Liaoyang. It was decided that it wouldn't do to have the prince die in battle, and so he was to be transferred to General Headquarters. But when the orders came through, the battle of Shaho was already underway. Prince Kan'in proceeded to the battlefield with his cavalry.

* * *

Tremendous pressure was then being brought to bear against the army by the main force of the Russian Army, especially against Kokura's Twelfth Division, and most particularly against the Shimamura brigade on a hill east of Lake Benxi. Outnumbered three to one and poorly armed, the Shimamura brigade was in imminent danger of being wiped out.

Fujii Shigeta had often been warned by Yoshifuru that, in the hands of an ordinary tactician, cavalry was no better than so many tin soldiers. Only with a superior tactician at the helm could cavalry carry out a surprise attack that might turn the tide of war. With the prince's brigade at his disposal,

Fujii decided that this was the time to use it in a surprise attack. Unfortunately, the cavalrymen were scattered, carrying out their primary duty of reconnaissance. He tried to assemble them, but, in the meantime, he sent out the Fifteenth Cavalry Regiment and a machine gun unit in advance, with the main force of the brigade to follow.

Along the way, they passed through extremely difficult, mountainous terrain. When they finally reached the southern bank of the Taizi River, there was no sign of the enemy. They proceeded then toward Lake Benxi, but the hills were so forbiddingly steep that they made little progress.

The brigade had been supplied with machine guns only at Yoshifuru's adamant insistence. This was the new weapon that the Russians at Port Arthur had in huge numbers and that took the lives of so many Japanese soldiers there. In the entire Japanese Army, only the cavalry had machine guns.

Yoshifuru had piled them in horse-drawn wagons, but Prince Kan'in could see that pulling these along the narrow mountain paths was impossible. On the spot, he had them dismantled and altered to be carried on horseback. While he was at it, he fixed them so that they could be planted firmly on the ground with tripods for better firing. This change was to have an enormous impact.

When, after great difficulty, the cavalrymen struggled to the northern base of Mt. Pingding—"Flattop"—on the southern bank of the Taizi, they found Shimamura's brigade fighting alone on the edge of disaster. They went straight into action, raking the left side of the Russian Army with blistering automatic fire.

The Russians had no machine guns. With incredible ease, the new weapon wreaked havoc. Roughly two battalions of infantry took to their heels first, heading east, followed by seven companies of cavalry and two infantry battalions that had come as far as the south bank of the Taizi. All of this happened in the space of barely an hour's fighting.

The machine guns of Prince Kan'in's cavalry were then turned against the Third Eastern Siberian Rifle Corps, fighting east of Lake Benxi, causing panic and retreat. After the war, it was found that the panic of Russian soldiers in the east sector had spread throughout the Russian Army.

* * *

By going on the offensive in the battle of Shaho, the Russian Army had gained the upper hand. To keep from being put on the defensive, the Japanese Army had been forced to respond with a counteroffensive—albeit one that lacked a grand purpose such as making the long march to Mukden.

The superior Russian forces were vigorously engaged all around the dispersed Japanese forces. Kuropatkin wanted to breach the Japanese line somewhere, anywhere. Once his men had created a gap, they could pour through it, head straight to Ōyama's headquarters in the rear, and overturn it. From the beginning, this had been Kuropatkin's goal. His troops were well supplied with all they needed, including ammunition, which they used lavishly. For every time a Japanese field gun or mountain gun was fired, the Russians returned fire a dozen or more times. Journalists traveling with the Russians reported that the army's vigor was nothing short of amazing.

After their various engagements with Japan, moreover, the Russians had come to understand Japanese ways of fighting. First and foremost was the Japanese fondness for night attacks. At first, these had caused the Russians to retreat in consternation, but by the time of the battle of Shaho they themselves were carrying out night attacks frequently and continued firing all night to guard against possible attacks by the Japanese.

The Russians were also used by now to Japanese-style hand-to-hand combat. In the beginning, the sight of Japanese troops charging with drawn swords and bayonets had taken them by surprise, but at Shaho they met the onslaught and held their ground, fighting with valor. Sometimes they too charged Japanese positions.

In any case, the Japanese were outnumbered two to one. Fighting was extremely brutal. The Japanese troops fought tooth and nail, barely managing to stave off disaster. "Japanese Army in danger"—that was the story initially sent out by foreign correspondents.

"God is with us. Victory is assured." The spirit of these words at the end of Kuropatkin's proclamation to the Russian Army seemed to swell the hearts of every unit, to the last man.

On October 12, there was vicious hand-to-hand combat at the enemy's main attack point of Daling. Some three regiments of the Russian Army made a bayonet charge. The lone Japanese regiment that met this charge was virtually annihilated, and the hilltop territory it occupied was lost. The Japanese Army then launched its own bayonet attack to recover the lost territory, and finally did so. Among the piles of Russian dead was the body of Lieutenant Colonel Vladimir Pekuta of the Eastern Corps, Stakelberg's aide. Orders were found in his pocket. The orders were from Stakelberg to the three corps under his command, the mixed mounted and infantry brigade, and Rennenkampf's division. They read, "The army's left flank is to drive the Japanese Army away from Lake Benxi and attack Field Marshal Ōyama's main force from northeast of Liaoyang."

* * *

At the battle of Shaho, the Russian Army showed its inherent strength. Russian noncommissioned officers and privates, taken from farming villages, followed orders faithfully and displayed remarkable tenacity in position warfare. But when it came to sentry duty or scouting, their Japanese counterparts were several times superior. The Japanese were far more skilled at alertly detecting changes in the overall situation, checking them out, and evaluating them appropriately. They were also better trained. The fighting skills of Japanese platoons and squads in particular were outstanding.

In terms of the quality of mid- and low-level officers, Japan also had the edge. Its officers were not simply valorous. More of them than the Russian officers fully understood their unit's strategic importance within the army as a whole, and had the spirit and ability to sacrifice their unit spontaneously for the sake of all when necessary.

In the Second Division (from Sendai) of Kuroki's army, there was a Major Nihira Senjun. He commanded the First Battalion in the Sixteenth Infantry Regiment (from Shibata). On October 13, Kuroki's two divisions were stuck on a southern slope in a range of mountains that spread east and west, fighting Russian troops at the summit. The Russians had established defensive positions on every outcrop and from there shot down on Kuroki's men. Kuroki, having decided that taking any one of those peaks would enable his army to break down the Russian line, ordered his Imperial Guard Division and Second Division to attack early that morning. The attack was a complete failure. Japanese losses only mounted as the day wore on.

Nihira's battalion had been crouched down since the day before on the south slope of one of the hills in the area, in a fissure that formed a natural trench. They were 1,000 feet above sea level, where the night air was bitterly cold. Conditions were worsened by nighttime rains that turned the bottom of the trench to mud. The battalion spent two days and one night mired in that mud, from the morning of the twelfth until the afternoon of the thirteenth, without fresh ammunition or rations. For two days and one night, they went without sleeping or eating, fighting desperately against the enemy until finally they burst out together and charged up the slope in bloody hand-to-hand combat. Almost everyone from the officers on down were killed or wounded in the charge, but the hundred or so who survived took the summit.

Before this death charge, Nihira addressed his men, who numbered over a thousand. "I have lost many men already," he told them, "at the battle of Liaoyang and in fighting at Jiulian. The last thing I want to do is to kill any more of you. But, for the army to achieve its strategic aim, this battalion has got to be sacrificed. I intend to die here. You, too, must abandon all thought of going home alive."

Nihira's style of leadership, as he prepared to hurl his men into certain death, was to convince them about the strategic significance of their mission. Only then did he ask them to give up their lives. The battalion's fight to the death was indeed of momentous significance as it set in motion events leading ultimately to the enemy's retreat.

*　*　*

The battle of Shaho began on October 8, and as of October 13 neither side had gained the advantage. Yoshifuru was still on the army's left flank, advancing along the eastern bank of the Hun River with his brigade. Just past a village called Toutaizi, however, all of a sudden, he found the way ahead blocked by a huge Cossack cavalry formation—the equivalent of two Japanese brigades, nearly double the size of his outfit.

He was struck with admiration by the Cossacks' skill at fighting on horseback. Their movements were swift and synchronized. Those in front held carbines. To be effective, mounted shooting requires extensive training, but these men handled their weapons with apparent ease. The front row advanced, shooting as they moved, while the back row drove forward as an assault force, their long spears aloft.

"Now that's a cavalry!" Yoshifuru murmured to himself, gazing appreciatively. Then he swiftly did what was necessary. He never panicked. He had no need to, for he knew that, even outnumbered, his meticulously crafted cavalry brigade had the formation, equipment, and tactics to stand up to any foe.

Seeing what the Japanese then did, the Cossacks must have thought, "Damn funny way for a cavalry to act!" With a battle about to begin, the Japanese cavalrymen all dismounted, thereby ceasing to be cavalrymen. They fired prone, like infantry.

And, because cavalry was inevitably weak on defense, Yoshifuru always had with him the infantry unit on loan from the army, which he now deployed. But this still wasn't enough to defeat the Cossacks. He also had his artillery unit, which promptly set to work deploying a battery in the rear. By firing shells to explode over the Cossacks' heads, they intended to throw them into disarray.

These three different types of soldiers functioned together as smoothly as clockwork in Akiyama Yoshifuru's detachment. Not even the mighty Cossacks, said to be the world's strongest cavalry, were a match for them.

Moreover, the enemy knew only one trick: making a mounted dash. Predictably, on this occasion too, the Russians came storming forward in repeated waves without a thought of defending themselves. Each time, Yoshifuru's defensive firing tactics won the day, until finally the Cossacks withdrew, leaving the ground littered with the corpses of their fallen comrades.

Fighting had begun around ten o'clock in the morning and ended a little past noon. Cossacks were known for not leaving their dead behind. Normally, while fleeing, they would reach down from the saddle to scoop them up, but this time they left behind over fifty bodies as well as a large number of weapons—in all, some five hundred carbines and spears. Yoshifuru's brigade, meanwhile, got off very lightly, suffering only twenty or so casualties.

* * *

There would be no miracles for either side at the battle of Shaho. The fierce terrain ruled out surprise attacks, the ace card of the underdog. Victory in a pitched battle against a foe twice as big, achieved while pushing relentlessly forward, must be counted rare in the annals of war. After a desperate fight, Japan won this victory.

Looking back on this battle that began on October 8, it is clear that the thirteenth marked a turning point. The Japanese Army had no sense of having turned a corner at the time, however, as their exchanges with the Russians that day were extremely fierce. By the sixteenth, with the turning point far behind and the outcome of the battle clear, a salient of the Japanese came under heavy fire and its defenders retreated. This incident went down in Russian history as the "perfect victory at Wanbaoshan."

The unit that had advanced on Wanbaoshan was a detachment led by Major General Yamada Yasunaga, consisting of two regiments of infantry, two companies of field artillery, and one battalion of mountain artillery. As military units go, it was quite small. This unit carried out the clumsiest retreat of any Japanese force in the entire Russo-Japanese War. Normally, when the artillery flees, care is taken to drag any cannons along, and, if that isn't possible, then the breech mechanisms are removed and discarded to make the weapons unusable. In this case, however, a dozen or so guns were left behind untouched. That was the one and only time such a thing happened in the war.

The leaders who participated in this battle at Wanbaoshan, including Yamada and his two regiment commanders, were known for their bravery. The two regiments were the Forty-first Infantry Regiment of Hiroshima and the Twentieth Reserve Infantry Regiment of Fukuchiyama. Both of them participated in the frontal assault at Liaoyang and won recognition for their valor. Neither the officers nor the men, in other words, were inferior. Rather, they were victims of bad luck, that perennial battlefield visitor.

On the night of the sixteenth, sensing that his detachment had moved too far forward and was in danger, Yamada had his men begin to pull back. While they were so engaged, a large Russian force came after them, and during the resulting confusion a second Russian force arrived and attacked from the side. Even though the Russians outnumbered their quarry by a factor of three, this must be called a tactically perfect victory for the Russians.

The Japanese force, threatened from the rear while retreating, was in a weak position from the first. The retreat itself was done by the book. First to fall back was the mountain gun corps, followed in turn by the field gun corps, then Lieutenant Colonel Takeshita Heisaku's Twelfth Reserve Infantry Regiment and, bringing up the rear, Lieutenant Colonel Uzawa Soshi's Forty-first Infantry Regiment, consisting of regulars. Though the retreat was faultless, the Russians' pursuit and attack was superb. Four regiments pounded Uzawa first. One went around behind him and cut off the main Yamada detachment, and another attacked the Japanese artillery and transport corps. It was a real drubbing.

The Yamada detachment was decimated in gruesome fighting. The Russian soldiers were pitiless in the extreme, stabbing and clubbing to death all the unarmed transport soldiers as well as the wounded. It could well be called a massacre.

In short, the battle of Shaho was peculiar. It never came to a proper end. But October 13 definitely marked the turning point. That was the fourth day after the Japanese forces began their united advance.

During this time, Kuropatkin's brain was working overtime. His misfortune was that the wheels in his brain spun so much faster than those of an ordinary person. "Where is the greatest danger now?" he would ask himself, concerned less with where pressure was being brought to bear on the enemy than with the peril facing his own troops. His considerable brainpower was not used much for calm judgments regarding the war situation, but revolved rather around this issue, which caused him much psychological pain. In the end, strategy and command are not clear-cut, but depend on a general's personality and psychology.

The Russians have generally been held to be a phlegmatic race. They were roundly criticized for this by Europeans and so acquired an inferiority complex. Kuropatkin's discernment and shrewdness put him in a class by himself. Before the war began, he was famous in court and military circles as a non-Russian Russian. Everyone in Russia believed him to be their finest general. You could say his fame grew directly out of the Russian inferiority complex.

On October 13, he decided to retreat. This was the same man who had declared to his army on the eve of battle, "Victory is assured." In his proclamation, he had also said, "The forces of the Manchurian Army are strong enough to begin forward movement. Nevertheless, you must remain unceasingly mindful of the victory to be gained over our strong and gallant foe. From the lowest to the highest, the firm determination must prevail to gain victory, whatever the sacrifice." Ironically, the most extreme reaction to those sacrifices came not from Kuropatkin's men, high or low, but from the general himself.

Kuropatkin's decision to retreat was brought about by the actions of Oku's army on the evening of October 12. Kuropatkin learned that Oku's army had surrounded the left flank of the western corps. General Bilderling, commander of the western corps, asked General Leonid Sobolev of the Sixth Siberian Army Corps to send reinforcements but was refused, and so he retreated. This opened a big breach between the western and eastern forces into which Kuroki's army poured with vigor enough to sever the Manchurian Army in two.

"This is a state of emergency!" Kuropatkin yelled, pounding his desk. The actions of Oku and Kuroki's armies did not come from any planned strategy. All the troops did was attack wholeheartedly. Kuropatkin was the sort of general who, in the confusion of battle, was always quick to acknowledge defeat.

In the end, the Russian "retreat" only amounted to ceding a small bit of territory in the north. The Manchurian Army upheld the honor of being the world's strongest military force by not crossing the Shaho to flee but halting on the river's south bank. Positioning one's troops with a river at their back is one of Sunzi's "desperate situations." Only a commander with the utmost faith in his troops would put them in such a dire situation.

The Japanese Army's push forward all the way to the Shaho on October 13, meanwhile, was a staggering feat. None of the troops slept that night. They mounted a continual, sleepless attack. "The Japanese Army's continual night assaults wore us out," wrote one Russian in his account of the battle. The Japanese troops did not attack just once that night, but again and again.

Oku's army made great strides forward on the thirteenth. Normally, after such a night, fighting would slacken in the morning, but, strangely, even after dawn on the fourteenth, the Japanese Army kept up its fierce attack without letup.

Kuropatkin came to the perfectly natural conclusion that the Japanese had plenty of reserves. It was military common sense that after an all-night advance, fresh troops would take over the next day. Kuropatkin assumed that the Japanese Army had brought in a huge supply of fresh troops to replace the battle-fatigued men at the front.

Understandable as this conclusion was, it was wrong. Men who had fought through the night without sleep or rest continued their onslaught at dawn. Reserves are an essential element in war strategy, the equivalent to pieces in hand (captured pieces that can be put back into play) in the chess-like game of shōgi. The value of reserve forces lies in being able to call up support in large numbers whenever it is tactically necessary. Kuropatkin assumed that Ōyama and Kodama had abundant reserves, but, in reality, they did not have a single soldier in reserve. They possessed no pieces in hand.

The game had to go forward with only the pieces on the board. Those being moved were ready to drop with fatigue. But, given the lack of replacements, nothing else could be done.

The Takashima battalion, part of the Third Division (from Nagoya) of Oku's army, advanced as far as the northern edge of the fort at Shaho, capturing fourteen enemy guns and several dozen caissons. But they advanced too far and were cut off without support.

No words can convey the fierceness of the Russian attack. Superior gunners surrounded the battalion on three sides and focused their firepower with a noise to split the heavens. To escape the bombardment, men dove into trenches. The landscape was transformed. Local houses were blown to bits, while trees, stripped clean of twigs and branches, turned into blackened poles. The Takashima battalion was not alone in getting battered. Every Japanese force in the area met the same fate.

What saved the Japanese Army was a torrential rain that began around four o'clock in the afternoon on the fourteenth, a deluge so epic that it seemed the heavens had tipped over. In the downpour, the Russians lost sight of their targets, and their cannon fire let up. The Japanese seized the chance to curl up in their trenches and grab some precious sleep.

*   *   *

Of all natural phenomena, none infringes so deeply on human affairs as rain. This is equally so on the battlefield. The deluge that started late in the afternoon of the fourteenth soaked the soldiers and their weapons, and by nightfall the fires of war were squelched. Knowing that the Russians would not keep up the fight in such heavy rain, the Japanese troops settled down to repair the ravages of sleepless fighting. Russian soldiers were no less exhausted. Moreover, having gone on the defensive in the latter half of the battle, the Russian line was in zigzag disarray and needed to regroup. Kuropatkin set about reorganizing his troops that night.

The Japanese also needed to dress ranks. Ōyama and Kodama issued orders that night to do so in preparation for the next advance. Some staff officers scoffed that General Headquarters didn't know the first thing about war. Now, when the Russian Army was reeling, was the time to deliver a knockout punch. This criticism was voiced with considerable conviction—but it was only idle criticism.

Suppose Ōyama and Kodama had had three fresh divisions at their disposal with plenty of ammunition on the side. Had they hurled those reserves at the Russian front on the night of the fourteenth, lighting into the exhausted soldiers, they might easily have driven them into the Shaho, a blow that would very likely have proved fatal.

Delivering a fatal blow was the one crucial thing that the Japanese Army had failed to do since the start of the war. Victory in war is impossible without delivering that fatal blow. With their backs to the river, the Russian troops were in an exceedingly vulnerable position, but the Japanese troops lacked the necessary reinforcements and ammunition to press their advantage. Their hands were tied.

On October 13 and 14, Ōyama climbed to the top of a hill in the village of Silitaizi to check on the battle's progress. On the evening of the fourteenth, he descended the hill in the pouring rain, turned to his chief of staff Kodama, and said, "Looks like a victory."

Kodama too could sense that momentum was on their side. Still, it was not a victory in the strictest sense of the word. There hadn't been such a victory since Jinzhou, Nanshan, and Liaoyang. In sword-fighting terms, the Japanese Army had lunged forward and, with only light wounds of its own, made a gash in the opponent's flesh. The opponent had merely stepped back, its strength undiminished. However big a step forward the army might have taken, the blow it delivered was far from a drastic, fatal stroke. Though wounded from head to toe, the enemy was still standing and had merely retreated a few steps. That was why Ōyama could only say, "Looks like a victory." The purpose of the battle of Shaho had been to defend by attacking, and the enemy had obligingly withdrawn, thus fulfilling the purpose of the battle. They had to content themselves with that.

Kodama spoke softly. "Shall we end it here, then?"

* * *

Japanese casualties at Shaho totaled 20,497—the equivalent of two full divisions. Russian casualties were even more horrific. Bodies of Russian soldiers abandoned on the battlefield numbered 13,333, and 709 men were taken prisoner. Russian casualties exceeded sixty thousand, but with its rich supply of reserves, the Russian Army was well able to recover. The Trans-Siberian Railway would soon apply balm to Russian wounds, in the form of nine trains bringing fresh troops daily. From that perspective, the Japanese Army's situation was desperate.

When the rain let up on October 16, fighting was still continuing on every front. Kodama sent a telegram to Yamagata Aritomo in Imperial Headquarters. He began by summing up the enemy's situation. "The enemy is still halted on the northern bank of the Hun River, dressing ranks. It appears they plan to switch to the offensive as soon as they are ready." He added, "Now is the optimal time to deliver another blow. For now, our troops have the advantage in both strength and morale." This was undoubtedly true, since they had just inflicted a loss of over sixty thousand men. "Alas, lack of ammunition prevents us from doing this. I deeply regret that there is nothing to do but hold the line, dig in, and wait for a fresh supply of ammunition."

"Message received," Yamagata instantly replied in his wire. "Re ammunition, I am exploring all avenues, including increasing production and purchasing from abroad. Despite utmost effort, to my extreme regret an ample supply cannot be quickly obtained. Recently at the prime minister's residence I stressed that no expense must be spared in procuring supplies for the armed forces, and not one cabinet member present disagreed. The administration is aware of the need. Unfortunately, supply capacity cannot be readily expanded."

The battle of Shaho petered out on October 18. The Russian Army retreated behind the Shaho and began to dig in, a ploy to gain time until it had regained its strength. On the twentieth, Manchurian Army headquarters ordered the Japanese Army to strengthen its defenses as well. The two armies ended up staring at each other from their respective trenches.

So began the celebrated "face-off at Shaho," but first the Japanese Army, known for its ferocious attacks, had to build solid field defenses. They entrenched, leaving a distance of only several hundred meters from the enemy at the closest point. In the end, they made a great trench line extending dozens of kilometers, with crisscrossing communication trenches between camps.

By November, there were already signs of winter in Manchuria. The two armies hunkered down and prepared for the winter ahead.

* * *

Following the battle of Shaho, men at the rear of the Japanese supply line were quick to sense that a winter lull was coming. They were the ones responsible for amassing foodstuffs and ammunition sent from the Japanese mainland, and getting them to the front. "With this little ammunition, there's no way the army can fight a war," they figured. "All they can do is dig a hole for the winter and crawl inside." The commissary in the rear had a better grasp of what was going on than did those at the front. They had no doubt that the war effort hinged on supply.

Akao Seiboku, the commissary general, realized that a vast amount of charcoal would be needed and so took steps to secure it, sending an army of merchants out to collect charcoal all across Manchuria and felling timber in the nearby hills to produce it locally. With the entire Japanese Army forced to camp outdoors in subzero temperatures, charcoal would be a life necessity. Ammunition might have been scarce, but charcoal was a different story. In short order, Akao assembled a vast amount, over 1,800,000 kilograms in all, in a pile over 6 meters high that looked from a distance like a Chinese-style wall.

Those in the rear were thus farseeing, whereas the chiefs of staff and commanders at the front were so involved in what was happening under their noses that they made no systematic plans for the winter. In the beginning, they dug only the usual firing trenches and counterguards. When November came, and they finally saw that this was going to be a contest of endurance, they tinkered with the trenches to make them winter-proof, and also constructed fortresses and other semi-permanent works. Communication trenches and tunnels were added later. By then, the grass had withered, the snow had turned to ice, and the ground was frozen solid a meter down, defying the soldiers' pickaxes. Still, the entire army was eventually able to burrow underground.

The battle of Shaho was basically called off for lack of ammunition. Yamagata Aritomo used the vague expression "years of halfhearted planning" as his excuse. In other words, from the first, the Japanese Army had suffered from a persistent systemic flaw, the lack of a basic concept of supply.

The standing army consisted of thirteen divisions, a fighting force of two hundred thousand men. Adding in the standby reservists, to be called up in time of war, made a total of three hundred thousand. This system of mobilization was, of course, borrowed from the West; headquarters always maintained this scale, even in time of peace. But they forgot one important thing: the need to manufacture sufficient ammunition in time of war. The navy did a far better job of understanding this need and preparing accordingly. During the war, they had ample production capacity.

What are we to make of this? It may be unbelievable, but from its very inception the Japanese Army suffered from what can only be called a total lack of common sense.

5

THE STORMING OF PORT ARTHUR

Meanwhile, the death struggle at the fortress in Port Arthur went on. General Nogi's Third Army followed their second all-out attack of September 19 with another on October 26. Both ended in wretched failure. Total casualties since the start of this battle numbered upwards of twenty thousand, an appalling figure.

This was no longer war, but disaster.

"We would like the focus of attack to be confined to 203-Meter Hill." The navy's messages took on a pleading tone. Capturing 203-Meter Hill would suffice, since all they still wanted was to look down on the harbor from the hilltop. The General Staff Office in Tokyo was well aware of this. Yamagata Aritomo, chief of the General Staff, understood perfectly.

The only dissent came from Nogi's on-site headquarters, which responded, "That will be unnecessary." They clung stubbornly to the same method of attack, lining up soldiers in front of the fortress and marching them relentlessly forward—thus sending vast numbers of their countrymen to meaningless deaths. Never before had incompetence at the helm caused a disaster of such proportions.

Voices calling for Nogi's dismissal were by now a concerted majority in Tokyo's Imperial Headquarters. Even Yamagata, Nogi's diehard supporter, concurred. But Nogi could not be removed without the approval of his direct superior, Commander in Chief Ōyama Iwao, who dismissed the proposal out of hand: "That would only have a harmful effect." The commander of an army was a symbolic figure, and switching commanders in mid-campaign would be detrimental to morale. Strategy and morale were the twin keys to victory.

Ōyama was adamant. "When there is a failure of strategy, staff should be prodded to deal with it. No personnel changes are called for. We will leave things in place and try another approach." Firing Nogi's chief of staff Ijichi would be simple enough, but that would only drive home to everyone in the Third Army, top to bottom, that he and Nogi were entirely to blame for the deaths of so many of their comrades. The army would be rocked, a general collapse of morale perhaps impossible to stave off. That was Ōyama's fear. By "try another approach," he meant sending Kodama Gentarō to Port Arthur, even though that wasn't his sphere, and having him take charge behind the scenes. That way, Nogi and Ijichi would not lose face and a collapse of morale could be prevented.

But Ōyama, taciturn by nature, did not spell out this plan in so many words. Besides, Kodama was embroiled in the ongoing battle at Shaho and could not be in two places at once. Knowing it was impossible to send Kodama to Port Arthur just yet, Ōyama bided his time.

No one in Ōyama's General Headquarters had faith in Nogi's abilities; in the obstinacy of his strategy, advisor Ijichi inspired universal loathing. There were dark murmurings. "Ōyama knows the pointless carnage at Port Arthur is Ijichi's doing, but still he doesn't dismiss him. It can only be because they're both from Satsuma."

* * *

Japan's army was running out of soldiers. Imperial Headquarters jealously guarded its few reserves on the mainland, the Seventh Division (Asahikawa) and Eighth Division (Hirosaki). While Russia had another million men in reserve, Japan had only these two divisions in the wings, numbering roughly thirty thousand men. This state of impoverishment was a crisis in itself. Such were the conditions of the Japanese Army in the summer of 1904, leading up to the battle of Liaoyang.

But every battle in Manchuria entailed immense bloodshed. Amid the chronic manpower shortage, it gradually became clear that further confrontation with the huge Russian force was impossible without sending over one of the two reserve divisions. Around July or August, opinion in Tokyo and Manchuria coalesced. "Send one division anyway." The problem was: send it where? To the main battleground on the Manchurian plains or to Port Arthur? Both were in flames.

Nogi's headquarters in Port Arthur wasted no words. "Just send us some men."

Imperial Headquarters couldn't decide what to do. Without resolving the issue, they mobilized the Eighth Division, concentrating the troops in Osaka to await orders. From there, the troops could board ship as soon as their orders came through.

The battlefields thirsted for fresh blood. Troop strength fell with every skirmish and so far had been bolstered with conscripts. The consensus regarding conscripted reserves was that they consisted of older, mostly married men who as fighters didn't hold a candle to the regulars. This was a fact. The Seventh and Eighth divisions, however, were made up of crack soldiers in active service.

"How can we possibly send those men to Port Arthur? The division is too precious to be ground up during a pointless campaign." Such was the unanimous sense at Imperial Headquarters. Nogi's headquarters wanted fresh blood without any adjustment in military tactics.

Nagaoka Gaishi called the idea "the height of folly." Though everyone may have agreed with this assessment, they still couldn't come to a decision. Imperial Headquarters continued to waver between the two alternatives, finally arriving at a highly irregular solution: let Emperor Meiji decide. This must have felt like drawing lots.

* * *

The Eighth Division, on standby in Osaka, consisted of men from the northern prefectures of Aomori, Iwate, Akita, and Yamagata. They assembled in Osaka in early September, their hearts heavy with apprehension. Would they be sent to Port Arthur? Troops ordered there suffered such a decline in morale that they were said to become like "sick sheep." This vaunted division, the strongest in the Japanese Army, was no exception.

Fortunately, the Eighth Division was spared the fate of Port Arthur. While they cooled their heels in Osaka, over a dozen communications flew back and forth between Imperial Headquarters and Kodama Gentarō, until finally Kodama agreed to abide by whatever Imperial Headquarters decided. Emperor Meiji's answer came down on September 27: "Send them north." Use the reserves on the Manchurian plains, in other words, not at Port Arthur.

The division commander was Lieutenant General Tatsumi Naobumi, a native of Kuwana (present-day Mie Prefecture), who, as an officer on the shogunal side in the Boshin War, gave considerable grief to Yamagata Aritomo, then head of the imperial forces. Tatsumi was a brilliant field commander, and people said that his coming to the battlefield would in itself give the army a great boost.

The soldiers were transported by sea from Osaka and arrived at the battlefield after the battle of Liaoyang. They just managed to participate in the final stages of the battle of Shaho, where their contribution figured decisively in the victory. Kodama sent Imperial Headquarters this highly unusual wire: "I am supremely grateful for the enlightened imperial decision."

In the meantime, Nogi's headquarters, that cancer eating away at the army, expressed displeasure that the Eighth Division had been sent north and made repeated requests for the Seventh Division. Once the Seventh Division was deployed, mainland reserves would be down to zero. "And, if we send those troops to Port Arthur, most will die in the first charge." This was Imperial Headquarters' fear.

September passed, and the end of October came. When the all-out attack on Port Arthur ended again in massive bloodshed and failure, replacements were, of course, needed—a need made all the more urgent by the Baltic Fleet's imminent approach. Even so, Imperial Headquarters continued to debate the appropriateness of sending the lone remaining standby division to Port Arthur. Lack of faith in the strategic brains in Nogi's headquarters was to blame for such waffling over a decision that ought to have been clear-cut. Weighed down with worry, Imperial Headquarters went round and round in circles.

* * *

Ijichi, of course, didn't attribute his repeated strategic failures to any flaw in his approach. He buttonholed every messenger from Tokyo to make his case that headquarters wouldn't provide the necessary ammunition. "The trouble is Imperial Headquarters."

This judgment was unfair. Imperial Headquarters had called a temporary halt to production of field guns and mountain guns in order to manufacture ammunition for siege guns. Kodama, who was then commanding a field operation, had personally approved the measure. Desperate for ammunition as he was, he had taken a broad view of the war situation and agreed that Port Arthur should have priority. Ijichi seemed incapable of similar objectivity. His continual habit of blaming his own mistakes on others, moreover, gave his character a somewhat effeminate tinge.

Ijichi's accusations eventually reached Yamagata's ears in Tokyo. Unable to let the matter pass, Yamagata fired off a lengthy message to Nogi.

> It has come to my attention that your chief of staff has made frequent statements attributing the lack of satisfactory progress in the attack on Port Arthur primarily to a shortage of ammunition. Stop and consider. Given the dearth of production facilities in our country, it should be evident that army commanders must content themselves with a small amount of ammunition. But, as the accompanying documents attest, by and large, we have sent all the ammunition you have requested. In order to get

ammunition to Port Arthur, everyone involved, from the prime minister on down, has labored night and day to come up with extraordinary measures, doing everything from increasing production to making purchases abroad. These efforts have resulted in a generous increase despite our straitened circumstances. For the chief of staff to make such claims not only harms military prestige and undermines morale in the siege army but is inimical to the interests of the chief of staff himself. He would have been better advised to discuss his opinion on the ammunition shortage before going overseas.

Before his assignment to the front, Ijichi had been inspector of field artillery in the Inspectorate General of Military Training. Though this was his area of expertise, he had been completely unaware of the situation until leaving the country. Yamagata pressed the point home: "How is it possible that he would become aware of the lack of ammunition and discuss it openly only after ordering a number of attacks?"

Then, perhaps fearing he had gone too far, he added a final comment: "Of course, I have only heard rumors of your chief of staff's imprudent remarks and have not verified the facts. But, if the rumors are true, be sure to chastise him thoroughly."

Although a man of high ideals who was hard on himself, General Nogi never raised his voice to his subordinates. He tended to do as Ijichi wanted. Even though Third Army headquarters was clearly so far to the rear that keeping up with the brutal fighting conditions at the front was impossible, Nogi made no attempt to move closer despite others' urging. The reason was that Ijichi had told him that farther to the rear, away from the din of gunfire, he could plan strategy better as he could hear himself think.

Nogi never said a word to Ijichi about Yamagata's blistering comments.

* * *

Here a digression. Kodama Gentarō's two main commanders were Major General Iguchi Shōgo and Colonel Matsukawa Toshitane. Iguchi, a Shizuoka man, was in the second graduating class of the Army Academy. An indifferent strategist, he was something of a critic and after the battle of Shaho dished out praise or censure to the various army staffs. He sent his comments to Nagaoka in a letter, the contents of which were highly inflammatory.

"The man is poison." This was his scathing denunciation of Fujii Shigeta, Kuroki's talented chief of staff and a man with a solid record of achievement. Fujii had a reputation for using ingenious machinations to oust subordinates he disliked. He also apparently attempted to hog credit for his subordinates' accomplishments. In short, although as chief of staff he was a man of rare ability, he was very much a man with the weak moral character generally found in those praised for their ability. War with Russia was a risky tightrope, wrote Iguchi, and having a man of this ilk in authority at such a time made a questionable contribution to army leadership. His criticism was couched in the most scathing terms. "Let him go on as he is, and there is no telling what sort of mischief he may get up to from selfish motives. He is a most virulent poison."

It makes sense that from Iguchi's perspective, a man with a razor-sharp mind like Fujii's would have seemed poisonous. As a critic, Iguchi was solid in his thinking. In opposing an offensive attack in the battle of Shaho, he showed his cautious and moderate temperament, which was incapable of flights of imagination. Indeed, after the war, he was unable to grasp the future shape of the army and quickly found himself outmoded as a strategist. For someone of Iguchi's plodding nature, Fujii's acrobatic mind and abilities would have stood out less for their virtues than for the dangerous traits hidden behind them.

Harsh as Iguchi was in his assessment of Fujii, he was even more emphatic in his denunciation of Nogi's chief of staff Ijichi Kōsuke, whom he referred to mockingly as "His Honor of the Third Army." He wanted Fujii and Ijichi consigned to oblivion. "Don't you have some way of getting rid of them?" He acknowledged that this would be hard to do. Though Fujii was from Hyōgo Prefecture and not in the Satsuma or Chōshū military clique, Iguchi wrote that he had proven skillful at earning the trust of his superiors— "a master of manipulation" was how he put it. Iguchi said of Ijichi, "Due to his relationship with Field Marshal Ōyama, I believe it would be difficult to take steps to get rid of him here in Manchurian Army headquarters."

In the midst of a hard-fought war, the pettiness of the world inhabited by these chiefs of staff was clear, due perhaps to the nature of their duties. Or perhaps the pettiness was a feature of the Japanese Army overall. The navy doesn't seem to have suffered from it very much.

* * *

Be that as it may, the Third Army at Port Arthur, its strategy in the hands of a chief of staff derided behind his back as a "superannuated anomaly," was engaged in a desperate struggle. At no other time in history did one man's brains and temperament go on causing disaster over such an extended period of time. In the meantime, the Russian Baltic Fleet, a continual source of terror to the entire nation of Japan, had set off from the Russian mainland.

Naval headquarters in Tokyo was busy working out what course to take should the fleet unluckily arrive before the fall of Port Arthur. The answer they came up with was invariably the same: Japan would lose the war.

Even under those circumstances, Tōgō's fleet would probably be victorious over the Baltic Fleet. "We can win all right." Navy Minister Yamamoto Gombei was unconcerned on that point. He had created the Japanese fleet for the express purpose of defeating the Russian fleet. Indeed, in the qualitative effectiveness of its fleet and the abilities of its seamen, Japan was leagues ahead of Russia. That was why Yamamoto Gombei was positive that the Japanese Navy would under no circumstances suffer a crushing defeat.

But in the case of the navy's overall strategy, just winning a victory wasn't enough. We must not forget that every last ship in the Baltic armada had to be sunk. If several of the enemy's huge warships survived and managed to find safe harbor at Port Arthur, sea transport of men and supplies would be endangered. Slowly but surely, the Japanese forces in Manchuria would lose. This probable outcome was as plain as day.

"Sink every last ship." Here lay the key to the grand design of winning the war. The trouble was, no naval battle in history had ever ended with an enemy armada being sent wholesale to the bottom of the sea. "Impossible or not, it's got to be done, or Japan cannot survive." This was Yamamoto Gombei's opinion. No mere argument or sophistry, his opinion was based on hard fact, like the answer to a math problem.

Once Yamamoto Gombei pointed this out, Yamagata Aritomo conceded that it made sense and offered encouragement to Ōyama and Kodama, who both understood the situation without being told. Like Yamamoto, they based their actions on a grand view of the war, following the identical thought process. But Nogi's headquarters, which was nominally under their command, was extremely insensitive to this grand strategy. Every staff meeting would end with the conclusion: "The navy is in too much of a hurry. We in the army have our own way of doing things"—thus dragging the discussion down from the level of grand strategy to a confrontation between the two branches of the military. That was why Nogi's headquarters kept rejecting the navy's persistent request for an attack on 203-Meter Hill.

But reality was marching on. The Baltic Fleet had begun its epic voyage.

* * *

Rear Admiral Rozhestvensky, commander of the Baltic Fleet, bore a considerable resemblance to Terauchi Masatake, army minister during the Russo-Japanese War. Neither man was imaginative; they both lacked the wits to try exercising their imaginations. They were methodical types, sticklers for administrative work who did all they could to keep things organized. They delighted in strict discipline and took inordinate interest in ferreting out disciplinary lapses among their subordinates. Temperamentally, both men were less military commanders than military police. On top of that, both were supremely secure in their positions and status. Rozhestvensky was the favorite of Tsar Nicholas II, and Terauchi was administrative head of the Chōshū faction headed by Yamagata Aritomo. Fortunately for Japan, Terauchi landed in the administrative position of army minister and had no say in strategy. Meanwhile, Rozhestvensky sped across the waves as head of a great fleet bound for a fateful encounter with Japan.

Originally an aide-de-camp to the tsar, Rozhestvensky had an unusual fixation on grandeur and spotless surroundings that had served him well in that ceremonial post. A headwaiter's job would have best suited his temperament. Nicholas II believed him to be Russia's ablest admiral, but the men who served under him privately disagreed. It seems to have been Count Witte, that enlightened Russian statesman, who first saw him for the fool he was.

At the start of the war, Rozhestvensky had the weighty office of acting chief of the Navy General Staff. It was a "weighty office" in Japanese terms. The Japanese Navy was a brand-new organization, highly streamlined and efficient, the division of duties clear-cut; the Japanese chief of the Navy General Staff was in charge of devising naval strategy, and his orders penetrated every corner of the navy. But the Russian nation and navy were highly antiquated in structure. For example, the Russian chief of the Navy General Staff had virtually no say over naval strategy in the Far East. Instead, Far Eastern viceroy Alexeyev, the tsar's favorite, did as he pleased.

During a court council at the start of hostilities, Rozhestvensky stressed the importance of inspecting every foreign commercial ship that entered the ports of European Russia. He refused to entertain any other opinion on the matter. His reasoning was that Japanese ships were sneaking into the ports disguised as foreign commercial ships. When Witte, who was present at the meeting, heard this, he thought, "This man is either an idiot or a coward." In his memoirs, he wrote, "I could only marvel at him."

* * *

The Baltic Fleet was established on April 30, 1904. What was until then called the "Pacific Fleet" consisted of the Far Eastern fleets based at Port Arthur and Vladivostok. As shown by the literal meaning of Vladivostok—"conquer the east"—Russia's naval presence in East Asia was for the purpose of intimidation, to aid in the invasion of China and Korea. The Pacific Fleet alone was comparable to the entire navy of any of the world's first-rate powers, but it was under continual pressure from Tōgō, and the death of its commanding officer Makarov dealt a heavy blow to Russian prestige.

But Russia still had its main fleet, and the decision was made to send this to the Far East. Warships in various waters around Europe were gathered together and newly organized on the Baltic Sea, and this was christened the Second Pacific Squadron—more familiarly known as the Baltic Fleet.

"You be commander in chief," the tsar told his favorite aide-de-camp, and so Rozhestvensky (who was also chief of the Navy General Staff) took the job. He threw himself wholeheartedly into the preparations, his days a crazy whirl of activity as he did everything from plan which warships to include and which to exclude, fit out the ships, and put the assembled fleet through maneuvers.

Rozhestvensky's talent was that of a government official, nothing more, but the man himself, who was possessed of a handsome and dignified appearance, didn't see it that way. He was confident that if he and the fleet in his command went to the Far East, they would emerge victorious. What lay at the bottom of that confidence was neither an accurate assessment of each side's fighting strength nor a winning strategy. Like the tsar who bestowed such favor on him and who referred to the Japanese even in official documents as macaques or "monkeys," he merely had a white man's sense of superiority. From the start, Rozhestvensky was convinced that white men could not possibly lose to members of an inferior race from an island country in the Far East.

Sending the Baltic Fleet to the Far East was an intrinsic element of the Russian grand strategy for the war. By dispatching the fleet to the seas near Japan, they could destroy the Japanese fleet, isolate the Japanese Army in Manchuria, and starve them out. This was the strategic significance of the move.

But would the strategy prove successful? Doubts floated about even within the navy and among the various cabinet ministers. There was the voyage to the Far East, to begin with. Not only was the distance involved a staggering 18,000 nautical miles, but also the fleet itself was of such monstrous size that refueling along the way posed an enormous challenge. Keeping up the men's morale was another consideration. In any case, a voyage by a fleet of such size was in itself a historic undertaking. Was it even possible? Naval experts were doubtful.

* * *

The strategic success of the voyage depended above all on arriving safely. There was also the question of whether the fleet could indeed win the coming battle. Here the Slavs showed their superiority to Japan's army leadership in the subsequent war against the United States. Many battle-ready Russian officers made the coolheaded judgment that victory was impossible. Captain

Nikolai Bukhvostov, the captain of the *Alexander III*, for example, predicted that half the fleet would be lost on the voyage due to mechanical problems or other reasons. This dire prediction did not come true. Rozhestvensky entered into the decisive battle with his full armada.

"Even if that doesn't happen," Bukhvostov went on, "the Japanese fleet will probably give us a licking. Their navy is better than ours, and the crews' abilities are very impressive."

Even though he was commander of a battleship in the fleet, Captain Bukhvostov made these remarks in a speech at a farewell party attended by civilians the evening before the fleet's departure. Leaving aside the question of whether or not his remarks were appropriate for that setting, Bukhvostov had the cool judgment of a true expert. Experts had verified the quality of the Japanese Navy each in his own area of expertise. Russian officers were strongly patriotic, however, and even the levelheaded Bukhvostov was second to none in that respect.

"We will never surrender," he concluded his speech. "That is our only resolve."

Let us get back to our story, and the debate over whether sending the Baltic Fleet to the Far East was the right thing to do. A majority felt that doing so would serve no purpose. "Everybody—not just experts, but anybody with the ability to think straight—could see that the operation was doomed," wrote Witte.

The final council to debate the issue was held on August 23, at Peterhof. On August 10, the Port Arthur Squadron had suffered grievous damage in the battle of the Yellow Sea. The better part of the squadron was destroyed by Tōgō, and the remaining ships fled back to the harbor at Port Arthur.

The tsar naturally attended the council. Everyone knew his opinion on the matter. He wanted to send the Baltic Fleet, and he was confident of victory.

A dazzling array of prominent people attended the council. Besides Grand Duke Alexei Aleksandrovich and Grand Duke Aleksandr Mikhailovich, there were Navy Minister Fyodor Avellan, War Minister Viktor Sakharov, Foreign Minister Vladimir Lamsdorf, and Zinovy Rozhestvensky. Every one of them masked their real feelings with a polite expression suitable to a court affair, but they didn't look happy.

* * *

This court conference would no doubt have bemused Japanese politicians of the day. Although most of those prominent figures privately thought that sending the fleet would mean Russia's defeat, no one spoke up and said so. Civilians and military officers alike worried more about the safety of their own positions and status in the bureaucracy than about the preservation of the nation. Any mention of defeat would put the tsar out of humor, and whoever offended the tsar was sure to be demoted in the end. Witte was not present because he had already been removed from office, but he wrote, "I had attended such conferences many times. Everyone present already either knew or surmised the tsar's intention regarding the topic under discussion and avoided going against it. Anyone whose opinion was at variance with His Majesty's held his tongue."

In an antiquated bureaucracy, everything works this way. Japan was not an imperial dictatorship when it took the illogical and unthinkable step of provoking war with the United States in 1941, but, at that time, its antiquarian bureaucracy was no less autocratic than that of tsarist Russia. In the face of the army's insistence, or bluster, about starting a war with the United States, everyone stayed quiet to save his own skin. Within the army bureaucracy, the few people of calm judgment were all demoted. As a result, the wildest, most fanatical opinion carried the day, and, by letting it pass, the others clung with relief to their personal safety.

In this case, the fanatic was Rozhestvensky himself. He met almost daily with the tsar in his twin roles as chief of the Navy General Staff and aide-de-camp. (This was how things worked in tsarist Russia. Sakharov also was both war minister and aide-de-camp. It boiled down to tsarist despotism.)

"What can we do to teach Japan a lesson?" the tsar asked.

Rozhestvensky fleshed out his idea of putting together a Second Pacific Squadron and sending it to the Far East. Its mission would be to send the Japanese Navy to the bottom of the sea and isolate Ōyama in Manchuria. He expressed no doubt about whether or not this fleet could win. To suggest that the Russian Imperial Navy was capable of defeat would have been disrespectful to the tsar and a serious breach of court etiquette. Besides, Rozhestvensky was convinced that the fleet would certainly sink every last Japanese ship.

He may have thought so because of his personality. Most of all, however, his conclusion had to do with his being chief of the Navy General Staff despite having no battle experience whatever—unbelievable as that may seem. Equally unbelievably, the greater part of his service in the navy had been shore duty; he had basically never served aboard an actual fleet. He had been chosen for his post based on his smart-looking appearance and his skill at making his way around court.

"Rozhestvensky, what do you think?" asked the tsar, last of all. He, of course, knew before asking what the rear admiral's answer would be.

* * *

"We can send the Japanese fleet to kingdom come." Rozhestvensky didn't actually say this in so many words. He may have wanted to, but extreme language and straightforward talk went against etiquette at the Russian court, where refinement came first. Rozhestvensky was second to none in his deference to the tsar in such matters.

"This grand expedition will be fraught with danger," he said. "But if Your Highness orders me to, I will lead it gladly and set off to do battle with Japan."

What did he really think? True enough, he had suggested that the tsar organize a Second Pacific Squadron to defeat the Japanese Fleet. This the tsar had done. All well and good—but Rozhestvensky may not have counted on being appointed commander in chief. When he first made the proposal back in spring 1904, inciting the tsar to action, he had been a mere rear admiral, far too lowly a rank for the command of such a great fleet.

Somebody else would do it. Based on that assumption, he may have promoted the plan as chief of the Navy General Staff with his usual knowing air, unconcerned about the consequences. There are signs that that was the case.

Russia was a big country with a huge population, and it possessed a great navy, yet, strange to say, compared with Japan it had far fewer admirals of real value. Still, the shortage was not so desperate that a rear admiral had to be made commander in chief. There were admirals, not to mention veteran vice admirals ready for promotion. But the tsar's favor centered on Rozhestvensky because he was "clever and stylish." For this same reason, he had favored and made much of Kuropatkin in the army.

An inferiority complex vis-à-vis the West made Russians perceive themselves as dull-witted, coarse, and slovenly. Overall, they saw themselves as semi-Asiatic, and they were hypersensitive to the fact that Westerners saw them that way too. The Russian court was afflicted by a congenital sense of inferiority dating back to the time of Peter the Great. Much was made of officials with a preponderance of German blood. Among those of Slavic ancestry, anyone with European-style agility of character and mind was habitually valued above his ability.

This was true of Rozhestvensky, who deliberately showed off his "European" mental quickness to ingratiate himself at court. As a result, an idea took root in the tsar's mind: Rozhestvensky would pull off a victory. The seed of that idea was planted by Rozhestvensky himself.

* * *

The Baltic Fleet collected at the port of Liepaja on the Baltic Sea before setting off on its grand voyage. Witte referred to Liepaja bitterly as a "cursed port." Before the outbreak of the Russo-Japanese War, opinion in the Russian government and navy had split down the middle over whether or not to construct a port there.

On the face of it, there could be no better site for a port. Russia was a continental country with few coastal areas suitable for the construction of seaports. Those it did have mostly froze over in the winter. Even Kronstadt, the main port charged with protection of the Russian capital of St. Petersburg, was icebound three to five months of the year. As the country expanded, the desire for ice-free ports grew hot enough to give off black smoke. To be sure, there were some in the Black Sea, and, in the Far East, Russia had possession of the harbor at Port Arthur. Still, a commercial and military harbor near St. Petersburg, the heart of European Russia, was wanting. Liepaja filled the bill. A port there could remain operational all winter long.

But Witte, along with certain elements of the Russian Navy, opposed the idea because of the narrowness of the channel. As they saw it, as soon as war broke out, the enemy would blockade the harbor, rendering it useless. The Russians habitually looked at things in a negative light. For this reason, a majority felt that, rather than Liepaja, Murmansk, located on Kola Bay, would make a better naval base. Witte sided with this opinion.

The debate between these two plans had surfaced in the last years of the reign of the former tsar, Alexander III. On his deathbed, he told his aides, "I want to choose Murmansk," but died soon afterward with the matter unresolved. Then, when his successor, the ruling Nicholas II, took the throne, he lost no time in issuing an order to build a naval base at Liepaja. Oddly enough, he did so in the name of the previous tsar, who he claimed had supported that plan. He even announced that the commercial harbor would be named Liepaja, the military one, "Port Alexander III." Witte surmised that one of his aides must have deceived the tsar.

This was how construction of a great Russian naval base at Liepaja got underway. The budget for the project was gigantic, earning the new facility the moniker "Money-gobbling Harbor."

Before war broke out, Hirose Takeo had toured the harbor. Afterward, he sent Tokyo a detailed report, with sketches, as "secret information." At the time of his visit, the port was still under construction, and, even when the Baltic Fleet assembled there, it remained unfinished.

"Liepaja is dangerous because it's ice-free." Some members of the Russian Navy were actually of this opinion, Hirose wrote. They reasoned that if ships were docked at a port where the sea was frozen then the enemy couldn't attack, so the Russian fleet would be safe. Hirose was surprised by the morbid intensity of Russia's defensive mindset. For that matter, Witte's opinion was not all that different. He cursed Liepaja, going so far as to say that constructing a warm-water port on the Baltic Sea was what had led Russia to do a damn fool thing like sending the Baltic Fleet to the Far East in the first place. In his opinion, Russia had no business embarking on any such costly and risky military adventure, and he blamed the existence of a warm-water port for making it possible.

* * *

The name of the battleship *Oryol*, one of the newest and largest ships in the Russian fleet, means "Eagle."

"I was a seaman aboard the warship *Oryol*," wrote Alexei Novikov-Priboy in the preface to his book *Tsushima*. He participated in the battle of Tsushima, though still a young seaman at the time. A ship of the same type as Rozhestvensky's flagship *Prince Suvorov*, the *Oryol* was first anchored in Kronstadt, where there was a naval station, but was later sent to the harbor at Liepaja, which was to become a sad memorial for Russia. "The buildings, factory chimneys, and giant cranes of the military harbor were all wrapped in fog," Novikov-Priboy wrote of the ship's entrance into the harbor.

Due to the flow of fresh water from nearly two hundred rivers, the water in the Baltic Sea is not very saline. Effectively sealed off by the embrace of the mammoth Scandinavian Peninsula, the sea is covered with heavy fog in spring and autumn. It was not an easy body of water for the crews to navigate. Liepaja Harbor was just then being enlarged, and in the scene before the men's eyes everything was under construction. The *Oryol* slipped inside the enormous stone breakwater with its fellow ships and dropped anchor.

In the eyes of Novikov-Priboy, who had until then sailed cruisers, the imposing appearance of this ship was magnificent. Generally regarded as the world's finest battleship, it was one of a set of four of the same class. The others were *Suvorov*, *Borodino*, and *Alexander III*, all with a displacement of 13,516 tons.

"Russia's existence and glory depend on its military," Witte had maintained. "If Russia should suffer a military defeat, that would spell the end of Russian existence and Russian glory." It was up to these four battleships, the world's biggest and newest, to protect the glory of the Russian Empire. They formed the nucleus of the Baltic Fleet. In addition, there were three other battleships, eight cruisers, nine destroyers, and six special service ships. Together, these made up the Second Pacific Squadron. Later, they would be joined by the Third Pacific Squadron (one battleship, one cruiser, three coast defense ships) to form the official Baltic Fleet, but at this point the Third Pacific Squadron had not yet been formed.

The hills above the harbor at Liepaja were already dusted with snow. Rozhestvensky was already aboard the *Suvorov*, which he had boarded in

Kronstadt. The day after leaving Kronstadt, the ship entered the port at Reval, which the Russians had once pillaged, and anchored there for a while. After a short time (about a month), the tsar came to inspect the fleet, visiting each ship in turn. When finally he came on the deck of the *Oryol* and addressed the seamen, he seemed worn out, his voice flat. He called on them to "destroy the insolent Japanese who have troubled the peace of Holy Russia." The tsar was a small man. Behind him, the towering figure of Rozhestvensky, resplendent in his full-dress uniform with golden epaulets, looked all the more imposing.

* * *

The Baltic Fleet departed Liepaja on October 15, setting out on its long, long voyage. First to leave at nine o'clock in the morning and puffing enormous clouds of black smoke was the cruiser *Almaz*. On the dock, a military band played while a crowd of spectators cheered. The *Suvorov* began to move out at noon.

Everything was done in the solemn Russian style. On the eve of departure, prayers for a safe crossing had been held on the *Suvorov* and on the other ships as well. The flag of St. Andrew, the Russian naval ensign, fluttered on every ship. The weather was glorious. The Baltic Sea was a deep ultramarine, as smooth as smooth could be.

"I don't believe in the success of this fleet." These words were written in the journal of Engineer Evgeny Politovsky, a shipbuilder on the *Suvorov*. Politovsky was an able construction engineer, and this was his first cruise. Normally, he worked in the St. Petersburg naval yard constructing warships, but, just when the Baltic Fleet was set to leave for the Far East, all of a sudden he was ordered aboard. The only way to keep this historic voyage of 18,000 nautical miles from ending in dismal failure was to pluck a shipwright from his peaceful workplace and take him along. There was no telling what repairs might become necessary, and they would have to be carried out while the ships were in motion—a daunting feat. Divers would be needed at times, and on occasion the engineer himself would have to don diving gear and go underwater. Politovsky was the right man for the job. Still only thirty, he knew more than anyone about the structure of battleships like the *Suvorov*.

He left a young wife at home. From the first, he was desperately unhappy, writing to her that he was "utterly disappointed in this fleet." He knew the quality of the men around him. Neither the gunners nor the firemen had any engineering ability to speak of. He knew too how the long haul ahead—18,000 nautical miles, a ridiculously long journey from an engineer's perspective—would adversely affect the ships' capabilities. Above all, he was skeptical as to whether morale could be maintained during a voyage so long. Anti-imperialist sentiment was spreading already among Russian workers and sailors, as he knew better than anyone. They would be lucky if no rebellion broke out before they reached the theater of war.

"I can only feel assured that no one can escape his fate," Politovsky wrote. "Should I live to return home, I will tell you all." During the journey, he was kept extremely busy repairing damage and performed his duties admirably. But he was never to return home to his wife. On the Sea of Japan, he was killed by a Japanese shell.

* * *

"He may be a terrible coward."

This character flaw, which Witte observed in Rozhestvensky, may well have rendered the man the least fit to command such a large fleet. From the time they left Liepaja, not only Rozhestvensky but the men under him too were possessed by a delusion. The rumor was that a squadron of Japanese destroyers was lurking in the Denmark Strait to ambush them. The idea was patently ridiculous, as a cursory look at Japanese naval strength would have shown. Was it even possible to send destroyers weighing barely 200 or 300 tons all the way to the North Sea in Europe? That would have necessitated taking along an auxiliary ship for repairs, as well as a couple of protected cruisers. Japan didn't have that kind of strength.

But even before engaging the enemy, the Baltic Fleet was dominated by fear of Japan. If anyone could pull off such a feat, they felt, it was Japan. Above all, Rozhestvensky himself was convinced of this. He and his aides had no doubt that at the very least Japan must have laid mines in the Baltic Strait along the southern tip of Sweden.

The fleet's speed was 8 knots.

On the evening of their second day out, as they neared the suspected danger zone, Rozhestvensky gave orders to prepare for combat and instructed everyone to sleep with their clothes on. All the ships' guns were readied for firing on an instant's notice.

Speculation was rife, but, on the seventeenth, they arrived safely at Denmark's Langeland Island and dropped anchor. Still, they couldn't let up their guard. The danger of Japanese torpedoes or mines wouldn't end until they had squeezed through the narrow strait, leaving the Baltic Sea behind and entering open sea. That at least was Rozhestvensky's judgment.

His judgment may not have been entirely a cowardly delusion. Even the Danish Navy sensed danger, sending a cruiser and a torpedo boat out in the open sea off Langeland Island where the Baltic Fleet lay at anchor, wary lest the Japanese Navy adopt the outlandish strategy of attacking the anchorage of a neutral country.

The following day, October 18, the fleet stayed at anchor. The above-mentioned journal of Engineer Politovsky consisted of letters to his wife, and every time the fleet dropped anchor like this he would go ashore and send a letter home. On the eighteenth, Rozhestvensky received a wire from the tsar making him vice admiral.

Already, only three days out of Liepaja, ships were breaking down one after another. The destroyer *Bystry* collided with the battleship *Oslyabya*, opening a great gash in its own side. The cruiser *Zhemchug*'s steam launch was damaged, and the bow of the destroyer *Bravy* was smashed, so that it took on some water. Repairs had to be carried out every time the fleet was at anchor, giving rise to qualms over the long ocean crossing ahead.

* * *

"Japanese torpedo boats are lurking in the North Sea."

The fleet was plagued by this terrifying yet utterly absurd delusion. No one laughed at the notion. Nobody knows who spread this delusion through the fleet. The probable source of the rumor was the Russian naval command in St. Petersburg. The Russian Empire's strategic center, which should have been cool rationality, believed it possible. Rozhestvensky himself, having transferred to the fleet from a building in naval headquarters, was a believer.

This incident alone disqualified him from commanding so vast a fleet. Even assuming that the delusion running riot among the men was not of his personal making, as commander, he was the one who should have quashed it. That was the minimum duty of a commander in chief. Uniting men's minds, raising their fighting spirit, eliminating all trace of defeatism—these were the abilities and the actions that the nation expected and demanded from its military leadership. Strategy could be left in the hands of staff officers.

"If we start to lose the war, I will take command." These words of Ōyama Iwao, the commander in chief of the Manchurian Army, epitomize the nature of top leadership. The commander's job is to purge the military of mass fear, delusions, and defeatism. In that sense, Nogi Maresuke's leadership deserves full marks. That the troops attacking Port Arthur never succumbed to mass defeatism despite their resounding losses owed in large measure to his powers of leadership.

Rozhestvensky himself suffered from defeatism.

"I am not a coward." So he may have declared, but whatever his personality traits, he was a leader who sowed panic in the entire fleet. Barely three days out of Liepaja, he issued orders so incomprehensible that they seem designed for the sole purpose of fomenting panic. "Everyone sleep in your clothes. All ships be ready to fire at a moment's notice." His actions at that point were not those of a commander but rather of someone out to create chaos.

In the military, the supreme command has access to the greatest amount of information. All the rest, from junior officers down, are merely laborers at their respective posts, not privy to information. Informing subordinates is actually undesirable in a military situation, so that they have no choice but to trust their superiors. In psychological terms, a millimeter of oscillation in the top command predictably expands in amplitude to a meter of oscillation below. Rozhestvensky's shivers naturally created a mood of what can only be called blind panic.

*　*　*

This expeditionary fleet of a scale unmatched in history saw Denmark's northern tip, Cape Skagen, on October 20, six days out from Liepaja. The entire fleet anchored off the cape, and coaling got underway. For the crews, this was backbreaking labor.

The skies were clear. At three in the afternoon, a Swedish steamboat drew near and signaled that it had an "important communication." This was a steamboat employed by Russian intelligence, bearing important information. Rozhestvensky took the message, which turned out to be vague. "A three-masted schooner has set sail from an inlet. Highly suspicious."

"It must be a Japanese spy ship, gone out to inform a flotilla of torpedo boats lying in ambush somewhere." Rozhestvensky's imagination was wilder than that of any writer of fiction. The idea that Japanese torpedo boats would be lurking in the North Sea was unrealistic, but even if it were true, they would hardly use a sailing vessel to convey an urgent message. Rozhestvensky's imagination wasn't grounded strongly in reality. He possessed great pride, but it's possible that excessive pride derives from morbid fear.

As a military man, he should have kept his fears locked in the privacy of his own mind. Susceptibility to fear isn't necessarily a disgrace in the armed forces. Down the ages, many of the greatest generals and strategists have had that trait. Human inventiveness arises less from brave spirits than from spirits subject to great fear. But the greatest generals in history kept their fear to themselves, not letting even their closest subordinates know. That may be the secret of successful high command.

Rozhestvensky did just the opposite, putting his fear on display to the entire fleet by staging a show. He issued orders that all gun muzzles be turned on every passing ship. The fleet was not out on distant seas, but was approaching the North Sea, which thronged with traffic. The North Sea is bounded by the coastlines of Norway, Denmark, Germany, and England. Commercial fishing boats of each of those countries were sure to pass in the vicinity of that great fleet of imperial Russia. Every time one did, the fleet's warships were to reposition their guns and train their sights on it. The idea was sheer madness.

Or, rather, it was perhaps something like a psychological warm-up exercise meant to induce madness. If anyone had cared to conduct an experiment in instilling an entire fighting force with mass terror, this method of Rozhestvensky's would have been just the way to go about it.

"Everybody's nerves were keyed up." So wrote Engineer Politovsky.

* * *

Could Rozhestvensky defeat Tōgō? Some of the seamen in the Baltic Fleet were already beginning to worry. From the first, the name "Tōgō" was well known to the Russian Navy as belonging to the supreme commander of the Japanese Combined Fleet, but of the man himself no one knew anything at all. Even in the top naval countries of Europe, people wondered what sort of fellow he was and what his strengths were. Japanese seamen too had no way of knowing anything about a man who until the outbreak of war had kept a low profile as port admiral. In comparison, Rozhestvensky was rather well known internationally from his treatises on the art of gunnery.

But at issue was each man's ability as commander in chief. What's funny about military men is that they always want their leader to be someone of powers so outstanding as to be mystical, and, when they believe that he is such a man, they want to place a kind of religious faith in him. When all the troops share that same faith, then and only then is the high command a success.

Ever since the war began, Tōgō had increasingly been inspiring that sort of mystical faith in his men. In particular, he had gained the greatest trust of his closest aides, commanders, and ship captains during an episode we have already described, when the two great battleships, the *Hatsuse* and the *Yashima*, were lost at once when they hit Russian mines on May 15 of that year. The Combined Fleet lost thirty-three percent of its battle capability in that single day. Everyone had assumed that all hope of winning was gone.

But Tōgō never batted an eyelash. The British naval captain William C. Pakenham was aboard the battleship *Asahi* as an observer, and he soon met with Tōgō to offer condolences for the devastating loss that might determine the fate of the Japanese nation. Tōgō thanked him with a calm smile. Years later, when Pakenham met with Akiyama Saneyuki, he reminisced. "Never did I sense the greatness of the human spirit so strongly as I did then." By suppressing the intensity of his inner turmoil, Tōgō succeeded brilliantly in preventing the fleet from succumbing to pessimism.

But Rozhestvensky took his personal fear as the script for a show he staged using the entire fleet. They were about to enter the North Sea. The crews were sleepless, on the lookout for phantom Japanese torpedo boats. Every gun was loaded, and every gun barrel swung in unison, following each new craft that came along. "Even if we came upon a small lighter, our destroyer went off after it like blazes," recorded one witness.

* * *

In this drama of fear, tension ratcheted up at every step. The alarming news that Japanese torpedo boats were in the vicinity made the fleet quickly weigh anchor and enter the North Sea. That night there was a dense fog, as thick as mud. As the fleet pushed on through the murky fog, each ship in turn sounded its foghorn to prevent collisions. Depending on the ship, this sounded like the bellow of a giant, the strangled sob of a young girl, or even the spirited shriek of a madwoman. The sounds heightened everyone's fear.

The wireless communication system that enabled ships to trade information served to intensify the climate of fear all the more. Out of an abundance of caution, every ship sent out a stream of messages, reporting weird goings-on that were mere hallucinations, churning out unsubstantiated reports as if they were pelting each other with stones.

When the sun rose on the morning of October 21, the fog had lifted. At last able to verify the state of their fleet with their own eyes, the men felt relieved. Some whispered their fear of the night to come. Rumor had it that one of the captains had gone insane.

Night fell. Ever since evening, the wind and waves had been high. The fleet steamed ahead, washed broadside by waves. Before nine o'clock, a shocking radio message came in, piercing the men's hearts. "We are being chased by Japanese torpedo boats."

The message was from the *Kamchatka*, the repair ship. Named for the peninsula that the Russian Empire had annexed in 1707, the little boat was loaded with equipment, shipbuilders, and engineers to carry out repairs as needed on the rest of the fleet. The *Kamchatka* belonged to the First Cruiser Division in the van of the fleet but had been slowed by engine trouble and so lagged behind, bringing up the rear all alone. This must have inflamed the crew's terror all the more.

The *Suvorov* was steaming through wind and waves when the *Kamchatka*'s startling report came in, spurring Rozhestvensky to an immediate response. He ordered all battleships cleared for action and instructed the *Kamchatka* to keep him fully informed. Russian radio equipment was strikingly inferior to the domestically made equipment of the Japanese Navy. Nevertheless, the radio operator kept up a strenuous tapping and got the message through. The reply that came in was way off the mark, a fact attributable less to the state of the equipment than to the psychological stress of the *Kamchatka*'s captain.

"They are coming at us from all directions," he reported. Asked how many enemy ships there were, he replied, "Eight torpedo boats."

Rozhestvensky never doubted it. A moment's calm reflection would have shown him how preposterous the claim was. Even if Japan had somehow managed to send a squadron of torpedo boats all the way to the North Sea in Europe, why deploy it against a mere repair ship? Why surround that ship with eight boats and attack it from all sides?

At the end of his exchanges with the *Kamchatka*, Rozhestvensky advised the repair ship to change course and get out of the path of danger. "When you have evaded the enemy, advise us of your longitude and latitude, as well as your course."

But the *Kamchatka*'s response was: "Afraid to reveal." They feared the worst if enemy torpedo boats overheard them radioing in their position.

Time passed.

At eleven o'clock at night, the *Suvorov* again sent out a wireless message. "What is happening? Do you still see Japanese torpedo boats?" The radio waves flew through wind and rain, but no immediate response came from the *Kamchatka*.

Rozhestvensky went into a fury. "Damned cowards!"

At length, there came a chastened reply. "No sign of them."

Rozhestvensky was relieved. He should have let the matter rest, but his overactive imagination lit up the dark North Sea bright as day. In the world of his imagination, eight Japanese torpedo boats were coming after the Baltic Fleet, plowing through the waves. He gave the order to prepare for action. His move was based on peculiar reasoning: "*Kamchatka* reports no sign of the enemy. That just goes to show the enemy has given up on the *Kamchatka* and is coming after the battleships." If there is a mental disposition that sees things only through the prism of fear, then Rozhestvensky's disposition may well belong in that category.

Time ticked away, and the great fleet steamed uneventfully on across the dark North Sea

But the seamen in the fleet hunched sleepless at their posts. Novikov-Priboy wrote that although it was permissible for some crew members to sleep, few if any did. The captain's psychology of fear had infected his entire fleet.

In the dead of night, rain came riding on the wind. "If only there was a moon!" The men cursed the weather. They were exhausted from fighting with their own imaginations in the pitch dark.

* * *

The fleet was steaming across the shallow North Sea. Formerly a plain, the land subsided in the diluvial epoch and became sea. In roughly the center of the sea is a vast shallow area known as Dogger Bank, a mere 11 meters deep at its shallowest point. The entire bank is a prime breeding ground for fish, teeming with cod, herring, flatfish, and flounder.

The Baltic Fleet commander should have known that the fleet was approaching Dogger Bank. Among sailors, it was common knowledge that fishing boats from Britain and other countries clustered there year-round, hard at work; Rozhestvensky should have foreseen that fishing boats would be out in large numbers even at night. Had this information, known to every sailor in Europe, been available to him and his aides as they assessed the situation, the great panic that they eventually unleashed might never have taken place.

Shortly after one in the morning, a tricolor signal flare went up in front of the *Suvorov*. After the war, a survey to determine which British fishing vessel had sent up the signal flare concluded that no signal had ever been released. In any case, the fleet was in an abnormally heightened state of nerves, and so the point was never clarified. What is clear is that the *Suvorov*, with Rozhestvensky aboard, turned on its searchlight to sweep the darkness. Given everyone's state of mind at the time, this was equivalent to an order to start fighting. The captain of every warship must have gasped in surprise. Aboard the *Suvorov*, the bugle call to prepare for action rang out. Rozhestvensky issued battle orders to the entire fleet.

Their opponents were trawlers. The searchlight caught a single-funnel fishing boat in a light so bright that "the red- and black-painted hull stood out clearly," wrote the *Suvorov*'s ship engineer Politovsky. It was a British fishing boat. The fleet as a whole, however, mistook it for a Japanese torpedo boat and let fly a thunderous cannonade.

"At the time I was on the fore bridge," wrote Politovsky to his wife, "but my ears were so deafened by the roar of the cannons and my eyes so blinded by the gunfire that I could not stand it and bolted below, hands over my ears, to watch the spectacle from the upper deck."

The mad party began.

Every warship in the fleet switched on its searchlight and frantically began firing its guns. Every time a cannon went off, the heavy air over the North Sea was rent in two and flashes of light slashed the darkness. It wasn't just one or two Japanese torpedo boats (actually British trawlers) that the Baltic Fleet set upon. The more quickly the searchlight crews worked, the more vessels they were able to locate. There was no lack of targets.

At some point, a cluster of fishing boats found itself hemmed in by the armada. The first boat that had been subjected to volley after volley of fire from the *Suvorov* made no effort to escape for some reason and just stayed put, cowering like a small forest animal waiting for a storm to blow over. There was no sign of anyone on board.

The one bit of good fortune for the trawlers was that the Russian gunners were poor marksmen. Had even one shell scored a direct hit, its target would surely have been blown to splinters, but mostly they landed harmlessly in the sea, sending up monster clouds of spray. The smaller shells were more successful. Every time one hit its mark, a chorus of huzzahs went up from some ships.

The fleet steamed straight ahead. Some fishing boats flipped over like newts, exposing red bellies, while two or three others were on fire. Determined to sink them, the fleet kept shining its searchlights and never let up on the attack.

Although some eyewitnesses may have reported, "No sign of anyone on board," others described seeing people run around on the narrow decks in a vain attempt to flee, waving their arms up and down in entreaty. The sight of the fishing crews' hapless confusion made some Russian sailors chortle. "The Japanese Navy is weak!" In this "war theater" built on a grand illusion, there was no compassion for the "enemy." The fishermen were unable to jump into the sea, which was boiling under the bombardment. Anyone foolish enough to jump in would have been instantly ripped to pieces.

The "battle" continued for a dozen minutes, and then one of the ships located another supposed enemy: "Japanese armored cruiser sighted." And so the *Aurora* (6,731 tons), a member of the Russian First Cruiser Division, came under concentrated friendly fire. Many of the shells scored bull's-eyes. By the time the *Aurora* radioed in the plaintive message "We are hit," the damage was done. There were four perforations above the waterline, the funnel was shot off, the chaplain had lost a leg, and the chief gunner was wounded.

By then, Rozhestvensky had realized the strangeness of this naval "combat" and issued a ceasefire, but the noncommissioned officers and crew manning the guns, too excited to control themselves, kept right on shooting. It was a long time before the sea regained its serenity.

* * *

"How humiliating!" Engineer Politovsky wrote to his wife back home. "We made fools of ourselves before the whole world." True enough, the madness of this incident set the world laughing at the Baltic Fleet. But to Britain, the victim of the attack, there was nothing funny about it.

Twenty-one fishing vessels, counting only those whose names are known, had been working that night in the shallows of Dogger Bank, the scene of the nightmarish incident. When the sun rose, the extent of the damage gradually became clear. As they returned to Hull, their base on England's east coast, the fishermen cursed. "Damn Russians ripped into us like a pack of mad dogs and then lit out." Some boats had gone down, others had as many as sixteen holes in their hulls. One boat brought back the decapitated bodies of its captain and chief engineer. Others limped into port, barely afloat.

British public opinion took a hard line. Parliament and newspapers dubbed the fleet the "Mad Dog Squadron." The unprovoked brutality of the Russians' attack on peaceful fishing vessels was bad enough, but still more despicable, went the argument, was the way the Russians had gone off and abandoned their victims without any offer of help. In that age, the nation was the wellspring of value and honor. Britain responded quickly to the "humiliation and brutality" inflicted on its citizens.

The British government issued standby orders to the navy. Not only that, the Russian ambassador, Count Aleksandr Benkendorf, was issued a warning. "Until the issue is resolved, the Baltic Fleet's progress across the North Sea must be halted. If the fleet insists on proceeding, please understand that Britain will enter into a state of war with Russia one week from now."

Foreign diplomacy in that era was backed by military power. The British government not only issued a warning but also instructed two of its own fleets, the Channel Fleet and the Mediterranean Fleet, to be ready for action. Behind this overly harsh response lay, needless to say, the Anglo-Japanese Alliance.

The stance of the British government, Parliament, and the leading newspapers gave the impression that war with Russia might break out at any moment, even though war was not in Britain's interest. The sort of machismo that refused to back down from the possibility of war was a source of diplomatic energy in that era.

Several factors mitigated against war. First and foremost were the alliances. At that time, France was allied with Russia and also had established an Entente Cordiale with Britain. The French government was quick to appeal to the governments of Britain and Russia, declaring its willingness to take on the role of peacemaker. The squabbling countries accepted the offer. Britain's brand of fighting diplomacy counted on the appearance of such a mediator to keep the peace.

* * *

Amid this international ruckus, the Baltic Fleet continued to steam south.

The British press and news agencies began by calling the fleet a mad dog and ended by branding it "piratical." The press insisted that the fleet be halted and detained, and that commander Rozhestvensky and his staff be sent packing. The drubbing they received in the press was extremely unfortunate for Rozhestvensky and the fleet, who certainly had no piratical intent when they did what they did. In the darkness, the crews had simply fallen prey to ungovernable fear, and neither Rozhestvensky nor his staff had been able to bring them under control.

The Russians hated the British and, when reviling them for their cunning, called their country "Perfidious Albion." At noon on the day after the unfortunate incident of firing on fishing boats, the Baltic Fleet passed through the English Channel. The sea was covered with fog, the British mainland invisible.

"This black-hearted land." Engineer Politovsky, a devoted husband, wrote those words to his wife while looking toward Britain from the deck of the *Suvorov*.

Though the fleet was reviled as the "Pirate Squadron" or "Mad Dog Squadron," its crews were human. Many different kinds of birds flew across the English Channel. On spotting the great warships, they would alight on their masts and turrets or rest in the shade of their funnels to ease the fatigue of flight. Some were too exhausted to fly away when anyone approached. The seamen gave the birds water and food before setting them free again.

Rozhestvensky was as quick as ever to berate his men for less than crisp salutes or appearance, but overall the mood of the fleet was somber, the sense of mortification deep.

Ever since leaving the Russian port of Liepaja, the fleet had yet to put in at any port. During the six days since the Dogger Bank affair, they had steamed on nonstop. There were internal rumors that they might stop at the port of Brest, France, but instead they passed it by. Then it was whispered that they were going to cross over the Bay of Biscay without stopping, and they did. The great bay, which lies along the northern coast of Spain and the western coast of France, was unpopular with sailors. The weather there was unpredictable, and, once it turned stormy, the crossing was extremely heavy going.

Fortunately, they had good weather. The problem was rather that, since they stayed at sea, they were unaware of the world's reaction to their blunder. Rozhestvensky himself was blithe to his aides. "Nothing much will come of it."

* * *

The ill-starred fleet first stopped to rest at the Spanish port of Vigo.

They were greeted by a cluster of rocks on the western coast of Spain, lit by the morning sun. The area had a jagged ria coastline, and the port was narrow and deep, geographically suitable to accommodate a large fleet. High mountains surrounded Vigo, and along the narrow coast was a scattering of fishing villages.

Vigo was a major fishing port. An old castle nestled at the foot of a mountain, and here and there in the mountains modern fortifications had been constructed, each flying the Spanish flag in a corner.

The Baltic Fleet fired off a gun salute in honor of the Spanish national flag. Clouds of smoke went up, and the hills rang with the sound of gunfire. The Spanish fortress guns returned the salute. The Russian crew looked forward to recuperating at Vigo, but British and French newspapers brought to them made clear that this was a vain hope. They learned that their action of firing on unarmed British trawlers in Dogger Bank and then steaming on their way had become hot news around the globe. The British government and Parliament were taking an extremely hard line, even calling the British Navy into play. They also learned that the Russian capital of St. Petersburg was receiving heated protests from Britain, which was demanding that the fleet's progress be halted until the matter was resolved.

Britain had already begun to take action. The crew of the Baltic Fleet carelessly failed to notice it at the time, but later they found that four British cruisers were hidden deep in a neighboring cove, keeping a sharp lookout.

But the tsar's expeditionary force also had friends—German steamers. To procure the vast amount of coal the fleet consumed, Russia had entered into a contract with a company in Germany, its ally. Four German colliers were in the harbor waiting for the fleet when it arrived.

The fleet tried to begin coaling immediately. The colliers each drew alongside a battleship, but then unexpectedly a Spanish official came aboard the *Suvorov*. "Spain is a neutral country," he stated firmly. "We cannot allow you to load coal in a neutral harbor."

"I've never heard anything so damned stupid!" Rozhestvensky pounded the table in fury when this development was reported to him in his stateroom. If Russia purchased German coal with its own money, what right did any country in the world have to interfere, he wanted to know—but in the end there was nothing for him to do but wire the Foreign Ministry in St. Petersburg and ask the foreign minister for help. Only by having the foreign minister back home send the Russian ambassador in Madrid scurrying could the fleet's peculiar difficulty be resolved.

* * *

The root of British diplomatic strength was the British Navy. From the Russian perspective, Britain's use of its strength was crafty; Britain was apparently carrying out abominable intrigues on the seven seas.

"The hand of Britain is behind it," Politovsky wrote shrewdly of the Spanish harbor administrator's haughty refusal to allow coaling in Vigo. This was so. Britain was not only faithful to its obligations under the Anglo-Japanese Alliance, but actively took the initiative. As the Baltic Fleet departed Europe to wipe out a small naval power in the Far East, Britain did all it could to interfere. Knowing Spain to be neutral, Britain appealed to the Spanish government. This was the gist of their proposal:

> The Baltic Fleet committed a heinous act in Dogger Bank, the North Sea, one without any precedent. They intend to continue on their way without clearing up this incident, but Britain, as victim, wishes to prevent that by any means possible. For instance, although the Baltic Fleet may try to replenish its coal in neutral Spanish territory, we wish Spain to deny it permission to do so. For the Spanish government to let the Russian fleet refuel in its territory would clearly violate Spanish neutrality.

And so the Baltic Fleet was stuck in the fishing port of Vigo. The harbor administrator who came aboard the flagship to issue the prohibition was a little, clean-shaven man in his mid-thirties. "Spain does not wish to violate its neutrality." He said this over and over. One little man succeeded in halting the progress of a mammoth fleet.

The pride of the Russian Empire was forced to lie at anchor under supremely humiliating conditions. When the prohibition went into effect, coal ships were already positioned alongside the battleships, fastened with ropes at the bow. "There could be no greater humiliation," wrote Politovsky.

Two days went by.

During that interval, how many telegrams must have flown back and forth between Madrid and St. Petersburg? Finally, at one in the afternoon on the second day, the Spanish government relented—with one proviso. Each battleship could load only 400 tons of coal.

The crews swung into action. Even the brig was emptied to get the job done. Russian officers normally did not participate in such manual labor, but this time they pitched in. Coal dust flew, turning faces and clothes black. As night came on, lanterns were lit on all the ships and coaling continued, wrapping up finally at nine in the morning.

The Baltic Fleet was forced to stay five long days in the Spanish port of Vigo. Strategically, those five days were of great benefit to Japan. The Japanese Army had yet to breach the fortifications at Port Arthur.

The Baltic Fleet, meanwhile, felt compelled to reach the Far East while the Russian fortifications and fleet at Port Arthur were still intact. Otherwise, the strategic value of the expedition would be much less, or practically nil.

The five days of enforced idleness took a marked toll on the crews' morale. "This is our glorious expeditionary force?" That thought was on everyone's mind. Where was the dignity of their fatherland?

The tsar's fleet was stuck in a remote Spanish fishing port at the whim of the port administrator. Even the most ignorant sailor knew full well that behind that state of affairs lay the might of Great Britain, ruler of the seven seas. The educational level of Russian sailors was low, and many of them were illiterate, but, even so, to a man they longed for the greater glory of their native land. Even the revolutionaries among them, men who had lost faith in the tsarist regime, were without exception angry and disappointed that the dignity of the St. Andrew warship flag should be treated so lightly and meanly.

"Spanish fools." Many of them were upset with the harbor administrators who served as checkpoint officials. Engineer Politovsky, who greatly admired the fine natural harbor at Vigo, was puzzled that the Spaniards had not made it into a thriving port. Though blessed with such a fine harbor, the locals made no effort to boost economic development and were content to eke out a living by exporting sardines, no more. Vigo was one step above a tiny fishing village, its lone industry a sardine-processing plant. The town was squalid, the people mired in poverty. "It's because Spaniards are extraordinarily lazy," Politovsky thought.

Eventually the fleet had to depart without ever having had shore leave. The next stopover, they all knew, would be at Tangier, on the African coast.

The ships left Vigo early in the morning and entered the open sea single file, in line-ahead formation. Skies were clear, the sea a bright blue that hurt the eyes. The men were happy. If only there had not been the prospect of war at journey's end, they might have waved their caps in eager affirmation of life and all things on earth.

But in short order they realized that they had picked up an unwelcome tail.

* * *

The tail consisted of British cruisers that had been hiding in a nearby port. The Baltic Fleet became aware of their presence after sunset. Around ten at night, a report came in of "mysterious ships aft. Apparently four or five." It soon became clear that these were remarkably swift warships, four in number.

In the dead of night, there was no moon or stars.

The British squadron flew over the dark sea as swiftly as if it were broad daylight. And they made provocative moves—or, rather, they mocked the Russian fleet. One moment all four ships would be bright with lanterns, the next the lights would be snuffed out, plunging the squadron into blackness. They did this over and over again. Not only that, they picked up speed, passing ahead of the Russian fleet and circling around in front. It was an acrobatic performance.

Speculation was rife. "They mean to report to the Japanese," some said. Others figured that they intended to goad Rozhestvensky into opening fire and so set off another international incident, thereby causing the expedition further delay. Both theories were correct. Sometimes a cruiser would pull in so close that it seemed in danger of colliding, then suddenly dart off again. The dexterity of these maneuvers was phenomenal.

As Rozhestvensky observed this cheeky behavior from the conning tower of the *Suvorov*, he drew on his meager store of self-control to keep from boiling over in rage. The following morning, he would strike his orderly for a trifling offense, but that night, up in the conning tower, he controlled himself. He even turned to his staff with a smile. "See there—now that's a navy!"

Rozhestvensky's dissatisfaction was reserved for the Russian Navy, which was under his command. He sometimes said the Russian Navy was "no good," sounding like a foreigner speaking ill of Russia. It was true that Russia did not have a single captain who could pull off clever maneuvers like those, and the training of Russian seamen left much to be desired.

Not that Rozhestvensky was lax with his crews. Far from it. He was a demon for practice and saw that every ship's day began with the signal for maneuvers: "Prepare for action!" He was especially insistent about gunnery practice. There were a total of 250 gunners in the fleet, and all of them practiced daily until they were worn out. Rozhestvensky was determined to polish the men's abilities in the remaining interval before they encountered the Japanese.

"The British squadron is terrific." Admiration burned in everyone's mind. At the same time, there was a flicker of apprehension. Would Tōgō's fleet be on the same level? If so, the sailors realized, they might find themselves overwhelmed.

* * *

That Rozhestvensky's fleet had left the port of Liepaja was known to Tōgō's fleet, which was then blockading the harbor at Port Arthur. They also knew from the newspaper that the fleet had caused an international uproar by firing on British fishing vessels in the North Sea. Akiyama Saneyuki and his mates learned the news at their base behind the Changshan Islands.

"On a night crossing, it could happen," Tōgō deadpanned, according to his aides. The moral code of Bushidō, the way of the warrior, had been in place since the Tokugawa period and lingered still among officers in their thirties and above. Tōgō was not so flippant as to mock this blunder by an enemy fleet he had yet to encounter.

Saneyuki's response was unusual. "How many British fishing boats sank?" That was all he wanted to know. He was interested in finding out the destructive force of the Baltic Fleet. He wired headquarters in Tokyo asking for particulars on the "illusionary war" in the North Sea.

"If we were as good marksmen as the Japanese, and if Russian shells had the explosive power of Japanese shells," then friendly fire might have sunk half the fleet, speculated Novikov-Priboy, the author of *Tsushima*.

As Novikov-Priboy observed, the marksmanship of Tōgō's gunners was extremely high, perhaps superior even to that of the British Navy at the time. Tōgō believed that in a naval engagement the key to victory lay, if anywhere, in the accuracy of the big guns. The outcome of the battle depended on whether you hit or missed your targets. That's why he insisted that gunners in every squadron kept on practicing, whether they were engaged in a blockade, out at sea, or on standby at the base off the Changshan Islands. He did something else noteworthy, choosing crack shots from the entire fleet to man the main guns in the battleship squadron. In Tōgō's view, the main guns of the battleships exerted the greatest force in a sea battle. Accordingly, he chose aces for the teams that would launch heavy shells from the main guns. Great marksmen are born, not made, he maintained, and there was little to be gained from training someone of mediocre ability. This approach shows Tōgō's practicality.

So Novikov-Priboy's observation about Japanese marksmanship was accurate. Also, he was right about the explosive power of Japanese shells, which was owing to Shimose powder. He learned those two characteristics of Tōgō's fleet only as a result of the eventual sea battle, however, and at the time of the North Sea crossing knew nothing about them.

In any case, by finding out in detail about the Dogger Bank affair, Saneyuki sought to assess the capability of the enemy fleet.

* * *

"Rozhestvensky's voyage." Known to later generations by this name, the epic voyage and its tribulations were both unprecedented. As in the ancient Chinese phrase "an army sent 10,000 leagues," the fleet was traveling to distant enemy waters, embarked on a journey the like of which no fleet had ever undertaken before. By journey's end, both men and ships were certain to be worn out.

But Tōgō's fleet was in worse shape, already exhausted after continuous sea duty ever since the war began. The Russian general Stoessel, charged with the defense of Port Arthur, was holding Nogi at bay on land and keeping Tōgō pinned to the mouth of the harbor at sea. A man of aristocratic leanings, Stoessel was not only vain and short-tempered but also frequently constrained by the comments of his wife, Vera Alekseyevna. He may not have been the finest commander, but he had the Russian talent for defending a fortress in full measure. In all the Russo-Japanese War, no Russian commander did as much damage to the Japanese Army and Navy as he.

Tōgō's crews were in a truly pitiable state. Even with the Baltic Fleet on its way, the siege of Port Arthur was making no headway. Protected by the sturdy fortress, the Port Arthur Squadron was alive inside the harbor. If Tōgō eased up on the blockade, the squadron was certain to come out and destroy military shipping routes in the Japan Sea and Yellow Sea.

There was even an unsubstantiated report that the Vladivostok Squadron had undergone repairs. In fact, the Vladivostok Squadron had been defeated in a sea battle with Kamimura Hikonojō off Ulsan. The prize high-speed cruisers *Rossiya* and *Gromoboy* had fled back to harbor little better than scrap heaps, never to come out again. Granted, any war vessel that stayed afloat could potentially be repaired. But while the Russians had a large ship-repair factory in Port Arthur, there was no such facility in Vladivostok. As a result, the Vladivostok Squadron led by the brilliant commander von Essen stayed put for the duration of the war. But Tōgō did not know this.

Tōgō was constantly on guard, never free from his fear that the Vladivostok Squadron might pop up at any moment. His fleet was exhausted, moreover, from its long blockade of the harbor. On hearing that the Baltic Fleet had left Liepaja, Tōgō was forced to issue this report on the condition of his warships: "Hulls and engines both extremely degraded." Carrying out repairs needed to restore the fleet to its full fighting strength would take over two months. In other words, the Third Army needed to capture Port Arthur at least two months before the Baltic Fleet appeared in the seas around Japan.

Meanwhile, the navy was actively cooperating on land with Nogi's Third Army. The heavy artillery unit of naval land forces went to work attacking the fortress and the town of Port Arthur (though all they did was aim by guesswork). The effect was great, but Nogi's chief of staff Ijichi treated this contribution rather as a nuisance, lodging frequent complaints about the use of naval artillery.

* * *

The death struggle at the Port Arthur fortress went on. The grisliness of that battle was surely unsurpassed in the history of European warfare.

Around that time, a young first lieutenant in the Russian Army cut through the besieging Japanese Army as Stoessel's envoy. A duke named Radziwill, he fled as far as the neutral ground of Yantai, where he entered the Russian consulate and succeeded in contacting his home country. The young duke horrified foreign reporters in Yantai with his description of appalling battle conditions.

"Why Japanese soldiers die in such numbers baffles me. On September 14, for instance, in the narrow space between the second and third batteries, I came on the bodies of two thousand six hundred Japanese soldiers piled high. Not even Russian military headquarters could come up with any tactical reason for the pathetic deaths of so many men."

The soldiers were killed not by Russian gunfire so much as by the order to die meaningless deaths, an order which they had no choice but to obey. The incompetence of Nogi's headquarters resulted in the virtual mass suicide of huge numbers of Japanese soldiers, tormenting the Russians with the stench of death. According to the duke, the unburied remains of a great many Japanese soldiers lay on a slope by one battery in the northeast sector of Port Arthur, exposed to the elements and rotting, the stink unbearable. At a battery barely fifty paces away, Russian soldiers worked in shifts because of the smell. Those on duty wore camphor-soaked handkerchiefs around the lower half of their faces and prayed for replacements to come soon.

"Japanese soldiers mostly died in front of the fortress, but occasionally some of them would make it inside, and then there would be bursts of fierce hand-to-hand combat. I personally inspected one stronghold and saw, mixed in the mounds of dead from each side, a pair of soldiers, Japanese and Russian, who had died locked together. I looked closer and saw that the Russian soldier had jabbed two fingers into the Japanese soldier's eye sockets, and the teeth of the Japanese soldier were embedded deep in the Russian's neck. The Japanese soldier was eyeless and the Russian soldier's windpipe was exposed. The sight was so gruesome that no one, however battle hardened, could have seen it without shivering."

Stoessel, a Slav, could mount a defense with amazing tenacity. One Russian lieutenant colonel, stationed at a particularly dangerous fortification at the front and unable to endure the ferocity of the Japanese attack, sent a message to Stoessel by horseback to try to persuade him to issue an order to retreat. Stoessel's reply was the same as on other occasions. "You might not be able to defend that fortification. But you can die."

The lieutenant colonel obeyed Stoessel's will and died in battle, along with every man in his unit. Stoessel then sent in another unit as replacement. He was determined not to give up even one stronghold to Nogi's forces. This was what First Lieutenant Radziwill told the foreign press. His intention was apparently not to extol Russian bravery but to tell about the war's brutality.

* * *

In November, the war situation looked still bleaker for Nogi's forces.

As before, Nogi's headquarters continued to reject the naval request to make 203-Meter Hill a main focus of attack. But Tokyo Imperial Headquarters was so insistent in its desire for this to happen that, on September 19, the First Division (from Tokyo) was deployed and made a token assault with a small force, withdrawing when they realized the strength of the opposition. If they'd had any tactical sense, they would have made another try. At that point, the defense of 203-Meter Hill was weak, consisting merely of a scattering of hillside trenches.

We also know that Stoessel noticed this canker sore. Seeing that 203-Meter Hill was the weak point of Russian defense, he hurriedly moved to shore it up. The halfhearted assault launched by Nogi's army effectively gave the Russians the idea of strengthening their defense. Of all the countless errors committed by Nogi's headquarters, this was perhaps the worst.

In the meantime, casualties were piling up in Nogi's army and so the urgent requests were flying out. "Send in the Seventh or Eighth Division." Imperial Headquarters was generally opposed to such a move. "If we give them to Nogi, he's only going to kill our crack divisions without achieving anything." With the Eighth Division sent to Liaoyang, the Japanese Army was down to its last reserve division.

"Send us the Seventh Division." Nogi's headquarters kept clamoring. Imperial Headquarters was reluctant, knowing that the men would only end up filling enemy trenches. So far, the style of fighting adopted by Nogi's headquarters had meant naked assaults with casualties numbering sixteen thousand, then five thousand. The Seventh Division would be wiped out in one go.

But with the looming threat of the Baltic Fleet's expedition to the Far East, Imperial Headquarters needed Port Arthur taken with all possible speed. They had no choice but to send in the Seventh Division after all.

The Seventh Division was formed of soldiers from Hokkaido and had its headquarters in the city of Asahikawa, with regimental headquarters in Sapporo, Hakodate, Kushiro, and Asahikawa. This division, the last that the Japanese Army held in reserve on the mainland, joined Nogi's setup. He planned to use the replacements to take 203-Meter Hill. Surprisingly, his headquarters was unaware that, unlike before, the hill was now heavily fortified. They had neglected to do the most basic reconnaissance. Forced by poorly informed superiors to go up against an iron wall, the Seventh Division was of all divisions the unhappiest.

* * *

The head of the Seventh Division from Hokkaido was Lieutenant General Ōsako Naotoshi, a Satsuma man. He had no formal education to speak of but was educated only as a samurai retainer of the lord of Satsuma domain. In that sense, he was no different from any army commander who had previously served as a samurai in the old domain system.

Emperor Meiji's preference in soldiers ran to old-style warriors of the caliber of reformer Saigō Takamori, swordsman Yamaoka Tesshū, and General Nogi Maresuke. Schemers like Yamagata Aritomo were not evidently to his liking. Ōsako, a man with the aura of a Saigō or a Yamaoka, first came to the emperor's attention when he was a colonel, head of the First Regiment in the Imperial Guard, and drew his favor.

But under the Japanese system the emperor himself, unlike the tsar, had no autocratic power. Judgment and execution of all political and military affairs was left to the cabinet and members of the Army General Staff Office (for the navy, the Navy General Staff). Such men served as "advisors to the throne" in a system where the emperor's mere existence had much meaning in everyone's mind. Therefore, even if Emperor Meiji favored Ōsako Naotoshi, their relationship was nothing like that between Nicholas II and his favorites. Let's just say that the emperor found him intriguing.

Although the emperor had no autocratic power, it did happen on rare occasions that the cabinet would ask him to pass judgment on some matter. Normally, such requests were seen as highly undesirable since they saddled the emperor with responsibility and prevented the cabinet from fulfilling its role as advisor. We have seen that when Nogi asked for the Eighth Division to be sent in, Imperial Headquarters, fearing the incompetence of Nogi's headquarters, wanted to send the division to the battle on the plains instead of to Port Arthur. Yet they could not cavalierly dismiss Nogi's request, so in the end they asked for an imperial decision. "By order of the emperor," they could then say to assuage Nogi's headquarters. This was the extent of Emperor Meiji's involvement in political and military affairs.

The emperor's fondness for Ōsako thus bore no tinge of politics. Since Ōsako knew only the vaguest sort of horsemanship, the emperor announced his intention to teach him. And so, while serving as a regimental commander in the Imperial Guard, Ōsako received a thorough schooling in the subtle arts of horsemanship directly from the emperor.

When the emperor heard from Yamagata that the Seventh Division was on its way to Port Arthur, he murmured, "So it's come to that!" and was silent. Once the Seventh Division went to war, Japan's reserves would be exhausted. Japan's own fate might be bitter, but so was that of this division. It was a foregone conclusion that everyone in it would end up filling enemy trenches at the Port Arthur fortress. The emperor's heart was heavy.

Ōsako himself, as captain of the Seventh Division, was unhappy that his outfit alone remained stuck on the Japanese mainland. Time and again, he traveled to Imperial Headquarters in Tokyo to push his request for orders to the front. He was every inch a Meiji warrior. When the orders finally came through, he made the journey again and met with Yamagata. After that, he called at the palace for a farewell audience with the emperor.

Both men were standing at attention. Ōsako reported that the division had finally been ordered to the front. Normally, the imperial audience of a division commander would then be over. But Emperor Meiji wanted a final exchange with this old man of Satsuma. Moreover, although Ōsako himself might be eager to go to the front, the emperor was concerned that the other officers and men in the division might be dreading their assignment to Port Arthur.

"How is troop morale?" the emperor inquired.

In his rich native dialect, Ōsako spoke forcefully about how keen the men were to fight. "Say we win the war, and after we do it turns out the Hokkaido division was the only one that never got in a lick—Yow! Hokkaido men could never turn their faces south to the rest of Japan ever again! The men've been in a right lather. But, luckily, now Your Majesty's given the order . . ."

The emperor couldn't help laughing. His sympathetic concern over the division being sent to certain doom was mitigated by Ōsako's humorous turn of speech. He himself had a humorous side and was drawn to anyone with a good sense of humor. Since Ōsako rarely used dialect in formal situations, his doing so now was undoubtedly a deliberate ploy to keep the emperor from dwelling on the harsh fate awaiting him and his Seventh Division.

Okazawa Kuwashi, chief aide-de-camp to the emperor, was present at this audience and later reminisced, "Never since the start of the war did His Majesty laugh so heartily."

Ōsako had no desire to be made into a tragic figure. His younger brother fought in the war and so did his son Sanji, a first lieutenant who was killed in battle. Like General Nogi, Ōsako knew the pain of losing a son in the war, but the two men's characters were as different as night and day. After the war, Nogi wrote a famous Chinese-style poem lamenting the many men he had sent to their deaths, with the line "In shame, how can I face their fathers?" Ōsako too wrote a similar tanka, likening his soldiers to flowers.

The flowers I took with me
have drifted away in the storm
I have nothing
to take back to those
who wait at home

* * *

"Dismiss Nogi Maresuke and his staff, and reconfigure Third Army headquarters."

This argument had been waged forcefully in Imperial Headquarters all along, but no one broached it any more. That was because, when Yamagata Aritomo once appeared at the palace to report on battle conditions at Port Arthur, Emperor Meiji had instructed him in no uncertain terms that Nogi was not to be dismissed.

The emperor was voicing the maxim that it was wrong to change leadership in the middle of a military operation, but when Nogi heard later about this injunction he was deeply moved. That shows the kind of spirit he had. Nogi had little sense of himself as a military official of the Japanese nation, seeing himself rather as the emperor's retainer, who was following the medieval concept of lord and vassal. This was something of a miracle. In the early days of the shogunate, a samurai identified himself by the name of his lord, for example, as "vassal of Lord Asano Takumi no Kami." Then the word *han*—domain—came into widespread use toward the end of the Tokugawa period. After that, the domain came to be seen as a kind of juridical person, and that is how contemporary samurai saw it. Loyalty to a flesh-and-blood lord took a back seat to loyalty to the domain.

Although Nogi Maresuke attained his majority in the Meiji period, curiously enough, his concept of the nation remained extremely vague. What stood out with crystal clarity in his mind was the figure of Emperor Meiji, and what made his devotion to the emperor so unswerving was undoubtedly the emperor's injunction that he, Nogi, should not be dismissed.

Yamagata Aritomo was deeply fond of Nogi, a fellow man of Chōshū, and from his youth had looked out for him. At the beginning of the war, when Nogi was a farmer in the village of Nasu, it was Yamagata who summoned him to Tokyo and restored him to active military duty. Now that Nogi was carrying on such an unbelievably inept campaign in Port Arthur, Yamagata felt responsible. Yet, as head of the Chōshū military clique, he wanted more than anything to protect Nogi and, if possible, straighten out what he was doing in Port Arthur.

After the decision to commit the Seventh Division, Yamagata went so far as to wire encouragement to Nogi. However, he wanted Nogi to make 203-Meter Hill the main focus of his attack, and this Nogi refused to do.

Yamagata even appealed to the emperor on Nogi's behalf and succeeded in getting his friend an imperial rescript of encouragement. Its message was essentially: "hurry and get the job done." Apparently still not satisfied, Yamagata then wired Nogi a poem of his own composition, written in classical Chinese.

> A hundred shells thunder, surprising heaven.
> Half a year of siege, ten thousand corpses sprawl.
> With a will stronger than iron
> Defeat the enemy in one blow at Port Arthur.

Implicit in the poem was a warning: fail in the next general assault, and you will be held responsible.

* * *

Nogi's headquarters behaved strangely. While carrying out a sorry campaign of obstinate bungling on a scale without parallel in history, they did not bother to send in proper reports. Although the headquarters of the Manchurian Army was his superior headquarters, with Ōyama Iwao as head, Nogi's chief of staff submitted only shoddy, minimal reports.

All the staff officers at General Headquarters were irate. Others pointed out that a shiftless, incompetent leader could no more write a report than he could map out strategy. A report was something you could write only if you were fighting battles worth reporting. How could men whose only strategy was relentlessly killing off their troops be expected to write reports?

It was all due to Ijichi Kōsuke's lack of competence and character, thought Kodama. But like the other staff officers, he never voiced this observation during the war. He felt sorry for Nogi. The two of them shared a common history—both were from Chōshū, and both joined the army after the Meiji Restoration to fight against Saigō Takamori's rebel army in Kumamoto as young majors. Kodama had been a staff officer under Tani Tateki, the defending general in Saigō's siege of Kumamoto Castle, while Nogi led the so-called "peasant soldiers" consisting of the nation's first conscripts—and got soundly thrashed at every turn by the Satsuma forces. Kodama was well aware that Nogi had been an ineffective commander from the first. Ineffective though he might be, he was fiercely loyal, had a strong sense of responsibility, and was in many ways the image of his distant relative Yoshida Shōin, the great educator and reformer. Of all Nogi's friends, no one knew him so well as Kodama.

Kodama knew also that Nogi was totally unqualified to lead an engagement of as great import in modern warfare as the assault on Port Arthur.

Ijichi would come to his aid, Kodama had thought, but Ijichi himself was a disappointment, and Nogi seemed constitutionally incapable of taking him to task.

At this juncture, Kodama Gentarō sent a letter to Nogi in Port Arthur. "As I wrote in my last letter, we lack adequate battle reports from your army and are rather better informed about the situation from the navy's reports." He was advising Nogi to write more detailed reports. Of course, Nogi himself had no need to pick up a pen. What Kodama meant was "light into Ijichi and make him write in greater detail." But this request was never fulfilled.

"What is the use?" Ijichi protested. "What will General Headquarters do to aid in our assault on Port Arthur? If they responded by sending a division, then it would be worth the trouble, but what have they ever done for us?"

Despite heavy criticism, Ijichi and Nogi's Third Army headquarters was still located in a safety zone where no bullets flew.

* * *

In late November, the third (or fourth, depending on how you calculated it) general assault on Port Arthur would begin. Nogi's headquarters conveyed this message to General Headquarters in Liaoyang and Tokyo's Imperial Headquarters, creating a mood of heightened anxiety and expectation. But Nogi's headquarters itself was almost totally lacking in confidence. Instead of changing strategy, they were going to continue carrying out the same failed plan—what Nagaoka Gaishi called "useless slaughter." Yet they had clearly lost confidence in slaughter as a tactic of warfare.

Like idiots incapable of learning more than one thing, Nogi's headquarters made the familiar preparations for the familiar style of assault. Normally, a campaign headquarters preparing for an attack crackles with excitement, but the staff's enthusiasm had waned. "Chief of Staff Ijichi is downcast." So reads a report filed by a messenger from Imperial Headquarters on the eve of the assault. This was not the face of a military strategist about to launch a major campaign. Trained in Germany, Ijichi had always had a vaguely Teutonic air, carrying himself with haughtiness, but he lacked the brains to come up with a plan on his own. When he formulated one using borrowed ideas, he tended to place unshakable faith in it. To shield the plan from outside criticism, he was impelled to become arrogant and make it into an article of faith. His being "downcast" probably means that his faith had begun to waver.

The military profession justifies not just killing enemy soldiers but even more so, killing one's own. Remaining long in the profession gradually dulls the conscience on that point, so that leaders can easily become defective as human beings. Ijichi undoubtedly felt vague horror at the prospect of killing so many of his compatriots, proving that his mind had not been altered to that extent. Even so, like so many military strategists, he put on a bold front. "There's nothing wrong with our approach." That's what he told the emissary from Imperial Headquarters, but he said it with a dejected look.

The emissary in question was Ōsawa Kaiyū, a staff officer born in Aichi Prefecture who also met with Nogi Maresuke. In his eyes, Nogi too did not carry himself like an officer about to send tens of thousands of soldiers to storm an enemy stronghold. The general had gone sleepless for three full days. His insomnia was due in part to his harried schedule, but, in fact, his nerves were stretched to breaking point by the war. To Ōsawa, Nogi did not appear confident of victory.

"I am doing all I can." Nogi spoke from the heart, looking haggard. "I do not know what more I can do." He must have been truly exhausted, for then he let slip something no commander should ever say. "If there were anyone else fit for the job, I would like to yield the right of command in Port Arthur."

Listening to these statements by Nogi Maresuke, a man he did not know well, Ōsawa apparently could not summon any sympathy in response.

* * *

"We've got one nagging sister-in-law in Tokyo and another in Liaoyang," complained a young staff officer in Nogi's headquarters who accosted a liaison officer from Tokyo. "It's hard to take."

There was some truth to this. The chain of command was vague from the first, as Nogi's army owed allegiance both to Imperial Headquarters in Tokyo and to General Headquarters, the headquarters of the Japanese Manchurian Army—yet neither one had power to issue a direct command. Offering opinions by way of suggestion was as much as they could do. "Why not try this?" Nogi's headquarters took all such remarks as nagging.

It must be stressed again that the Japanese Army probably ought to have separated Nogi's army from the Manchurian Army of Ōyama and Kodama, and attached it directly to Imperial Headquarters from the first. Ōyama and Kodama, embroiled in conducting open-air warfare on the Manchurian plains, had no time or energy to spare for a completely dissimilar campaign, that of storming a fortress. "Port Arthur is in Nogi's hands." That was the prevailing logic. Nogi's headquarters was free to design and carry out any strategy it wished. Such wide authority, free of restrictions from any quarter, should have lent zest to the command. If a military genius had been operating Nogi's headquarters, he would have taken full advantage of that freedom.

But to a mediocre leader, nothing is so disheartening as complete freedom to exercise one's power of discretion. "We are orphaned." That must have been how it seemed to them. In that sense, Nogi Maresuke and Ijichi Kōsuke were both orphans.

These orphans had the troops under their command replenished and also had the Seventh Division, Japan's last remaining standby division, sent over from the mainland; the conditions were right for them to hurl this vast supply of fresh blood at the fortress. So began the third storming of Port Arthur, but beforehand Nogi suffered from a nervous disorder and was unable to sleep, and Ijichi lost his usual oily vigor.

Neither man had the least confidence of victory.

All the liaison officers from Tokyo sensed this state of mind. "Headquarters is executing a battle plan that the commanders themselves have no faith in, killing soldiers out of sheer habit." This was the impression they all received. The expression "useless slaughter" coined by Nagaoka Gaishi conveys the general impression of the visiting "sisters-in-law."

In the history of warfare, no battle plan is as idiotic as this third assault on Port Arthur carried out by Nogi and Ijichi. Never abandoning the idea of a frontal attack, they rested the success of the plan solely on Japanese bravery. "Charge!" Third Army headquarters merely issued this death order, not functioning as a center of planning or judgment. As for 203-Meter Hill, which the navy and the "sisters-in-law" kept yammering about, they attacked it in dribs and drabs in order to quiet the yammering—an ill-advised way to carry out an attack if there ever was one.

* * *

The third general attack on the Port Arthur fortress took place on November 26. The attack targets were Pine Tree Hill for the First Division (from Tokyo) on the right column; Twin Dragons Hill for the Ninth Division (from Kanazawa) in the central column; and the East Cockscomb Hill for the Eleventh Division (from Zentsūji) on the left column. It was to be a complete frontal attack.

Added to this, there was to be another assault carried out by a large suicide force of elite troops. Dubbed the Shirodasukitai, "White Sash Troop," they would later become renowned as a symbol of the fighting at Port Arthur. Its members, over three thousand one hundred in all, were chosen from each division. From the first, Nogi and Ijichi planned to have Major General Nakamura Satoru lead this special unit. Believing it unethical to send only soldiers to their deaths, they wanted a general in command. Nakamura was then head of the Second Infantry Brigade.

Hailing from the Hikone domain, which came in for particularly harsh treatment in the Meiji Restoration, Nakamura entered the army school for noncommissioned officers in 1872. Three years later, he was a second lieutenant in the army, and during the First Sino-Japanese War he served as aide-de-camp to Emperor Meiji, who was extremely fond of him.

"Nakamura will command the White Sash Troop, will he?" When the sovereign heard this report, it is said that his expression turned gloomy.

Nakamura's military record dated back to the Satsuma Rebellion, when, shortly after the Conscription Ordinance was issued, he had difficulty leading a band of garrison soldiers. Known as "peasant soldiers," garrison soldiers of the day would scatter and flee when they encountered shock troops of the former samurai class.

"Soldiers are prone to cut and run." This impression stuck in Nakamura's mind. In the interim, twenty-odd years of training had left Japanese soldiers stronger than the samurai-class fighters of years past. Their mettle had been tested in the First Sino-Japanese War, although Nakamura did not take part in that campaign. His last experience of a hail of bullets came in the Satsuma Rebellion.

Before departing for the front as head of the Second Infantry Brigade, Nakamura inspected his men at the Aoyama parade ground and admonished them in ringing tones. "For the duration of this war, let the word 'retreat' be obliterated." Famous in the army for his musical voice, he spoke so loudly that his words carried to every corner of the parade ground. No doubt memories of his younger days in the Satsuma Rebellion moved him to admonish the men that way.

The "no retreat" suicide squad of over three thousand men came under heavy fire at the Port Arthur fortress and suffered fifteen hundred casualties in a bloodbath.

* * *

Nothing shows the dearth of ability in Nogi's headquarters so much as this ill-omened idea of a suicide squad. The technical military term for such a squad is an assault group. By rights, an assault group should be used for surprise attacks and exists for the tactical purpose of making a sudden move against the enemy from the rear. But Nogi's headquarters used theirs in a frontal attack.

Nor was it merely a frontal attack: the squad was ordered straight down the middle, where the enemy's strongest defenses were concentrated.

"Headquarters must have been deranged when it set about carrying out this plan." This was the gist of a written comment by Satō Kiyokatsu, an officer in the commissariat. A hysteria-prone person attempting to escape distress will go into a fit of hysterics, and similarly an incompetent military commander in utmost distress will implement tactics of extreme foolishness. Hysteria is said to be common in women, but among men it is common in military personnel. Hysterical foolishness is particularly common in the military profession. This means that grown men act infantile. Overall, General Nogi's headquarters may well have been in a state of hysterical foolishness.

The plan that Nogi's headquarters gave to Nakamura's White Sash Troop was to lead a bayonet charge up the main thoroughfare, capture Pine Tree Hill, the strongest fort in all Port Arthur, and then pour into the streets of town. They were dreaming.

"Nakamura will bring it off," Nogi said confidently to Ijichi. General Nakamura Satoru was the one who had told his brigade to obliterate the word "retreat." Though his philosophy of warfare was old-fashioned, he was known for his bravery. Nakamura was then fifty-one, and whether he had the physical stamina for a dash up the main thoroughfare was open to question, but he was chosen in order to raise morale—to show that even a general would dauntlessly throw himself into the jaws of death. Too many soldiers had been killed at Port Arthur, and so the high command needed to sacrifice one of its own. Three thousand men was the equivalent of three regiments and could have been headed by someone of the rank of colonel.

The name "White Sash" comes from the white sash each man wore from the right shoulder to the left armpit to make identification easier in the dark of night.

Nakamura did not criticize the tactics of the military headquarters but expressed thanks for his assignment. "I have gained a place to die." Given the state of affairs at Port Arthur, he believed that a general had to die there, and he was sincerely honored to have been chosen for the purpose. His response shows what a thoroughgoing military man of the Meiji period he was.

* * *

All of the men were doomed to be slain by the efficient killing apparatus of the fortress, but even if this visionary plan had somehow come true—assuming, in other words, that all three thousand men broke through unscathed and poured into the streets of Port Arthur—what were they supposed to do then? Armed only with Japanese swords and pistols, they were bound to be subjugated in street warfare.

Nogi's headquarters, which had come up with this fantastic plan, was the target of constant whispers at Imperial Headquarters in Tokyo and at General Headquarters in Manchuria. "No one over there has a clue about what's really going on." Not once since the start of the battle had staff officers leaped into the thick of the fray for reconnaissance. Not only that, despite being criticized for locating their headquarters too far back from the front, they had done nothing to remedy the situation. It was obvious that their detached location prevented them from designing strategy that took in any sense of the front.

From the first, Ōyama Iwao had never once interfered in Nogi's conduct of the battle, but after this he had had enough and, on December 1, sent Nogi a scolding letter of admonition. "The position of your headquarters and reserve troops is too far back, preventing you from coming to the aid of your troops in the event of a counterattack." How did he think he could fight a war that far back from the action?

Let us return to the White Sash Troop.

The doomed men began action at dawn on November 26, 1904, gathering just north of Kuropatkin's battery north of Longyan and dressing ranks. In the evening, General Nogi came by, accompanied by his adjutant, to address the troops.

> A massive increase in enemy troops is taking place on the continent, and at sea the coming of the Baltic Fleet is not far off. The safety of the nation hinges on how our besieging army fights ... You who are about to enter the jaws of death—I look upon you with the most ardent expectations. This very day you are called upon to give your lives for your country. Would that you exert yourselves to the fullest.

The words were written out on paper. The general read them aloud, and when he had finished it was reported that "Sadness filled the camp, amid hushed silence."

* * *

The previous day, on the morning of the twenty-fifth, the Russian general Stoessel issued orders to his whole army. "Tomorrow, on the thirteenth"—according to the Russian calendar—"Nogi is going to come at us with a general attack. There are signs in the air, so make sure you carefully patrol each battle station. If you find anything out of the ordinary, however small, report it."

It seems as if he was gifted with divine powers of perception, but actually that was not the case. Nogi had a peculiar habit which all the Russian officers from Stoessel down were aware of. They noted that "on the twenty-sixth"—the thirteenth by the Russian calendar—"he always begins a bombardment loud enough to rattle heaven and earth, and sends out waves of shock troops." For the Russians, this made defense easy. Every month as the twenty-sixth drew near, all they had to do was take up their posts, stockpile ammunition in their fortifications, and then, armed to the teeth, sit back and wait. It was a sure thing that Japanese troops would materialize over the ridgeline of the hills. It was as if they came in order to be killed. All the Russians needed to do was throw them in the blender with a hail of shells.

The story of the "twenty-sixth of the month" was this: the Third Army's first incursion into Port Arthur forts was the June 26 attack on Sword Hill, followed by a July 26 attack on Anziling mountain range. The first general assault, moreover, took place around August 20, when the army suffered heavy casualties. The next attack started on September 19 and lasted several days, followed by another all-out assault on October 26, when Nogi's forces were dealt a crushing blow. Since then, they had received reinforcements from the home country and so were likely to be planning a fresh assault. Stoessel anticipated that the next assault was sure to take place on November 26.

Why did Nogi invariably choose the same day of the month to make his move? This point mystified Stoessel and his aides. They weren't the only ones who found it mysterious. The General Staff at Imperial Headquarters was equally puzzled. "All they're doing is allowing the enemy time to prepare, killing soldiers needlessly. What the hell do Nogi and Ijichi mean by picking the twenty-sixth of the month every single time?" Both Yamagata Aritomo and Nagaoka Gaishi wanted to know. On the occasion of the coming third general assault, they sent a special emissary, one Lieutenant Colonel Mori Kunitake, to call at Nogi's headquarters in Liushufang and find out. The explanation Ijichi gave was unexpected.

"There are three reasons. One is the need to prepare ammunition. Detonating fuses last a month—after that they deteriorate and are less effective. Therefore, attacks need to be spaced a month apart." This scientifically debatable and strategically meaningless point was the first reason cited by Ijichi.

"Second, the day we attacked and broke through at Nanshan was the twenty-sixth. It's good luck."

And there was more.

"The third reason is that twenty-six is an even number and splits evenly in two. That means we can split the fortress."

Beside him, Nogi gave a firm nod. This was the level of the brains behind the attack on the modern fortifications at Port Arthur. Soldiers would die.

* * *

Stoessel's warning to his troops to "watch out for the thirteenth"—the twenty-sixth, by the Japanese calendar—was spot on that day.

According to reports from every stronghold in the fortress, from around eleven in the morning to about four in the afternoon on the twenty-fifth, Russian observers watched from afar as Nogi's troops continuously moved rolling stock from Anziling mountain range toward Wangjia Dianzi. They judged this to be an ammunition-transport unit, whose increased movement was a harbinger of a major offensive.

"Hasn't Nogi ever studied the part in the tactical textbook that says hide your intention to attack?" Stoessel wondered. In a similar situation, the Russian Army would go to extraordinary lengths to conceal its operations.

At noon on the twenty-fifth, Stoessel issued orders to all units to prepare for battle. In the meantime, one of Stoessel's most valiant officers, Major General Kondratenko, received an urgent message from Captain Romanovsky, who was scouting the Pigeon Bay area. "Enemy activity in this area picking up fast." Kondratenko responded by dispatching the Tenth Company of the marines. This is merely one example of Russian precautions. On this day, all the Russian troops in the fortress were engaged in energetic activity. Here reinforcements were sent in, there troops were transferred out.

And, on the twenty-sixth, Nogi's offensive took place right on schedule.

Russian gunfire rent the air. An array of Japanese guns—everything from siege guns and 28-centimeter howitzers to field guns and mountain guns—returned fire, aiming at the hills of Port Arthur.

The Third Army's advance was underway.

Around sunset, under the leadership of General Nakamura Satoru, the three thousand men in the White Sash Troop—men whom Nogi had exhorted, "The success of this battle hinges on your efforts"—began to move. They were huddled at the foot of the elevation north of Shuishiying, invisible to the Russians.

The White Sash Troop set out at six in the evening. East of the campsite was a small stream. They followed that stream until they were spotted by enemy searchlights and subjected to heavy concentrated fire. Survivors pushed forward, and at eight-forty the entire troop fixed bayonets, ready to engage in hand-to-hand combat. The immediate goal was to capture the supporting fort at Pine Tree Hill.

"Storm the streets of Port Arthur!" The three thousand men in the White Sash Troop who were given this preposterous order began to fight at eight-forty in the evening, and an hour later were crushed.

The whole idea of them invading the streets of Port Arthur was a fantasy born of Nogi's madness and ignorance. The town was surrounded by dense fortifications, piled layer on layer like fish scales. At the very first layer, in front of a supporting fort, one half of the three thousand became casualties.

But the valor of Japanese soldiers was great, probably without parallel anywhere in the world at that time. The surviving soldiers cut through barbed-wire entanglements and infiltrated enemy territory, leaping into enemy trenches in strategically senseless heroics. Those who made it into the trenches were hit with grenades and died.

Though killed in great numbers by Russian soldiers, the Japanese invading the trenches managed to dispatch a number of the enemy. But killing a small number of Russian soldiers in trenches did not change the fact that their main goal, invading the town of Port Arthur, was a physical impossibility. Even so, Japanese soldiers continued to believe that their deaths would somehow contribute to victory and went on dying like dogs. They were fortunate in one thing only, that they died never knowing that the headquarters of their army, with their lives in its hands, was one of the most spectacularly unfit command centers in the history of war. The soldiers mostly believed that the generals' way of thinking was right, but there were a few doubters. Some division and brigade commanders were skeptical and thought the behavior of headquarters strange.

The ablest and bravest generals in the Port Arthur offensive and defensive were Kondratenko on the Russian side and Ichinohe Hyōe (from Tsugaru) on the Japanese side, both of them major generals. Even Ichinohe was frustrated. "Why does command keep coming up with orders that make no sense, that have nothing to do with our actual situation?" Yet he said nothing, afraid to disturb morale, and silently devoted himself to leadership at the front.

Of all the Russian soldiers at Port Arthur, those under Kondratenko were much ahead of the rest in strength. When the White Sash Troop under Major General Nakamura, even after suffering a crippling blow, still managed to continue forward in part and penetrate enemy trenches, the Russians rained bombs on them, and the two sides stabbed and killed each other. Into this hellish scene, a peculiar Russian soldier suddenly appeared.

He swiftly descended the hill with seven or eight grenades strapped to his body in front, back, and on either side. All the fuses were lit. He dove into a cluster of White Sash soldiers, seeking to blow himself up and take a large number of Japanese with him. He died just as he intended to. His body was blown to bits and simultaneously the bodies of several Japanese soldiers flew sky high.

* * *

"The indolence of your headquarters is killing soldiers for no reason. I don't know what you think you're doing, but the only ones you're killing are Japanese soldiers!" Kodama Gentarō would later rip into Ijichi Kōsuke partly for authorizing this suicide operation. The one he wanted to yell at was Nogi. Fearing that he might damage Nogi's authority as the high command, he took Ijichi to task instead.

Nogi had seriously expected the troop's assault to succeed. But, by ten that night, most of the men lay dead or wounded on the slope amid barbed-wire entanglements. Nakamura himself, gravely wounded, was replaced by Colonel Watanabe Mizuya. The casualties included sixty-six officers; in the end, command of every unit went to lower-echelon or noncommissioned officers. By one in the morning, the battlefield was littered with the wounded and dead. The few surviving Japanese soldiers were trapped, unable to engage in systematic fighting.

Having instructed his own brigade to "obliterate the word 'retreat,'" Major General Nakamura could not very well retreat himself. But he was severely wounded in the fighting and yielded command to Colonel Watanabe, who made the decision to retreat. Watanabe finally scraped together some able-bodied soldiers and sent for new orders.

Nogi's headquarters at Liushufang was far away, but eventually, when Nogi took in Watanabe's report, disappointment was written large on his face. "So it didn't work." He felt he had run out of options. Yet something had to be done, and quickly. After dawn, when the sun lit up the slope, all the wounded men stranded there would be run through and killed by Russian bayonets.

Nogi gave the order to retreat.

Like the White Sash Troop's surprise attack, the systematic attacks carried out by the other divisions also failed utterly. Whole battalions and companies were virtually wiped out everywhere. The 28-centimeter howitzers that Nogi's headquarters had initially rejected, dismissing them as "unnecessary," proved potent. Together with the siege guns, they destroyed the fort on the north slope of East Cockscomb Hill and the outer walls of the forts of Twin Dragons and Pine Tree Hills. Even so, the forts continued to function.

The Eleventh Division had taken on those ruined strongholds, sending out wave upon wave of shock troops. But in front of the batteries were fields full of landmines and tangles of barbed wire, with automatic rifles and rapid-firing guns all around. When one Japanese unit was wiped out, the next would attack, climbing over the bodies of their fallen comrades. Rarely, a few soldiers would manage to scale the breastworks, but beyond lay still more automatic rifles, and any who managed to dash through safely would only encounter still tighter defense at the vital points within. Penetrating all those layers of defense was beyond human power.

* * *

At this point, Ōyama and Kodama's General Headquarters had moved north from Liaoyang as far as Yantai. North of them was Kuropatkin's vast field army, but all the enemies did was glare at each other, neither side willing to launch a heroic battle.

For days, every time Kodama Gentarō opened his mouth, all that came out was "What's the news from Port Arthur?" He could say nothing else. The safety of the entire Japanese force in Manchuria now rested in the hands of Nogi's army in Port Arthur. Indeed, if the outlook worsened any for Nogi's army and its attack on Port Arthur, Japan's entire army and navy strategy would collapse, and the nation itself would be doomed. The key to the fate of Japan rested with the wits of two of the most foolish and obstinate of men.

General Nogi, mused Kodama, might well end up like General Grouchy if he wasn't careful. At Waterloo, when Napoleon fought against British and Prussian coalition troops led by the Duke of Wellington, he had General Emmanuel de Grouchy lead a detached force in pursuit of the Prussian Army, another wing of the enemy. His intention was to have Grouchy defeat the Prussians.

Grouchy was a general of no redeeming feature beyond blind obedience to orders. What he did at that time was also in accord with his honest-to-a-fault personality. Not knowing where to find the Prussians that Napoleon had ordered him to deal with, he marched steadily on until he came within earshot of fierce gunfire far off in the direction of Waterloo. The battle of the main force was underway.

Grouchy should have gone straight there. His staff urged him to do so, some of them in exasperation, but Grouchy wouldn't listen. "The emperor ordered me to find the Prussian Army." That was all he would say, and stuck to his prearranged plan. In the meantime, Napoleon was defeated at Waterloo. If Grouchy had had the flexibility and decisiveness to adapt to changing circumstances, if he had rushed to Waterloo and attacked Wellington's British troops from the side, Napoleon's fate might well have been different. But fate itself abandoned Napoleon, killing off all his able generals and leaving only a figurehead like Grouchy to command a military wing of such crucial importance. Grouchy destroyed Napoleon's power.

Nogi's army in Port Arthur was in a sense a detached force of the Manchurian Army. Just as Grouchy not only failed to find the Prussian Army but also stubbornly defined his own strategic function, so Nogi insistently clung to his bizarre policy of frontal assault on the fortress at Port Arthur. While Grouchy failed to be of any strategic use to Napoleon, at least he managed not to get any of his own men killed. Nogi, by contrast, had for all practical purposes taken on the task of single-handedly using up soldiers in the Russo-Japanese War. In that sense, the sin of his stubborn folly may outweigh Grouchy's.

* * *

On November 26, the date of the third assault on Port Arthur, Kodama Gentarō awoke before dawn in the headquarters in Yantai. He was too worried to sleep.

He put on his uniform, wearing the cap sideways, and stepped into the corridor. The night sentry gave a startled salute. Kodama merely grunted in reply, not bothering to return the salute. Few military men were as incapable of observing the military formalities as he. He generally had a button or two undone and sometimes even wore his shoes on the wrong feet.

The latrine was behind the headquarters building. Kodama relieved himself and had just stepped back outside when all of a sudden his surroundings grew light. The sun was coming up.

Kodama paused by the side of the latrine, pressed his small, childlike palms together, and bowed his head in worship. By rights, he was a man of little religious inclination, but concern over Manchurian strategy had led him to acquire the habit of praying to the rising sun. He needn't have done his worshipping beside the latrine, of all places, but that's the kind of man he was.

At first, none of his aides realized what he was doing, and only the noncommissioned officers and soldiers attached to headquarters knew; but one day Colonel Matsukawa Toshitane went into the latrine after him and witnessed the scene. He never mentioned this to Kodama, figuring that anything he said would only embarrass the general.

On the morning of the Port Arthur attack, when Kodama prayed to the rising sun for success, he was skeptical of Nogi's chance of victory. Normally, he himself worked out a battle strategy by mulling various options until he had them narrowed down to two, but choosing between those final two was always an agonizing experience for him, and he had never yet made the choice with confidence. The nation's survival hinged on the success or failure of the plan he selected, and, since both alternatives had solid reasoning behind them, it was like drawing lots. That was Kodama's own expression—"drawing lots."

You could cudgel your brains till they bled, he believed, but brainpower had its limits, and in the end it all came down to luck. He faced the rising sun and prayed—for a winning lot. It was a truly artless prayer, but in the end what else could he have prayed for?

Whether Nogi's headquarters in Port Arthur had put any great effort into choosing their final plan was doubtful. Port Arthur strategy had been left in Nogi's hands, with Kodama completely on the sidelines. His invocation to the rising sun that morning was purely and simply a prayer for the gods to "be with Nogi."

Glossary

Ashigaru: light foot soldier, lowest rank in the samurai class.
Boshin War: (1868–1869) a series of civil war battles around the time of the collapse of the Tokugawa shogunate.
Bushidō: the moral code of the samurai, stressing loyalty, mastery of the martial arts, and death with honor.
Chōshū: present-day Yamaguchi Prefecture; one of the two major domains, together with Satsuma, that led the overthrow of the Tokugawa shogunate (1603–1868).
Genrō: elder statesmen who were "founding fathers" of the modern state of Japan and the chief advisors to the emperor.
Geta: high wooden clogs with a V-shaped cloth thong that passes between the first and second toes.
Go: board game in which two players, Black and White, alternately place black and white stones on a large ruled board to compete for surrounding territory.
Haikai: a form of linked verse from which haiku evolved.
Hakama: formal divided overskirt, worn over a kimono, tied at the waist, and falling almost to the ankles.
Haori: a traditional formal jacket worn over a kimono, with short cord fasteners tied at chest level.
Hatamoto: direct vassals of the Tokugawa shogunate.
Jōruri: a form of narrative chanting accompanied by the three-stringed samisen, commonly associated with the puppet theater.
Kokinshū: classical imperial anthology of waka poetry compiled ca. 905.
Koku: a unit of rice equivalent to about 180 liters (5 bushels); in Tokugawa Japan, land value for taxation purposes was expressed in koku of

rice; one koku was generally viewed as enough to feed one person for a year.

Kumi: groups of samurai that made up the organizational structure of the feudal domains.

Man'yōshū: Japan's earliest extant collection of poetry, compiled in the eighth century.

Meiji Restoration: overthrow of the Tokugawa shogunate and restoration of the emperor's direct rule of Japan in 1868.

Minamoto no Yoshitsune: a general (1159–1189) of the Minamoto clan, regarded as one of the most famous samurai fighters in the history of Japan and a tragic hero who was forced to commit suicide by his brother Yoritomo, founder of the Kamakura shogunate.

Oda Nobunaga: warlord (1534–1582) who began Japan's reunification after the hundred years of civil war known as the era of Warring States.

Okachi: low-status samurai (but higher than the ashigaru); light foot soldiers.

Rin: unit of Japanese currency equal to 1/1000 yen (1/10 sen), used from the beginning of the Meiji era until 1953.

Rōnin: masterless samurai.

Ryō: a unit of currency used during the Tokugawa period; the standard gold coin was equivalent to one ryō.

Satsuma Rebellion: 1877, the last major armed uprising against the new central government, started by disgruntled former Satsuma samurai with Saigō Takamori as their leader.

Satsuma: present-day Kagoshima Prefecture; one of the two major domains, together with Chōshū, that led the overthrow of the Tokugawa shogunate (1603–1868).

Sen (money): unit of Japanese currency equal to 1/100 yen, used from the beginning of the Meiji era until 1953.

Seppuku: ritual suicide by disembowelment, originally reserved for samurai warriors only.

Shinkokinshū: classical imperial anthology of waka poetry compiled ca. 1205.

Shinsengumi: the group of elite swordsmen who served as a special police force in the late Tokugawa period.

Shōgi: Japanese chess, in which a player wins by checkmating the opponent's king; unlike Western chess, players can use captured pieces, and their own pieces can be promoted, sometimes several ranks higher at a time, from pawn to gold, for example.

Tanka: (see waka).

Three hundred feudal lords: this phrase refers to "all feudal lords," for there were roughly three hundred feudal lords (daimyo) across Tokugawa Japan.

Tokiwa Society: educational support organization sponsored by the lord of the former Matsuyama domain to promote the study in Tokyo of talented young men from around Matsuyama.

Tokugawa period: rule of Japan by the Tokugawa shoguns 1603–1868; also called the Edo period, after the name of the capital Edo (now Tokyo).

Toyotomi Hideyoshi: warlord (1537–1598) of humble origin who completed a reunification of sixteenth-century Japan begun by his lord Oda Nobunaga.

Tsubo: a unit of area, roughly 3.3 square meters, corresponding to two tatami mats.

Waka (also tanka): a classical form of poetry dating to the eighth century, with thirty-one syllables in the pattern 5-7-5-7-7.

CPSIA information can be obtained
at www.ICGtesting.com
Printed in the USA
LVHW080812230420
653743LV00006B/55